Addressing Multicultural Needs in School Guidance and Counseling

Simon George Taukeni
University of Namibia, Namibia

A volume in the Advances
in Educational Marketing,
Administration, and Leadership
(AEMAL) Book Series

Published in the United States of America by
  IGI Global
  Information Science Reference (an imprint of IGI Global)
  701 E. Chocolate Avenue
  Hershey PA, USA 17033
  Tel: 717-533-8845
  Fax: 717-533-8661
  E-mail: cust@igi-global.com
  Web site: http://www.igi-global.com

Library of Congress Cataloging-in-Publication Data

Names: Taukeni, Simon George, 1973-
Title: Addressing multicultural needs in school guidance and counseling /
  Simon George Taukeni, Editor.
Description: Hershey PA : Information Science Reference, [2020] | Includes
  bibliographical references. | Summary: "This book examines counseling
  approaches and interventions to deal effectively with psychosocial
  issues facing students and their families"-- Provided by publisher.
Identifiers: LCCN 2019021154 | ISBN 9781799803195 (hardcover) | ISBN
  9781799803201 (softcover) | ISBN 9781799803218 (ebook)
Subjects: LCSH: Educational counseling--Study and teaching. | Student
  counselors--Training of. | Multicultural education. | Behavior disorders
  in children. | Life skills--Study and teaching.
Classification: LCC LB1027.5 .A44 2020 | DDC 371.4--dc23
LC record available at https://lccn.loc.gov/2019021154

This book is published in the IGI Global book series Advances in Educational Marketing,
Administration, and Leadership (AEMAL) (ISSN: 2326-9022; eISSN: 2326-9030)

British Cataloguing in Publication Data
A Cataloguing in Publication record for this book is available from the British Library.

All work contributed to this book is new, previously-unpublished material.
The views expressed in this book are those of the authors, but not necessarily of the publisher.

For electronic access to this publication, please contact: eresources@igi-global.com.

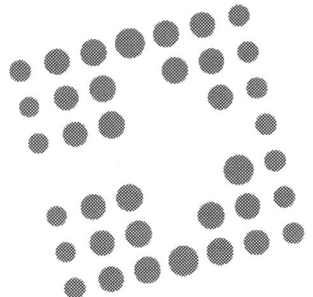

Advances in Educational Marketing, Administration, and Leadership (AEMAL) Book Series

ISSN:2326-9022
EISSN:2326-9030

Editor-in-Chief: Siran Mukerji, IGNOU, India & Purnendu Tripathi IGNOU, India

MISSION

With more educational institutions entering into public, higher, and professional education, the educational environment has grown increasingly competitive. With this increase in competitiveness has come the need for a greater focus on leadership within the institutions, on administrative handling of educational matters, and on the marketing of the services offered.

The **Advances in Educational Marketing, Administration, & Leadership (AEMAL) Book Series** strives to provide publications that address all these areas and present trending, current research to assist professionals, administrators, and others involved in the education sector in making their decisions.

COVERAGE

- Educational Management
- Educational Finance
- Advertising and Promotion of Academic Programs and Institutions
- Faculty Administration and Management
- Academic Pricing
- Governance in P-12 and Higher Education
- Consumer Behavior
- Students as Consumers
- Technologies and Educational Marketing
- Educational Marketing Campaigns

IGI Global is currently accepting manuscripts for publication within this series. To submit a proposal for a volume in this series, please contact our Acquisition Editors at Acquisitions@igi-global.com or visit: http://www.igi-global.com/publish/.

Titles in this Series

For a list of additional titles in this series, please visit:
https://www.igi-global.com/book-series/advances-educational-marketing-administration-leadership/73677

Strategic Leadership in PK-12 Settings
Johnny R. O'Connor (Lamar University, USA)
Information Science Reference • copyright 2020 • 291pp • H/C (ISBN: 9781522592426)
• US $175.00 (our price)

Handbook of Research on Social Inequality and Education
Sherrie Wisdom (Lindenwood University, USA) Lynda Leavitt (Lindenwood University, USA) and Cynthia Bice (Miami Dade College, USA)
Information Science Reference • copyright 2019 • 556pp • H/C (ISBN: 9781522591085)
• US $245.00 (our price)

Women's Influence on Inclusion, Equity, and Diversity in STEM Fields
Ursula Thomas (Georgia State University, USA) and Jill Drake (University of West Georgia, USA)
Information Science Reference • copyright 2019 • 333pp • H/C (ISBN: 9781522588702)
• US $185.00 (our price)

Intergenerational Governance and Leadership in the Corporate World Emerging Research and Opportunities
Julia Margarete Puaschunder (Columbia University, USA & Princeton University, USA & The New School, USA)
Business Science Reference • copyright 2019 • 216pp • H/C (ISBN: 9781522580034) • US $205.00 (our price)

New Age Admissions Strategies in Business Schools
Shalini Kalia (S.P. Jain School of Global Management, India) and Lubna Nafees (Appalachian State University, USA)
Business Science Reference • copyright 2019 • 346pp • H/C (ISBN: 9781522590736) • US $225.00 (our price)

For an entire list of titles in this series, please visit:
https://www.igi-global.com/book-series/advances-educational-marketing-administration-leadership/73677

701 East Chocolate Avenue, Hershey, PA 17033, USA
Tel: 717-533-8845 x100 • Fax: 717-533-8661
E-Mail: cust@igi-global.com • www.igi-global.com

Table of Contents

Section 7
Bullying

Section 8
Support Provision

Detailed Table of Contents

Section 1
Orphans, Marginalized, and Other Vulnerable Children

At the core of the education system in Namibia lies the philosophical underpinning of inclusivity and its underlying principle of equal participation. Thus, to exclude any individual or societal group, directly or indirectly, from participation in education is tantamount to violating the primary meaning of democracy as it pertains to education. This assertion is consistent with the United Nation's SDG 4, which strives at ensuring "Inclusive and Equitable Quality Education and Promote Lifelong Opportunities for All," and SDG 16, which is aimed to provide "Peace, Justice, and Strong Institutions." Two ethnic groups in Namibia, the Ovahimba and the San, are regarded as marginalized, and this marginalization cuts across all spheres of their lives. This research-informed chapter provides an insight into experiences of children from indigenous communities in schools. It further presents an argument for culturally responsive approaches to counseling for learners from indigenous communities.

Orphan-hood is a natural occurrence event of life and not a personal choice. It is a natural life event of losing a parent or a primary caregiver in the life of an orphan child. This chapter focuses on the psychological and social issues that orphans and other vulnerable children experience when their parents are no longer alive. Using literature as a source, most psychosocial issues affecting orphans and other vulnerable children are categorized and justified. Possible solutions and recommendations are clearly illustrated for possible intervention and prevention strategies. Lastly, the chapter ushers future research directions regarding psychosocial issues affecting orphans and other vulnerable children.

Section 2
Anger Management

Anger in young people is on the increase worldwide and effective anger treatment services are in demand. However, the lack of research on the construct of anger and little evidence-based practice makes it difficult to ascertain the best service for these angry young people. Moreover, there is a lack of extensive evidence and qualitative research in the combination of psychoeducation and positive psychology interventions in anger management programmes for young people. Therefore, this chapter will summarise a phenomenological study of an existing psychoeducational anger management programme in the UK and discuss its findings. This chapter will present anger and positive psychology in the context of developing an effective anger management programme and provide a simple anger management strategy to use as a foundation for developing anger management programmes in schools.

A review of childhood secondary trauma is presented. Secondary trauma involves the transfer and acquisition of negative affective and dysfunctional cognitive states due to prolonged and extended contact with others, such as family members, who have been traumatized. As such, secondary trauma refers to a spread of trauma reactions from the victim to those who have close contact with the traumatized individual. Assessment devices are reviewed and most of these appear to be designed to assess secondary or vicarious traumatization in therapists rather than in the general population of adults. The majority of scales lack cutoff scores and this is a significant weakness. The modified Stroop procedure is presented as non-paper and pencil method of assessing secondary trauma reactions. The evaluation of the efficacy of therapeutic interventions for secondary traumatization is virtually non-existent. Systematic studies of secondary trauma are in their infancy and a good deal of further research is needed.

Student trauma can set up challenges and obstacles to a student's academic success. The correlation between experienced childhood trauma and negative medical and social problems is significant, creating problems at school with academic work, behaviors, and social interactions. Further compounding this issue are cultural differences in traumatic resolution and the hidden curriculum of education, especially as the globalization of school communities increases. The complexity of this issue generates an ideal situation for a multidisciplinary team approach, with precise defining of each team member's role to increase comprehensive services for teachers, students, families, and the administration. Essential members of the multidisciplinary team are school administration, teachers, family members, guidance staff, counseling staff, school social workers, school nurses, and community resources that can coordinate with the school to create individualized plans to optimize student success. The chapter is a compilation of scholarly research through desktop research.

Section 4
Child Abuse and Neglect

Syed Najmah Jameel, Department of Psychology, University of Kashmir, Hazratbal, India

Shawkat Ahmad Shah, Department of Psychology, University of Kashmir, Hazratbal, India

Child abuse and neglect is a global problem which needs attention from every corner of the world. This chapter aims to investigate the definitions, types and causes of child neglect and abuse, as well as their impacts on children, risk and protective factors associated with child abuse and neglect, and child abuse neglect prevention and intervention. This chapter will provide an insight into problems faced by child abuse and neglect victims in particular because they are extremely vulnerable and incapable of defending themselves. This will in turn provide a base for school counsellors to have introspection on the existing frame of strategies/policies with this sensitive section of the population. It may provide baseline for designing new strategies in accordance with the needs of the victims of child abuse. Further it will be a unique way to address this complex social problem.

Stephen Oluwaseun Emmanuel, Adeyemi College of Education, Ondo, Nigeria

This chapter provides a groundwork for school counselors. It amplifies their roles and responsibilities to neglected children and also discusses the issues that should be considered in the assessment and treatment of neglected children and their families. The chapter provides professional guides to therapists who specialize in the treatment of neglected children and school counselors who meet with the neglected children occasionally. The methodology adopted for the assessment and treatment of neglect in this chapter is child-centered, family-focused, and culturally receptive. The author posits that dealing with child neglect will be more effective when school counselors leave the four walls of the school to provide support for neglect children and thus integrating them into the school system.

    Joyce Mathwasa, University of Fort Hare, South Africa
    Zoleka Ntshuntshe, University of Fort Hare, South Africa

Children worldwide begin life with greater vulnerability as they suffer from various forms of mistreatment, discrimination, and exploitation at the hands of those who are supposed to protect and provide for them. This chapter focuses on how the rights of the child are violated through child abuse and neglect based on socioeconomic status in multi-religious and multi-cultural societies. Child abuse and neglect are social ills that threaten to diminish the social and moral obligation of every parent causing moral decay in the youth populace. While neglect may be viewed as parental behaviour of failure to nurture children, children suffer various forms of abuse from trusted relatives, caregivers, and strangers. Factors such as political instability, famine, and poverty have robbed children of their right to normal life. The chapter will also explore the criticisms or loopholes in the children's rights so that parents and caregivers can infuse them in their nurturing of the child.

Section 5
Stress

    Daya Weerasinghe, Federation University Australia, Australia

The aim of this chapter is to discuss parent-child stress among different cultures in relation to parents' perceptions and their involvement in mathematics homework and children's academic achievement. Several decades of research have demonstrated that parental involvement in children's achievement is associated with a variety of positive and negative academic and motivational outcomes. It is argued that parents' involvement may matter more for some children than for others and parents are active participants rather than passive observers in children's education. This chapter provides insights on how parental involvement in homework can make a difference and why excessive involvement of parents can cause stress for both parents and children. Further, it is discussed how the cultural differences between Asian and European groups appear to narrow down with acculturation over the years.

Section 6
Anxiety

Chapter 10

Joyce Mathwasa, University of Fort Hare, South Africa
Lwazi Sibanda, National University of Science and Technology,
Zimbabwe

It has always been said 'Knowledge is Power' and that knowledge is gained through education, an idea as old as humanity. Learners acquire life skills such as cognitive ability, interpersonal, psychosocial, and social skills that help learners in decision making, problem solving, critical thinking, creative and effective communication. These skills are learnt through the numerous subjects within a curriculum. Dewey's assertion is that education is life itself, but it focuses on the examinations, yet life depends on the examination outcomes. This chapter focuses on how learning institutions use tests and examinations to grade learners which affects their future. The examination process causes anxiety due to lack of relevant information, inadequate preparation, and overloaded curriculum content. The pressure to achieve a certain level of excellence, family pride, academic recognition, and social mobility is stressful. The chapter will also explore the sources of stress, the levels of stress and stress management tactics.

Section 7
Bullying

Chapter 11

Johannes Ntshilagane Mampane, University of South Africa, South
Africa

Homophobic bullying in schools is a global phenomenon. However, on the African continent, the phenomenon is rife because homosexuality is regarded to be un-African and is often linked to Western culture and colonial influence. These misconceptions about homosexuality have resulted in a culture of homophobia being inculcated into major structures of the society including schools. In this regard, this chapter aims to explore and describe the problem of homophobic bullying in South African schools. Particular attention is paid to cases of school-based homophobic bullying as primary sources of data as well as secondary sources of data from extant literature, textbooks, and journals articles. The chapter employs the Epstein Theory of Overlapping Spheres of Influence to proffer practical solutions and recommendations to address the problem of homophobic bullying in South African schools. These are school-, family-, and community-based solutions and recommendations based on the principles of social justice, inclusion, diversity, and equality.

Section 8
Support Provision

Chapter 12

    Minda M. B. Marshall, LectorSA, South Africa
    Simon George Taukeni, University of Namibia, Namibia
    Rheinhold Disho Muruti, University of Namibia, Namibia
    Gibert Likando, University of Namibia, Namibia
    Cynthy Kaliinasho Haihambo, University of Namibia, Namibia
    Mathilde Shihako, University of Namibia, Namibia
    Chamelle De Silva, University of Namibia, Namibia
    Marshall M., LectorSA, South Africa

This chapter foregrounds the Lab-On-Line project, a technological innovation developed to enhance visual processing skills, improve memory and vocabulary, and increase reading fluency with the explicit aim of improving comprehension. Thirty (30) 3rd year students at one of the University of Namibia campuses participated in the pilot study. A pre-test was conducted for placement purpose. Subsequently, the selected sample commenced with the Lab-On-Line program that consists of 20 lessons that were carried out twice a week over a period of five months. Thereafter a Standardized Reading Evaluation was performed to determine their language proficiency, reading speed per minute and comprehension ability. Results show that the majority of participating students had improved their perceptual development and reading speed (VPF), cognitive development and comprehension skills (CDF), and relative reading efficiency (AIUF).

Chapter 13

    Nonzukiso Tyilo, University of Fort Hare, South Africa
    Jenny Shumba, University of Fort Hare, South Africa

The education system in South Africa is exacerbated with challenges that influence the effective teaching and learning in school, for example, discipline, substance abuse, teenage pregnancy, low self-esteem, lack of positive role models, peer pressure, poor study habits, poverty, etc. Guidance and counselling nurture learners to make informed decisions and about life and this deepens learners' self-knowledge, beliefs, interests, etc. Since the dawn of democratic government in South Africa, guidance was phased out in schools and replaced with Life Orientation (LO). LO as a compulsory subject focuses on self in relation to others and society. It addresses skills, knowledge, and values for people to adopt a healthy lifestyle, involved in solving problems and make informed decisions. The teaching LO in schools prepares and empowers learners to become responsible citizens. The chapter aims to help LO teachers to understand the key role of LO in schools, in the midst of the challenges.

Chapter 14
Noxolo Mafu, Vaal University of Technology, South Africa

Along the dynamic freedoms of democracies of the 21st century, counselling pupils for social justice is a radical democratic process of learning. This is within awareness of metacognitive application of critical thinking that transforms prior obtained frame of reference. It also ignites, without imposing, critical self-reflection as a deliberate cognitive activity on experiences that bring about perspective transformation. Ironically, that school counselling continues to be less regarded as a management role in schools is a misconstrued perspective that not only disadvantages the pupil but also alienates counsellors while also deflating effectiveness of teaching efforts. The teaching and learning process is a collaborative effort that can only succeed when existing school's networks are utilised in the most effective manner especially for a transformative and democratic education. This chapter explores avenues of school counselling along post-constructivist perspectives determining a democratic pupil as sought to be a change catalyst for good citizenship in the society.

Preface

The importance of guidance and counseling in a global space cannot be overemphasized. It is for that sole ethos that this book is well placed to take up its rightful space in knowledge creation and dissemination. While the world has been integrating and becoming a global village, scientists are busy ensuring that multicultural diversities and beliefs become at a center stage as a road map of who we are and where we are going. It is therefore important to reemphasis the role of guidance and counseling in shaping the lives of our children and students in the current era of globalization. This book plays a significant role by ensuring that its content provides the best guidance to students on how to deal with their emotional, social, cultural, academic and personal issues. Authors in the book provided the most practical ways how to deal with: Trauma, stress, child abuse and neglect, anger, anxiety and bullying. There are also some authors who wrote about how best to support children who are marginalized, orphans and other vulnerable children.

IN THIS BOOK

In the first chapter, the author provided insight into experiences of children from indigenous communities in schools. She further presented an argument for culturally responsive approaches to counseling for learners from indigenous communities.

The second chapter focused on the psychological and social issues that orphans and other vulnerable children experience when their parents are no longer alive. Using literature as a source, most psychosocial issues affecting orphans and other vulnerable children were categorized and justified.

The third chapter discussed prevalent problem of aggressive behavior among young people within schools as recorded to be on the increase, therefore, research on discovering the best solution to preventing angry students is imperative. For that reason, the central theme for this chapter is to address the need for suitable anger management treatments and discuss a phenomenological study on the experience and impact of Tristone Coaching's - Children's Healthy Anger Management Programme (CHAMP) in four adolescent males.

A review of childhood secondary trauma is presented in the fourth chapter. Secondary trauma involves the transfer and acquisition of negative affective and dysfunctional cognitive states due to prolonged and extended contact with others, such as family members, who have been traumatized. As such, secondary trauma refers to a spread of trauma reactions from the victim to those who have close contact with the traumatized individual. Children can acquire secondary trauma reactions from parents who have PTSD. School mental health workers might also acquire secondary trauma reactions from the children with whom they work.

The fifth chapter discussed contemporary research concerning childhood trauma and how common and paradoxical manifestations of behavior can spill over into the classroom. Additionally, cultural differences and the hidden curriculum of classrooms can create another layer of difficulty for students—often students who are already at a disadvantage due to being displaced, adjusting to new surroundings, communication difficulties, on-going negative dynamics of being a member of an oppressed and marginalized people group, and lack a peer support group.

Different forms of child abuse and neglect namely: physical or emotional maltreatment, sexual abuse, neglect or commercial or other exploitation, which results into harm to the child's health, existence, development, or decorum in the context of a relationship of responsibility, trust or power were covered in sixth chapter.

In the seventh chapter, the author discussed the concept, forms and causes of child neglect as well as its attendant effects on the affected population. The chapter provides some recommendations about how school counselors can offer a helping hand to this teeming population.

The eighth chapter focused on how the rights of the child are violated in child abuse and neglect through socioeconomic status in multi-religious and multi-cultural societies. Child abuse and neglect are social ills that threaten to diminish the social and moral obligation of every parent causing moral decay in the youth populace. While neglect may be viewed as parental behaviour of failure to nurture children, children suffer various forms of abuse from trusted relatives, caregivers, and strangers. Factors such as political instability, famine, poverty have robbed children their right to normal life. The chapter also explored the criticisms or loopholes in the children's rights so that parents and caregivers can infuse them in their nurturing of the child.

In the ninth chapter, the author provided insights on how parental involvement in homework can make a difference and why excessive involvement of parents can cause stress for both parents and children. He further discussed how the cultural differences between Asian and European groups appear to narrow down with acculturation over the years.

In the tenth chapter, the issue of examination anxiety was discussed. The examination process causes anxiety due to lack of relevant information, inadequate preparation and overloaded curriculum content. The pressure to achieve a certain level of excellence, family pride, academic recognition and social mobility is stressful. The chapter also explored the sources of stress, the levels of stress and stress management tactics.

The eleventh chapter explored and described the problem of homophobic bullying in South African schools. Particular attention was paid to cases of school-based homophobic bullying as primary sources of data as well as secondary sources of data from extant literature, textbooks and journals articles. The chapter employed the Epstein Theory of Overlapping Spheres of Influence to proffer practical solutions and recommendations to address the problem of homophobic bullying in South African schools.

Authors in the twelfth chapter introduced a new Lab-On-Line project, a technological innovation developed to enhance visual processing skills, improve memory and vocabulary, and increase reading fluency with the explicit aim of improving comprehension.

In the thirteenth chapter, authors demonstrated how Life Orientation subject addresses skills, knowledge, and values for students to enable them to adopt healthy life-style as they are involved in solving problems and making decisions about their lives. The subject links to guidance and counseling, for example, career and career choices, study skills and development of self. This implies that the teaching Life Orientation in schools prepares students for the outside world as they socially engage to become responsible citizens. The main of this chapter is to help Life Orientation teachers to understand the important role that Life Orientation can play in guiding and counseling the learners in schools, particularly in the midst of all the challenges taking place in schools.

The last chapter explored the challenges faced by mainly counsellors of the 21st century's pupils and why it has become insurmountable to improve counselling strategies for learner access, retention and success. Many pupils who start school encounter various challenges from diversity, under-resourcefulness or differences at school.

CONCLUSION

I, as the editor, believe without any doubt that this book is best fitting in all school programs and in both undergradute and postgraduate programs especially for the courses such as Guidance and counseling, Life skills, Inclusive/Special Education and Life Orientation to mention but a few.

Section 1

Orphans, Marginalized, and Other Vulnerable Children

Chapter 1

Inclusive Approaches to School Counseling:
Arguing for Culturally-Responsive Psycho-Social Support for Learners From Indigenous Communities

Cynthy K. Haihambo
University of Namibia, Namibia

ABSTRACT

At the core of the education system in Namibia lies the philosophical underpinning of inclusivity and its underlying principle of equal participation. Thus, to exclude any individual or societal group, directly or indirectly, from participation in education is tantamount to violating the primary meaning of democracy as it pertains to education. This assertion is consistent with the United Nation's SDG 4, which strives at ensuring "Inclusive and Equitable Quality Education and Promote Lifelong Opportunities for All," and SDG 16, which is aimed to provide "Peace, Justice, and Strong Institutions." Two ethnic groups in Namibia, the Ovahimba and the San, are regarded as marginalized, and this marginalization cuts across all spheres of their lives. This research-informed chapter provides an insight into experiences of children from indigenous communities in schools. It further presents an argument for culturally responsive approaches to counseling for learners from indigenous communities.

DOI: 10.4018/978-1-7998-0319-5.ch001

INTRODUCTION

This study was situated within Maslow's hierarchy of needs. Towards the end of the chapter, suggestions are made for culturally responsive counseling to support the inclusion of children by helping them deal with institutions of stigmatization and discrimination in schools and establish resilience, while fostering the transformation of institutions. The desired outcome of culturally responsive counseling is to help children understand why they are treated in certain ways and build their resilience, while creating schools in which all children feel welcome, irrespective of their cultural backgrounds.

In Namibia, ethnic minority populations are regarded marginalized on the basis of their lifestyles which set them at the margin of what many regard as development, using economic variables as indicators for this so-called development. The Ovahimba own and value cattle; maintain semi-nomadic lifestyles, maintain unique traditional dress codes and kept their original cultural practices with limited western influence. Cattle-rearing, an activity mostly performed by children under parental supervision, is an important part of their culture. The San, who are regarded as the First peoples in Southern Africa, do not believe in property possession. Their family systems are their property. They were highly nomadic and depended on nature for survival. Now they are forced by conservation laws and by-laws to limit hunting and the harvesting natural resources, they had to adapt to being more stationed, rendering them vulnerable to influences of mainstream society to whom they are dependent for their day to day needs. Some of their traditional skills, such as hunting, collecting veld food, tracking, healing people) have become redundant in modern times. Other skills of the San people are under-valued in terms of monetary compensation. In order for them to be absorbed in the labor market and maintain an average living standard, they need education. According to Article 20 of the Namibian Constitution, (1990) education is a basic human right as stated in; Convention on the Rights of the Child, 1990; the Dakar Framework for Action,1990; UN Sustainable Development Goals, 2015). To this end, many nations over the globe used education as a tool to overcome challenges such as poverty, diseases, inequality, and social injustices. Therefore, exclusion of the indigenous communities is tantamount to intentionally marginalizing them and purporting their poverty.

In Dakar, a commitment was made to the pursue of broad-based strategies for achieving learning needs for all through expanding and improving early childhood education, especially for the marginalized and most vulnerable; ensuring that all children have access to and complete free primary education; offering of equitable access to learning for both children and adults, eliminating gender disparities and improving the quality of education, especially recognized and measurable learning outcomes (UNESCO, 2000, p. 15).

The qualitative, multiple case-study research that informs this chapter was conducted in piece meals over a period of five years, from 2012 -2017. This chapter discusses the realities of the lives of children from marginalized Ovahimba and San communities and their consequent psycho-social support needs.

Background

Since attaining independence on March 21, 1990, Namibia has made tremendous strides in the inclusion of learners from indigenous communities in mainstream schooling. Not only did the country manage to convince the Ovahimba and San communities to consider formal education as part of their lifestyles, but strides were also made in creating inclusive education environments for them. One such effort for the Ovahimba was the establishment of the Ondao Mobile School in the Kunene region. This school, consisting of various units, was developed as a compromise between communities and the education sector. Its main aim was to ensure that learners can attend to their traditionally assigned roles of which cattle herding is central, and still have the opportunity to attend formal schooling. The school reaches out to learners in their natural community environment in the form of tents equipped with learning material and a teacher or two to facilitate teaching and learning. If the semi-nomadic community decides to move from one place to another, the unit of the school follows them.

An example of a unit of the Ondao Mobile School

In response to the traditions of the San people, the Nyae-Nyae Village School was established as a model of community-based education in 1992 in the Tsumkwe, Otjozondjupa region. The school was to offer education through the learners' mother tongue. The San, having a culture of close-knit kinship, do not like being separated from their children, hence the units of the village school in the villages. Learners do not have to be separated from their parents for long periods for the sake of receiving education. However, not all San children attend the Nyae Nyae Village School and not all Ovahimba children attend the Ondao Mobile School, which is only a primary school in any case. Disputes between culture and school were often problematic issues for community schools. The school rules rarely fit into the traditional ways of operation. Similarly, the communities struggled to integrate the way school functions into their traditional operations participate (Haihambo, Brown,

Figure 1. One of the units of the Ondao Mobile School in the Kunene region

Figure 2. Inside a classroom of a Mobile School unit

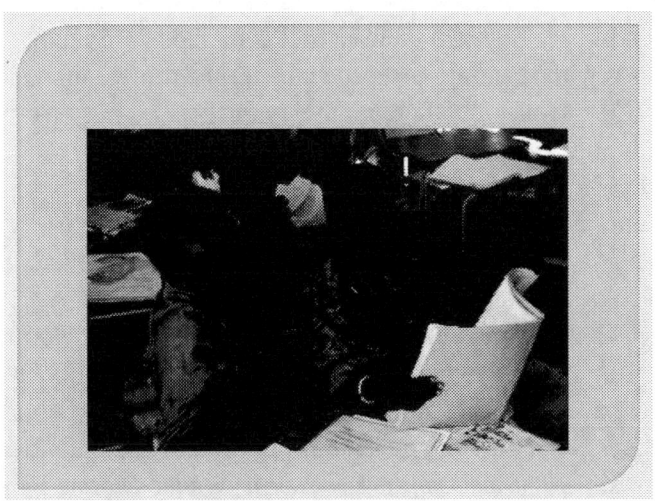

Ndimwedi & Claassen, 2012). One such source of conflict was the requirement that the children had to be at school at a certain time five days a week, wear school uniforms and read from books.

With the exception of those that are close to areas where these community schools operate, the majority of children from indigenous Ovahimba and San communities attend mainstream schools wherever they find themselves. It is in these schools where learners from indigenous communities experience various patterns of exclusion and stigmatization. Psycho-social support interventions are thus needed. These interventions ought to consist of counseling approaches that are not only relevant, but also responsive to the culture and livelihood of indigenous communities.

At the heart of the philosophy of inclusive education lies the idea of citizenship/ citizenry, which implies a sense of belongingness. Unfortunately, in most of the mainstream schools that have dominant groups, there exist structural and non-structural tenets of power, rendering those from ethnic minority groups vulnerable (Olukoshi, 2017). In these diverse school settings, the unique needs of children from minority populations are likely to be overlooked. Their knowledge and realities are barely acknowledged, let alone being used to form building blocks for teaching and learning. Schools operate according to set rules, most of which are rigid conventional structures that have been normalized. Anything outside these structures is perceived as mischievous, disrespectful, or simply unfit for learning. Learners from the Ovahimba and San communities often enter school with totally different sets of pre-literacy

Figure 3. Learners in an "inclusive school"

and pre-numeracy skills and values. They enter these "alien" institutions which have no acknowledgement of their knowledge and values. Not only does the mainstream school system undermine their existing knowledge, but it also unintentionally tries to "erase" it. In most of the schools, learners are prohibited by way of school rules, from speaking their mother tongue on the school premises as a way of encouraging them to learn the medium of instruction or official language. While this could be a good strategy in the process of learning a second or foreign language, it is not always good for self-identity, especially in the case of minority populations. In addition, research revealed that learners from indigenous communities asserted that their opinions were not valued and this made them shy to participate (Haihambo, Brown, Ndimwedi & Claassen, 2012). Learners are mostly at a loss and need psycho-social support to find their space in this new school environment and situate themselves in terms of equality and equity. According to Hansen (2009: 172), diversity implies that there is a "multiplicity of different units and dimensions in which interaction and behavior are guided or conditioned by coexistence and interaction between different groups". The concept entails breaking down rigid perspectives of social differentiation, such as "either/or", and permit into our inner circle a new logic of "not only/but also" (Beck, 2009; Vertovec, 2015). Despite the Sector Policy on Inclusive Education (2013) highlighting children from marginalized communities as a key population and advocating for their inclusion, these learners are mostly regarded as "minorities" and the treatment that comes with this label requires more than ordinary counseling to make them adapt. Schools do not seem to transform at the same pace as the policies, and fail to identify the learners from indigenous communities' needs for protection from institutions of stigma and "othering" while in their care. As a result, learners from the San and Ovahimba communities keep running away from school. Therefore the Department of Marginalized Communities in the Office of the Vice-President introduced a campaign titled: *Back to School and Remain in School*. Part of the efforts of this campaign involves officials of the Ministry of Education Arts and Culture as well as the Office of the Vice-President going into communities to trace children who left school or were never in school and convince them and their families to go to school. Although these learners are provided with basic needs such as food, cosmetics, blankets, school uniforms and stationeries, it has been observed that they go into hiding when they see cars because they do not want to go to school. Their refusal to go to school can be attributed to pull factors in the communities (stress-free life) as well as push factors (overt and covert stigma, harassment) in schools. Without culturally-responsive approaches to counseling of learners from marginalized communities, investments such as these will be futile. Although many of the complexities are situated beyond the boundaries of the school fence, schools should make extra efforts for transformation of schools from spaces where stigma and discrimination are allowed to exist, to becoming true inclusive education spaces where diversity is valued.

Marginalization as an Institution

Marginalization can be described as *"a form of acute and persistent disadvantage rooted in underlying social inequalities"* (The United Kingdom's Global Monitoring Report, 2010). Marginalization is thus a form of structural disadvantage which results from social inequality, emanating from any form of diversity that has become the norm. Marginalization and exclusion occur when people are structurally and systematically excluded from meaningful participation in economic, social, political, cultural and other forms of human social activities.

Namibia, like any other country, boasts with a multi-lingual, multi-cultural and multi-ethnic population in which diversity is appreciated and embraced. The harmony could be a reality among dominant groups. However, it seems that the indigenous communities have not been fully integrated into the society. If schools are to be the spaces in which children should learn about tolerance for diversity and experience acceptance do not fulfill these duties, the society should be worried about future harmony between and among groups. It is from this background that transformation of schools into inclusive spaces is undertaken. One avenue of transformation is through strengthening the "marginalized" while re-educating the "marginalizers". In making propositions for culturally responsive counseling, the researcher provides the context and historical background.

Indigenous communities/ marginalized communities generally face various challenges. They have faced displacement for many generations as rightly stated by Martinez-Cobo (1984).

Those having a historical continuity with pre-invasion and pre-colonial societies that developed on their territories, consider themselves distinct from other sectors of societies now prevailing in those territories, or parts of them. (p. 27)

Both the Ovahimba and San communities form at present non-dominant sectors of society and are determined to preserve, develop, and transmit to future generations their ancestral territories, and their ethnic identities, as the basis of their continued existence as peoples, in accordance with their own cultural patterns, social institutions and legal systems (Martinez-Cobo, 1984). Both groups continue to record high learner drop-out rates from schools. Both groups also practice early parenthood and early marriages. It is normal for youth to get married and have children before they turn 18 years. This implies that their concept of adulthood is different from that

7

of the mainstream society and by implication the legal definition. Dropping out of school to assume these adult roles might be perceived irresponsible and bordering to a violation of human rights by the country's laws and internationally ratified conventions, but for these indigenous communities, it is normal, and in some corners it is even encouraged.

REALITIES OF THE LIVES OF CHILDREN FROM MARGINALIZED COMMUNITIES IN MAINSTREAM SCHOOLS[1]

Issues Affecting Ovahimba Learners in Schools

There are a number of issues affecting Ovahimba children in schools. The researcher starts by focusing on those issues affecting Ovahimba children in the mobile school units, which are only applicable to the primary school phase, before shifting the focus to mainstream primary and secondary schools.

Lack of the Community's Acceptance for Formal Education

During interviews with teachers and learners, it came to light that parents and communities are yet to appreciate the value of formal education for them and for their culture. Teachers continuously repeated the view that parents do not urge children to go to school when they chose not to go to school, the family celebrates. In fact, there have been several cases observed where parents came to the school to fetch their children from school to attend to household chores. These findings are supported by Ndimwedi (2014) who asserted that:

Otjomotjira is a village in the Omatendeka Conservancy, which has had limited exposure to the outside world and hardly has had any social, physical and/or economic development. Schooling seems to have been a foreign concept in this village since "nobody in the village has ever been attending a government school (ibid. p. 24).

A teacher at one of the Mobile School units who was interviewed affirmed:

My biggest problem is children coming to school whenever they wish. What is worse is that the parents are happy when they do not come to school. Also, some families rotate children. [What do you mean with rotating?] Two go to school today, while the other two or three herd cattle and assist at home. Then tomorrow, those that went to school yesterday go for cattle herding and the others come to school or come when they are done with some of the chores. This makes continuity very difficult. I am already doing multi-grade teaching. Because of this practice, I always have to go back to work I covered already, as learners keep missing chunks of work. Trying to discuss with parents is a daunting task. They think they are doing you a favor by doing this. (TOK 4).

One leaner reported his ordeal of going to school against his parents' will:

When I heard about school where one can learn how to write, I decided to go to school. My father (actually referring to the grandfather) send people to come and fetch me. After a while, I ran away from home again to come to school. I started writing my name. First we were writing our names on the ground, and later on a paper. My father sent people to come and fetch me and they beat me. But I kept coming back until they gave up. Now my father is the one that brags about me reading. He keeps his papers until I come from school to read for him! (16 year old boy in Grade 4).

In this case, it took perseverance on the side of the child for parents to realize the value of education. The researchers can attest to these facts. During interviews and observations in communities, questions like these were often asked: "*Who should herd cattle if you want all the children to go to school? Can they eat school?*" During the data collection phases of this study, upon enquiring why certain children were not in school, the researchers would be informed that: *They take care of cattle.* Therefore, there is need for culturally responsive conversations with communities to establish a balance between culture and traditions and the importance of education so as to avoid further marginalization in education.

Cultural Beliefs

The Ovahimba cannot be separated from their cattle. It can be said the cattle are the lifeline of the being of the Ovahimba. Even in severe droughts, selling or slaughtering their cattle is not an option. Therefore, for children to herd cattle is a higher priority than going to school. Secondly, for parents to understand the school curriculum, they need to come closer to the school. But they perceive the school as alien. The distance between the two widens the rift between them. It is important for counseling that is relevant to these communities to support not only children, but also their parents and communities.

Another cultural aspect is that of kinship. The Ovahimba ethnic group has a very complicated and close knit form of kinship, which is further complicated by polygamy. Homesteads consists of inter-dependent multi-layered family members, each with their responsibilities. Their daily interaction can be equated to a cultural school. Within this network, children learned their culture and tradition and how to survive, respect others and become accepted members of their group. Formal schooling disrupted this process. Worse still, when children went to school, they were exposed to another set of knowledge and connections were barely made between their cultural knowledge and the formal school curriculum (Matengu, Likando, Haihambo, 2018). The Mobile School enabled learners to participate in the parallel curricula by moving between the two rather distinct spaces namely the home and the school. The Mobile School units are also within the community and parents/ adults had easy access both literally and figuratively to it. Date however revealed that the acceptance of formal schooling is taking much longer than anticipated, with limited inroads here and there. The two institutions remain in unhealthy competition and the children, who move between the two, often find themselves on the wrong side in both settings. Schooling is perceived as interfering in the arrangement of kinship. Communities are of the view that the school does not transform the knowledge that the families expect of their children and youth. It is therefore argued that, while the Mobile School is a welcome intervention of bringing education to indigenous communities, there is a need to build bridges between the school and culture so that both setting can collaborate and accommodate each other.

The situation was more complicated in regular schools. To start with, leaners had to get rid of their traditional gear, which is part of their identities. In regular schools, learners have to wear school uniforms. The food, the teaching, learning approaches, school rules and school cultures were often at loggerheads with what learners have learned at home. Ovahimba children's physical appearance distinguishes them from learners from mainstream dominant groups. They are often termed uncivilized and often, their intellectual capacities do not match their academic performance. This can be attributed to biased forms of assessment that do not acknowledge traditional knowledge. Learners in these schools end up frustrated and targeted by their peers who are made to believe that they have arrived in modernity.

Another cultural aspect that clashes with schooling that of early marriages, that leads to early parenthood. Girls are engaged and ultimately married off early to much older men. In some schools, these young engaged or married women do attend school. They often find themselves in a dilemma, having to choose between their expected traditional roles and school in which one does not experience belongingness and success. More often they opt for leaving school and being full-time housewives. In these cases, inclusive, equitable education remains a target too high to reach.

Issues Facing San Learners in Education

One prominent issue affecting the education of San learners is poor school attendance and high school dropout figures. Not all San children attend the Nyae-Nyae village school. Those that attend this school have recorded good school attendance at primary school phase, but with each grade into secondary education, the numbers of San children in secondary education begin to dwindle. Their school drop-out is linked to push factors in the school and pull factors in the community. A study by Brown and Haihambo, 2012, cited statistics obtained from the Tsumkwe Secondary School, which is part of the Village School. These statistics indicate that the majority (70%) of Learners' enrolment in this school in 2011 was San children in 2011. The majority of San children were found in lower grades. Their figures dwindled with every grade. In 2011, there were 138 San learners in Grade 8; 77 in Grade 9; 55 in Grade 10; only one in Grade 11 and none in Grade 12. These findings are supported by Kavari (2012) who found that San children in Omaheke Region had fewer difficulties attending primary schools as these are close to their villages, but secondary school attendance was impaired by long distances of the schools from their homes. A circular was issued by the Ministry of Education, supported by the Department of Marginalized Communities for children of indigenous communities to be given preference for boarding facilities. Although this was a good attempt to ensure that these children are not missing out on education due to distances, their separation from their families for a whole term without visiting their families had detrimental consequences. They ran away from school and were exposed to dangers (Kavari, 2011).

There were many push factors in the school. These include the lack of respect for the San culture, the undermining of the knowledge children from the San communities bring to school. These factors fuelled complex institutions of stigma and inferiority imposed on San children by their peers from dominant groups and sometimes also by teachers and hostel staff. The lack of support in school and further marginalization by teachers were common. In some cases, sexual and physical abuse of San children in schools and hostels were heightened by the absence of adults in the school whom they can trust and who understands them. Most of the teachers and hostel matrons and supervisors are from non-San dominant groups (Women's Leadership Center, 2017).

In the midst of these push factors were the pull factors. These included the San children's desire to be with their families. The San culture values family coherence. Almost everything is done in a group. When children are separated from their families to stay in school hostels, and there is barely any representation of the family in the school, children from the San communities find the adjustment difficult. The experiences of San children in education can be summarized in this poem narrated by young San girls:

Education
Education
You intimidate my people!
Making our culture inferior!
Education
Can you for the sake of our children
Reconcile with San cultures?
To embrace you,
We need to find
Something about ourselves
In you ....
Where is the much-researched
Knowledge of our people?
Where are the stories
of our San ancestors?
Where are our priceless
Songs and dances?
We want to get to know you
Come closer to us
With early childhood education
In our San languages (Women's Leadership Center, 2017: 26)

The poem above speak volumes regarding the perceptions, fears and feelings toward education systems that are not responsive to the community's culture, language, knowledge and needs. (Hays, 2012). Many San people expressed a desire to maintain their traditional cultural knowledge, but neither the school nor the mainstream society seems to acknowledge such knowledge.

The issues threatening the education of San learners in schools were known to teachers. When asked to enumerate reasons for the drop-out of San learners, teacher-counsellors/ counselling support teams in schools mentioned the following reasons:

1. Change of the environment from primary to secondary Schools
2. Poverty
3. Being bullied
4. No parental support

All the teacher-counselors interviewed explained at length how poverty negatively affected the education of San learners. One teacher counselor said:

... *"because these learners not on-par with their peers in terms of basic needs. Even if they are exempted from school-related fees, are transported to and from school; receive school uniforms, the fact that they do not have cosmetics, extra food and other necessities other children have result in feelings of inferiority and also attract bad treatment by others". (Teacher Counselor).*

When asked how these school counselors try to mitigate school drop-out and support San learners, they referred to general methods of psycho-social support/ counseling which they use for all learners. These included: *"I talk to them"; "I encourage them to work hard"; I tell them about other San people who made it in life"; I tell them not to worry with those that tease them"; and "San children are clever. If they focus and do not escape from school and disappear for weeks, they do very well, hence I tell them about the importance of education to change their lives."* (Teacher-counsellors from Kunene, Omaheke and Otjozondjupa regions).

It can be concluded that children from indigenous communities in Namibia face challenges with schooling. These challenges can be associated with the non-acceptance of schooling by these communities and the non-acceptance of the in indigenous communities by the dominant groups.

The above education-related experiences of Ovahimba and San learners reveal gaps in the existing in-school approaches to mitigate them. The researcher thus argue for culturally sensitive approaches which implies a shift from comfort zone approaches to those interventions that calls for us to dig deep into the lives of learners from indigenous communities and approach counselling from an insider-position.

Arguing for Culturally-Responsive Counseling for Learners from Ovahimba and San Communities

Article 20 of the Namibian Constitution states that education is a basic human right Ministry of Information and Broadcasting (1990). The high drop-out of learners from indigenous communities, if left unchallenged, will continue to reinforce marginalization of these communities and broaden the gap between them and dominant communities in terms of employment, access to health and life expectancy: all which are co-dependent on the level and quality of education. One way of mitigating early drop-out and low performance of learners from indigenous communities is by embarking on counselling approaches that are culturally responsive. Such counselling methodologies should speak to the actual needs of learners from indigenous communities that uphold their African cultures. Culturally responsive counselling goes hand in hand with culturally-sensitive pedagogies. In such pedagogy and counselling, the facilitators of knowledge, the education space and the community expectations are in synch with one common goal: that of helping learners experience success.

The following are some of the elements of culturally-sensitive counselling and pedagogies:

- Affirmation of learners: helping learners to be proud of their culture and who they are. Teachers will only be able to manage affirmation if they know and are empathetic toward their learners.
- Build relationships (with learners and parents): learners from indigenous communities
- Unify the class to work together and support one another. Often, learners who have support from their peers do not need to seek counseling from adults.
- Nurture learners' minds by creating enabling environments for self-esteem building. These include de-stigmatization of indigenous communities; listening to learners; identifying learners' needs through differentiated strategies rather than depending on self-disclosure.
- Engage families and communities (Even if you do not live in the community, you can walk through the community)
  Adapted from Blackwell (2017).

The above stated approaches should be identifiable in schools attended by learners from indigenous communities. If culturally sensitive pedagogies and culturally responsive counseling are applied, learners at risk of drop-out due to unwelcoming school environments will be identified early and early intervention will take place. Such learners will be assisted and empowered and equipped with resilience skills to enable them to not only be present in schools, but to experience citizenship in their educational spaces which in turn will lead to meaningful participation and performance.

RECOMMENDATIONS

The study recommends that Ovahimba and San communities be engaged in developing the kind of school they think their children would love, and help government to adapt schools to the architectural design of these communities while negotiating and compromising on aspects deemed important by both indigenous communities and national education administration .

Pre- and in-service teacher-education should include teaching in indigenous communities as part of their inclusive education curricula and expose students to culturally responsive pedagogies and culturally-sensitive counseling.

The curriculum should engage various discourses of knowledge construction and that no one form of knowledge is superior over the other. These will lead to the equalization of opportunities and the ultimate end to marginalization in education. Although schools have counseling structures in place, there is no evidence that the culturally responsive element is consciously considered.

It will be important to consider the inclusion of teachers, auxiliary staff, hostel staff from indigenous communities in schools, even if it means making use of affirmative action regulations. Their presence will help learners from indigenous communities to have people to whom they can relate easily and who will protect them at levels of decision making.

IN CONCLUSION

It was clear in this study that the Government gave thought to the poverty in which the indigenous communities find themselves. For this reason, they made provision for the basic needs of these children by giving them food, cosmetics, and other amenities. However, these only addressed the basic needs of children from indigenous communities (Maslow, 1982). The higher level needs for safety, belongingness and self-actualization remained highly neglected.

Although the teachers entrusted with the psycho-social needs of all learners were aware of such learners needs, they had limited skills to respond to the complex psycho-social needs of these learners and their communities.

In order for governments and countries to guarantee inclusive and equitable quality education for all children, governments must invest in resources and structures that will enhance enrolments and retention of all children, including those from marginalized communities. Often, children from indigenous communities are forced to assimilate as opposed to acculturate when they enter education settings. The education system does not seem to consider the cultural backgrounds of learners from marginalized communities.

If all students are to succeed, we must pay much more attention to community-based learning as a strategy for engaging and motivating students and for strengthening the relationship between schools and communities (Melaville, Berg and Blank, 2006: iii)

FUTURE RESEARCH DIRECTIONS

Based on the outcomes of this research, it proposed that participatory research, involving indigenous communities, should be conducted. Such research should be driven by indigenous communities and should lead the design of the school that the Ovahimba and San people would want for their children.

Research that targets teachers employed in indigenous communities should be embarked upon to unpack their attitudes and deep lying perceptions and expectations, but also their skills to teach and render counseling to these learners.

CONCLUSION

The multiple case study research that informs this chapter concludes that, although children from indigenous communities are prioritized for inclusive education and are identified as a vulnerable group, their education attainment remain at risk due to a two-fold threat:

1. Culture that is in conflict with the modern school institution and the modern school institution is not aligned to the cultures and traditions of the indigenous communities. Government has attempted to mitigate this mismatch with initiatives such as the Ondao Mobile School and the Nyae-Nyae Village School. To a large extent, these were more successful in the primary schools rather than in secondary schools where puberty and adolescence contribute to self-awareness and self-identity.
2. Unfortunately, data seems to suggest that, the structural adjustments made to accommodate indigenous communities in education are at the base of Maslow's hierarchy of needs with a focus on physiological needs (food, shelter, and clothing). The higher order needs such as safety, self-esteem and self-actualization needs are yet to be achieved. As a result, when schools are not successfully offering these, learners opt to flee to the safety of their homes and communities.

Furthermore, the data reveals that the modern school institution has brought with it a western approach to teaching, learning and counseling, which promotes assimilation rather than acculturation. Given this situation, teachers' mindsets are not geared tpwards adjusting to the needs of learners as advocated for in the Sector Policy on Inclusive Education (2013) and are thus not culturally responsive. The schools, even those within the very communities they are intended to serve, do not seem to acknowledge the sociological and psychological tenets of such communities.

In the contrary, they seem to subconsciously expect learners to fit in/ adapt to this new form of learning. Even the counseling of learners seems to try and encourage learners to adapt and endure forms of stigmatization such as othering and abuse. The desirable approach should be that of adjusting the school to the needs of all learners. While acknowledging the multiple efforts made by the Government of the Republic of Namibia to provide education to indigenous communities and by so doing starting the journey of de-marginalization, the lived experiences of Ovahimba and San children suggest that inclusive education remain highly compromised. In order to achieve equity, the current status quo of *Culture versus Education* should be transformed into *Culture and Education*.

ACKNOWLEDGMENT

The author wishes to thank her co-researchers in all three pieces of research that informed this chapter, namely: Prof. Anthony Mashego-Brown, MS. Pamela Claassen, Mr. J. Ndimwedi. Mr. E. Louis, Prof. G. Likando and Prof. K. Matengu.

This research was supported by the University of Namibia Research and Publication Committee while the second research was funded by the Chinese Funds in Trust and the Faulty of Education. The last research was funded by the researchers.

REFERENCES

Blackwell, A. (2017, July). *Teaching in the Spirit of Ubuntu.* Paper presented at Public Lecture of the University of Namibia.

Blom Hansen, T. (2009). *Sovereigns beyond the State: On Legality and Authority in Urban India. In Sovereign Bodies: Citizens* (pp. 169–191). Migrants, and States in the Postcolonial World. doi:10.1515/9781400826698.169

Brown, A., & Haihambo, C. K. (2015). Developmental issues facing the San people of Namibia: Road to de-marginalization in formal education. University of Namibia Press. doi:10.2307/j.ctvgc619h.20

Haihambo, C. K., Brown, A., Ndimwedi, J., & Claassen, P. (2012). *The crisis of education for the San and Ovahimba in Contemporary Namibia.* Conference Paper. Education Conference, University of Namibia, Windhoek, Namibia.

Hays, J. (2012). In OSISA 2012. The Indigenous World 2013. Retrieved from osisa. org/indigenous-peoples/regional/osisa-and-indigenous-world-2013

Martinez-Cobo. (1984). Study of the Problem of Discrimination against Indigenous Populations. Final report submitted by the Special Rapporteur. United Nations, Department of Economic and Social Affairs.

Matengu, K. K., Likando, G., & Haihambo, C. K. (in press). Inclusive education in marginalised contexts: The San and Ovahimba learners in Namibia. *British Council.*

Ndimwedi, J. (2014). *Educational Barriers and Employment Advancement among the Marginalized People in Namibia: The case of the OvaHimba and OvaZemba in the Kunene Region* (Master's dissertation). University of the Western Cape.

Olukoshi, A. (2017). *The conceptual and legal basis for inclusive democracy and integration/mainstreaming of marginalized groups in society. Paper presented on 16 February 2019.* Windhoek: International IDEA.

UNESCO. (2000). The Dakar framework for action. In Education for all: meeting our collective commitments. Paris: UNESCO.

Vertovec, S. (2019). Talking around super-diversity. *Ethnic and Racial Studies, 42*(1), 125–139. doi:10.1080/01419870.2017.1406128

Women's Leadership Center. (2017). *CEDAW through San Young Women's Eyes: Claiming out Rights! Demanding dignity!* Olof Palme International Center.

ADDITIONAL READING

Ainscow, M., & Sandill, A. (2010). Developing inclusive education systems: The role of organizational cultures and leadership. *International Journal of Inclusive Education, 14*(4), 401–416. doi:10.1080/13603110802504903

Bagele, C. (2012). *Indigenous Research Methodologies*. Los Angeles, CA: SAGE.

KEY TERMS AND DEFINITIONS

Democracy: Democracy is one of the key pillars or the Namibian education system. Democracy in education means involving learners, on a regular basis and in developmentally appropriate ways, in shared decision making that increases their responsibility for shaping and reshaping the education landscape in order to make it a good place to be and learn.

Diversity: It is an understanding and acknowledgement that each individual is unique, and recognizing our individual differences. These can be along the dimensions of race, ethnicity, gender, sexual orientation, socio-economic status, age, physical abilities, religious beliefs, political beliefs, or other ideologies.

Equity: Equity in education is a process of levelling the play field to ensure that every child has an equal chance for success, irrespective of the complexities of their lives. That requires understanding the unique challenges and barriers faced by individual learners or by vulnerable groups with a likelihood to miss out on education due to barriers they face. It requires that schools provide additional support to help them overcome those barriers.

Inclusive Education: Inclusive education means that all learners should attend and be welcomed by their neighborhood schools in age-appropriate, regular classes and are supported to learn, contribute and participate in all aspects of the life of the school. Such schools should respond to the needs of all learners and render support to enable them to succeed, both academically and socially.

Marginalized Communities: In general terms, marginalized communities are communities confined to the lower or peripheral edge of the society. Such a group is denied involvement in mainstream economic, political, cultural and social activities due to their living conditions, lifestyles or exclusion. In Namibia, the Ovahimba and San communities are among those regarded as marginalized communities.

Ovahimba: The Himba are an ethnic group of nomadic pastoralists who inhabit the Kaokoland area of the Kunene Region of Namibia.

Psycho-Social Support: Psychosocial support is a method of responding to psycho-social factors posing barriers to learning and development of human beings. It helps individuals and communities to heal the psychological wounds and rebuild social structures following an event or systemic traumatic experiences. In the Namibian education system, school counseling is one method of psycho-social support built into the curriculum, with teachers who receive basic training to render such counseling.

Resilience: Resilience is a skill that enables human beings to cope in spite of setbacks, or barriers, or limited resources. Young people are strengthened and capacitated to bounce back after traumatic events.

San: The San are a Khoe-san group of people who maintain a nomadic lifestyle. They are regarded as one of the marginalized communities in Southern Africa as they found themselves at the periphery of society.

Stigmatization: It is the discriminating process of ascribing shame and humiliation to an individual on the basis of the diversity they present. In Namibia, many children from indigenous communities experience various forms of stigma in schools because of their appearance, language or lack of resources.

Chapter 2
Psychological and Social Issues Affecting Orphans and Vulnerable Children

Zoleka Ntshuntshe
University of Fort Hare, South Africa

Simon G. Taukeni
University of Namibia, Namibia

ABSTRACT

Orphan-hood is a natural occurrence event of life and not a personal choice. It is a natural life event of losing a parent or a primary caregiver in the life of an orphan child. This chapter focuses on the psychological and social issues that orphans and other vulnerable children experience when their parents are no longer alive. Using literature as a source, most psychosocial issues affecting orphans and other vulnerable children are categorized and justified. Possible solutions and recommendations are clearly illustrated for possible intervention and prevention strategies. Lastly, the chapter ushers future research directions regarding psychosocial issues affecting orphans and other vulnerable children.

INTRODUCTION

This chapter makes a contribution towards a subject matter called psychosocial issues affecting orphans and other vulnerable children. It seeks to expand the debate and create further awareness on the plight of the orphans and vulnerable children globally. By so doing, more intervention and prevention strategies would be devised

DOI: 10.4018/978-1-7998-0319-5.ch002

in order to address the plight of orphans and other vulnerable children. The chapter highlighted the most critical psychological and social issues with the support of evidence as provided in the current literature.

Background

A large body of empirical evidence demonstrates that most orphans and other vulnerable children are generally being affected by psychosocial issues compared with non-orphans (Escueta et al., 2014). Certain things make children to be viewed as vulnerable, namely: being orphaned by the death of one or both parents, living on the street, living in poverty, living with disability, affected by armed conflicts, abused by parents, other family members and caregivers, being HIV positive and being affected by HIV and AIDS, being marginalized, being stigmatized and even discriminated against, being child laborers including domestic workers, street vendors and victims of human trafficking (UNICEF, UNAIDS, PEPFAR, 2006; UNICEF, 2007).

The challenges facing orphans and other vulnerable children have been partially known especially the ones in the developing world. Pillay (2014) found that sub-Saharan Africa has been identified as the world's poorest region with the largest proportion of vulnerable children in the world. It was further estimated that the highest number of orphans in the world of over 48.3 million were in sub-Saharan Africa (UNICEF, UNAIDS, PEPFAR, 2006). The loss of one or both parents often affects the psychosocial well-being of orphaned children. Psychosocial well-being is defined as a positive age and development stage appropriate outcome of children's psychological, physical and social development embedded in the child's natural abilities to cope in his or her environment (Richter, Foster & Sherr, 2006).

Literature has been consistent reporting that whenever a child happens to lose his or her parents, many of the orphans lack psychosocial support. Philippi et al (2006) defined psychosocial support as an ongoing process of meeting the physical, emotional, mental, spiritual and social needs of a child. Psychosocial support is the basic right of every child for his or her psychological, emotional, mental, physical and social development (Repssi, 2008). In their study, they warn that if psychological issues are not addressed satisfactorily, orphans and other vulnerable children would end up involving themselves in risk behaviors such as alcohol, drug abuse, prostitution and other risk behaviors that are not acceptable in the community. Not only that, orphans and vulnerable children are at higher risk of developing psychological problems such as anxiety, depression, trauma, mental health, mood swings and other somatic symptoms (Makame, 2002).

Psychological issues such as stigma and marginalization are among the many risks to which orphans and other vulnerable children are subjected to in many societies (Caserta, 2017). Link and Phelan (2006) studied the forms associated with stigma and marginalization to include: labeling, stereotyping, separation, status loss, and discrimination. Regarding social issues facing orphans and other vulnerable children, FHI and USAID (2001, as cited in [Mwoma & Pillay, 2015]) noted the overwhelming number of OVC live with either one parent, elderly grandparents who also need care and support, or with poor relatives who struggle to meet their own needs. There are also other orphans living in child-headed households (Theron, 2012) caring for their younger siblings (Ramphele, 2012). Children in such circumstances are at risk of losing opportunities for schooling, clothing, decent living and meeting their psychosocial needs (Mwoma & Pillay, 2015). UNAIDS (2013) asserts that orphan-hood is frequently accompanied by prejudice and increased poverty, factors that could disrupt children's chances of completing their education.

These are some of the psychological and social issues facing orphans and other vulnerable children this chapter discusses in detail. Even though the authors made specific reference to sub-Saharan Africa, the discussion of orphans and other vulnerable children go beyond the regional block, race, gender, ethnicity, color, geographical location and status. An orphan child is an orphan child; it does not matter whether the child is an African, American, European, Asian or Caribbean. The chapter's focal point is to take the discussion of orphans and other vulnerable children broadly and globally in the context of psychosocial issues facing them. Therefore, the next section presents the psychological and social issues facing orphans and other vulnerable children.

PSYCHOLOGICAL AND SOCIAL ISSUES AFFECTING ORPHANS AND VULNERABLE CHILDREN

Orphans experience psychological and emotional problems before and after the death of parents, which sometimes makes it difficult for them to cope and adjust in school and social settings (UNAIDS/UNICEF 2007; Luther, 2004). Psychological impact occurs when the child loses a parent to whom an attachment was formed. Some children have to watch their parents going through different stages of illness and eventually lose them through death. This experience may be too traumatic for them and may stay with them for a long time which, in turn, may disturb their learning at school. This is evident from studies by Tsheko (2007) and Ntshuntshe (2012) which revealed that some orphans had gaps in memory and could not remember what was taught in class because of the trauma of losing their parents. It can also lead to long periods of absenteeism and even dropping out of school (REPSSI, 2012). This results in the realization that the child has lost a parent and possibly all his hopes of finishing school and a bright future ahead may be diminished.

Following this traumatic experience orphans and vulnerable children are often victims of stigma and discrimination. Due to their situation, these children often find themselves isolated from social settings and in school as well (REPSSI, 2012). Sometimes orphans lose parents through HIV & AIDS. To this day and age people perceived to be infected or affected with HIV still experience isolation within their homes and in public and workplaces (Regional Psychosocial Support Initiative (REPPSI), 2012). Due to this stigma of HIV and illnesses associated with the disease, children often find themselves isolated from social settings and in school as well (REPSSI, 2012). Studies have shown that stigma can lead to other children teasing their classmates who have lost parents to HIV/AIDS (Gilborn, Nyonyintoro, Kabumbuli and Jangwe-Wadda, 2001). These results in children often hiding their parents' status and even their own because of the urge to protect them from stigma and ostracism associated with HIV. Consequently, the burden of keeping this secret also becomes an additional stressor for some of them (Murphy, Roberts & Hoffman, 2002). Stigma and discrimination often mean loss of dignity and self- esteem on the part of the sufferer and it tends to inhibit the growth of orphans who are already distressed (Nyawasha, 2006). Children who are often stigmatized and discriminated against, can even internalize the stigma to which they are subjected. Furthermore, stigmatization and discrimination must be understood as social processes linked to making the person feel unequal and excluded (Shilubana & Kok, 2004). Often times orphans are labeled, patronized, exploited and rejected (Jackson, 2008). As a result of all these prejudices, orphans repeatedly face fear and harassment. The child may not only feel isolated by adults but also feel victimized by other children, further lowering the orphan's self-esteem and confidence (Jackson, 2008).

Self-esteem is a term used to describe a person's overall sense of self-worth or personal value. It can also be described as how an individual sees himself, how he/she perceives his value to the world, and how valuable he/she thinks he/she is to other people (Olegbeleye, 2013). People are often described as having high self-esteem, in which case they think very well of themselves and their abilities, or low self-esteem, filled with doubts and criticism about themselves and their abilities. Self-esteem is important because it is an essential human need that is vital for survival and normal healthy development (Olegbeleye, 2013). According to Maslow (1943), psychological health is not possible unless the essential core of a person is fundamentally accepted, loved and respected by others and by himself. Self-esteem also allows people to face life with more confidence, benevolence, and optimism, thereby easily reaching their goals to self-actualize (Cherry, 2012). Hence negative experiences of stigmatization, labeling can lead to withdrawal and isolation, which can have major impairments to their psychological and social development.

Orphans are also affected economically and socially since many of them take on the responsibility of heading their homes at an early age. This is a result of the disappearance of African kinship where relatives used to take in orphaned children. The result is that these children have greater needs than children who reside in homes that are normally headed by adults (Barnett & Whiteside, 2002). They are unable to cope financially; consequently, they have limited access to vital resources like health, education and social security (Hepburn, 2005; Heat, 2002; UNICEF, 2006). The financial burden experienced by these children at home forces them to drop out of school and look for work to supplement the family income. This, in turn, forces children to become victims of child labor; crime and girl children are predisposed to becoming victims of human trafficking, prostitution, sugar daddies and early marriage (UNAIDS 2012). In addition to this, orphaned children often suffer a lack of school needs, such as uniforms and books, which often contributes to their dropping out of school. Due to these challenges some orphaned children are withdrawn from school by caregivers/parents who are not able to meet these school demands (Skinner & Davids, 2006). Such frustrations cause orphans to prioritize finding work rather than staying at school (Heat, 2002).

Case and Ardington (2006) also observed that orphans are less likely to be enrolled in school and are also likely to drop out of school after the death of a parent due to increased household demands on the orphaned children. The same narrative applies to going to school as well since schooling is likely to be disrupted because of socio-economic conditions in their homes. Moreover, Ardington (2007) found that there are poor planned educational opportunities among most orphans than non-orphans in South Africa.

In addition to this there is evidence that, in poor households, orphans may experience discrimination in the allocation of resources against children who are direct biological children (Hepburn, 2005).

In a study conducted in Tanzania, it was found that orphans were more likely to go to bed hungry than non-orphans (UNAIDS, 2006; UNICEF, 2006). In addition to this, research carried out in Lesotho found that children, who had migrated to other homes as a result of the death of a parent or parents, reported being given different food from other children in the household, being beaten up, often overworked and being given inadequate clothing (Skinner & Davids, 2006). This implies that orphans can also become victims of neglect, in which case, neglect can be defined as the absence of due care (Nyawasha, 2006). People often neglect orphans and other vulnerable children because they associate their condition with immoral tendencies of which they do not approve (Nyawasha, 2006).

SOLUTIONS AND RECOMMENDATIONS

In light of the issues raised in the preceding section, studies have found that orphans and vulnerable children need varying types of support starting from the home to the school. Studies have shown that a coordinated program can ensure an effective support provision for orphans and vulnerable children as it includes professionals from social workers, psychologists, police, nurses, and educators. Studies have shown that training of teachers in providing psychosocial support to orphans and vulnerable children is of the essence as psychological and behavioral problems are seemingly on the rise and teachers mostly rely on simply referring all these cases to centers outside the school. Training teachers on psychosocial support would equip them with the knowledge and skills needed to provide psychosocial support to orphaned learners in schools.

It is a fact that some countries have already introduced courses in which teachers can be trained in psychosocial support. In Zambia, an official course in psychosocial support (Teacher's Diploma in Psychosocial Care, Support and Protection) was launched in 2013 (Ministry of Education, Science, Vocational Training, and Early Education (MESVTEE); REPSSI, 2013). Training teachers in psychosocial support is based on the premise that education is expected to bring normality in these challenging situations, due to its stable environment. In the event of a traumatic experience (losing a parent), the healing process can begin at school as the school and the teacher represent a familiar, friendly and trustworthy environment. Follow up on this, is the possibility that on-going training for teachers could be done along the lines of in-service training programs which are normally organised by Departments of Education in order to equip, uplift and enhance the teacher capacity for those already in service. This is in keeping with the sentiment that the continuous professional development of teachers at school is essential in order to address the gaps in training that can arise through time and change in curriculum and learner situations. Studies have shown that educators who had received some training were better equipped to handle learner problems they faced at school as they were closer in order to respond and support them.

Secondly, this position placed teachers in a strategic position to be able to refer learners to professionals outside the school who can further assist them. Training of teachers is recommended as teachers have a primary role to play as they are the first adults with whom orphaned learners and vulnerable children come into contact at school.

In addition to this, it is recommended that teachers utilise widely accepted ways of providing psychosocial support like utilising families, forming partnerships with communities and forming peer and youth groups. The important role played by communities can never be overlooked because communities are an important resource that can be used to foster resilience for orphans. The dynamic interaction between the orphaned learner and the community can give a child a sense of belonging as well as help in strengthening his social relationships with other people. Therefore, schools can be urged to start embarking on the process of forming meaningful partnerships with communities to assist the psychosocial provision of orphaned learners. In these settings, issues like child-headed homes, poverty, and stigma can be monitored and it can be made sure that children receive the necessary support.

This can be further extended to peer groups as well. In order for orphaned learners to gain self-esteem and lost confidence, there are things that can assist them in regaining dignity and hope for the future. Therefore, schools are encouraged to rekindle those activities which used to bring the youth together, things like camps, Christian fellowships and peer and youth support groups in schools. Orphan-hood goes with separation and loss and by re-establishing relations with peers is another way of dealing with loss and bringing orphans and vulnerable children back into the community. In these settings, children can be supported by other youth where they can learn survival skills such as personal hygiene, interpersonal skills, self-esteem and responsibility in order to maintain a healthy and successful lifestyle. The donation of food and money is not enough for orphaned children to survive on. It is within groups like these that children can learn important skills. In addition, this is an example of children receiving support from other youth within their own communities. The skills they will learn will enable them to make empowered decisions, co-operation and may even give them opportunity to put the skills they have learned to use.

This can also be aligned with another strategy where children who have been through a traumatic time are welcomed back into society. This "return" to school encourages learners to return to school after the bereavement period. The learner at this stage needs validation of the experience which is the recognition and acceptance that what the learner has just gone through is valid (Hall, 2012). Validation is important when it comes to achieving psychological well-being. Validation entails listening; therefore painful experiences will be acknowledged which will, in turn, improve communication between the learner and the teacher/peers (Hall, 2002). When a teacher/peer validates a child, they create a safe space for the learner to express his/ her fears, worries and other issues that make them uncomfortable. All those painful experiences and concerns that are expressed, acknowledged and validated by a trusted listener will diminish. Thus by being validated the child gains that reassurance which gives him/her hope for the future and regains lost confidence. Reassurance can actually go a long way in making people feel that they are not alone and that other people are backing them. All the above processes play an important role in making the learner to feel emotionally secure and helping him/her to persevere.

Teachers can also be trained in identifying learners who are in need of support, and in this way orphans and vulnerable children can be spotted and assisted promptly. The identification of learners needing support is very critical as it forms the basis on which all subsequent support might be based upon. Teachers are also in a better position to observe all forms of vulnerability such as inadequate and torn uniforms, behavioral problems, and absenteeism from school, poor nutrition, children showing signs of abuse, impaired concentration, and many others. Early identification of children ensures timely referral and that appropriate support is rendered. Hence it is important for teachers to have knowledge and skills to be able to identify orphaned and vulnerable learners successfully, which would lead to successful intervention and well-informed referrals. Importantly, teachers are in a better position to identify some practical peer-to-peer programs to empower orphans and other vulnerable children in meeting their psychosocial needs both at school, home and in their local communities. Mwoma and Pillay (2015) assert that school being the place where learners spend most of their time; it could be the right place to advocate programs to ensure that OVC receive psychosocial support. A school may offer programs such as peer support, group guidance, provision of safety and security and encouragement to share orphans' feelings in a productive and meaningful manner (Taukeni, 2011) through role-plays and drama. Other programs may include: support groups, psychological debriefing, home visiting, play groups, cash transfer, material assistance and skills building programs (King, et al, 2009).

FUTURE RESEARCH DIRECTIONS

Even though authors made a considerable effort to discuss most psychosocial issues affecting orphans and vulnerable children, there is still further need for in-depth research to explore the best strategies and interventions to address the plight of our children. For example, specific interventions may be focusing on bereavement counseling, accessing social grants, and education opportunities and providing resilient skills to adjust to life-changing circumstances including how to run households and maintaining family bonds. Lastly, the authors are of the opinion that research on orphans peer-to-peer programs that seek to benefit them with much needed psychosocial support and development should be explored in the future research.

CONCLUSION

The chapter covered many psychological and social issues facing orphaned and other vulnerable children, namely: trauma, neglect, stigmatization, labeling, isolation, discrimination, exploitation, rejection, stress, poor self-esteem and poverty. It further covered issues about the limited access to vital resources such as health, education and social security that are facing orphaned and other vulnerable children.

REFERENCES

Ardington, C. (2007). *Orphan-hood and schooling in South Africa: Trends in the Vulnerability of Orphans between 1993 & 2005*. Academic Press.

Barnett, T., & Whiteside. (2002). AIDS in the Twenty First Century: Diseases and Globalization. Palgrave McMillan.

Case, A., & Ardington, C. (2006). *The impact of Parental Death on School Outcomes: Longitudinal Evidence from South Africa*. Academic Press.

Caserta, T. A. (2017). *The psychosocial wellbeing of orphans and youth in Rwanda: Analysis of predictors, vulnerability factors and buffers* (Academic dissertation). University of Helsinki, Finland: Department of Social Science 36, Social Psychology.

Cherry, K. (2012). About.com. *Psychology (Irvine, Calif.)*.

Gilborn, L., Nyonyintoro, R., Kabumbuli, R., & Jwagwe-Wadda, G. (2001). *Making a difference for children affected by AIDS: Baseline findings from operations research in Uganda*. Washington, DC: Population Council.

Hall, K. (2012). What is validation and Why Do I Need to Know? *Psych Central*. Retrieved on October 23, 2014, from http://blogs.psychcentral.com/emotionally-sensitive/2012/02/levels-of-validation

Hall, K. (2012). Validation of experience. *Psychology Central*. Retrieved on August 25 2014 from http://blogs.psychcentral.com/emotionallysensitive/2012/02/levels-of-validation

Heat. (2002). The EFA 2002 Assessment Country Report, Zimbabwe, Harare.

Hepburn, A. (2005). *Early Childhood Mental Health Consultation*. Georgetown University.

Jackson, M. A. (2008). *A study of children and grief: living through bereavement* (Dissertation). University of KwaZulu-Natal.

King, E., De Silva, M., Stein, A., & Patel, V. (2009). Interventions for improving the psychosocial well-being of children affected by HIV and AIDS. Cochrane Database of Systematic Reviews, 2. doi:10.1002/14651858.CD006733.pub2

Luther, S. (2004). *Resilience and Vulnerability (Adaptation in the context of childhood Adversities)*. Cambridge University Press. Retrieved from assets.cambridge.org/97 805218/07012sample/9780521807012wspdf.PDF

Murphy, A., Roberts, K., & Hoffman, D. (2002). Article. *Journal of Child and Family Studies*, *11*(2), 191–202. doi:10.1023/A:1015177609382

Mwoma, T., & Pillay, J. (2015). Psychosocial support for orphans and vulnerable children in public primary schools: Challenges and interventions strategies. *South African Journal of Education*, *35*(3), 1–9. doi:10.15700aje.v35n3a1092

Ntshuntshe, Z. (2012). *An assessment of the implementation of intervention programmes which ensure the right to education for orphans in King William's Town District* (Unpublished Master of Education dissertation). University of Fort Hare.

Nyawasha, T. (2006). Psychosocial Support to Orphans and Vulnerable children. Rapports. AIDS in Africa: UNAIDS country by country.

Olegbeleye, A. O. (2013). *Predictors of the Mental Health of Orphans and Vulnerable Children in Nigeria*. Ife Psychologia. Retrieved from http://www.readperiodicals.com/201309/3093274031.html

Pillay, J. (2014). Challenges educational psychologists face working with vulnerable. In T. Corcoran (Ed.), *Psychology in Education: Critical Theory-Practice*. Rotterdam: Sense Publishers. doi:10.1007/978-94-6209-566-3_7

Ramphele, M. (2012). *Conversations with my sons and daughters*. Johannesburg: Penguin Books.

REPSSI. (2013). *REPSSI launches Teacher's Diploma Course in Psychosocial Care, Support and Protection in Zambia*. Retrieved from http://www.repssi-launces-teachers-diploma-course-in-psychosocial-care-support-in-Zambia

REPSSI. (2013). *REPSSI launches Teacher's Diploma in Psychosocial Care, Support & Protection*. Retrieved from http://www.riatt-esa.org/updates/repss-launces-teachers-diploma-psychosocial-care-support-and-protection

Richter, L., Foster, G., & Sherr, L. (2006). *Where the heart is: Meeting psychological needs of young children in the context of HIV/AIDS*. The Hague, The Netherlands: Bernard van Leer Foundation.

Shilubana, M., & Kok, J. C. (2004). Learners without adult care at home who succeed in school. *Education as Change*, *9*(1), 101–107. doi:10.1080/16823200509487105

Skinner, D., & Davids, A. (Eds.). (2006). *A situational Analysis of Orphans and Vulnerable Children in Districts of South Africa*. HSRC Press.

Taukeni, S. (2011). *A phenomenological study of orphaned learners' experiences with regard to psychosocial support provisioning in Endola Circuit, Namibia* (PhD thesis). University of Fort Hare.

The Regional Psychosocial Support Initiative (REPSSI). (2012). *Mainstreaming Psychosocial Support within the Education Sector*. Author.

Theron, L. C. (2012). Resilience research with South African Youth: Caveats and ethical complexities. *South African Journal of Psychology. Suid-Afrikaanse Tydskrif vir Sielkunde, 42*(3), 33–345. doi:10.1177/008124631204200305

Tsheko, G. N. (Ed.). (2007). *Our Children Our Future. From Vision to Innovative Impact. Community Responses to Vulnerable Children. Qualitative Research Report on Orphans and Vulnerable Children in Palapye*. Botswana: HSRC Press.

UNAIDS. (2006). *Report on the global AIDS Epidemic 2006*. Retrieved from http://www.unaids.org./en/HIVdata/2006GlobalReport/default.asp

UNAIDS. (2013). *Global report: UNAIDS report on the global AIDS epidemic*. Geneva: UNAIDS.

UNAIDS/UNICEF. (2007). *Global Study on Child Poverty and Disparities 2007-2008*. Author.

UNICEF. (2006). *Africa's orphaned and Vulnerable Generations: Children affected by AIDA*. New York: United Nations Children's Fund.

UNICEF, UNAIDS, & PEPFAR. (2006). Africa and Vulnerable Generation: Children Affected by AIDS. Authors.

UNICEF. (2007). *State of the World's Children*. Author.

ADDITIONAL READING

Bennel, P. (2003). *The impact of the AIDS Epidemic on schooling in Sub-Saharan Africa*. Johannesburg: University of Witwatersrand.

Cluver, L., & Gardner, F. (2006). *The psychological well-being of children orphaned by AIDS*. Cape Town, South Africa.

De Wagt, A., & Connolly, M. (2005). *Orphans and the Impact of HIV/AIDS IN Sub-Saharan Africa*. Tumushabe.

Skinner, D., & Davids, A. (Eds.). (2006). *A situational Analysis of Orphans and Vulnerable Children in Four Districts of South Africa*. HSRC Press.

UNAIDS (Joint United Nations Programme on HIV/AIDS). (2006). *2006 Report on the Global AIDS Epidemic*. Geneva: UNAIDS.

UNICEF. (2003). *Africa's orphaned generations*. New York: UNICEF.

UNICEF. (2007). *2004. The State of the World's Children*. New York: UNICEF.

Wood, L., & Goba, L. (2011). Care and support of orphaned and vulnerable children at school: Helping teachers to respond. *South African Journal of Education*, *31*(2), 275–290. doi:10.15700aje.v31n2a484

KEY TERMS AND DEFINITIONS

Child Abuse: When a caregiver or teacher causes bodily harm or injury or death to a child of under 18 years of age. Forms of abuse are neglect, physical abuse, sexual abuse, exploitation, and emotional abuse.

Child Labor: The exploitation of children under the age of 18 years through any form of work that deprives children to have a normal childhood development resulting in affecting them negatively; physically, psychologically, mentally, emotionally, morally, spiritually, and socially.

Loneliness: An unpleasant emotional response that is felt by a child because he or she does not have anyone to talk to like a friend or any significant person.

Orphans and Vulnerable Children: A child under the age of 18 whose mother, father or both parents and or a primary caregiver has died and who is in need of care and protection.

Psychological Issues: These are internal needs that include feelings, thoughts, emotions, understanding and perceptions, and decision making.

Social Issues: These are external needs such as food, shelter, clothing, education, medical care, security, love, and a sense of belonging, which are basic needs for human survival and development.

Suicidal Thoughts: The act of intentionally thinking to end one's life, due to overwhelming feelings of hopeless, useless, unwanted, or unneeded by others.

Well-Being: State of being comfortable, healthy, or happy.

Section 2
Anger Management

Chapter 3
Addressing the Need for Anger Management in Young People:
Using Positive Psychology Interventions

Tanya Heasley
https://orcid.org/0000-0001-5492-694X
University of East London, UK

ABSTRACT

Anger in young people is on the increase worldwide and effective anger treatment services are in demand. However, the lack of research on the construct of anger and little evidence-based practice makes it difficult to ascertain the best service for these angry young people. Moreover, there is a lack of extensive evidence and qualitative research in the combination of psychoeducation and positive psychology interventions in anger management programmes for young people. Therefore, this chapter will summarise a phenomenological study of an existing psychoeducational anger management programme in the UK and discuss its findings. This chapter will present anger and positive psychology in the context of developing an effective anger management programme and provide a simple anger management strategy to use as a foundation for developing anger management programmes in schools.

INTRODUCTION

In an ever-increasing society of angry individuals across the globe, and limited evidence-based practice available (Glancy & Saini, 2005), it is unclear to determine what anger management programme (AMP) would best treat all angry people

DOI: 10.4018/978-1-7998-0319-5.ch003

(Glancy, & Saini, 2005). Furthermore, there has been relatively little evidence and qualitative research in the combination of psychoeducation and positive psychology interventions (PPIs) in AMPs.

More importantly, the need for suitable AMPs to improve relational interactions with each other is required (Thomas, 2001) as aggressive anger is occurring more frequently within our homes, workplaces and schools (Kassinove & Sukhodolsky, 1995). A prevalent problem of aggressive behaviour among young people within schools is on the increase (Campano & Munakata, 2004) therefore, research on discovering the best solution to preventing angry learners is imperative. For that reason, the central theme for this chapter is to address the need for suitable anger management treatments and discuss a phenomenological study on the experience and impact of Tristone Coaching's - Children's Healthy Anger Management Programme (CHAMP) in four adolescent males.

CHAMP is an existing psychoeducational AMP that consists of PPIs and has been facilitated within schools in the United Kingdom (UK) for the past three years. The programme ran for six one-hour sessions weekly and focused on teaching the participants strategies, emotional regulation and assertive communication skills that would enable them to use their anger positively and improve their self-esteem. Each session contained both psychoeducational element and a PPI relevant to that specific session. A phenomenological approach was used to examine the lived experience of the participants from a rural school in the UK and explore their interpretations of its effects on their anger. These interpretations will contribute to the solutions in developing a suitable AMP later in the chapter.

Firstly, in order to determine adequate AMPs, it is essential to develop a different perspective to anger and see its positive benefits rather than try to eliminate it. In other words, to understand what anger is, why it is needed and what treatments are effective in managing it. Therefore, this chapter will also define the concept of anger, present positive psychology, define psychoeducation and end with practical suggestions of anger management strategies for parents, teachers, counsellors and facilitators in service delivery.

ANGER IN PERSPECTIVE

There are many layers to the construct of anger (Spielberger, 1999), as well as many ways an individual can express their anger - for instance; verbally, physically, self-sabotage and suppressing. Therefore, it is difficult to define or distinguish its core characteristic and its benefit. Nevertheless, according to researchers, anger is neither healthy or unhealthy (Kashdan, Goodman, Mallard, & Dewall, 2015), it is a primary emotion (Ekman, 1992) and how it is expressed determines whether it is healthy or not. Furthermore, anger is subjective, while some perceive it as a negative emotion, others utilise its energy for positive change. In other words, anger can be a useful emotion rather than an unwanted emotion. However, some consider internalised anger and low emotional regulatory can lead to aggressive behaviour (Eisenberg et al., 2001), while others suggest anger itself is not aggression (Kassinove, & Tafrate, 2002), anger is instead, an emotional feeling (Kassinove, & Sukhodolsky, 1995).

At its primary function, when anger is activated, it initiates the fight or flight response (survival instinct) (Lotfali, Moradi, & Ekhtiari, 2016), provides motivational tendencies (Kashdan, et. al., 2015) and somatic energy to respond towards, a perceived threat, or escape from it. Therefore, anger has beneficial properties, in that it provides the energy required to get out of danger. However, suppressing this energy over long periods of time interrupts or disconnects the pathways used to transmit messages between the limbic system and the prefrontal cortex in the brain, fundamentally altering its structure which can eventually lead into the development of depression (Gresham, Melvin, & Gullone, 2016) and other mental health issues.

In view of this, research indicates that anger-related issues are often the main cause of an adolescent's referral to the mental health service (Blake, & Hamrin, 2007). Moreover, according to The World Health Organization (WHO, 2013) estimates that, in any given year, 20% of adolescents worldwide, may experience a mental health problem. More importantly, evidence for the need of early interventions is borne out by research that shows 70% of children and adolescents experiencing mental health problems need adequate support at an early age (Children's Society, 2008). While early intervention is key in the prevention of mental illness in children and adolescents, research in determining suitable interventions is sparse, particularly psychoeducational interventions for anger related depression. This gives further rationale of the need for more studies to ascertain suitable anger treatment services for adolescents.

Anger and Aggression

When an individual expresses their anger unhealthily, such as aggressively - not only are they perceived negatively within society, but also self-consciously (Tracy, Robins, & Tangney, 2008). To give an illustration, when a young person expresses their anger aggressively, they are usually masking underlying emotions such as hurt, fear and shame and this can become perpetuated by their negative self-perception of behaving aggressively (Heasley, 2018). When discussing this form of anger expression, it is important to note that negative self-perception can develop into social anxiety disorder (Moradi, Ghahari, Gheytarani, & Safari, 2016). For instance, fear and anxiety, when suppressed, can develop into depression (Moradi, et al., 2016) as well as lead to repressed anger. In other words, feeling sad, depressed and angry correlates to negative self-image (Kernis, Grannemann, & Barclay, 1989). Furthermore, it is suggested that lower self-acceptance is associated with more frequent externalisation of anger in both an indirect and direct way (Kruczek, 2017).

Considering anger is neither healthy or unhealthy (Kashdan, et al., 2015), the way anger is expressed determines whether the outcome is healthy or not (Kashdan, et al., 2015). To give an illustration, aggressive anger could be seen in a learner who has hit another learner because they borrowed a pencil without asking: this explosive behaviour would be deemed as expressing anger unhealthily (Kashdan et al., 2015; Silove, et al., 2017). In addition, another unhealthy expression of anger is when it is directed internally towards the self (Spielberger, 1999), in other words - implosive anger (Spielberger, 1999).

In view of this, it can be argued that there is a fundamental need for anger-coping strategies for young people (Chin, & Ahmad, 2017). Having said that, with the lack of resources and suitable AMPs it is no wonder that young people are finding it hard to express their anger healthy. However, it is important to mention that not all angry young people behave aggressively (Golden, 2004), even though it is without question that all adolescents experience anger as a basic emotion (Ekman, 1992), and most find anger difficult to manage (Phillips-Hershey & Kanagy, 1996).

As mentioned earlier, there is a lack of research on a young person's anger, with more studies focusing on aggression (Burney, 2001), even though aggressive behaviour resulting from anger, is prevalently seen in young people (Feindler & Engel, 2011), therefore, further research on the construct of anger rather than the action of aggression (Saini, 2009), is important when determining solutions for reducing a young person's explosive and implosive anger.

Anger and Shame

Implosive anger can have deleterious effects, such as manifesting into the development of self-harming behaviour (Laye-Gindhu, & Schonert-Reichl, 2005), depression and shame (Shamshikova, Ermolova, & Belashina, 2018). Furthermore, research indicates a strong link between anger and shame (Tangney, et al., 2007) and feelings of shame often precede the expression of anger (Lewis, 1971). Likewise, in a study by Nasir, & Ghani, (2014) show adolescents often felt regret after expressing their anger. Regret positively correlates to shame when one reflects on one's behaviour and uses it as an internal barometer for morals and values (Tracy, et al., 2008). Whereas, counterfactual regret is created through the internalising shame that consequently turns toxic (Bradshaw, 2015) and the individual no longer acknowledges a mistake that has been made, yet perceive their self as a mistake (Bradshaw, 2015). Therefore, shame negatively correlates to self-esteem (Tangney, Wagner, Fletcher, &

Gramzow, 1992). Moreover, low self-esteem is more likely linked with anxiety and depressive disorders (Leary & MacDonald, 2003) and affects well-being (Righetti, & Visserman, 2017).

Although shame is associated with anger and aggression (Tangney, et al., 1992), it has a serving value when reinforcing or developing what is wrong (Harris, 2017). According to Tracy, et al., (2008), the self-conscious emotions: shame, guilt, embarrassment and pride arise when one reflects on one's behaviour and act as an internal barometer for morals and values depicted within individuals and the society (Tracy, et al., 2008). However, shame-bound individuals are more likely to blame others, experience intense feelings of anger, express their anger in destructive ways and are more aware of their anger as the cause for negative long-term consequences for themselves and their relationship with others (Tangney, et al., 2007). Brene Brown's (2006) shame resilience theory, proposes that shame is a three-part construct containing psychological, social and cultural components: psychological relating to emotions, thoughts and behaviours; social relates to the interpersonal context tied to relationships and connections; and cultural points to meeting expectations within society (Brown, 2006). Brown's (2006) grounded theory study of women and shame could not consider shame to be excluded because of any psychological, social or cultural reason and that psychoeducational group work is important in building shame resilience (Brown, 2006). Therefore, incorporating a shame resilience module into a psychoeducational anger management programme would potentially benefit angry young people.

A REVIEW OF ANGER AND ANGER MANAGEMENT RESEARCH

With angry behaviour on the rise worldwide (Ambrose & Mayne, 1999), and the growth of aggressive anger in young people (Feindler & Engel, 2011), it is fundamentally necessary to provide AMPs to a progressively angry society (Glancy & Saini, 2005). Furthermore, there is a great need to improve relationships (Thomas, 2001), as according to Kassinove & Sukhodolsky, (1995), our homes, workplaces and schools are consequently affected by the frequent occurrence of aggressive anger. Moreover, a major problem has subsequently developed due to the aggressive behaviour of young people within society (Feindler & Engel, 2011), particularly within schools (Campano & Munakata, (2004), therefore, it is imperative for empirical research to discover the best intervention for angry young people. In addition, the lack of evidence-based practice available makes it difficult to ascertain the best AMP suitable for angry individuals (Glancy & Saini, 2005). Also, according to Akande (2001) not one treatment suits all, and yet anger management programmes are on the increase, so too are the effectiveness of treating anger disorders (DiGiuseppe, & Tafrate, 2003), such as intermittent explosive disorder (Coccaro, 2012).

Lench, (2004) proposed that developing an anger diagnostic tool is essential in establishing suitable interventions and prevention strategies for angry individuals (Lench, 2004). That said, the limited research on the phenomenon of anger (Kassinove, & Sukhodolsky, 1995), makes defining an anger disorder problematic. Not only is defining an anger disorder problematic due to the lack of scientific study of anger (Kassinove, & Sukhodolsky, 1995), but researchers using a logical-empirical positivist model tend to neglect the phenomenological approach to anger and rely on measurable results through self-reporting, rather than talking to people about their phenomenal experiences (Kassinove, & Sukhodolsky, 1995). Furthermore, not only has there been much less research on the correlates of maladaptive anger expression in young people than in adults (Kerr, & Schneider, 2008), but there are more published studies on depression and anxiety than anger (DiGiuseppe & Tafrate, 2003; Kassinove & Sukhodolsky, 1995), even though in psychotherapy anger is the most challenging of emotions (Norcross & Kobayashi, 1999). Moreover, there is insufficient research on a young person's anger. For instance, according to Burney, (2001), previous studies have only focused on aggressive behaviour (Burney, 2001), and not on the construct of anger, even though this is worth considering when determining the most effective interventions for angry young people and aggression.

Nevertheless, according to Kassinove, & Tafrate, (2002) anger is not aggression, it is the result of various factors contributing to anger that facilitates aggressive behaviour (Nasir, & Ghani, 2014; Neighbors, Vietor, & Knee, 2002; Averill, 1993). In other words, it is the individual's reaction to certain anger-triggering events that leads to aggression (Kashdan, et. al., 2015). Having said that, it is suggested that suppressed anger and limited emotional regulation, leads to aggressive behaviour (Eisenberg et al., 2001) and emotional dysregulation (D'Agostino, Covanti, Monti, & Starcevic, 2017). This theoretical concept according to Rothbart, Ahadi, & Hershey, (1994) asserts that aggression in a young person is caused by their inability to inhibit their emotional impulses. To put it another way, their emotional regulation is impaired. Moreover, researchers have linked insufficient emotional regulation with aggressive behavioural difficulties (Eisenberg, et. al., 2007). Nonetheless, a growth in aggressive behaviour, caused by anger, is seen extensively in young people (Feindler & Engel, 2011), yet, more attention is given to researching the correlates of maladaptive anger expression in adults, rather than in young people (Kerr, & Schneider, 2008).

Despite the lack of attention on the study of anger (DiGiuseppe & Tafrate, 2003), findings in five meta-analytical reviews of treatment for anger and aggression (Beck & Fernandez, 1998; Bowman-Edmonson & Cohen-Conger, 1996; Del Vecchio & O'Leary, 2004; DiGuiseppe & Tafrate, 2003; Tafrate, 1995), demonstrates some beneficial effects of treatment on various aspects of anger. The results appear to suggest that relaxation-based treatments (Tafrate, 1995; Bowman-Edmonson &

Cohen-Conger, 1996; DiGiuseppe's & Tafrate's, 2003) and treatments containing cognitive-behavioural components (Beck & Fernandez, 1998; DiGiuseppe's & Tafrate's, 2003; Del Vecchio & O'Leary's, 2004) as the most effective in improving anger expression (Bowman-Edmonson & Cohen-Conger, 1996; Del Vecchio & O'Leary's, 2004), and anger control (Beck and Fernandez, 1998), as well as treating anger suppression (Del Vecchio & O'Leary's, 2004) and reducing aggressive behaviour (DiGiuseppe's & Tafrate's 2003).

However, limitations to these meta-analytical reviews include; methodical limitations due to few studies being reviewed and the low number of subjects in the studies (Tafrate, 1995; Bowman-Edmonson & Cohen-Conger, 1996); the investigation consisted mostly of an aggressive population with clinical anger (Beck and Fernandez, 1998); the interventions were mostly based on cognitive, behavioural, or cognitive-behavioural models (DiGiuseppe's & Tafrate's, 2003); lacked specific population (Tafrate, 1995; Beck & Fernandez, 1998) and does not include interventions for children (Del Vecchio & O'Leary's, 2004). For the most part, researchers in these studies relied on measurable results through self-reporting, rather than using a phenomenological approach to study the subjective experiences of the participants (Kassinove, & Sukhodolsky, (1995). That said, cognitive-behavioural and skills-based approaches are the most frequently studied and empirically supported treatment for anger and aggression in youth (Blake, & Hamrin, 2007). Nonetheless, in DiGiuseppe, & Tafrate's (2003) meta-analytic review on anger treatments, there is no mention of psychoeducational treatments or positive psychological interventions. This suggests they have not been empirically tested, or they are not available to young people, (DiGiuseppe, & Tafrate, 2003). In view of this, there is insufficient research on the use of PPIs to draw any firm conclusions about the positive effects they have on negative emotions such as anger and shame, as well as reducing aggressive behaviour.

Positive Psychology

The science of positive psychology measures the different mechanisms that induce happiness and subjective well-being, as well as assist individuals and societies to flourish through exploring the positive elements of human functioning (Seligman & Csikszentmihalyi, 2000). Rather than focusing on negative emotions and treating mental health disorders, the intention is to enhance performance and flourishing in an individual or community using a *what's right* approach (Seligman, 2002; Seligman & Csikszentmihalyi, 2000). In other words, the scientific approach to positive psychology is to study the thoughts, feelings and behaviour of an individual and focus on their strengths, rather than their weaknesses - with the intention to build them up, instead of concentrating on repairing what might be broken. Having said that, positive psychology is not about negating negative feelings or dismisses suffering, on the contrary, as according to Seligman, Steen, Park, & Peterson, (2005), to relieve suffering and increase happiness, understanding the two concepts and how they interact with each other is important and can be achieved through a complete science and practice of psychology as well as the use of validated PPIs (Seligman et al., 2005).

The Use of Positive Psychology Interventions

It is postulated that positive psychology enhances performance and flourishing in an individual using PPIs, as well as increases optimal human functioning (Seligman, 2002; Seligman & Csikszentmihalyi, 2000), relieve suffering, cultivates happiness (Seligman, et al., 2005) and enhances positive emotions (Fredrickson, 1998). According to Sin and Lyubomirsky (2009, p. 467), PPIs are programmes, practices, treatment methods or activities *aimed at cultivating positive feelings, positive behaviours, or positive cognitions* (Sin, & Lyubomirsky, 2009, p. 467). For instance, in two meta-analyses of PPIs, research has found that they can enhance psychological well-being, subjective well-being and reduce depressive symptoms (Sin, & Lyubomirsky, 2009; Bolier, et al., 2013), as well as improve happiness, well-being, and enhancing positive emotions (Fredrickson, 1998).

To illustrate, in a study of positive psychology and evidence-based coaching programme for young people, on the impact of their mental health and well-being, results indicate an increase in the levels of their engagement, hope and wellbeing (Ewan & Green, 2013; Dulagil, Green, & Ahern, 2016). Moreover, findings in a study on a further twelve positive psychology school-based interventions were positively related to the wellbeing and academic performance in young people (Waters, 2011).

Having said that, although positive psychology improves the wellbeing in young people, there is a lack of qualitative research on what effects these PPIs had on reducing anger and alleviating shame in young people. Moreover, not all PPIs are suitable to everyone, or an appropriate fit (Lyubomirsky, 2008), therefore, this further gives the reason for research on the effects and impact of PPIs, in addition to exploring suitable anger management treatments for young people from a positive psychology perspective.

Psychoeducation

Psychoeducation has evolved since its first conception noted in an article by John Donley (Donley, 1911), although he had not used the term *psychoeducation*, in fact, the word psychoeducation was first used in a book written by Brian Tomlinson, (Tomlinson, 1941). However, it was not until Anderson, (1980) popularised the term after using it to help patients with schizophrenia.

According to the American Psychiatric Association (APA) (2000), psychoeducational interventions should follow treatment guidelines for individuals with mental health problems, specifically schizophrenia (APA, 2000). However, in using a multidimensional approach to integrating PPIs into a psychoeducational AMP, suggests giving a broader range of constructs for the treatment of anger problems. Therefore, it is apparent that learning to manage anger through psychoeducation equips a young person with emotional dysregulation and inadequate executive function (Rhodes, & Parra, 2017) to first, understand the psychological theory of their thoughts and feelings, and second, learn the mechanisms of anger, coping strategies, and relaxation skills (Rhodes, & Parra, 2017).

Therefore, considering anger-related issues in young people can negatively affect their mental health, a multidimensional approach to using psychoeducation and PPIs could become indispensable adjunctive psychotherapy. Moreover, through psychoeducation, understanding the cause of anger-related behaviour and learning coping-strategies can empower and equip the young person to manage their anger better. For example, according to Reyes, (2010) with an improved understanding of the causes and effects of the problem, psychoeducation broadens the person's perception and interpretation of the problem, and this refined view positively influences the individual's emotions and behaviour (Reyes, 2010). In other words, understanding the concept of anger, its relation to behaviour and other emotions and why an individual experience it, is fundamental to include within AMP.

Considering cognitive-behavioural and skills-based approaches as the most frequently studied and empirically supported treatment for anger and aggression in youth (Blake, & Hamrin, 2007), psychoeducational interventions to manage anger for young people have not been well documented. In addition, there is insufficient research on the use of PPIs to draw any firm conclusions about the positive effects they have on negative emotions such as anger and shame.

RECOMMENDATIONS FOR FUTURE ANGER MANAGEMENT DEVELOPMENT

A Phenomenological Study of An Anger Management Programme

As previously discussed, there is an essential need for the provision of strategies for young people to learn appropriate ways to manage their anger (Chin, & Ahmad, 2017). Furthermore, early intervention is key when tackling anger problems in young people, as well as the ongoing need to determine suitable anger management programme for young people. With that in mind, this section will discuss the findings of a study conducted by Heasley, (2018) of Tristone Coaching's CHAMP. Heasley, (2018), explored the experience and impact in four adolescent males participating on the psychoeducational AMP in the UK, to further contribute to the research in addressing the need to reduce angry behaviour in young people (Heasley, 2018).

Although positive psychology is a science that can be measured (Seligman, et al., 2005) and majority of PPIs have been researched using the quantitative approach, which seeks to measure and uses numerical data to analyse (Carter & Little, 2007), Heasley, (2018) used a qualitative approach to explore, describe and interpret the experiences of the participants (Smith, & Osborn, 2009), and centred on the young person's perception of their anger, shame and their experience of CHAMP (Heasley, 2018). To guide enquiry, an Interpretative Phenomenological Analysis (IPA) was chosen as the methodology to provide a voice, for under-researched children, to be heard (Petalas, Hastings, Nash, Dowey, & Reilly, 2009), and with theoretical underpinnings in phenomenology, hermeneutics and an idiographic perspective (Shinebourne, 2011), IPA was used to enable the researcher to examine the lived experience of the participants (Smith, Flowers, & Larkin, 2013), and provide a detailed account of the participant's interpretation of their practical engagement with the programme (Shinebourne, 2011).

However, not only can IPA present some limitations and has similarities in method as Grounded Theory and Thematic Analysis (Langdridge, & Hagger-Johnson, 2013), its phenomenological analysis can be descriptive, rather than interpretative (Tuffour, 2017), language can be over-simplistic (Langdridge, & Hagger-Johnson, 2013) and bracketing can be problematic (Langdridge, & Hagger-Johnson, 2013). In addition, its subjective research approach means two analysists working on the same data may evaluate different interpretations (Tuffour, 2017). Considering this, a double hermeneutic position was taken due to the two levels of interpretation within IPA, allowing both the researcher and participant to interpret the activities (Shinebourne, 2011), giving a rich and detailed understanding of the AMP from the participant's perspective.

According to the findings, CHAMP alleviates and ameliorates the anger in young people, while also enhancing their psychological wellbeing (Heasley, 2018). Moreover, the experience and impact in four male adolescent participants attending the programme, demonstrated a non-judgmental relationship with the facilitator, provided practical support, developed interpersonal skills and improved their ability to manage their anger (Heasley, 2018). An overview of the emerging themes from the study can be found in Table 1.

The aim of the study was to contribute to the lack of research on suitable AMPs for angry adolescents in looking through a phenomenological lens at a psychoeducational AMP that incorporates PPIs. In general, the participants experienced the programme as beneficial. This benefit is further supported by the positive impact the programme

Table 1. Overview of themes of Tristone Coaching's CHAMP (Heasley, 2018)

	Main Theme	Subordinate Theme
Part One: The overall experience of the programme	• Practical Support • Non-judgmental Relationship	• Helpful • Coping Strategies • Intrinsic Motivation • Someone to talk to • Trust
Part Two: Impact of a child's experience	• Acceptance and Improved interpersonal skills • Improved ability to manage anger	• Improve relationships • Self-worth and self-esteem • Identity • Self-control • Alleviates anger • Ameliorates anger

had on the participant's anger and shame and psychological wellbeing (Heasley, 2018) as well as alleviating and ameliorating their anger. In view of this, the following section will provide a brief overview of the evidence-based solutions to developing a suitable AMP within schools.

Practical Support

To understand the anger and learn coping strategies for managing anger, the psychoeducational element of anger management programmes should aim to be easy, fun and helpful (Heasley, 2018) as well as provide practical components to prevent boredom from developing (Heasley, 2018). Furthermore, according to Reyes, (2010), *With an improved understanding of the causes and effects of the problem, psychoeducation broadens the person's perception and interpretation of the problem, and this refined view positively influences the individual's emotions and behaviour* (Reyes, 2010).

In the study conducted by Heasley, (2018) psychoeducation can increase positive thoughts about personal anger, regulate emotions and produce behavioural change (Heasley, 2018; Kauffman, 2018). These findings are consistent with research literature according to Kauffman, (2018), that children need to be taught skills that are relevant to their needs, as well as productive, autonomous and increases their ability to thrive in their environment (Kauffman, 2018). Moreover, combining practical interventions with the opportunity to talk openly, will benefit young people with concentration issues (Heasley, 2018).

In view of this, it is important to provide a nurturing space to conduct the AMP, such as a classroom, a listening room or a quiet space within the school that will not have interruptions from other learners, teachers, staff, etc. (Heasley, 2018). This is to enable new insight and self-awareness to grow, as well as provide the opportunity to experience something that was inherently enjoyable and rewarding, which can result in cultivating a sense of wellbeing (Heasley, 2018).

In positive psychology, wellbeing can be described as, *true happiness found in the expression of virtue and what is worth doing* (Hefferon, & Boniwell, 2011, p.77). Therefore, it can be postulated that the AMP should be engaging for participants to experience happiness and worthwhile (Heasley, 2018). For instance, Tefler, (1980) suggests that enjoying an activity that leads to learning a skill, develops happiness. To further illustrate, the participants of CHAMP interpreted the programme as helpful and something they enjoyed (Heasley, 2018), therefore, learning anger management strategies can lead to the cultivation of happiness (Heasley, 2018).

Having said that, the effectiveness of the method of delivery, quality of an AMP and rapport between the participants and the facilitator, is an important factor to consider when determining psychoeducation as a requisite for a successful anger management treatment (Heasley, 2018).

Non-Judgemental Relationship

The opportunity to talk to someone and share personal information is an important feature when developing an AMP (Heasley, 2018). Furthermore, trust is an important feature for participants to feel confident and assured that they would not be judged by the facilitator (Heasley, 2018). Therefore, to facilitate adaption and behavioural change in an individual (Ryan, Stiller, & Lynch, 1994) there should be a positive representation in the interpersonal experience between the participant and the facilitator (Heasley, 2018). To achieve this, the participant needs to feel their relationship with the facilitator as supportive and having a connection (Heasley, 2018; Ryan, et al., 1994).

Furthermore, it is worth considering the participant's internalised representation of the facilitator as a contribution to the beneficial factor of an AMP (Heasley, 2018), and it is suggested that perceived autonomous support is fundamental to the adolescent's feelings of relatedness to the facilitator (Ryan, 1992). Not only does this increase self-esteem, but adolescents are more likely to be intrinsically motivated to engage with the AMP (Ryan, et al., 1994) when feeling connected to the facilitator. In addition, positive relationship with facilitators is crucial in establishing a space for belonging, and where confidence, trust, and self-belief can grow (Hanrahan, & Banerjee, 2017; Heasley, 2018).

Despite this, readiness is a key characteristic of their internalised representation of the facilitator (Heasley, 2018). In other words, a potential difficulty in establishing rapport between the young person and adult would impede the effectiveness of the AMP when the young person is not ready to participate (Deffenbacher, 1999;

Howells & Day, 2003). For instance, according to Bowlby, (1969), young people develop attachment styles that continue throughout life. These attachment styles can be considered as secure, anxious/ambivalent and avoidant (Ainsworth, Blehar, Waters, & Wall, 1978).

Moreover, the internalised representation of adults, teachers, practitioners or facilitators, play an important role as attachment figures in the socialisation and development of young people (Ryan, et al., 1994), as well as important predictors of self-esteem, adjustment and motivation (Ryan, et al., 1994). The perception of the facilitator can also drive the motivation and responses of the participant (Mehrabian, 1981).

Acceptance and Improve Interpersonal Skills

Social acceptance and identity are key to managing anger in young people (Heasley, 2018). This can be achieved through improving adolescent relationships and cultivating their sense of belonging, from attending an AMP that provides a supportive environment in which the young person feels valued and accepted (Heasley, 2018). These are essential ingredients for developing positive self-perception (Moradi, et al., 2016).

According to Ryan & Deci's, (2000), self-determination theory, fulfilling the following basic psychological needs: competence, autonomy, and relatedness - fuels the formation of identity (Luyckx, Vansteenkiste, Goossens, & Duriez, 2009). To put it another way, the self-determination theory approach is the foundation for self-development and identity. It has been posited that young people find forming an identity challenging (Luyckx, et al., 2009). In addition, young people experience new self-belief and competence when receiving positive feedback from friends and teachers (Heasley, 2018), subsequently resulting in intrinsic motivation (Hanrahan, & Banerjee, 2017). Therefore, an AMP must positively support participants in the identification of the self (Heasley, 2018), and allow an autonomous motivation to grow their non-contingent self-esteem (Deci, & Ryan, 1995). In other words, provide them with the opportunity to verbalise their self-worth and allow them to be harmonious with their true inner self (Waterman, 1993). When a young person has been given this freedom to express themselves, they feel accepted, connected to, and valued by the facilitator (Heasley, 2018) as well as extrinsically motivated (Ryan, & Deci, 2000).

Improve Ability to Manage Anger

An effective AMP should positively impact the young person's anger and shame, as well as their strategy-use, self-regulation, and focused attention (Heasley, 2018). In other words, their executive functioning skills develop – therefore, enhancing psycho-social behaviour, emotional regulation (Rhodes, & Parra, 2017), and reduced aggressive behaviour (Castillo-Eito, Rowe, & Norman, 2018). Building on from the idea that strengths in executive function utilises anger healthily, this section illustrates that participants can positively identify an AMP as increasing their ability for self-control, reduce their feelings of anger, ameliorate their anger and increase their self-esteem (Heasley, 2018).

Another line of thought on executive functioning demonstrates that enhancing intrinsic motivation to better regulate emotions (Ryan, et al., 1994), can motivate a young person to want to do better at home or in school (Heasley, 2018). Similarly, emotional regulation correlates with motivation - particularly autonomous motivation which is suggested to reduce threatening behaviour (Hodgins, et al., 2010). Likewise, motivational strategies improve behaviour (Swaminath, 2009).

Positive Psychology Interventions for Managing Anger

With regards to improving behaviour and managing anger, it is important to mention that, although AMPs can help support a young person to handle their anger in a more healthy and appropriate manner, it does not prevent them from having the angry episode in the first place. Having said that, the following section provides a general discussion for managing and preventing anger from the findings of using three PPIs in Tristone Coaching's CHAMP that emerged from the experience of the participants on the AMP.

Mindfulness

Mindfulness is an emotional regulation strategy (Gross & Thompson, 2007) useful for anger management (Heasley, 2018). According to the findings in the study of CHAMP, the use of mindfulness in anger management alleviates anger and ameliorate its use in young people (Heasley, 2018). Furthermore, positive emotions mediate in the correlations between mindfulness, depressive symptoms, emotional regulation and self-acceptance (Jimenez, Niles, & Park, 2010) as well as self-concept (Cohen-Katz et al., 2005). Moreover, emotional regulation based on mindfulness is associated with vitality (Ryan & Brown, 2003), this correlates to positive psychology and the enhancement of psychological wellbeing (Seligman, et al., 2005).

Anger Journal

An anger journal is a modified version of Pennebaker's (1997) expressive writing intervention and can provide young people with a tool to understand, express and manage their anger better. Notably, one of the participants on the CHAMP considered their anger journal as a friend they could express their thoughts and feelings to (Heasley, 2018). Furthermore, writing about thoughts and feelings as experimental disclosure improves anger-related psychological health (Heasley, 2018). This is consistent with research literature suggesting expressive writing increases psychological wellbeing (Frattaroli, 2006). Moreover, in a meta-analysis review by Frattaroli, (2006) show experimental disclosure taking place at home provided the participants with comfortability and relaxation to engage more fully in the intervention (Frattaroli, 2006).

Moreover, in the study of Tristone Coaching's CHAMP the experience of a participant completing their anger journal at home, perceived this as a safe option and provide integration within their family, particularly cultivating a closeness with their parent (Heasley, 2018). This correlates with theoretical implications to self-regulation and social interaction theory (Frattaroli, 2006). The strength of such an approach is that self-regulating emotions through expressive writing affects a young person's health and wellbeing through social integration (Frattaroli, 2006). To illustrate further, expressive writing promotes a young person to talk about the events affecting their thoughts and feelings (Heasley, 2018), which in turn improves social relationships (Frattaroli, 2006).

Best Possible Self

The Best Possible Self (BPS) (King, 2001) PPI is a writing activity for the participant to imagine their future selves and that everything has worked out in the best possible way (King, 2001). Young people can identify this activity as a positive indicator for enhancing their self-worth and identity (Heasley, 2018). This intervention can also promote self-regulation and rationalisation of self-worth (Heasley, 2018). This is consistent with research suggesting that BPS PPI promotes emotional regulation and increases self-esteem (Loveday, Lovell, & Jones, 2016). Therefore, since the BPS not only increases self-esteem, it also improves self-regulatory emotions to improve the management of anger (Heasley, 2018).

A SIMPLE ANGER MANAGEMENT STRATEGY

The foundations to all anger management strategies consist of three parts: recognising the signs of anger, making the choice to calm down, and then communicating the situation in a positive way. The following section provides a demonstration of a simple anger management strategy:

Step One: Recognising the Signs of Anger (Breaking up your Anger)

Anger is a communicative emotion telling you something is not quite right and that you need to act. When anger has been triggered, it can be felt as a sensation within the body. Recognising the signs before you respond is key to managing anger. In addition, understanding and acknowledging your thoughts when anger is triggered can also equip an individual to think more and stop before reacting. Finally, taking ownership of your behaviour when expressing anger can highlight the potential consequences you may face.

Think about the times when you have been angry and answer the following:

1. What are the effects on your body (tick all that apply and add any others)?
    a. Muscles tense
    b. Heart beats faster
    c. Breathing becomes faster
    d. Making my hands into fists
    e. Stomach feeling knotted
    f. Sleep problems
    g. Headaches
    h. Sweating
    i. Problems swallowing
    j. Dry mouth
    k. Feeling unreal
2. What sort of things goes through your mind when you are angry (thoughts)?
3. How do you usually express your anger (behaviour)?

Step Two: Choosing to Calm Down (Anger Management is all About Thinking)

When anger is triggered, your primitive brain responds first to make you fight, flight or freeze. This is because the brain is not capable of thinking about responsibility and consequences of action. When this happens, the brain prevents you from *hearing* or understanding what others are saying. It causes you to think in a very black or white way – "I am right, and you are wrong", "I must win, and you will lose".

When this happens, you need to choose to engage your thinking brain as quickly as possible (refer to step one), for you to not do those things that you will later regret. This can be focusing on objects in the room, counting backwards from 20, or using the following breathing and focus strategy – called Rectangle Breathing

1. Locate a shape that is a rectangle – a door, window, book etc.
2. Look at the top left-hand corner and take a deep breath and hold for two counts.
3. Slowly let out your breath as you follow along the top side until you reach the top right-hand corner.
4. Take a deep breath and hold for two counts.
5. Slowly let out your breath as you follow along the right-hand side until you reach the bottom right-hand corner.
6. Take a deep breath and hold for two counts.
7. Slowly let out your breath as you follow the bottom line until you reach the bottom left-hand corner.
8. At the bottom left-hand corner take a deep breath and hold for two counts.
9. Slowly let out your breath as you follow the left-hand side until you reach the top left-hand corner.

Step Three: Clearing process (Communicating the Situation Positively)

As mentioned in step one, anger is communicative - therefore, anger management is essentially about communicating our thoughts and feelings effectively. This step is fundamentally about telling someone how you feel in a more assertive and healthy manner.

Consider every time that you feel angry with another person - you either express your feelings which triggers a reaction in them, or you do not express your anger which builds inside you until eventually you explode or implode. You are in conflict with that person and will remain so until you can resolve matters with them.

If this is not done it is likely that you will remain resentful or hostile towards them. This serves no-one and will evidently keep unhealthy anger alive. Often when it comes to expressing anger to others, there is fear about how to express it in such a way that it is clean, healing and empowering for both you and others.

Using the following basic clearing process, you will find that even in the most difficult and challenging situations you can confront someone, without it becoming a serious drama.

The following *Clearing Process* demonstrates an issue between two friends in school. One has taken a joke too far again, in class, and the other is now communicating their anger healthily to them.

Before starting the clearing process with someone - make sure you consider the following:

1. Be certain about the facts relating to the situation
2. Practice the clearing process with a support person

3. Be aware this is your issue, not theirs.
4. The other person does not need to justify their behaviour to you.
5. Tell the person you need them to listen to you.
6. Offer them the opportunity to give you feedback at the end of the clearing process.
7. Give yourself enough time to do the clearing and ask the person how much time they have available to do the process.
8. Do not be attached to the outcome; sometimes the process may not go the way you want it to.
9. There may be times in the clearing process where you will not have a behaviour to own
10. Do not mix or confuse judgments with feelings when stating the data.

The Clearing Process

Always start by saying the highlighted sentence in order, followed by what you think and feel.

- **I feel**.......... angry with you.
- **Because**.... I have asked you many times, not to make fun of me.
- **When**......the class laughs at me, I feel really upset and embarrassed.
- **What I want is**....... for you to respect me.
- **What I am willing to own about my behaviour is**......often I do not show you the same respect, and I know how hurtful that must be for you.

Keep in mind about clearing – it is about healing and not hurting each other.

SUGGESTIONS FOR FUTURE RESEARCH

Considering the central theme to this chapter is to address the need for suitable anger management treatments and discuss the main findings of the phenomenological study on the experience and impact of Tristone Coaching's CHAMP - in providing solutions to developing future anger management programmes, several limitations need to be acknowledged of the study. For instance, the participant sample was not varied enough - therefore, future studies should include mixed gender and a range of ages to provide a more general result. In addition, the methodology used for this study was an interpretative phenomenological analysis and highly reflexive. Furthermore, the interpretations of the participant's experience of the AMP can differ depending on the researcher's own interpretation of language and meaning. To put it another way, not only does language play an important role when discussing the limitations to this study, but language also shapes the symbolic representations of emotional experiences (Thompson, 1991). Furthermore, interpreting the discourse from the transcriptions depends on the symbolic representations of language in the interviewer. Moreover, two analysists reading the same transcription might provide different interpretations.

However, the key findings of the study on using PPIs in anger management and the solutions to developing future AMPs have contributed to the research recommendations in Richardson, & Halliwell's (2008) "Boiling Point". Published by *The Mental Health Foundation*, Boiling Point is a report about problem anger, how it affects individuals, families and communities and what can be done to reduce the harm it causes.

Despite this, suggestions for future studies should concentrate on determining individuals' anger expression styles. This can be achieved by using the Anger Expression Inventory (AEI) section of the State-Trait Anger Expression Inventory (Spielberger, et al., 1985). The AEI was designed to differentiate between how much anger individuals experience and the extent to what anger they express (Spielberger, Krasner, & Solomon, 1988). In addition, using the State Shame and Guilt Scale-Revised (Marschall, Sanftner, & Tangney, 1994) to determine the extent to whether shame decreases after an AMP.

CONCLUSION

Combining psychoeducation with positive psychology gives a broader range of constructs for the treatment of anger management. Learning to manage anger through psychoeducation equips the young person with emotional disturbances and behavioural struggles to first understand the psychological theory of their thoughts and feelings and second, learn the mechanisms of anger, coping strategies, and relaxation skills (Heasley, 2018).

Drawing on Fredrickson's broaden and build theory (1998), creating a psychoeducational anger management programme developed to promote anger as a positive emotion (Fredrickson, 2013), and an essential fuel for survival and change, will broaden the thoughts of an individual in the moment and serve them in building personal resources to aid the use of behaving constructively, proactively and productively or in a prosocial manner (Heasley, 2018).

According to the research conducted by Heasley, (2018), the study identified self-determined actions in the participants as acting autonomously, self-regulating behaviours, responding positively to events and acting in a self-realising manner (Heasley, 2018). In other words, the participants were taking personal responsibility and developed emotional regulation (Heasley, 2018). These findings are consistent with research showing that adolescents become more self-determined when given adequate support (Wehmeyer, & Abery, 2013) further closing existing gaps in evidence-based practices in young people (Wehmeyer, & Abery, 2013).

Finally, when a young person can fully understand the effects and sensations of their own anger, are able to recognise when and what triggers their anger, and then able to express it in a healthy way, this indicates successful anger management. However, the fundamental key to an effective anger management programme in a school - is the facilitator; whether that is the school counsellor, teacher or support staff. Not only do facilitators play an important role in integrating the participant into the AMP (Heasley, 2018), but it is also crucial for the facilitator to understand the concept of anger, that anger is triggered, the effects anger can have on the body, how others may express their anger, as well as comprehend and accept their own anger. In other words, the facilitators must first attend the AMP as a participant and work on their own anger issues before attempting to teach or facilitate to others.

REFERENCES

Ainsworth, M. D. S., Blehar, M., Waters, E., & Wall, S. (1978). *Patterns of attachment*. Hillsdale, NJ: Erlbaum.

Akande, A. (2001). A way of being: A program for aggression control of male children. *Early Child Development and Care, 167*(1), 127–148. doi:10.1080/0300443011670111

Ambrose, T. K., & Mayne, T. J. (1999). Research review on anger in psychotherapy. *Clinical Psychologist, 55*(3), 353–363. doi:10.1002/(SICI)1097-4679(199903)55:3<353::AID-JCLP7>3.0.CO;2-B PMID:10321749

American Psychiatric Association. (2000). *Diagnostic and statistical manual of mental disorders: DSM-IV-TR*. Washington, DC: American Psychiatric Publishing, Inc.

Anderson, C. M., Hogarty, G. E., & Reiss, D. J. (1980). Family Treatment of Adult Schizophrenic Patients: A Psycho-educational Approach. *Schizophrenia Bulletin, 6*(3), 490–505. doi:10.1093chbul/6.3.490

Averill, J. R. (1993). Illusions of anger. In R. B. Felson & J. T. Tedeschi (Eds.), *Aggression and Violence: Social interactionist perspectives* (pp. 171–192). Washington, DC: American Psychological Association. doi:10.1037/10123-007

Beck, R., & Fernandez, E. (1998). Cognitive behavioral therapy in the treatment of anger: A meta-analysis. *Cognitive Therapy and Research, 22*(1), 63–74. doi:10.1023/A:1018763902991

Blake, C. S., & Hamrin, V. (2007). Current approaches to the assessment and management of anger and aggression in youth: A review. *Journal of Child and Adolescent Psychiatric Nursing, 20*(4), 209–221. doi:10.1111/j.1744-6171.2007.00102.x PMID:17991051

Bolier, L., Haverman, M., Westerhof, G. J., Riper, H., Smit, F., & Bohlmeijer, E. (2013). Positive psychology interventions: A meta-analysis of randomized controlled studies. *BMC Public Health, 13*(1), 119. doi:10.1186/1471-2458-13-119 PMID:23390882

Bowlby, J. (1969). *Attachment and loss* (Vol. 1). New York: Basic Books.

Bowman-Edmondson, C., & Cohen-Conger, J. (1996). A review of treatment efficacy for individuals with anger problems: Conceptual, assessment, and methodological issues. *Clinical Psychology Review, 16*(3), 251–275. doi:10.1016/S0272-7358(96)90003-3

Bradshaw, J. (2015). Healing the Shame That Binds You. *Health Communication.*

British Psychological Society (BPS). (2000). *Code of conduct, ethical principles and guidelines.* Leicester, UK: BPS.

Brown, B. (2006). Shame Resilience Theory: A Grounded Theory Study on Women and Shame. *Families in Society, 87*(1), 43–52. doi:10.1606/1044-3894.3483

Burney, D. M. (2001). *Adolescent Anger Rating Scale: Professional Manual.* Lutz, FL: Psychological Assessment Resources.

Campano, J. P., & Munakata, T. (2004). *Anger and aggression among Filipino students.* The Free Library Sourced.

Carter, S. M., & Little, M. (2007). Justifying Knowledge, Justifying Method, Taking Action: Epistemologies, Methodologies, and Methods in Qualitative Research. *Qualitative Health Research, 17*(10), 1316–1328. doi:10.1177/1049732307306927 PMID:18000071

Castillo-Eito, L., Rowe, R., & Norman, P. (2018). Interventions to reduce aggressive behaviour in adolescents: A systematic review and meta-analysis. . doi:10.13140/RG.2.2.35740.39041

Children's Society. (2008). *The Good Childhood Inquiry: health research evidence.* London: Children's Society.

Chin, L. S., & Ahmad, N. S. B. (2017). Effect of cognitive behavioural therapy (CBT) anger management module for adolescents. *International Journal of Guidance and Counselling, 3*(2), 68–78.

Coccaro, E. F. (2012). Intermittent Explosive Disorder as a Disorder of Impulsive Aggression for DSM-5. *The American Journal of Psychiatry*, *169*(6), 577–588. doi:10.1176/appi.ajp.2012.11081259 PMID:22535310

Cohen-Katz, J., Wiley, S., Capuano, T., Baker, D. M., Deitrick, L., & Shapiro, S. (2005). The effects of mindfulness-based stress reduction on nurse stress and burnout: A qualitative and quantitative study, part III. *Holistic Nursing Practice*, *19*(2), 78–86. doi:10.1097/00004650-200503000-00009 PMID:15871591

D'Agostino, A., Covanti, S., Monti, M. R., & Starcevic, V. (2017). Reconsidering Emotion Dysregulation. *The Psychiatric Quarterly*, *88*(4), 807–825. doi:10.100711126-017-9499-6 PMID:28194549

Deci, E. L., & Ryan, R. M. (1995). Human autonomy: The basis for true self-esteem. In M. Kernis (Ed.), *Efficacy, agency, and self-esteem* (pp. 31–49). New York: Plenum Publishing Co.

Deffenbacher, J. L. (1999). Cognitive-behavioural conceptualisation and treatment of anger. *Journal of Clinical Psychology*, *55*(3), 295–309. doi:10.1002/(SICI)1097-4679(199903)55:3<295::AID-JCLP3>3.0.CO;2-A PMID:10321745

Del Vecchio, T., & O'Leary, K. D. (2004). The effectiveness of anger treatments for specific anger problems: A meta-analytic review. *Clinical Psychology Review*, *24*(1), 15–34. doi:10.1016/j.cpr.2003.09.006 PMID:14992805

DiGiuseppe, R., & Tafrate, R. (2003). Anger treatment for adults: A meta-analysis review. *Clinical Psychology: Science and Practice*, *10*(1), 70–84. doi:10.1093/clipsy.10.1.70

Donley, J. E. (1911). Psychotherapy and re-education. *The Journal of Abnormal Psychology*, *6*(1), 1–10. doi:10.1037/h0071950

Dulagil, A., Green, S., & Ahern, M. (2016). Evidence-based coaching to enhance senior students' wellbeing and academic striving. *International Journal of Wellbeing*, *6*(3), 131–149. doi:10.5502/ijw.v6i3.426

Eisenberg, N., Cumberland, A., Spinrad, T. L., Fabes, R. A., Shepard, S. A., Reiser, M., ... Guthrie, I. K. (2001). The Relations of Regulation and Emotionality to Children's Externalizing and Internalizing Problem Behavior. *Child Development*, *72*(4), 1112–1134. doi:10.1111/1467-8624.00337 PMID:11480937

Eisenberg, N., Ma, Y., Chang, L., Zhou, Q., West, S. G., & Aiken, L. (2007). Relations of Effortful Control, Reactive Under control, and Anger to Chinese *Children's Adjustment. Development and Psychopathology, 19*(02), 385–409. doi:10.1017/S0954579407070198 PMID:17459176

Ekman, P. (1992). An argument for basic emotions. *Cognition and Emotion, 6*(3-4), 169–200. doi:10.1080/02699939208411068

Ewan, W., & Green, S. (2013). Positive psychology goes to primary school. *Education Today, 13*(4), 22–23. Retrieved from http://www.educationtoday.com.au/article/Positive-psychology-goes-to-primary-school-388

Feindler, E. L., & Engel, E. C. (2011). Assessment and intervention for adolescents with anger and aggression difficulties in school settings. *Psychology in the Schools, 48*(3), 243–253. doi:10.1002/pits.20550

Frattaroli, J. (2006). Experimental disclosure and its moderators: A meta-analysis. *Psychological Bulletin, 132*(6), 823–865. doi:10.1037/0033-2909.132.6.823 PMID:17073523

Fredrickson, B. L. (1998). What good are positive emotions? *Review of General Psychology, 2*(3), 300–319. doi:10.1037/1089-2680.2.3.300 PMID:21850154

Fredrickson, B. L. (2013). Positive emotions broaden and build. *Advances in Experimental Social Psychology, 47*, 1–53. doi:10.1016/B978-0-12-407236-7.00001-2

Glancy, G., & Saini, M. A. (2005). An evidenced-based review of psychological treatments of anger and aggression. *Brief Treatment and Crisis Intervention, 5*(2), 229–248. doi:10.1093/brief-treatment/mhi013

Golden, B. R. (2004, January). Healthy anger: How to help your child/teen manage their anger. New Living Magazine.

Gresham, D., Melvin, G. A., & Gullone, E. (2016). The Role of Anger in the Relationship Between Internalising Symptoms and Aggression in Adolescents. *Journal of Child and Family Studies, 25*(9), 2674–2682. doi:10.100710826-016-0435-4

Gross, J. J., & Thompson, R. A. (2007). Emotion regulation: Conceptual foundations. In J. J. Gross (Ed.), *Handbook of emotion regulation* (pp. 3–24). New York: Guilford Press.

Hanrahan, F., & Banerjee, R. (2017). 'It makes me feel alive': The socio-motivational impact of drama and theatre on marginalised young people. *Emotional & Behavioural Difficulties*, *22*(1), 35–49. doi:10.1080/13632752.2017.1287337

Harris, N. (2017). Shame in regulatory settings. In P. Drahos (Ed.), *Regulatory Theory: Foundations and applications* (pp. 59–76). Acton, Australia: ANU Press. doi:10.22459/RT.02.2017.04

Heasley, T. (2018). *Experience and impact of a Psychoeducational Anger Management Programme including Positive Psychology Interventions in Adolescent Males: An Interpretative Phenomenological Analysis* (Unpublished master's dissertation). University of East London, London, UK.

Hefferon, K., & Boniwell, I. (2011). *Positive psychology: Theory, research and applications*. Maidenhead, UK: Open University Press.

Hodgins, H. S., Weisbust, K. S., Weinstein, N., Shiffman, S., Miller, A., Coombs, G., & Adair, K. C. (2010). The cost of self-protection: Threat response and performance as a function of autonomous and controlled motivations. *Personality and Social Psychology Bulletin*, *36*(8), 1101–1114. doi:10.1177/0146167210375618 PMID:20693387

Howells, K., & Day, A. (2003). Readiness for anger management: Clinical and theoretical issues. *Clinical Psychology Review*, *23*(2), 319–337. doi:10.1016/S0272-7358(02)00228-3 PMID:12573674

Jimenez, S. S., Niles, B. L., & Park, C. L. (2010). A mindfulness model of affect regulation and depressive symptoms: Positive emotions, mood regulation expectancies, and self-acceptance as regulatory mechanisms. *Personality and Individual Differences*, *49*(6), 645–650. doi:10.1016/j.paid.2010.05.041

Kashdan, T. B., Goodman, F. R., Mallard, T. T., & Dewall, C. N. (2015). What Triggers Anger in Everyday Life? Links to the Intensity, Control, and Regulation of These Emotions, and Personality Traits. *Journal of Personality*, *84*(6), 737–749. doi:10.1111/jopy.12214 PMID:26248974

Kassinove, H., & Sukhodolsky, D. G. (1995). Anger disorders: Basic science and practice issues. In H. Kassinove (Ed.), *Anger disorders: Definition, diagnosis, and treatment* (pp. 1–26). Washington, DC: Taylor & Francis. doi:10.3109/01460869509087270

Kassinove, H., & Tafrate, R. C. (2002). *Anger management: the complete treatment guidebook for practitioners*. Atascadero, CA: Impact.

Kauffman, J. M. (2018). Psychoeducational Technology: Criteria for Evaluation and Control in Special Education. *Focus on Exceptional Children*, 5(3). doi:10.17161/fec.v5i3.7377

Kernis, M. H., Grannemann, B. D., & Barclay, L. C. (1989). Stability and level of self-esteem as predictors of anger arousal and hostility. *Journal of Personality and Social Psychology*, 56(6), 1013–1022. doi:10.1037/0022-3514.56.6.1013 PMID:2746456

Kerr, M. A., & Schneider, B. H. (2008). Anger expression in children and adolescents: A review of the empirical literature. *Clinical Psychology Review*, 28(4), 559–577. doi:10.1016/j.cpr.2007.08.001 PMID:17884263

King, L. A. (2001). The health benefits of writing about life goals. *Personality and Social Psychology Bulletin*, 27(7), 798–807. doi:10.1177/0146167201277003

Kruczek, A. (2017). Relationship of self-image and self-acceptance with the expression of anger in girls diagnosed with conduct disorder. *Psychiatria I Psychologia Kliniczna*, 17(4), 314–324. doi:10.15557/PiPK.2017.0035

Langdridge, D., & Hagger-Johnson, G. (2013). *Introduction to research methods and data analysis in psychology*. Harlow: Pearson Prentice Hall.

Laye-Gindhu, A., & Schonert-Reichl, K. A. (2005). Nonsuicidal self-harm among community adolescents: Understanding the "whats" and "whys" of self-harm. *Journal of Youth and Adolescence*, 34(5), 447–457. doi:10.100710964-005-7262-z

Leary, M. R., & MacDonald, G. (2003). Individual differences in self-esteem: A review and theoretical integration. In M. R. Leary & J. P. Tangney (Eds.), *Handbook of self and identity* (pp. 401–418). New York, NY: Guilford Press.

Lench, H. C. (2004). Anger Management: Diagnostic Differences and Treatment Implications. *Journal of Social and Clinical Psychology*, 23(4), 512–531. doi:10.1521/jscp.23.4.512.40304

Lewis, H. B. (1971). *Shame and guilt in neurosis*. New York: International Universities Press.

Lotfali, S., Moradi, A., & Ekhtiari, H. (2016). On the Effectiveness of Emotion Regulation Training in Anger Management and Emotional Regulation. *Difficulties in Adolescents. Modern Applied Science*, 11(1), 114. doi:10.5539/mas.v11n1p114

Loveday, P. M., Lovell, G. P., & Jones, C. M. (2016). The Best Possible Selves Intervention: A Review of the Literature to Evaluate Efficacy and Guide Future Research. *Journal of Happiness Studies*, 19(2), 607–628. doi:10.100710902-016-9824-z

Luyckx, K., Vansteenkiste, M., Goossens, L., & Duriez, B. (2009). Basic need satisfaction and identity formation: Bridging self-determination theory and process-oriented identity research. *Journal of Counseling Psychology, 56*(2), 276–288. doi:10.1037/a0015349

Lyubomirsky, S. (2008). *The How of Happiness: A practical guide to getting the life you want.* London: Sphere.

Marschall, D., Sanftner, J., & Tangney, J. P. (1994). *The state shame and guilt scale.* Fairfax, VA: George Mason University.

Mehrabian, A. (1981). *Silent messages: Implicit communication of emotions and attitudes* (2nd ed.). Belmont, CA: Wadsworth.

Moradi, I., Ghahari, S., Gheytarani, B., & Safari, R. (2016). The relationship between identity style, fear of negative evaluation with social acceptance. *Social Sciences, 11*(14), 3549–3553. doi:10.3923science.2016.3549.3553

Nasir, R., & Ghani, N. A. (2014). Behavioral and Emotional Effects of Anger Expression and Anger Management among Adolescents. *Procedia: Social and Behavioral Sciences, 140*, 565–569. doi:10.1016/j.sbspro.2014.04.471

Neighbors, C., Vietor, A. N., & Knee, C. R. (2002). A Motivational Model of Driving Anger and Aggression. *Personality and Social Psychology Bulletin, 28*(3), 324–335. doi:10.1177/0146167202286004

Norcross, J. C., & Kobayashi, M. (1999). Treating anger in psychotherapy: Introduction and cases. *Journal of Clinical Psychology, 55*(3), 275–282. doi:10.1002/(SICI)1097-4679(199903)55:3<275::AID-JCLP1>3.0.CO;2-M PMID:10321743

Pennebaker, J. W. (1997). Writing about emotional experiences as a therapeutic process. *Psychological Science, 8*(3), 162–166. doi:10.1111/j.1467-9280.1997.tb00403.x

Petalas, M., Hastings, R. P., Nash, S., Dowey, A., & Reilly, D. (2009). "I like that he always shows who he is": The perceptions and experiences of siblings with a brother with Autism Spectrum Disorder. *International Journal of Disability Development and Education, 56*(4), 381–399. doi:10.1080/10349120903306715

Phillips-Hershey, E., & Kanagy, B. (1996). Teaching students to manage personal anger constructively. *Elementary School Guidance & Counseling, 30*(3), 229–234.

Reyes, C. (2010, October 22). *What is psycho-education? Psycho-educational teacher for students with behavioral issues.* Retrieved from http://thepsychoeducationalteacher.blogspot.co.uk/2010/10/what-is-psycho-education.html

Rhodes, S., & Parra, M. A. (2017). Executive Functioning. doi:10.1007/978-981-287-082-7_275

Richardson, C., & Halliwell, E. (2008). Boiling point: problem anger and what we can do about it. London: Mental Health Foundation.

Righetti, F., & Visserman, M. (2017). I Gave Too Much: Low Self-Esteem and the Regret of Sacrifices. *Social Psychological & Personality Science*, *9*(4), 453–460. doi:10.1177/1948550617707019

Rothbart, M. K., Ahadi, S. A., & Hershey, K. L. (1994). Temperament and social behavior in childhood. *Merrill-Palmer Quarterly*, *40*, 21–39.

Ryan, R. (1992). Agency and organization: Intrinsic motivation, autonomy, and the self in psychological development. Nebraska Symposium on Motivation. *Nebraska Symposium on Motivation*, *40*, 1–56. PMID:1340519

Ryan, R. L., & Deci, E. L. (2000). Self-determination theory and the facilitation of intrinsic motivation, social development, and well-being. *The American Psychologist*, *55*(1), 68–78. doi:10.1037/0003-066X.55.1.68 PMID:11392867

Ryan, R. M., & Brown, K. W. (2003). Why we don't need self-esteem: On fundamental needs, contingent love, and mindfulness. *Psychological Inquiry*, *14*, 71–76.

Ryan, R. M., Stiller, J., & Lynch, J. H. (1994). Representations of relationships to teachers, parents, and friends as predictors of academic motivation and self-esteem. *The Journal of Early Adolescence*, *14*(2), 226–249. doi:10.1177/027243169401400207

Saini, M. (2009). A meta-analysis of the psychological treatment of anger: Developing guidelines for evidence-based practice. *The Journal of the American Academy of Psychiatry and the Law*, *37*, 473–488. PMID:20018996

Seligman, M. E., & Csikszentmihalyi, M. (2000). Positive psychology: An introduction. *The American Psychologist*, *55*(1), 5–14. doi:10.1037/0003-066X.55.1.5 PMID:11392865

Seligman, M. E. P. (2002). *Authentic happiness: Using the new positive psychology to realize your potential for lasting fulfilment*. New York: Simon & Schuster Australia.

Seligman, M. E. P., Steen, T. A., Park, N., & Peterson, C. (2005). Positive psychology progress: Empirical validation of interventions. *The American Psychologist*, *60*(5), 410–421. doi:10.1037/0003-066X.60.5.410 PMID:16045394

Shamshikova, O. A., Ermolova, E. O., & Belashina, T. V. (2018). *Expression of Individual Psychological Personality Traits Depending on the Level of Anger Repression (A Case Study of a Sample Group of Law Enforcement Officers). DEStech Transactions on Social Science, Education and Human Science.* doi:10.12783/dtssehs/ichss2017/19577

Shinebourne, P. (2011). Interpretative Phenomenological Analysis. In N. Frost (Ed.), *Qualitative Research Methods in Psychology: Combining core approaches* (p. 4465). Open University.

Silove, D., Mohsin, M., Tay, A. K., Steel, Z., Tam, N., Savio, E., ... Rees, S. (2017). Six-year longitudinal study of pathways leading to explosive anger involving the traumas of recurrent conflict and the cumulative sense of injustice in Timor-Leste. *Social Psychiatry and Psychiatric Epidemiology, 52*(10), 1281–1294. doi:10.100700127-017-1428-3 PMID:28825139

Sin, N. L., & Lyubomirsky, S. (2009). Enhancing well-being and alleviating depressive symptoms with positive psychology interventions: A practice-friendly meta-analysis. *Journal of Clinical Psychology, 65*(5), 467–487. doi:10.1002/jclp.20593 PMID:19301241

Smith, J. A., Flowers, P., & Larkin, M. (2013). *Interpretative phenomenological analysis: theory, method and research.* London: Sage.

Smith, J. A., & Osborn, M. (2009). Interpretative Phenomenological Analysis. In J.A. smith (Ed.), Qualitative psychology: A practical guide to research methods. London, UK: Sage.

Spielberger, C. D. (1999). *State-Trait Anger Expression Inventory-2 (STAXI-2).* Odessa, FL: Psychological Assessment Resource Inc.

Spielberger, C. D., Johnson, E. H., Russell, S. F., Crane, R. J., Jacobs, G. A., & Worden, T. J. (1985). The experience and expression of anger: Construction and validation of an anger expression scale. In M. A. Chesney & R. H. Rosenman (Eds.), *Anger and hostility in cardiovascular and behavioral disorders* (pp. 5–30). New York, NY: Hemisphere.

Spielberger, C. D., Krasner, S. S., & Solomon, E. P. (1988). The experience, expression and control of anger. In M. P. Janisse (Ed.), *Health psychology: Individual differences and stress* (pp. 89–108). New York, NY: Springer-Verlag. doi:10.1007/978-1-4612-3824-9_5

Swaminath, G. (2009). Psychoeducation. *Indian Journal of Psychiatry, 51*(3), 171–172. doi:10.4103/0019-5545.55082 PMID:19881043

Tafrate, R. (1995). Evaluation of treatment strategies for adult anger disorders. In H.

Tangney, J. P., Stuewig, J., & Mashek, D. J. (2007). Moral Emotions and Moral Behavior. *Annual Review of Psychology*, *58*(1), 345–372. doi:10.1146/annurev. psych.56.091103.070145 PMID:16953797

Tangney, J. P., Wagner, P., Fletcher, C., & Gramzow, R. (1992). Shamed into anger? The relation of shame and guilt to anger and self-reported aggression. *Journal of Personality and Social Psychology*, *62*(4), 669–675. doi:10.1037/0022-3514.62.4.669 PMID:1583590

Telfer, E. (1980). *Happiness*. New York: St. Martin's Press. doi:10.1007/978-1-349-16325-0_2

Thomas, S. P. (2001). Teaching Healthy Anger Management. *Perspectives in Psychiatric Care*, *37*(2), 41–48. doi:10.1111/j.1744-6163.2001.tb00617.x PMID:15521301

Thompson, R. (1991). Emotional Regulation and Emotional Development. *Educational Psychology Review*, *3*(4), 269–307. doi:10.1007/BF01319934

Tomlinson, B. E. (1941). *The Psycho-educational Clinic by Brian E.* New York, NY: MacMillan Co.

Tomlinson, B. E. (1941). *The psychoeducational clinic*. New York, NY: MacMillan. doi:10.1037/11457-017

Tracy, J. L., Robins, R. W., & Tangney, J. P. (2008). *The self-conscious emotions: theory and research*. New York: Guilford.

Tuffour, I. (2017). A Critical Overview of Interpretative Phenomenological Analysis: A Contemporary Qualitative Research Approach. *Journal of Health Communication*, *2*, 52. doi:10.4172/2472-1654.100093

Waterman, A. S. (1993). Two conceptions of happiness: Contrasts of personal expressiveness (eudaiomina) and hedonic enjoyment. *Journal of Personality and Social Psychology*, *64*(4), 678–691. doi:10.1037/0022-3514.64.4.678

Waters, L. (2011). A review of school-based positive psychology interventions. *The Educational and Developmental Psychologist*, *28*(2), 75–90. doi:10.1375/aedp.28.2.75

Wehmeyer, M. L., & Abery, B. (2013). Self-determination and choice. *Intellectual and Developmental Disabilities*, *51*(5), 399–411. doi:10.1352/1934-9556-51.5.399 PMID:24303826

W.H.O. (2003). *Caring for children and adolescents with mental disorders*. Setting WHO directions. Geneva: World Health Organization. Available at: http://www. who.int/mental_health/media/en/785.pdf

ADDITIONAL READING

Deci, E. L., & Ryan, R. (2000). The "What" and "Why" of Goal Pursuits: Human Needs and the Self-Determination of Behavior. *Psychological Inquiry*, *11*(4), 227–268. doi:10.1207/S15327965PLI1104_01

Feindler, E. L., Marriott, S. A., & Iwata, M. (1984). Group Anger Control Training for junior high school delinquents. *Cognitive Therapy and Research*, *8*(3), 299–311. doi:10.1007/BF01173000

Fischer, K. W., & Tangney, J. P. (1995). Self-conscious emotions and the affect revolution: Framework and overview. In J. P. Tangney & K. W. Fischer (Eds.), *Self-conscious emotions: The psychology of shame, guilt, embarrassment, and pride* (pp. 3–24). New York: Guilford.

Humphrey, N., & Brooks, A. G. (2006). An evaluation of a short cognitive-behavioural anger management intervention for pupils at risk of exclusion. *Emotional & Behavioural Difficulties*, *11*(1), 5–23. doi:10.1080/13632750500392856

Phillips, R., & LaHaye, T. (2002). *Anger is a choice*. Grand Rapids, MI: Zondervan.

Reid, K., Flowers, P., & Larkin, M. (2005). Exploring the lived experience. *The Psychologist*, *18*, 20–23.

KEY TERMS AND DEFINITIONS

Anger Management Programme: A practical study of understanding personal anger and learning coping strategies and techniques on how to manage anger.

CHAMP: Tristone Coaching's Children's Healthy Anger Management Programme is a psychoeducational anger management programme designed to use positive psychology interventions to help young people manage their anger.

Interpretative Phenomenological Analysis: Interpretative phenomenological analysis is a qualitative research approach to a psychological phenomenon.

Positive Psychology: The scientific study of what is right about an individual.

Positive Psychology Interventions: Practical strategies to help an individual flourish and thrive.

Psychoeducation: A form of treatment that educates an individual about their mental health issue and teach them skills that can help them to manage their mental health problem.

Section 3
Trauma

Chapter 4
Secondary Trauma in Children and School Personnel

Robert Motta
Hofstra University, USA

ABSTRACT

A review of childhood secondary trauma is presented. Secondary trauma involves the transfer and acquisition of negative affective and dysfunctional cognitive states due to prolonged and extended contact with others, such as family members, who have been traumatized. As such, secondary trauma refers to a spread of trauma reactions from the victim to those who have close contact with the traumatized individual. Assessment devices are reviewed and most of these appear to be designed to assess secondary or vicarious traumatization in therapists rather than in the general population of adults. The majority of scales lack cutoff scores and this is a significant weakness. The modified Stroop procedure is presented as non-paper and pencil method of assessing secondary trauma reactions. The evaluation of the efficacy of therapeutic interventions for secondary traumatization is virtually non-existent. Systematic studies of secondary trauma are in their infancy and a good deal of further research is needed.

INTRODUCTION

Secondary trauma of childhood typically encompasses negative psychological experiences that are due to a child having a close bond with someone who has been traumatized. This bond could be with a parent, guardian, relative, or anyone else with whom the child is emotionally close. It is not appropriate to call these reactions "secondary PTSD" as there is little evidence that the trauma-exposed child actually

DOI: 10.4018/978-1-7998-0319-5.ch004

develops PTSD. In general, the term, "secondary trauma," refers to the experience of negative affective, cognitive, and behavioral states which result from extended and close contact with others who have been traumatized. School personnel who work extensively with traumatized children can also acquire secondary trauma reactions from the children with whom they work.

BACKGROUND

Those experiencing secondary trauma have not directly experienced a traumatic event but have acquired trauma symptoms vicariously, often through close contact with trauma victims (Figley, 1995; McCann & Pearlman, 1990). One might conceive of secondary trauma as a "spread of effect" of trauma from the impacted person or situation to those who have close involvement with the traumatized person. Hearing about or witnessing trauma situations, and an inclination to identify with those in the trauma situation, can also result in secondary trauma reactions, especially if these vicarious experiences evoke fear reactions in the witness (e.g., Marshall & Galea, 2004; Propper, Stickgold, Keeley, & Christman, 2007). The range of secondary trauma symptoms can include anger, anxiety, depression, low self-esteem, emotional exhaustion, difficulty concentrating, body aches, sleep problems changes in eating habits, startle responses, increase in addictive behaviors, and withdrawing from others. Not only is the study of secondary trauma is in its infancy and comparatively lacking in empirical studies, but systematic, controlled research on secondary trauma in children is almost non-existent.

Secondary trauma or vicarious trauma, are terms that have been used in somewhat different contexts. Secondary trauma, or secondary traumatic stress, parallel the diagnostic categories that are presented for posttraumatic stress disorder (PTSD) and acute stress disorder in the *Diagnostic and Statistical Manual of Mental Disorders*(4th ed., text rev.; *DSM-IV-TR;* American Psychiatric Association [APA], 2000). Vicarious trauma refers more specifically to the alteration of cognitive schemas and core beliefs. For example, therapists who have extensive contact with children who have undergone traumatic experiences may acquire the negative emotional states of these children. In vicarious traumatization the focus is the alteration of one's cognitions and basic life assumptions such as beliefs in environmental stability, safety, and a secure sense of self. However, it is increasingly recognized that vicarious trauma and secondary trauma are not entirely distinct concepts (Bober & Regehr, 2006; Jenkins & Baird, 2002) in that they both involve the transfer of trauma symptoms to others. For this reason the terms "secondary trauma" and "vicarious trauma" will be used synonymously in this review. The overarching issue between the terms is the disturbance of one's emotions and/or cognitions as a result of experiencing the impact of trauma on others.

MAIN FOCUS OF CHAPTER

The main focus of this chapter will be on understating what secondary trauma is, how it is measured, and how it impacts the school system. In one of the first documented investigations of secondary trauma, Rosenheck and Nathan (1985) presented a case history of a 10 year old son of a Vietnam veteran. This child had an unusually intense involvement in his father's emotional life and experienced high levels of guilt, anxiety, and aggressiveness, and a morbid preoccupation with traumatic events that his father had encountered. In another study, Parsons, Kehle, and Owen (1990) compared Vietnam combat veterans with PTSD to Vietnam era veterans without PTSD on their ratings of their children's social and emotional functioning. Overall, veterans with PTSD perceived their children as having substantially greater social and emotional difficulties, marked by an inability to initiate and maintain relationships. It was also found that children of veterans with PTSD were significantly more likely to demonstrate a lack of self-control resulting in more aggressive, hyperactive, and delinquent behaviors. In these examples, it is reasonable to state that the traumatic experiences of the parent negatively impacted the child and that a secondary traumatic process had therefore taken place.

There are a number of other situations in which secondary traumatization can occur. It has been reported to take place in families living with a traumatized family member (Catherall, 1992), in partners of those who have been sexually abused (Nelson & Wampler, 2000), in wives of combat veterans with PTSD (Waysman, Milkulincer, Solomon, & Weisenberg, 1993), in children of Vietnam veterans (Motta, Joseph, Rose, Suozzi, & Leiderman, 1997; Suozzi & Motta, 2004), in wives of police officers (Dwyer, 2005) in grandchildren of Holocaust survivors through intergenerational transfer of symptoms (Kassai & Motta, 2006; Kellerman, 2001; Perlstein, 2010), in family members of those with a serious illness (Boyer et al., 2002; Libov, Nevid, Pelcovitz, & Carmony, 2002; Lombardo, 2005), and in children of parents with serious emotional disturbance (Lombardo & Motta, 2008).

There are also numerous studies documenting secondary trauma reactions in personnel working with individuals who have been traumatized, such as children who have been abused (e.g. Brady, Guy, Polestra, & Fletcher-Brokaw, 1999; Figley, 1995; Ghahamanolou & Broadback, 2000; McCann & Pearlman, 1990, Pearlman & MacIan, 1995; Schauben & Frazier, 1995). School psychologists, social workers, and guidance counselors frequently encounter abused children in their daily work. Research suggests that exposure to reports of traumatic experiences can have a negative effect on one's cognitive schemas and emotional functioning. In this instance, cognitive schemas refer to beliefs, assumptions, and expectations as they relate to one's self-view and one's beliefs about the world (McCann & Pearlman, 1990). Previously held views of one's self and one's environment may be shaken or altered by trauma exposure or by on-going interaction with traumatized individuals. For example, one's view of the environment as being relatively safe and predictable may be altered to a more negative view in which the environment is perceived as threatening. Similarly one's self-view might be shifted from that of an assured, stable self-perception toward a more vulnerable and fragile perspective following on-going exposure to traumatized individuals. Pearlman and Saakvitne (1995) view "vicarious traumatization" as a process whereby an individual's self view is transformed through empathic exposure to the victim's trauma. Such exposure can lead to alteration in one's identity, how one views the world, and one's feeling of personal safety and trust. McCann & Pearlman state that vicarious traumatization may occur because one might "...experience painful images and emotions associated with ..... (the other's) traumatic memories..." (1990, p. 144).

Increasingly, mental health professionals within the schools are being called upon to treat survivors of childhood abuse, violent crime, terrorism, natural disasters, torture, and war-trauma. These school personnel may experience symptoms similar to those of the traumatized children with whom they work and these can result in changes in their occupational and personal relationships. Boscarino, Figley, & Adams (2004) found extensive secondary trauma reactions among social workers who were involved in helping those exposed to the September 11th, 2001 terrorist attack in New York City. Empathy and emotional contagion are also terms that have been used to explain vicarious or secondary trauma reactions. Empathy may be viewed as the ability to understand the child's experience of being traumatized. According to Pearlman and MacIan (1995) vicarious traumatization occurs through empathic engagement and reports of trauma. Similarly, emotional contagion involves the experiencing of another person's distress, but on an unconscious level. For example, a teacher or school mental health worker interacts with a child trauma victim and feels parallel emotions, but has no conscious awareness of the relationship between his or her feelings and those of the child (Figley, 1995). The above studies (e.g. Figley, 1995; Pearlman et al., 1995) highlight the conditions under which secondary trauma might occur but it remains unclear as to why many experience this condition.

SOLUTIONS AND RECOMMENDATIONS

Little to no research exists regarding the treatment of secondary trauma and an overall recommendation is that a greater focus be placed here. It is certainly advisable and recommended that school personnel to be supportive and attentive to students experiencing secondary trauma but little else is known regarding effective intervention. Available literature has not settled upon the specific mechanism by which secondary trauma reactions originate. It would appear that exposure to traumatized caretakers can alter a child's perceptions of self and their view of the safety of their milieu through an alteration of cognitive schemata. In addition to the disruption of one's cognitive schemas, secondary trauma might also be transmitted directly through observational learning as explained by Bandura's (1967) social learning theory.

In the social learning view, one need not alter one's cognitive schemata in order for secondary trauma to occur. Rather, social learning theory posits that simply observing the behavior of another can alter one's perception of events. A cognitive processing component, whether conscious or not, is not a requirement for learning to occur according to social learning theorists. Perhaps the best example of this can be found in the functioning of primates. Rhesus monkeys observing fear reactions in other monkeys will acquire the observed monkeys' fear reactions. This might be analogous to the situation where a child acquires the trauma reactions of his or her parents without the parents having verbalized their problems. What is even more surprising than the occurrence of this direct observational learning process among primates is the fact that rhesus monkeys will acquire fear reactions of monkeys displayed only in a video presentation with no actual contact with fearful monkeys (Mineka & Zinbarg, 2006).

The fact that monkeys acquire fear reactions by viewing videotaped material has implications regarding the degree to which children may acquire fear reactions by watching television. Trauma exposure by way of television may be one way in which secondary traumatization can occur, i.e. the acquisition of trauma responses through exposure to the trauma and violence occurring among others, as viewed on television (Marshall & Galea, 2004; Propper, Stickgold, Keeley, & Christman, 2007). In fact Singer, Flannery, Guo, Miller and Leibbrandi (2004) found that while there were many contributing factors to childhood trauma, exposure to violent material on television was an important element. This finding suggests that limitations on what children watch on TV might be well considered if one wishes to lessen the possibility of secondary traumatization.

FUTURE RESEARCH DIRECTIONS.

A question might be asked as to why we are so sensitive to acquiring the trauma reactions of others who have been traumatized? This is certainly an area for future research. It is possible that the ability to become affected or traumatized by experiencing the trauma of others has survival value and we are therefore genetically predisposed to developing these reactions. We are genetically programmed to be social beings and thus we are affected by the concerns of the members of our society (Cacioppo & Patrick, 2008). Historically, our ancient ancestors who were unaffected by the trauma experience of others may have been less capable of adapting to life threatening situations and therefore their survival prospects might have been compromised (e.g.,

Dawkins, 1976). The increased danger and threat to our ancestors who were unable to react to the trauma of others would be expected to lower their survival chances. Dawkins might take the position that the genes underlying secondary trauma would eventually become dominant among our ancestral survivors and we carriers of those genes would become more abundant than those not carrying the dominant genes. It is possible that individuals not carrying the genetic predisposition to acquiring secondary trauma reactions would have had lower survival prospects and therefore would be less likely to become our progenitors.

Another research direction has to do with the areas of assessment. Assessment of secondary trauma has been problematic because its effects are often less severe and consequently more difficult to detect than those seen in primary trauma and PTSD. There are no scales specifically designed to assess childhood secondary trauma. With the exception of research studies using a modified Stroop procedure, to be described below, virtually all assessment devices for assessing secondary trauma have relied on paper and pencil measures or interviews and are subject to measurement and interpretation errors. Another difficulty in secondary trauma research is the relative lack of psychometrically sound measuring instruments for assessing this phenomenon, in comparison to the relative abundance of measures that assess the primary traumatic experience of PTSD. While the Secondary Trauma Scale (STS; Motta, Hafeez, Sciancalepore, & Diaz, 2001) presents cutoff scores, all other measures of secondary trauma lack psychometrically validated cutoffs and so one's scores on the measures do not tell the researcher or clinician whether or not the individual being evaluated has a significant problem.

Figley, for example, developed the Compassion Fatigue Self-Test for Psychotherapists (CFST; Figley 1995). This scale is used specifically for mental health workers and although it lacks cutoff scores that would be indicative of emotionally troubled or pathological reactions, it has had wide usage and is well regarded. Similarly, Bride, Robinson, Yegidis, and Figley (2003) developed a 17 item Secondary Traumatic Stress Scale (STSS), which measures intrusion, avoidance, and arousal symptoms, associated with the stress of professional relationship between social work practitioners and traumatized clients. The scale shows strong psychometric characteristics but, like the CFST does not have cut off scores and is designed primarily for therapists. The same can be said for the Traumatic Stress Institute Belief Scale (TSI; Pearlman 1996), which measures disruption of beliefs of safety, trust, esteem, intimacy, and control among mental health professionals. A significant issue is that, except for the STS, the above noted scales have been designed with the clinician in mind. The scales assess the extent to which clinicians working with traumatized individuals are negatively impacted during the therapeutic process. Unfortunately, none of the existing paper and pencil scales have been designed specifically for use with children.

Unlike the other measures noted in this section which deal primarily with therapists' reactions to their clients, the Secondary Trauma Scale (STS; Motta, et al., 2001) has been validated with samples involving members of the community, students, and practicing therapists. The STS has a test-retest reliability of .87 for a one to two week interval, an alpha reliability of .89, and demonstrates sound concurrent and discriminant validity. There are 18 items that are rated on a five point scale and so the range of scores is from 18 to 90. Scores at or above 38 on the STS are suggestive of mild to moderate anxiety and scores of 45 or higher are indicative of moderate to severe anxiety. Similarly, scores of 38 or higher are associated with mild to moderate depression, while scores of 49 and higher can be indicative of moderate to severe depression (Motta, Newman, Lombardo, & Silverman, 2004). The availability of cutoff scores can be helpful to both the clinician and researcher in their efforts to better understand the nature and impact of secondary traumatization. When one's score on the STS is high, that person is likely to be experiencing significant emotional upset. Attempts at developing a psychometrically sound secondary trauma scale for children have not been successful.

As mentioned earlier, modifications of the Stroop procedure (Stroop, 1935) have also been used to assess secondary trauma. Specifically, a variant of the Stroop procedure sometimes referred to as the "modified Stroop" or "emotional Stroop," has been employed for this purpose. The standard Stroop procedure involves a series of color words such as RED, GREEN, YELLOW, etc. These words are printed in colors such that the color and the word do not agree with each other. The word RED, for example, might be printed in the color, green. Researchers note that participants take longer to name the color of the word, when the underlying word meaning and the word color don't agree with each other. When the word and the color in which it is printed do coincide, the time required to name of color of the word is lessened. The delay in color naming, when word meaning and word color do not coincide, is said to occur because of the cognitive and perceptual interference caused by the dissimilarity of word and color and is appropriately referred to as the Stroop "interference effect." A version of this procedure was used to study PTSD in children who had been sexually and physically abused (Dubner and Motta, 1999). One of the tasks required of the abused children was to name the colors of sex abuse words such as NAUGHTY, TOUCH, SEX, PRIVATES, and SECRET presented 50 times. Sexually abused children with PTSD took significantly longer to name the colors than other groups of children. The modified Stroop has also been used in assessing secondary trauma in the grandchildren of Holocaust survivors (Kassai & Motta, 2006; Perlstein, 2010) where the task is to color name stimulus words relevant to the Holocaust.

The modified or emotional Stroop procedure has been used in the assessment of affective difficulties related to war experiences. Here, war related words such as COMBAT, WEAPON, BLAST, etc. are printed in colors and the participant's task is to name the colors in which the words are printed, but not read the words themselves. Words that have emotional significance, as would the above words to a combat veteran, take longer to color name than neutral words (CHAIR, CAR, PAINT, etc.) or positive words (HAPPY, PLEASED, CONTENT, etc). Similarly non-combatants name the colors of the combat words faster than those who have experienced combat because the words have less emotional significance to them. This procedure has been used to evaluate response delays due to emotional concerns, both primary and secondary, related to war, rape, PTSD, interpersonal violence, and other traumas and sources of emotional distress (e.g., Foa, Feske, Murdock, Kozac, & McCArthy, 1991; McNally, Kaspi, Riemann, & Zeitlin, 1990). The Stroop's usage in assessing secondary trauma has been limited but nevertheless, useful.

In a study of secondary trauma, children of war veterans and those of non-veterans named the colors in which war related words were printed (Motta, Joseph, Rose, Suozzi, & Leiderman, 1997). Participants also completed a series of standardized measures related to in impact of war experience. A statistically significant difference in color naming time between the children of veterans and non-veterans was found only on the Stroop stimulus card containing war related words. There were other cards involving neutral, positive, and cleanliness related stimuli in addition to the standardized measures. These other measures did not show differences between children of veterans and children of non-veterans. This initial study suggested that the Stroop procedure involving words relevant to emotional concerns could be successfully used to assess secondary trauma. It also revealed that the modified Stroop procedure was able to detect secondary trauma effects while standard measures were not able to do so.

A related study of secondary traumatization using the Stroop was conducted (Suozzi & Motta, 2004). This study systematically investigated the relationship between intensity of Vietnam combat exposure and the transfer of trauma symptom to children of veterans. It was thus specifically designed to assess secondary traumatization effects due to combat. Forty male combat veterans who comprised high and low combat intensity groups were administered a series of measures designed to assess PTSD, depression, anxiety, intrusive thoughts, and avoidance responses. Veterans also completed an emotional Stroop procedure involving combat relevant and non-relevant stimuli. Offspring of veterans ($n=53$) completed similar measures. It was found that affective responses of the offspring were impacted by level of combat intensity of their fathers. The most pronounced effects occurred on the emotional Stroop stimulus card involving war related words, where children of high combat veterans showed the longest Stroop response latencies. Results of this study supported the Stroop paradigm as a research tool for investigating secondary trauma in parent-child dyads.

The value of the modified or emotional Stroop procedure is that it presents an objective methodology for assessing secondary trauma in children and adults. It is a highly sensitive procedure in that it will often pick up differences between secondary trauma groups where standardized measures will not. The procedure has three apparent drawbacks. First, it is necessary to use stimulus words that are relevant to the particular area of trauma, whether it be rape, war, combat exposure, interpersonal violence, etc. This can be a cumbersome and time consuming during initial stages of development of the relevant stimuli. Second, while the procedure does provide reliable and replicable outcomes, it, like many other measures of secondary trauma, lacks cutoff scores and therefore has inherent limitations. A third limitation is that because of its relatively limited use it has not been extensively validated as far as specificity and predictive power are concerned. Nevertheless, it is significantly correlated with both PTSD measures and with both anxious and depressive reactions (Suozzi et al., 2004).

Perhaps the real strength of the modified Stroop procedure is that it provides a means of validating the existence of secondary trauma reactions without a reliance on self-report. The data derived from the Stroop are simple response latency measures and as such are far less influenced by one's perceptions and beliefs than are the paper and pencil measures. The Stroop appears to be relatively impervious to social desirability influences as participants are characteristically unfamiliar with what constitutes an adaptive or maladaptive response, and this adds to its utility for both practice and research purposes.

Another research direction is a focus on treatment. There are virtually no agreed upon treatments that are specifically targeted for treating secondary traumatization in children or in adults. Generally, when treatments are attempted, they tend to follow those typically seen for treating PTSD. Thus, one sees a variety of interventions from re-exposure to trauma stimuli, pharmacotherapy aimed at reducing anxiety and depression, psychotherapy, peer participation, family therapy, etc. Elements of treatment involve establishing a therapeutic alliance, providing education, managing anxiety, facilitating re-experiencing, and integration of the trauma experiences. Exposure therapy has been used for at least the past two decades and is one of the more common ways of treating PTSD although its utility with children is less well established than with adults. It is assumed that it might also be useful in treating secondary trauma, although there are virtually no empirical studies in this area. Exposure therapy involves re-experiencing (for example, through verbal recounting, the use of imagery, or through other techniques such as virtual reality procedures) and re-processing traumatic material in a graded, controlled fashion and within the safe confines of the therapist's office or clinical setting. The vast majority of cognitive-behavioral interventions for dealing with PTSD and acute trauma reactions involve some form of re-exposure to, and re-experiencing of, formerly traumatizing events (e.g. Lyons 1987; Saigh, 1987). Therefore the assumption has been that a similar process might be of value for those suffering from secondary traumatization. As stated earlier, there are virtually no controlled and validated studies in this area.

It is important do determine effective interventions for treating secondary trauma in children and in mental health professionals who work with children, as they have high rates of burnout and turnover. This is especially true of therapists working in outpatient and inpatient settings where trauma victims are seen on a regular basis (Kottler, 1993). The question arises as to what can be done to protect therapists from secondary traumatization within these environments? According to Killian (2008), social support is the most significant factor in protecting against treatment induced psychological strain and in terms of enhancing employment satisfaction. "Maintaining peer contact and consultation provides an opportunity to share how one's work and personal life interact and affect each other, to examine what areas of one's life have been disrupted by this work, and to reality test by stepping back and assessing how much the work has increased one's cynicism or alienation" (p. 40).

A number of factors have been associated with increasing levels of secondary traumatization in child therapists. These include the number of cases typically seen, whether the therapist has their own work space, the degree of control the therapist has over such issues as how many days are worked and how many cases are seen, and whether or not the therapist has experienced personal traumas (Jenkins & Baird, 2002). Those who see many cases of traumatized children, and those who have little control over their schedules are more likely to develop secondary trauma. Killian (2008) suggests that agencies should take on the responsibility of modifying the variables that produce work stress and compassion fatigue in therapists rather than placing the onus of responsibility on therapists to take care of these matters themselves. Such an approach is proactive and attempts to prevent problems rather than allowing them to develop and then devising strategies for dealing with them.

Bober and Regehr (2006) found that while therapists agreed that having more time for leisure activity, social interactions, and other self-care activities such as exercise and hobbies, would be helpful in reducing their stress, they did not necessarily pursue these activities for themselves. They seemed much better at advising others to engage in these activities than in following their own advice. However, a qualitative study by Killian (2008) did not find significant correlations between the use of these various coping strategies and the reduction of secondary traumatization, but did find that lowering hours worked per week, having control over ones work environment and schedule, and social support were effective in reducing secondary trauma. Phipps and Byrne (2003) suggest that interventions for secondary trauma should include components that involve social support, normalization of the therapists' experiences, and the provision of some of the self-help strategies noted above. Similarly, Munroe et al.(2003) stress the importance of professional social support with an emphasis on advising therapists to pursue personal self-care strategies. Clearly, this is an area much in need of additional research as there are virtually no systematic studies with regard to the treatment of secondary traumatization among therapists or non-therapists.

CONCLUSION

Recent research and clinical observation shows that traumatic experiences have a contagious nature to them and can negatively impact children. The impact of trauma is experienced not only by the victims of trauma but also spreads to those who have close contact with the victims. It also spreads to those who strongly identify with trauma victims and who might be repeatedly exposed to trauma through video or TV. School psychologists are likely to see troubled children whose caretakers have been traumatized by a variety of experiences including war, community violence, terrorist attacks, family conflict, etc. The fact that fears can be acquired through observation has been seen at both the human and at the primate level and this suggests that we may be genetically "hard-wired" to acquiring secondary trauma reactions through vicarious exposure.

There is comparatively little research on secondary trauma measurement and the majority of the assessment devices that do exist tend to be designed for therapists and not for the general population nor for children. There is no systematic and controlled research focusing upon an evaluation of various therapeutic interventions for secondary trauma as seen in children and adults. These are areas that are much in need of further study. It is unfortunate that we, and especially the younger generation, are increasingly exposed to traumatic events such as terrorism on television. The existence of a "video generation" as we have today all but assures that terrorist acts, and other forms of trauma, will have an increasingly wider negative impact, particularly on the young. A good deal of additional research is needed in areas such as the nature of secondary trauma, the underlying process by which it spreads to others, its assessment and treatment. Research on treatment of secondary trauma in children is particularly needed, as there are no systematic, comparative studies in this area. Nevertheless, it is gratifying to see that secondary traumatization is increasingly recognized as a real phenomenon and this will doubtlessly lead to further research and the growth of our knowledge in this important area.

REFERENCES

American Psychiatric Association. (2000). *Diagnostic and statistical manual of mental disorders* (4th ed.). Washington, DC: Author.

Bandura, A. (1967). The role of modeling personality development. In C. Lavatelli & F. Stendler (Eds.), *Readings in childhood and development* (pp. 334–343). New York: Harcourt Brace Jovanovich.

Bober, T., & Regeher, C. (2006). Strategies for reducing secondary or vicarious trauma: Do they work? *Brief Treatment and Crisis Intervention, 6*(1), 1–9. doi:10.1093/brief-treatment/mhj001

Boscarino, J. A., Figley, C. R., & Adams, R. E. (2004). Compassion fatigue following September 11 terrorist attacks: A study of secondary trauma among New York City social workers. *International Journal of Emergency Mental Health, 6*(2), 57–66. PMID:15298076

Boyer, B., Bubel, D., Jacobs, S. R., Knolls, M., Harwell, V. D., Goscicka, M., & Keenan, A. (2002). Posttraumatic stress in women with breast cancer and their daughters. *The American Journal of Family Therapy, 30*(4), 323–338. doi:10.1080/01926180290033466

Brady, J. L., Guy, J. D., Poelstra, P. L., & Fletcher-Brokaw, B. F. (1999). Vicarious traumatization, spirituality, and treatment of sexual abuse survivors: A national survey of women psychotherapists. *Professional Psychology, Research and Practice, 30*(4), 368–393. doi:10.1037/0735-7028.30.4.386

Bride, B. E., Robinson, M. M., Yegidis, B., & Figley, C. R. (2003). Development and validation of the secondary traumatic stress scale. *Research on Social Work Practice, 13*, 1–16.

Cacioppo, J. T., & Patrick, W. (2008). *Lonliness: Human Nature and the Need for Social Conncetion*. New York: W.W. Norton & Co.

Catherall, D. R. (1992). *Back from the brink: a family guide to overcoming traumatic stress*. New York: Bantam Books.

(1995). Compassion fatigue as secondary traumatic stress disorder: An overview. InFigley, C. R. (Ed.), *Compassion Fatigue: Coping with Secondary Traumatic Stress Disorder in Those Who Treat the Traumatized* (pp. 1–19). New York: Brunner/Mazel.

Dawkins, R. (1976). *The Selfish Gene*. Oxford, UK: Oxford University Press.

Dwyer, L. A. (2005). *An investigation of secondary trauma in police wives* (Unpublished doctoral dissertation). Hofstra University, Hempstead, NY.

Foa, E. B., Feske, U., Murdock, R. G., Kozac, M. J., & McCarthy, P. R. (1991). Processing of threat-related material in rape victims. *Journal of Abnormal Psychology, 100*(2), 156–162. doi:10.1037/0021-843X.100.2.156 PMID:2040766

Ghahramanlou, M. A., & Brodbeck, C. (2000). Preditors of secondary trauma in sexual assault counselors. *International Journal of Emergency Mental Health, 1,* 229–240. PMID:11217154

Jenkins, S., & Baird, S. (2002). Secondary traumatic stress and vicarious trauma: A validation study. *Journal of Traumatic Stress, 15*(5), 423–432. doi:10.1023/A:1020193526843 PMID:12392231

Kassai, S. C., & Motta, R. W. (2006). An investigation of the spread of potential Holocaust-related secondary traumatization to the third generation. *International Journal of Emergency Mental Health, 8*(1), 35–47. PMID:16573251

Kellerman, N. (2001). Psychopathology in children of Holocaust survivors: A review of the research literature. *The Israel Journal of Psychiatry and Related Sciences, 38*(1), 36–46. PMID:11381585

Kottler, J. A. (1993). *On being a therapist* (2nd ed.). San Francisco: Jossey-Bass.

Libov, B. G., Nevid, J. S., Pelcovitz, D., & Carmony, T. M. (2002). Posttraumatic stress symptomology in mothers of pediatric cancer survivors. *Psychology & Health, 19*(4), 501–511. doi:10.1080/0887044022000004975

Lombardo, K., & Motta, R. W. (2008). Secondary trauma in children of parents with mental illness. *Traumatology, 14*(3), 57–67. doi:10.1177/1534765608320331

Lombardo, M. (2005). *Secondary trauma in individuals exposed to a person with a serious medical illness* (Unpublished doctoral dissertation). Hofstra University, Hempstead, NY.

Lyons, J. A. (1987). Posttraumatic stress disorder in children and adolescents: A review of the literature. *Developmental and Behavioral Pediatrics, 8*(6), 349–356. doi:10.1097/00004703-198712000-00007 PMID:3323244

Marshall, R. D., & Galea, S. (2004). Update on posttraumatic stress disorder. *Journal of Clinical Psychology, 65*(Suppl1), 37–43.

McCann, I. L., & Pearlman, L. A. (1990). Vicarious traumatization: A framework for understanding the psychological effects of working with victims. *Journal of Traumatic Stress, 3*(1), 131–150. doi:10.1007/BF00975140

McNally, R. J., Kaspi, S. P., Riemann, B. C., & Zeitlin, S. B. (1990). Selective processing of threat cues n posttraumatic stress disorder. *Journal of Abnormal Psychology, 99*(4), 398–402. doi:10.1037/0021-843X.99.4.398 PMID:2266215

Mineka, S., & Zinbarg, R. (2006). A contemporary learning theory perspective on the Etiology of anxiety disorders. *The American Psychologist, 61*(1), 10–26. doi:10.1037/0003-066X.61.1.10 PMID:16435973

Motta, R. W., Hafeez, S., Sciancalepore, R., & Diaz, A. B. (2001). Discriminant validation of the Secondary Trauma Scale. *Journal of Psychotherapy in Independent Practice, 24*, 17–24.

Motta, R. W., Joseph, J. M., Rose, R. D., Suozzi, J. M., & Leiderman, L. (1997). Assesment of secondary trauma with a modified Stroop procedure. *Journal of Clinical Psychology, 53*, 895–903. doi:10.1002/(SICI)1097-4679(199712)53:8<895::AID-JCLP14>3.0.CO;2-F PMID:9403392

Motta, R. W., Newman, C. L., Lombardo, K. K., & Silverman, M. A. (2004). Objective assessment of secondary trauma. *International Journal of Emergency Mental Health, 6*(2), 67–74. PMID:15298077

Munroe, J. F., Shay, J., Fisher, L. M., Makary, L. M., Rapperport, K., & Zimering, R. T. (2003). Preventing compassion fatigue: A team treatment model. In C. R. Figley (Ed.), *Compassion Fatigue: Coping with Secondary Traumatic Stress Disorder in Those who treat the traumatized* (pp. 209–231). Brunner /Mazel.

Nelson, B. S., & Wampler, K. S. (2000). Systemic effects of trauma in clinic couples: An exploratory study of secondary trauma resulting from childhood abuse. *Journal of Marital and Family Therapy, 26*(2), 171–184. doi:10.1111/j.1752-0606.2000.tb00287.x PMID:10776604

Parsons, J., Kehle, T. J., & Owen, S. V. (1990). Incidence of behavior problems among children of Vietnam war veterans. *School Psychology International, 11*(4), 253–259. doi:10.1177/0143034390114002

Pearlman, L. A., & MacIan, P. S. (1995). Vicarious traumatization: An empirical study of the effects of trauma work on trauma therapists. *Professional Psychology, Research and Practice, 26*(6), 558–565. doi:10.1037/0735-7028.26.6.558

Pearlman, L. A., & Saakvitne, K. W. (1995). Treating therapists with secondary traumatic stress disorders. In C. R. Figley (Ed.), *Compassion fatigue: Coping with secondary traumatic stress disorder in those who treat the traumatized* (pp. 150–177). New York: Brunner/Mazel.

Perlstein, P. (2010). *An evaluation of potential transgenerational transmission of Holocaust trauma in the third generation* (Doctoral dissertation). Hofstra University, Hempstead, NY.

Phipps, A. B., & Mitchell, K. (2003). Brief interventions for secondary trauma: Review and recommendations. *Stress and Health, 19*(3), 139–147. doi:10.1002mi.970

Propper, R. W., Stickgold, R., Keeley, R., & Christman, S. D. (2007). Is television traumatic? Dreams, stress, and media exposure in the aftermath of September 11, 2001. *Psychological Science, 18*(4), 334–340. doi:10.1111/j.1467-9280.2007.01900.x PMID:17470259

Rosenheck, R., & Nathan, P. (1985). Secondary traumatization in the children of Vietnam veterans with posttraumatic stress disorder. *Hospital & Community Psychiatry, 36*, 538–539. PMID:4007811

Saigh, P. A. (1987). In vitro flooding of childhood posttraumatic stress disorder. *School Psychology Review, 16*, 203–211.

Schauben, L. J., & Frazier, P. S. (1995). Vicarious trauma: The effects on female counselors of working with sexual violence survivors. *Psychology of Women Quarterly, 19*(1), 49–54. doi:10.1111/j.1471-6402.1995.tb00278.x

Singer, M. L., Flannery, D. J., Guo, S., Miller, D., & Leibbrandi, S. (2004). Exposure to violence, parental monitoring and television as contributors to children's psychological trauma. *Journal of Community Psychology, 32*(5), 489–504. doi:10.1002/jcop.20015

Stroop, J. R. (1935). Studies of interference in serial verbal reactions. *Journal of Experimental Psychology, 18*(6), 643–661. doi:10.1037/h0054651

Suozzi, J., & Motta, R. W. (2004). The relationship between combat exposure and the transfer of trauma-like symptoms to offspring of veterans. *Traumatology, 10*(1), 17–37. doi:10.1177/153476560401000103

Waysman, M., Mikulinger, M., Solomon, Z., & Weisenberg, M. (1993). Secondary traumatization among wives of posttraumatic combat veterans: A family topology. *Journal of Family Psychology, 7*(1), 104–118. doi:10.1037/0893-3200.7.1.104

ADDITIONAL READING

Lombardo, K., & Motta, R. W. (2008). Secondary trauma in children of parents with mental illness. *Traumatology, 14*(3), 57–67. doi:10.1177/1534765608320331

McCann, I. L., & Pearlman, L. A. (1990). Vicarious traumatization: A framework for understanding the psychological effects of working with victims. *Journal of Traumatic Stress, 3*(1), 131–150. doi:10.1007/BF00975140

Mineka, S., & Zinbarg, R. (2006). A contemporary learning theory perspective on the Etiology of anxiety disorders. *The American Psychologist, 61*(1), 10–26. doi:10.1037/0003-066X.61.1.10 PMID:16435973

Motta, R. W., Joseph, J. M., Rose, R. D., Suozzi, J. M., & Leiderman, L. (1997). Assesment of secondary trauma with a modified Stroop procedure. *Journal of Clinical Psychology, 53*, 895–903. doi:10.1002/(SICI)1097-4679(199712)53:8<895::AID-JCLP14>3.0.CO;2-F PMID:9403392

Motta, R. W., Newman, C. L., Lombardo, K. K., & Silverman, M. A. (2004). Objective assessment of secondary trauma. *International Journal of Emergency Mental Health, 6*(2), 67–74. PMID:15298077

Stroop, J. R. (1935). Studies of interference in serial verbal reactions. *Journal of Experimental Psychology, 18*(6), 643–661. doi:10.1037/h0054651

Van der Kolk, B. A. (2014). *The body keeps the score*. New York: Viking Press.

Van dernoot Lipsky, L. (2007). Trauma stewardship: An everyday guide to caring for self while caring for others. Las Olas Press.

KEY TERMS AND DEFINITIONS

Emotional Stroop: Similar to the Stroop Procedure but rather than using the names of colors, emotion evoking words are used. The delay in naming the color of these words, as opposed to emotionally neutral words, reveals their emotional impact.

Modeling: Enacting the behavior of another simply through observation.

Observational Learning: That form of learning that takes place simply through viewing another's behavior and not through a process of instruction.

Secondary Trauma: The spread of the negative emotional states due to trauma to others who have not been traumatized.

Secondary Trauma Scale: As scale developed specifically for assessing secondary trauma. It emphasizes the degree to which another person's trauma responses produce similar responses in the recipient, although the latter has not been traumatized.

Secondary Traumatization: The process of acquiring secondary trauma responses.

Stroop Procedure: A testing procedure developed by J.R. Stroop that examines the delay in naming the color of printed words when those words describe colors that are not congruent with the actual ink color in which the words are printed.

Vicarious Trauma: Is another term commonly used in the literature to describe secondary trauma. It is often used for the spread of trauma between clients and therapists.

Chapter 5

Student Trauma, the Hidden Curriculum, and Cultural Humility:
This Trio Needs a Team Approach

Dana C. Branson
Southeast Missouri State University, USA

ABSTRACT

Student trauma can set up challenges and obstacles to a student's academic success. The correlation between experienced childhood trauma and negative medical and social problems is significant, creating problems at school with academic work, behaviors, and social interactions. Further compounding this issue are cultural differences in traumatic resolution and the hidden curriculum of education, especially as the globalization of school communities increases. The complexity of this issue generates an ideal situation for a multidisciplinary team approach, with precise defining of each team member's role to increase comprehensive services for teachers, students, families, and the administration. Essential members of the multidisciplinary team are school administration, teachers, family members, guidance staff, counseling staff, school social workers, school nurses, and community resources that can coordinate with the school to create individualized plans to optimize student success. The chapter is a compilation of scholarly research through desktop research.

DOI: 10.4018/978-1-7998-0319-5.ch005

INTRODUCTION

The goal of educators is to provide students with a learning environment in which they can absorb, comprehend, synthesize, and apply information that is important for the future. While educating students has always involved challenges, the globalization of the classroom, amalgamated with childhood trauma and the hidden curriculum, are creating new obstacles that make learning difficult for some of schools' most vulnerable students. This chapter will discuss contemporary research concerning childhood trauma and how common and paradoxical manifestations of behavior can spill over into the classroom. Additionally, cultural differences and the hidden curriculum of classrooms can create another layer of difficulty for students—often students who are already at a disadvantage due to being displaced, adjusting to new surroundings, communication difficulties, on-going negative dynamics of being a member of an oppressed and marginalized people group, and lack a peer support group.

Due to the complexity of these intertwined issues, there is no simple or universal approach to effectively deal with these challenges to learning and classroom management. A multidisciplinary team is a realistic approach to a problem that is complicated and involves numerous individual factors. The team approach involves two important components: a well fashioned, multiple-player team with well-defined roles and the unity of the team toward an end goal. It is not enough to believe that a teacher or a guidance counselor should be able to "fix" a multidimensional problem. An ideal team comprises players from a student's home, school, and community to provide comprehensive assistance to all aspects of the issues, not just the behaviors in the classroom.

BACKGROUND

Research into childhood trauma has consistently found that experienced adversity is correlated with an increased risk of negative outcomes in several life domains, specifically physical, emotional, cognitive, social, and spiritual arenas (Asok, Benard, Roth, Rosen, & Dozier, 2013; Belsky, Schlomer, & Ellis, 2012; Danese & McEwen, 2012; Institute of Medicine and National Research Council, 2014; Power, et al., 2013). The importance of family is central to theoretical underpinnings and a starting point of investigation of both positive and negative life outcomes. For example, the family serves many roles, such as basic protection, affection, companionship, social status, means of reproduction, and regulation of sexual behavior, and constructs a world view for members through a complex lens of culture, temperament, personality, environment, and individual experiences (Zastrow & Kirst-Ashman, 2016). The family unit is the most foundational influence of culture for children, providing them with the lens through which they view the world, make sense of experiences, interpret the meaning of incoming information, and interact with the world through this highly delicate and complex creation of culturally-based norms (Schaefer, 2016). Ideally, the family unit is a buffer that protects children from negative life experiences and a source of whole-person nourishment with the hope of fashioning productive and well-adjusted adults (Belsky et al., 2012; Sperry & Widom, 2013). Unfortunately, a commonality of students struggling with academic performance, behavior in the classroom, and social aspects is the presence of poverty, absence of basic needs, childhood adversity, and dysfunctional families (Allen-Meares & Montgomery, 2014). Research surrounding negative life events and environments correlating to future challenges in adulthood is not new (Herman, 1997); however, its impact on the learning environment and ways to minimize negative effects are growing areas of inquiry and sophistication.

In addition to the presence of adversity that potentially creates negative outcomes for learning, there are challenges associated with the increase in diversity and disadvantaged children from cultures outside the mainstream of the educational environment (Richard & Sosa, 2014). In 2016, the United States admitted close to 100,000 refugees. While this number is decreasing due to political policies (Hartig, 2018), there is no shortage of refugee, displaced, and unregistered children in need of educational opportunities. Children of different cultures, ethnicities, and languages are being displaced into American classrooms. The United Nations High Commissioner for Refugees (UNHCR, 2018) estimates that less than 25% of refugees obtain secondary education services. Additionally, there are 5 million students in U.S. public schools who do not speak English. While Spanish is the most common primary language for non-English speaking students, schools are also grappling with other languages. The most common primary languages of non-English speaking students, after Spanish, are Chinese-Cantonese, Chinese-Mandarin, Vietnamese, and Arabic (Sanchez, 2017). With each people group and language comes different cultures. While today's teachers work to embrace the benefits of diversity in the classroom, these dynamics also create significant challenges that can potentially decrease the overall learning environment for all students. Balancing how to create a welcoming classroom with the rigor of the educational curriculum that must be covered in a limited time period challenges even the most culturally proficient teachers. Sanchez (2017) found that most non-English speaking students struggle in school, placing them at a higher risk for behavior issues and involvement in violence. Therefore, the need to help non-English speaking students assimilate and accommodate through communication acquisition and mainstream culture is a priority for schools. However, this task further depletes school resources of time, finances, and staff.

When thinking about cultural humility in classrooms, the stereotypical picture of a student from a different country who wears different style of clothes, eats different types of food, and speaks a different language may come to mind. However, it is important to consider that children from the same community that come together in a classroom and speak the same language can also come from very diverse cultures. Common pieces of culture especially important for teachers and schools to appreciate are the cultural priority of education, work ethic philosophies, level of parental support with homework, and conflict resolution methods (Vanalstine, Cox, & Roden, 2015). These are additional dynamics a teacher and school system should consider when creating an effective and inclusive learning environment. When looking at teachers in the U.S., the majority are middle-class, white females with an average of 14 years of teaching experience (Loewus, 2017). However, the composition of the classroom continues to change and become more diverse. Teachers must work to overcome common stereotypes of people groups, appreciate differences in work ethics, and adjust for priority of education in a student's culture, while also balancing group behavior, individual student behavior issues, mental health presentations, increasing paperwork, and less control over the content taught in their classrooms (Alsubaie, 2015). Due to the enormity of this task, teachers need assistance to ensure success for all students. Utilizing school and community resources, while also partnering with home-based supports, is most efficacious method of equipping students and teachers in their educational journey.

ADVERSE CHILDHOOD EXPERIENCES (ACE)

Felitti and Andas (1998) conducted the original Adverse Childhood Experiences (ACE) study and found a strong positive correlation between negative childhood events and negative health outcomes in adulthood. Copious amounts of research have explored the results and how ACE scores might correlate with other life dynamics. Prior studies reveal correlations between higher ACE scores and an increase in chronic health issues, unemployment, poverty, relationship conflicts, and a decrease in educational success (Miller-Cribbs et al., 2016). Other research indicates that higher ACE scores are more prevalent in different populations, specifically those struggling with poverty, adult smokers (current and former), adults who engage in heavy alcohol use, obese adults, American Indian/Alaskan Native population (Nurius, Greene, Logan-Greene, Longhi, & Song, 2016), lesbian, gay, and bisexual adults (Blosnich & Andersen, 2015), adult African American females (Corbin et al., 2013), victims of human trafficking (Reid, Baglivio, Piquero, Greenwald, & Epps, 2017), women struggling with depression (Honkalampi et al., 2005), baccalaureate social work students (Branson, Radu, & Loving, in press), and others. This list of populations with increased ACE scores is not exclusive; however, it provides evidence that vulnerable students in educational settings might also be struggling with elevated ACE scores.

The original ACE study population ($n = 9,508$) was primarily college-educated, employed, middle-class adults. Among medical histories, physical exam reports, and lab results, participants completed a 10-item questionnaire using a dichotomous response (yes/no) that assessed the presence of negative childhood events, specifically: emotional, physical, and sexual abuse; neglect; parental separation/divorce; witnessed abuse of one's mother-figure; presence of a family member with mental health issues; presence of a family member with substance abuse issues; and if a household member was incarcerated. The correlations between negative childhood experiences and negative health outcomes were significant. The study results indicated that as ACE scores increased, the more likely physical problems in adulthood were experienced. Elevated ACE scores are also correlated with a deficit of social determinants of health, such as health insurance, access to medical care, and/or positive health supports. Additionally, there is an increased prevalence of tobacco use, mental health issues, substance use disorder(s), high-risk sexual behavior, suicidal activities, and other negative behaviors (Anda et al., 1999; Dube et al., 2001; Felitti et al., 1998). Furthermore, ACE scores are common regardless of income level, culture, ethnicity, and race. In the original study, 2 out of 3 participants endorsed at least one ACE score. The research revealed that participants with an ACE score of 4 were two times more likely to suffer from heart disease and/or cancer. Participants with an ACE score of 5 were eight times more likely to struggle with alcohol use disorder, and participants with ACE scores of 6 or more were found to have a lower life expectancy, an average of 20 years less than participants with an ACE score of zero (Redford, 2015).

Because of the prevalence of childhood trauma established by the ACE study, educators must appreciate how the presence of past trauma plays out in their classrooms and the learning environment of students. Trauma is a fickle phenomenon in that it is highly individual. Two people can experience the same trauma at the same point in time, yet the outcomes will be vastly different for each person. Numerous factors contribute to a person's response to trauma, such as the nature of the event; intensity level; frequency of distress; individual genetics; biology; personality; temperament; accessible physical, logistical, and emotional supports; individual experiences and coping skills; cultural reaction and norms concerning trauma; and countless other neuroses (Caska & Renshaw, 2013; Enlow, Blood, & Egeland, 2013; Regehr, 2018; Regehr & Glancy, 2014). Several definitions of trauma exist; however, a commonly accepted definition is by the Substance Abuse and Mental Health Services Administration (SAMHSA) and will serve as the definition of trauma for this chapter:

Trauma refers to experiences that cause intense physical and psychological stress reactions. It can refer to a single event, multiple events, or a set of circumstances that is experienced by an individual as physically and emotionally harmful or threatening and that has lasting adverse effects on the individual's physical, social, emotional, or spiritual well-being. (SAMHSA, 2014, p xix)

Childhood trauma can especially be damaging to the developing brain and can alter its functionality (van der Kolk, 2014). Humans are made for survival. When trauma occurs, the brain has a specific biological and instinctual response that occurs. Essentially, when a person encounters a trauma, the hypothalamic-pituitary-adrenal center is activated. The hypothalamus is a small but important part of the autonomic nervous system that notifies the pituitary gland to start releasing survival stress hormones, especially cortisol (Burke-Harris, 2018). This chemical puts the entire mind and body on hyper-alert, creating a specific kind of stress that is uncomfortable and a desire to return to a normal state as quickly as possible. While in this hyper-altered state, one's heart rate goes up, pupils dilate, saliva decreases, digestion slows down, and numerous other physiological changes occur to make the threatened person run faster and farther (flight response), fight more aggressively (fight response), and/or take in the environment to decide to remain quiet, hide, and be undetected or allow damage to occur while minimizing the damage (freeze response; Duros & Crowley, 2014). While this system is superior in the animal kingdom for survival, it becomes corrosive to the host system if engaged on a regular or near constant basis due to on-going or significant unresolved trauma. This is referred to as toxic stress, and is considered a form of trauma in of itself if it is present too long or too often (Segal, Gerdes, & Steiner, 2019)

Children are especially vulnerable to the damaging effects of toxic stress due to the rapid rate of physical, emotional, and social development in childhood. Research has found that childhood trauma can affect several parts of the brain, such as decreased volume of the corpus callosum (large portion of brain, concentrated nerve connection activity), prefrontal cortices (cognitive function of pre-planning, social behavior regulation, and decision making), temporal lobe (sensory processing for emotional reaction and memory), hippocampus (appropriate behavior response and memory), and amygdala (emotional responses specific to adversity; De Bellis & Keshavan, 2006; Teicher, Samson, Polcari, & McGreenery, 2006). Additionally, research indicates that maltreatment in childhood can reduce the volume of gray matter (Tomoda et al., 2009), leading to an overall compromised structure and function of the brain.

By breaking down how trauma potentially disrupts different brain functions, resulting traumatic aftermath can be seen as logical. An example would be the commonality of memory disturbances around highly traumatic events. If Sara was in a terrible car accident, she might be asked by a police officer to report what happened. Sara may honestly state that she does not clearly remember the event, as the bits and pieces of the memory are fuzzy. The officer further presses Sara for details, saying, "How did the back window of the car get busted out?" Sara searches her memory and suddenly remembers, "Yes…now I remember, the car was rolling, and it was very loud! I could hear the metal of the car crunching, items in the car flying around, and the sound of glass breaking. I even remember being hit by shards of the glass." However, a week later when Sara goes to see the car with the insurance adjuster, the tow truck operator says, "Oh hey lady, sorry about the back window. I had to break it out to get a hook cable on it to pull it out of the ditch." Suddenly, Sara's clear memory of the glass breaking, including audio and tactile features, is discovered to be false. The brain wants so badly to fill in the gaps and make sense of traumatic events. In this scenario, the false memory is likely to be a harmless issue. However, in survivors of sexual abuse or sexual assault, memory glitches can potentially serve as disturbing gaps that irritate the healing process, contributing to self-blame and negative emotional aftermath, and/or produce a false memory implicating a person(s) not involved in the event. This can also lead to trauma survivors being labeled as poor historians and unreliable sources of information.

Resulting impairments to brain function and structure can contribute to negative or stunted psychological development, resulting in a host of behavioral and emotional impairments in students (Nurius et al., 2016). Specific areas of deficits that are central to a student's learning environment include exaggerated changes in mood, general emotional numbness, incongruent affect, poor emotional regulation, explosive anger and/or over-reaction to events, and increased sensitivity to non-verbal cues (SAMHSA, 2014). Additionally, students may struggle with cognitive issues, such as disturbances of attention, an inability to focus and concentrate, poor problem-solving, impulsivity, and increased use of aggression to deal with problems. Other problematic issues have been noted in interpersonal difficulties, resulting in problems with developing trust, poor social skills, poor boundaries, authority problems, ineffective perspective taking, low or inflated self-esteem, struggles with guilt and shame, and inaccurate locus of control. Traumatic aftermath may also be internalized physically, increasing a student's vulnerability to eating disorders, anxiety-related issues, self-mutilation behaviors, and somatic complaints (D'Andrea, Stolbach, Ford, Spinazzola, & van der Kolk, 2012). Below is a table of from SAMHSA (2014) of immediate and delayed traumatic symptoms.

Educators are familiar with household events creating problems in the classroom due to academic preparation and experience with students. Teachers quickly learn that when a child is struggling at school, the root of the problem could stem from problems at home or parents experiencing difficult life events. When looking at the extensive possible reactions to trauma, a student's behavior often makes logical

Table 1. Reactions to trauma (SAMHSA, 2014, p. 62-63)

Immediate Emotional Reactions: • Numbness and detachment • Anxiety or severe fear • Guilt (including survivor guilt) • Exhilaration as a result of surviving • Anger • Sadness • Helplessness • Feeling unreal; depersonalization (e.g., feeling as if you are watching yourself) • Disorientation • Feeling out of control • Denial • Constriction of feelings • Feeling overwhelmed	**Delayed Emotional Reactions** • Irritability and/or hostility • Depression • Mood swings, instability • Anxiety (e.g., phobia, generalized anxiety) • Fear of trauma recurrence • Grief reactions • Shame • Feelings of fragility and/or vulnerability • Emotional detachment from anything that requires emotional reactions (e.g., significant and/or family relationships, conversations about self, discussion of traumatic events or reactions to them)
Immediate Physical Reactions: • Nausea and/or gastrointestinal distress • Sweating or shivering • Faintness • Muscle tremors or uncontrollable shaking • Elevated heartbeat, respiration, and blood pressure • Extreme fatigue or exhaustion • Greater startle responses Depersonalization	**Delayed Physical Reactions** • Sleep disturbances, nightmares Somatization (e.g., increased focus on and worry about body aches and pains) Appetite and digestive changes • Lowered resistance to colds and infection Persistent fatigue • Elevated cortisol levels • Hyperarousal • Long-term health effects including heart, liver, autoimmune, and chronic obstructive pulmonary disease
Immediate Cognitive Reactions • Difficulty concentrating • Rumination or racing thoughts (e.g., replaying the traumatic event over and over again) • Distortion of time and space (e.g., traumatic event may be perceived as if it was happening in slow motion, or a few seconds can be perceived as minutes) Memory problems (e.g., not being able to recall important aspects of the trauma) Strong identification with victims	**Delayed Cognitive Reactions** • Intrusive memories or flashbacks Reactivation of previous traumatic events Self-blame • Preoccupation with event • Difficulty making decisions • Magical thinking: belief that certain behaviors, including avoidance behavior, will protect against future trauma • Belief that feelings or memories are dangerous • Generalization of triggers (e.g., a person who experiences a home invasion during the daytime may avoid being alone during the day) • Suicidal thinking
Immediate Behavioral Reactions • Startled reaction • Restlessness • Sleep and appetite disturbances • Difficulty expressing oneself Argumentative behavior • Increased use of alcohol, drugs, and tobacco • Withdrawal and apathy • Avoidant behaviors	**Delayed Behavioral Reactions** • Avoidance of event reminders • Social relationship disturbances Decreased activity level • Engagement in high-risk behaviors Increased use of alcohol and drugs Withdrawal
Immediate Existential Reactions • Intense use of prayer • Restoration of faith in the goodness of others (e.g., receiving help from others) Loss of self-efficacy • Despair about humanity, particularly if the event was intentional • Immediate disruption of life assumptions (e.g., fairness, safety, goodness, predictability of life)	• **Delayed Existential Reactions** Questioning (e.g., "Why me?") • Increased cynicism, disillusionment Increased self-confidence (e.g., "If I can survive this, I can survive anything") • Loss of purpose • Renewed faith • Hopelessness • Reestablishing priorities • Redefining meaning and importance of life Reworking life's assumptions to accommodate the trauma (e.g., taking a self-defense class to reestablish a sense of safety)

sense. If Seth experienced a terrible tornado and was traumatized by the event, it is understandable why he becomes overly anxious during thunderstorms. However, what about paradoxical reactions to trauma? These are often the behaviors that cause confusion, incorrect assumptions, and hurtful judgements from others that can further compound the negative behaviors being displayed. The term *paradoxical reaction* is usually seen in the medical community to denote an opposite reaction to a medication or treatment protocol (Farkas, 2015). However, trauma reactions can also be paradoxical; behaviors that are cogently the opposite of how one "should" react after being exposed to an aversive event. If Seth experienced a significant trauma due to a devastating tornado that destroyed his home and resulted in the death of his youngest child, it might be considered odd or unhealthy for him to suddenly become a storm chaser and seek out the very destruction that created such a negative experience.

Paradoxical reactions to trauma are also evident in classrooms and affect potential learning. When a sexual assault victim returns to the areas when she was attacked dressed in seductive clothing, one might mistakenly assume that she enjoys being sexually assaulted and welcomes being raped. An observer might think that this woman should have learned her lesson and changed the places she spends time and the clothing she wears. In reality, this behavior is a pathological attempt to regain control. Examples that might baffle a teacher in a classroom could be students who: (a) complete their homework, but do not turn it in to receive points, (b) refuse to complete seemingly easy assignments for needed points, (c) refuse to comply with classroom directives that are to their benefit, (d) achieve success and appear to be making sustain goal obtainment, then suddenly and purposefully revert to behaviors that sabotage progress, and (e) establish a trusting relationship with a teacher, then purposefully steal a personal item from the teacher as a means of destroying the relationship. Other common behaviors are identifying with an abuser, a victim becoming a predator, or the student who is so involved with being the class clown that he is willing to sacrifice his academic future rather than set aside his façade and comply with authority (Fecser, 2015).

As evidenced by this long litany of possible negative outcomes, cultural differences, personal influences, and environmental factors, the responses to childhood trauma vary greatly. Problems with any one of these dynamics places a student at an increased risk of non-compliance or exhibiting behaviors that receive negative consequences. Additionally, complications of trauma rarely present in a singular fashion, meaning that students struggling with unresolved trauma may exhibit numerous problematic behaviors, making it difficult to be fully present, physically, emotionally, and socially in a classroom for learning.

Cultural Differences

An additional lens to consider when looking at trauma and aftermath that could create barriers to education is through cultural differences. Addressing the dynamics of an increasingly diverse classroom is a significant educational challenge (Chan & Ross, 2014). A useful illustration for appreciating the power of culture and the need for recognizing difference is Hall's (1976) cultural iceberg model. When looking at the iceberg, it is divided into three different layers. The surface layer consists of observable differences in culture that do not involve a great deal of emotion. These are cultural items located at the top of the iceberg that often stimulate curiosity for outsiders to explore differences. Common examples are eating ethnic foods or observing different cultural activities, such as performance arts, music, or traditional dress. The next layer of the cultural iceberg is the shallow culture, which is located just beneath the water's surface and involves cultural differences that evoke more emotion. Shallow culture is the unspoken rules that govern behavior. Examples of shallow culture include items like type of eye contact, how one shows courtesy, ideas of modesty, and how respect is shown. When cultural differences clash, it can create judgements, defensiveness, and anger, which can create negative ideas, prejudices, and discriminatory practices (Vanalstine et al., 2015). The final layer of Hall's iceberg is deep culture. These are the unconscious rules that when intersecting with cultural differences can create intense emotion. These are often bits of culture that are believed to be universal; therefore, discord results when cultural differences clash. Examples of deep culture include ideas of cleanliness, level of pain or illness threshold before seeking medical attention, attitudes concerning privacy, and child rearing practices (Hall, 1976). Cultural differences from the surface, shallow, and deep end can create dilemmas in a classroom setting and with the learning management style of the teacher. While it is easy to imagine this with students coming from a foreign country who look and speak very different from others in the classroom, these same levels of cultural difference occur with students within the same ethnicity, community, and school district. Understanding these unspoken rules and appreciating cultural variance is a significant step toward effective management of difference.

Additional elements of culture that are essential to consider when trying to understand how trauma aftermath is expressed through behaviors in classrooms are culturally influenced communication styles. American, Canadian, and Northern Europeans tend to be more comfortable with aspects of an individualistic culture. They care more about individual preferences and desires. Collective cultures, however, believe the group is more important. Asians and some South Americans are more comfortable with collective culture values (Adler, Rosenfeld, & Proctor, 2017). Consequently, when a trauma is experienced in an individualistic culture, the focus is on the individual response of victims — what do individuals need to recover, specific preferences for assistance, what emotions are involved for the individual, and what does the trauma mean to the individual personally. However, in a collectivistic culture, trauma is likely to be viewed differently. What does the trauma mean for the group, family, or community? How do others feel about the trauma and what does the group need to recover? Additionally, the collective response to the trauma is likely to be heavily influenced by history and how similar situations were processed in the past, leaving little room for individual preferences (Adler et al., 2017).

Another cultural value that influences communication that need to be recognized is the difference between high and low verbal contexts. Members who use high context communication rely heavily on nonverbal cues and the nature of the relationship with the receiver of the information to convey meaning. This creates tendencies to talk around delicate topics, trying to give illustrations and cues to communicate content. Low context members communicate in a more straightforward manner, with words and tones that convey meaning in a more blunt and clear manner (Adler et al., 2017). A typical problem that might occur in a classroom could be a high context teacher working to resolve a conflict with a low context student who speaks in a blunt tone, causing the teacher to feel disrespected. This could result in the student receiving a punishment, a setback in development of a relationship with the teacher, an increased negative attitude concerning the teacher and the class, and/or low motivation to perform and conform in the classroom.

Individualism versus collectivism and high versus low verbal context cultures influence the type and level of communication expressed. This is important, as individuals in individualistic/high content cultures are more likely to feel free to verbally process and express their experiences, whereas those from a collectivist/low content culture are less likely to share traumatic experiences openly. Appreciating these cultural differences in communication styles is especially salient regarding trauma resolution (Lam, 2015). Research supports the processing of traumatic events with others, especially with trained professionals or others with similar experiences who can relate and empathize as a positive means toward traumatic growth and increase in resilience (Ben-Porat, 2015; Tassie, 2015). There has also been research concerning the benefits of using artistic methods and drama-related storytelling as tools to process traumatic events toward resolution (Barnett, 2018; Palidofsky & Stolbach, 2012; Zerrudo, 2016). While some cultures would embrace this methodology, others would be off-put by such a personal exposure of vulnerability. It is important for schools and teachers to take cultural differences in expression and processing of trauma into consideration when implementing possible classroom interventions, assignments, or activities that are geared toward introspection of past aversive events. While these activities may be healing to some students, they could be harmful to another. Due to the complex nature of trauma, culture, and manifestations of behavior, highly trained professionals are valuable resources for teachers and schools. Fortunately, certified school social workers can provide these services to students, while also supporting the mission of the school and the individual goals of teachers (Allen-Meares & Montgomery, 2014; Richard & Sosa, 2014).

The Hidden Curriculum

An additional phenomenon that can be the source of problematic behavior, yet rarely accounted for in a multi-cultural classroom, is the hidden curriculum. The hidden curriculum can be defined as the unspoken behaviors that are considered universal in the classroom (Schaefer, 2016). Beyond what is considered compliant and non-compliant behavioral aspects of the hidden curriculum are mainstream values and practices that set students up for success. While some aspects of the hidden curriculum find their way into posted classroom rules, the majority are invisible and are taught through the socialization process (Rahman, 2013). Furthermore, the hidden curriculum is based on the values and practices of the dominant culture (Safta, 2017). In the United States, this is commonly white, middle-class, protestant values, which might be in direct opposition to other students' values (Rahman, 2013). Students who belong to a dominant group are often more successful at assimilating and demonstrating compliance to the hidden curriculum due to its familiarity, providing an additional advantage to school success that students from non-dominant groups do not have. Students from oppressed, marginalized, and non-dominant groups already have socially and institutionally based barriers to overcome due to their cultural membership (Sue, Rasheed, & Rasheed, 2016). The hidden curriculum becomes yet another barrier that requires accommodation and assimilation of a student's culture to excel.

Examples of the hidden curriculum include placing the right hand over one's heart then reciting the Pledge of Allegiance, raising one's hand to ask a question, asking permission to leave the classroom, being on time for class, and dismissing to a bell. Students unfamiliar with these standards of behavior may unknowingly engage in disobedient behavior, receiving negative attention from teachers and other students, reinforced feelings of not belonging, and increased social isolation. This commonly results in students not speaking up for their academic needs or engaging school officials with concerns. This can also create an initial impression to a new teacher and school district that the non-compliant student is a troublemaker. Although some of the bits and pieces of the hidden curriculum are adapted to quickly, other parts may be an assault on a student's cultural identity, creating seemingly on-going non-compliance and rebellion. In reality, it may be a student's attempt to integrate the hidden curriculum while preserving who he is and his connection to his culture (Safta, 2017). Additionally, because the hidden curriculum is a significant part of positive group behavior and overall classroom control, it must be enforced to avoid chaos. When taking these different facets of culture and cultural difference together, it becomes easier to understand why students outside of a mainstream group might struggle in school (Rahman, 2013). If a student comes to the classroom from a culture that embraces peer-group instruction and work, he might be considered lazy or cheating if he attempts to work with others on an individual assignment. A student from a highly private culture that believes it is disrespectful to discuss personal bathroom needs might leave the classroom without asking permission, only to be apprehended in the hallway by a resource officer and humiliated when she must explain her behavior. A student from a culture where obedience to authority is highly favored may ask numerous clarifying questions to the teachers, being seen as "needy" and lacking in self-confidence, whereas a student that comes from a culture where being subservient to a woman is seen as a weakness to his manhood might feel obligated to be defiant in the classroom and dismissive of directives from female teachers.

The examples of problematic scenarios due to the hidden curriculum are endless and can create potential barriers to educational attainment at any level, pre-k through university-higher learning. Once the hidden curriculum is appreciated by members of the institution, it can be dismantled, accounted for, and minimized as a barrier. Commonly, the charge to ensure that educational services are culturally appropriate for the student and family will fall to the guidance staff and/or school social worker. Research and educational practitioners have suggested methods to increase student comfort in the learning environment and to navigate the hidden curriculum:

- Present oneself as a learner and engage students as experts of their experiences and culture
- Embrace diversity with genuine interest as a classroom
- Provide clear spoken and written instructions for assignments and welcome requests for clarification
- Share with students the expectations for the classroom
- Provide an environment free of stereotypes and prejudice
- Engage in universal learning design, i.e. be innovative, flexible, and open to multiple methods of learning and assessment (Alsubaie, 2015; Chan & Ross, 2014)

Awareness and implementation of purposeful strategies to increase cultural humility and decrease barriers will help schools, learning environments, teachers, and students more richly enjoy the benefits of diversity of the student body (Rahman, 2013; Safta, 2017; Vanalstine et al., 2015).

Multidisciplinary Approach

Due to the complexity of students struggling with multiple co-existing issues, interventions that come from a multidisciplinary team are more likely to be successful. The team approach is not a new concept for schools; however, there are common logistical and social challenges that decrease its effectiveness. School multidisciplinary teams are constructed around the goal of enhancing the overall well-being of students. Leadership boards and committees focus on the institution, maintaining and achieving high educational standards and accreditations. However, when individual students are falling behind academically, rarely is the sole problem a deficit in educational performance. Physical and invisible disabilities, unresolved childhood adversity, on-going toxic stress, family discord, cultural differences, and social inadequacies are just a few of the problems that schools are now expected to deal with, along with the arduous task of educating students with a full and robust curriculum that continues to expand with higher standardized expectations of competence. However, oftentimes schools find that they do not have the time and/ or manpower to effectively address the barrage of dynamics that plague their most vulnerable students. Additional challenges are lack of funds to employ the needed members of a multidisciplinary team, causing present members to be overwhelmed by the multiple roles they must balance while also being held accountable to the educational needs to an entire school.

Guidance staff are often called upon to assist with at-risk students. However, the guidance staff has their own full agenda of ensuring that students are getting the required course work they need to move forward in classes and graduate on time. Additionally, they are tasked with creating schedules that fit diverse curriculums, enrichment opportunities, required recreation hours, and getting everyone to lunch, while ensuring teachers have enough time for classroom planning and collaboration with other colleagues. Therefore, when the guidance staff is also called upon to deal with students struggling with a myriad of issues, they are too overwhelmed to provide the level of supports they would like. Two specific initiatives can be highly effective to increasing the school's collective approach to dealing with at-risk students: hiring of certified school social workers and establishing a multidisciplinary team that represents a student's individual, family, school, and community systems.

The multidisciplinary team approach is an established best practice in several divisions of social work (Segal et al., 2019). This is also ideal for school settings, as it is a method that helps to ensure the development of a comprehensive, individualized, and effective plan of action. However, schools currently struggle to employ the members needed for a multidisciplinary team. There are presently more security guards in American public schools than school social workers (Willingham, 2018). School administration, faculty, and support staff are overwhelmed with job duties, and the laundry list of what is expected continues to grow (Allen-Meares & Montgomery, 2014). Richard and Sosa (2014) found five major trends that create the necessity for school social workers: adoption of the response to intervention movement to ensure that at-risk students are identified early and provided appropriate services, use of evidence-based practices, growth in the demand for school-based mental health services, accreditation and government accountability standards, and data-driven decision making. School social workers are distinctively trained to provide the clinical and skill-based services to help schools address these growing operational trends and to support other school personnel in performing their duties more effectively (Ayasse & Stone, 2015).

School social workers provide a host of unique services to schools. They can conduct detailed biopsychosocial assessments that can provide vital information and understanding regarding the negative manifestations teachers deal with in and out of the classroom. Additional supports include networking services for students struggling with deficits in basic needs (food, clothing, shoes, school supplies, etc.), substance use disorders, mental health issues, academic performance problems, suicidal/homicidal ideation, and supports for especially vulnerable students, such as unregistered, homeless, LGBTQ+, emancipated, and/or pregnant students. School social workers can provide ongoing therapeutic relationships with students, allowing them to provide informal case management, crisis intervention, attendance monitoring, home visits, and advocacy for students (Kelly et al., 2015; NASW, 2010). Rarely does a school system struggle to justify the need for a dedicated school social worker; however, budget issues and misunderstandings concerning what school social workers do and the role of the guidance counselor are common barriers that keep school districts from acquiring school social worker positions (Gherardi & Whittlesey-Jerome, 2018).

Once acquired, a school social worker can be an invaluable part of a multidisciplinary team to ensure a student's overall success with school and future plans (Allen-Meares & Montgomery, 2014). However, a vital factor to the success of the team is well-defined roles for each member of the team and the team's understanding and respecting of each team member's role. The precise defining of each team member's role increases comprehensive services for teachers, students, families, and the administration. Once defined, the multidisciplinary team needs to be fully vested in collective work, while also respecting the delineation of each member's role. Failure to do so creates over and underutilization of team members, sets up resentment between team members, and creates gaps in service provision (Kelly et al., 2015). A strong team can be confident in their members, reaches out in times of need, partners to assist challenges as presented, celebrates in progress, encourages each other in student regressions, and continuously evaluates the team collectively and independently for ways to improve and evolve (Ayasse & Stone,

2015; Richard & Sosa, 2014). Needed members of the multidisciplinary team are school administration, teachers, family members, guidance staff, school social workers, school nurses, and community resources that can partner with the school to create individualized plans to optimize student success. The precise method for defining each team member's role is highly dependent on the school size, student body composition, school faculty and staff, community resources, and community support of the school. However, time invested in this venture has potential for substantial returns in individual, group, and community domains.

SOLUTIONS AND RECOMMENDATIONS

When looking at the complex issues involved with childhood trauma, the spill over of negative behavior into classrooms, the further complications of the hidden curriculum that adds an additional barrier of inequality and challenge to students who are already set apart by difference, and the increasing globalization of the classroom, it becomes clear that additional supports are needed. Teachers, school administrators, identified students in need, the student body, and affected families could all benefit from an increased presence of trained school social workers. Currently in the U.S.A., the presence of police outnumbers school social workers. Schools rarely struggle to demonstrate and justify the need for a school social worker, however, budgetary costs are a common barrier from school districts obtaining this position in a sustainable manner. Even when a school social worker is hired, the position is often district wide, creating a caseload that is too enormous to be effective. Therefore, school social workers need to be hired at the ideal ratio to students to be able to provide services to schools that create a positive difference. Additionally, the role of the school social worker needs to be well-defined, along with the other roles and positions in the school community to increase effectiveness and decrease pseudo-turf wars between other educational professionals and staff.

Commonly, schools that could benefit the most from the presence of a school social worker are also the schools with the lowest financial supports. This makes hiring and keeping a school social worker even more challenging. Grants and community supports are ideal ways to create positions at schools for a school social worker, but sustainability of the position needs to be planned for from the beginning of acquiring the position. One possible solution that has been successful is a community partnership with an identified school over a 5-year period to establish a school social worker position. A community level social service agency, for example, the United Way, agrees to fund a school social worker position at a school for one year, providing 100% of the school social worker's salary and benefits. The second year, the community agency provides 75% of the salary and benefits, while the school picks up the other

25%. The third year, the community agency and school each provide equal parts of funding for the position. The fourth year the community agency provides 25% and the school 75%, and by the fifth year, the school is fully funding the position. Additionally, by the fifth year, the school social work position has become such a vital part of the school community and student success, that the position is no longer seen as an extra or luxury, but a needed part of the educational environment. Regardless of the presence of a school social worker, on-going educational/professional development opportunities and faculty/staff trainings concerning cultural humility, trauma-informed care, and ways to reduce barriers to student holistic learning and development should be part of a school's comprehensive strategic plan.

FUTURE RESEACH DIRECTIONS

Due to the commonality of childhood trauma, the increase in the multi-cultural classroom, and the identified cultural barriers of the hidden curriculum, additional research is needed to determine best methods for combating these dynamics to increase the academic efficacy of vulnerable students. Increased understanding of the connection between childhood trauma, brain development, and resulting trauma-induced behaviors is needed. Additionally, development of more effective and realistic interventions that support both the student and the classroom milieu are also needed. Schools using innovative approaches that show promise in elevating overall wellness of students and educational success should be assessed for themes and patterns that can be augmented for other education programs. Finally, the presence of a school social worker and the increase in school-based services for at-risk students should be reviewed on a national and international level to provide school districts with empirical data to support the development and maintenance of school social work positions in schools.

CONCLUSION

Today's school administrators, teachers, guidance staff, school social workers, and other support staff are being asked to do more and more with fewer resources, training, and time. Schools must deal with ever changing educational standards, state and federal policies, meeting accommodations for students with disabilities (physical and emotional), safety concerns, outcomes of school violence, the mental health of students, substance use disorders of the student body and family members, reproductive health issues, bullying issues, LGBTQ+ needs, as well as students who struggle with issues including poverty, lack of resources, and compromised support systems. Each of these dynamics has a cultural lens that must be appreciated when creating effective interventions. Schools must also deal with the effects of childhood trauma and toxic stress on academic performance and behavior compliance in the classroom. Schools are also dealing with an increase in the globalization of their student body. This presents more cultural dimensions to school governance, increasing the concentration of issues that accompany populations who are oppressed and marginalized. Due to the workload generated by these issues and related responsibilities, there is a need for understanding of trauma-related issues, increased cultural humility by the school community, specific training for guidance staff and school social workers, and a need to embrace a multidisciplinary team approach to student challenges. The summation of these dynamics creates considerable challenges for today's schools. However, a multidisciplinary team working together can tackle these issues more effectively and turn problems into opportunities for productive change in the educational community and a source of personal growth for students.

REFERENCES

Adler, R. B., Rosenfeld, L. B., & Proctor, R. F. (2017). *Interplay: The process of interpersonal communication* (14th ed.). New York, NY: Oxford University Press, Inc.

Allen-Meares, P., & Montgomery, K. L. (2014). Global trends and school-based social work. *Children & Schools*, *36*(2), 105–112. doi:10.1093/cs/cdu007

Alsubaie, M. A. (2015). Examples of current issues in the multicultural classroom. *Journal of Education and Practice*, *6*(10).

Anda, R. F., Croft, J. B., Felitti, V. J., Norenberg, D., Giles, W. H., Williamson, D. R., & Giovino, G. A. (1999). Adverse childhood events and smoking during adolescence and adulthood. American Medical Association, 282(17), 1652-1658.

Asok, A., Bernard, K., Roth, T. L., Rosen, J. B., & Dozier, M. (2013). Parental responsiveness moderates the association between early-life stress and reduced telomere length. *Development and Psychopathology*, *25*(3), 577–585. doi:10.1017/S0954579413000011 PMID:23527512

Ayasse, R. H., & Stone, S. I. (2015). The evolution of school social work services in an urban school district. *Children & Schools*, *17*(4), 215–222. doi:10.1093/cs/cdv025

Barnett, J. (2018). Setting the stage for bridging disability and trauma studies: Reclaiming narrative in Amy and the Orphans. Word & Text: A Journal of Literary Studies & Linguistics, 8, 129–148.

Belsky, J., Schlomer, G. L., & Ellis, B. J. (2012). Beyond cumulative risk: Distinguishing harshness and unpredictability as determinants of parenting and early life history strategy. *Developmental Psychology*, *48*(3), 662–673. doi:10.1037/a0024454 PMID:21744948

Ben-Porat, A. (2015). Vicarious post-traumatic growth: Domestic violence therapists versus social service department therapists in Israel. *Journal of Family Violence*, *30*(7), 923–933. doi:10.100710896-015-9714-x

Blosnich, J. R., & Anderson, J. P. (2015). Thursday's child: The role of adverse childhood experiences in explaining mental health disparities among lesbian, gay, and bisexual U.S. adults. *Social Psychiatry and Psychiatric Epidemiology*, *50*(2), 335–338. doi:10.100700127-014-0955-4 PMID:25367679

Branson, D. C., Radu, M. B., & Loving, J. D. (in press). Adverse Childhood Experiences (ACE) scores: When social work students and trauma mix. *The Journal of Baccalaureate Social Work*.

Burke-Harris, N. (2018). *The deepest well: Healing the long-term effects of childhood adversity*. London: Bluebird.

Caska, C. M., & Renshaw, K. D. (2013). Personality traits as moderators of the associations between deployment experiences and PTSD symptoms in OEF/OIF service members. *Anxiety, Stress, and Coping*, *26*(1), 36–51. doi:10.1080/10615806.2011.638053 PMID:22129461

Chan, E., & Ross, V. (2014). Narrative understandings of a school policy: Intersecting student, teacher, parent and administrator perspectives. *Journal of Curriculum Studies*, *46*(5), 656–675. doi:10.1080/00220272.2014.911352

Corbin, T. J., Purtle, J., Rich, L. J., Rich, J. A., Adams, E. J., Yee, G., & Bloom, S. L. (2013). The prevalence of trauma and childhood adversity in an urban, hospital-based violence intervention program. *Journal of Health Care for the Poor and Underserved*, *24*(3), 1021–1030. doi:10.1353/hpu.2013.0120 PMID:23974377

D'Andrea, W., Ford, J., Stolbach, B., Spinazzola, J., & van der Kolk, B. A. (2012). Understanding interpersonal trauma in children: Why we need a developmentally appropriate trauma diagnosis. *The American Journal of Orthopsychiatry*, *82*(2), 187–200. doi:10.1111/j.1939-0025.2012.01154.x PMID:22506521

Danese, A., & McEwen, B. S. (2012). Adverse childhood experiences, allostasis, allostatic load, and age-related disease. *Physiology & Behavior*, *106*(1), 29–39. doi:10.1016/j.physbeh.2011.08.019 PMID:21888923

De Bellis, M. D., Keshavan, M. S., Shifflett, H., Iyengar, S., Beers, S. R., Hall, J., & Moritz, G. (2006). Cerebellar volumes in pediatric maltreatment-related posttraumatic stress disorder: A sociodemographically matched study. *Biological Psychiatry*, *52*(11), 1066–1078. doi:10.1016/S0006-3223(02)01459-2 PMID:12460690

Dube, S. R., Anda, R. F., Felitti, V. J., Chapman, D. P., Williamson, D. F., & Giles, W. H. (2001). Childhood abuse, household dysfunction, and the risk of attempted suicide throughout the life span: Findings from the Adverse Childhood Experiences study. American Medical Association, 286(24), 3089-3095.

Duros, P., & Crowley, D. (2014). The body comes to therapy too. *Clinical Social Work Journal*, *42*(3), 237–246. doi:10.100710615-014-0486-1

Enlow, M. B., Blood, E., & Egeland, B. (2013). Sociodemographic risk, developmental competence, and PTSD symptoms in young children exposed to interpersonal trauma in early life. *Journal of Traumatic Stress*, *26*(6), 686–694. doi:10.1002/jts.21866 PMID:24490247

Farkas, J. (2015, September). *Recognizing and managing paradoxical reactions from benzodiazepines and propofol.* Retrieved from: https://emcrit.org/pulmcrit/ recognizing-and-managing-paradoxical-reactions-from-benzodiazepines-propofol/

Fecser, M. E. (2015). Classroom strategies for traumatized, oppositional students. *Reclaiming Children and Youth*, *24*(1), 20–24.

Felitti, V. J., Anda, R. F., Nordenberg, D., Williamson, D. F., Spitz, A. M., Edwards, V., ... Marks, J. S. (1998). Relationship of childhood abuse and household dysfunction to many of the leading causes of death in adults: The Adverse Childhood Experience (ACE) study. *American Journal of Preventive Medicine*, *14*(4), 245–258. doi:10.1016/ S0749-3797(98)00017-8 PMID:9635069

Gherardi, S. A., & Whittlesey-Jerome, W. K. (2018). Role integration through the practice of social work with schools. *Children & Schools*, *40*(1), 35–43. doi:10.1093/ cs/cdx028

Hall, E. T. (1976). *Beyond trauma.* New York, NY: Anchor Books.

Hartig, H. (2018, May 18). Republicans turn more negative toward refugees as number admitted to U.S. plummets. *Pew Research Center.* Retrieved from: http:// www.pewresearch.org/fact-tank-2018/05/24/republicans-turn-more-negative-towards-refugees-as-number-to-u-s-plummets/

Herman, J. (1997). *Trauma and recovery: The aftermath of violence-from domestic abuse to political terror.* New York, NY: Basic Books.

Honkalampi, K., Hintikka, J., Haatainen, K., Koivumaa-Honkanen, H., Tanskanen, A., & Viinamaki, H. (2005). Adverse childhood experiences, stressful life events, or demographic factors: Which are important in women's depression? A 2-year follow-up population study. *The Australian and New Zealand Journal of Psychiatry, 39*(7), 627–632. doi:10.1080/j.1440-1614.2005.01636.x PMID:15996145

Institute of Medicine and National Research Council. (2014). *New directions in child abuse and neglect research*. Washington, DC: The National Academies Press; doi:10.17226/18331

Ionescu, C. L., & Binţinţan, M. D. B. (2018). Project for the multidisciplinary team and their management in the context of special education. *Palestrica of the Third Millennium Civilization & Sport, 19*(2), 123–126. doi:10.26659/pm3.2018.19.2.123

Kelly, M. S., Frey, A., Thompson, A., Klemp, H., Alvarez, M., & Cosner-Berzin, S. (2016). Assessing the National School Social Work Practice Model: Findings from the Second National School Social Work Survey. *Social Work, 61*(1), 17–28. doi:10.1093wwv044 PMID:26897995

Lam, K. Y.-I. (2015). Disclosure and psychological well-being of sexually abused adolescents in Hong Kong. *Journal of Child Sexual Abuse, 24*(7), 731–752. doi:10.1080/10538712.2015.1077364 PMID:26479960

Loewus, L. (2017, August 15). The nation's teaching force is still mostly white and female. *Education Week*. Retrieved from: http://www.edweek.org/articles/2017/08/15/the-nations-teaching-force-is-still-mostly.html

Miller-Cribbs, J. E., Wen, F., Coon, K. A., Jelley, M. J., Foulks-Rodriguez, K., & Stearns, J. (2016). Adverse childhood experiences and inequalities in adult health care access. *International Public Health Journal, 8*(2), 257–270.

National Association of Social Workers. (2010). *Social workers in schools: Kindergarten through 12 grade occupational profile. NASW Center for Workforce Studies and Social Work Practices*. Washington, DC: Author.

Nurius, P. S., Green, S., Logan-Greene, P., Longhi, D., & Song, C. (2016). Stress pathways to health inequalities: Embedding ACEs within social and behavioral contexts. *International Public Health Journal, 8*(2), 241–256. PMID:27274786

Palidofsky, M., & Stolbach, B. C. (2012). Dramatic healing: The evolution of a trauma-informed musical theatre program for incarcerated girls. *Journal of Child & Adolescent Trauma, 5*(3), 239–256. doi:10.1080/19361521.2012.697102

Power, R. A., Lecky-Thompson, L., Fisher, H. L., Cohen-Woods, S., Hosang, G. M., Uher, R., ... McGuffin, P. (2013). The interaction between child maltreatment, adult stressful life events and the 5-HTTLPR in major depression. *Journal of Psychiatric Research, 47*(8), 1032–1035. doi:10.1016/j.jpsychires.2013.03.017 PMID:23618376

Rahman, K. (2013). Belonging and learning to belong in school: The implications of the hidden curriculum for indigenous students. *Discourse (Abingdon), 34*(5), 660–672. doi:10.1080/01596306.2013.728362

Redford, J. (Producer). (2015, September 21). *ACES primer* [Video file]. Retrieved from https://vimeo.com/139998006

Regehr, C. (2018). *Stress, trauma, and decision-making for social workers.* New York, NY: Columbia University Press. doi:10.7312/rege18012

Regehr, C., & Glancy, G. (2014). *Mental health social work practice in Canada* (2nd ed.). Toronto, Canada: Oxford University Press.

Reid, J. A., Baglivio, M. T., Piquero, A. R., Greenwald, M. A., & Epps, N. (2017). Human trafficking of minors and childhood adversity in Florida. *American Journal of Public Health, 107*(2), 306–311. doi:10.2105/AJPH.2016.303564 PMID:27997232

Richard, L. A., & Sosa, L. V. (2014). School social work in Louisiana: A model of practice. *Children & Schools, 16*(4), 211–220. doi:10.1093/cs/cdu022

Safta, C. G. (2017). Between flexibility and conventionalism. Elements of hidden curriculum with implications in managing conflicts in education. *Jus et Civitas, 68*(1), 95–101.

Sanchez, C. (2017, February 23). English language learners: How your state is doing. *NPR.* Retrieved from: http://www.npr.org/sections/ed2017/02/23/512451228-5-million-english-language-learners-a-vast-pool-of-at-risk

Schaefer, R. T. (2016). *Sociology: A brief introduction* (12th ed.). New York, NY: McGraw-Hill Companies, Inc.

Segal, E. A., Gerdes, K. E., & Steiner, S. (2019). *An introduction to the profession of social work* (6th ed.). Boston, MA: Cengage Learning.

Sperry, D. M., & Widom, C. S. (2013). Child abuse and neglect, social support, and psychopathology in adulthood: A prospective investigation. *Child Abuse & Neglect, 37*(6), 415–425. doi:10.1016/j.chiabu.2013.02.006 PMID:23562083

Substance Abuse and Mental Health Services Administration. (2014). *Trauma-Informed Care in Behavioral Health Services. Treatment Improvement Protocol (TIP) Series 57. HHS Publication No. (SMA) 13-4801.* Rockville, MD: Author.

Sue, D. W., Rasheed, M. N., & Rasheed, J. M. (2016). *Multicultural social work practice: A competency-based approach to diversity and social justice* (2nd ed.). Hoboken, NJ: John Wiley & Sons.

Tassie, A. K. (2015). Vicarious resilience from attachment trauma: Reflections of long-term therapy with marginalized young people. *Journal of Social Work Practice, 29*(2), 191–204. doi:10.1080/02650533.2014.933406

Teicher, M. H., Samson, J. A., Polcari, A., & McGreenery, C. E. (2006). Sticks, stones, and hurtful words: Relative effects of various forms of childhood maltreatment. *The American Journal of Psychiatry, 163*(6), 993–1000. doi:10.1176/ajp.2006.163.6.993 PMID:16741199

Tomoda, A., Suzuki, H., Rabi, K., Sheu, Y. S., Polcari, A., & Teicher, M. H. (2009). Reduced prefrontal cortical gray matter volume in young adults exposed to harsh corporal punishment. *NeuroImage, 47*, T66–T71. doi:10.1016/j.neuroimage.2009.03.005 PMID:19285558

United Nations High Commissioner for Refugees. (2018). *Turn the tide: Refugee education in crisis.* Geneva, Switzerland: UNHCR UN Refugee Agency.

van der Kolk, B. (2014). *The body keeps the score: Brain, mind, and body in the healing of trauma.* New York, NY: Penguin Books.

Vanalstine, J., Cox, S. R., & Roden, D. M. (2015). Cultural diversity in the United States and its impact on human development. *Journal of the Indiana Academy of the Social Sciences, 18*, 125–143.

Willingham, A. J. (2018). US schools now have more security guards than social workers. *CNN.* Retrieved from: http://www.cnn.com/ampstories/us/us-schools-now-have-more-security-guards-than-social workers

Zastrow, C., & Kirst-Ashman, K. K. (2015). *Empowerment series: Understanding human behavior and the social environment* (10th ed.). Boston, MA: Cengage Learning.

Zerrudo, M. R. (2016). Theater of disaster, folk stories as vehicles for healing and survival. *Teaching Artist Journal, 14*(3), 161–170. doi:10.1080/15411796.2016.1 209073

ADDITIONAL READING

Astor, R. A., Jacobson, L., Wrabel, S. L., Benbenistity, R., & Pineda, D. (2017). *Welcoming practices: Creating schools that support students and families in transition*. Oxford, United Kingdom: Oxford University Press.

Cori, J. L. (2007). *Healing from trauma: A survivor's guide to understanding your symptoms and reclaiming your life*. Boston, MA: Da Capo Lifelong Books.

Diamond, S. (2011). *Social rules for kids-the top 100 social rules kids need to succeed*. Shawnee, KS: AAPC Publishing.

Gillardo, M. E. (2014). *Developing cultural humility: Embracing race, privilege and power*. Thousand Oaks, CA: SAGE Publishing, Inc.

Hackett, E., & Muhanji, J. (2017). *Lessons from cross-cultural collaboration: How cultural humility informed and shaped the work of an American and a Kenyan*. Eugene, OR: Wipf and Stock.

Phifer, L., Crowder, A., Elsenraat, T., & Hull, R. (2017). *CBT toolbox for children and adolescents: Over 200 worksheets & exercises for trauma, ADHD, autism, anxiety, depression & conduct disorders*. Eau Claire, WI: PESI Publishing and Media.

Rippey-Massat, C., Kelly, M. S., & Constable, R. (2015). *School social work: Policy and research* (8th ed.). Oxford, United Kingdom: Oxford University Press.

Scaer, R. (2005). *The trauma spectrum: Hidden wounds and human resiliency*. New York, NY: W. W. Norton and Company.

Smith, B. (2015). *Mentoring at-risk students through the hidden curriculum of higher education*. Lanham, MD: Lexington Books.

Tough, P. (2012). *How children succeed: Grit, curiosity, and the hidden power of character*. Wilmington, MA: Mariner Books.

van der Kolk, B. (2015). *The body keeps the score: Brain, mind, and body in the healing of trauma*. London, United Kingdom: Penguin Books.

Varianides, A. (2012). *The school social work toolkit: Hands-on counseling activities and workshops*. Washington, DC: NASW Press.

Villarreal-Sosa, L., Cox, T., & Alverez, M. (2016). *School social work: National perspectives on practice in schools*. Oxford, United Kingdom: Oxford University Press.

Section 4
Child Abuse and Neglect

Chapter 6
Child Abuse and Neglect

Syed Najmah Jameel
Department of Psychology, University of Kashmir, Hazratbal, India

Shawkat Ahmad Shah
Department of Psychology, University of Kashmir, Hazratbal, India

ABSTRACT

Child abuse and neglect is a global problem which needs attention from every corner of the world. This chapter aims to investigate the definitions, types and causes of child neglect and abuse, as well as their impacts on children, risk and protective factors associated with child abuse and neglect, and child abuse neglect prevention and intervention. This chapter will provide an insight into problems faced by child abuse and neglect victims in particular because they are extremely vulnerable and incapable of defending themselves. This will in turn provide a base for school counsellors to have introspection on the existing frame of strategies/policies with this sensitive section of the population. It may provide baseline for designing new strategies in accordance with the needs of the victims of child abuse. Further it will be a unique way to address this complex social problem.

INTRODUCTION

Worldwide child abuse and neglect is recognised as a significant public health concern which has adversely affected children's mental and physical health and has both immediate as well as long term effect on child's development. Child abuse or includes all forms of physical or emotional maltreatment, sexual abuse, neglect or commercial or other exploitation, which results harm to the child's health, existence, development, or decorum in the context of a relationship of responsibility, trust or

DOI: 10.4018/978-1-7998-0319-5.ch006

power (Butchart, Phinney & Furness 2006). Research studies have highlighted that children who experience abuse and neglect in their early life are more vulnerable to have problems in social relationships and academic profile (Raby, et.al 2018).

Canadian Red Cross [CRC] (2019) defined child abuse and neglect as, *child abuse is any form of physical, emotional and/or sexual mistreatment or lack of care that causes injury or emotional damage to a child or youth.*

World Health Organization[WHO] (1999) defined child abuse as *"Child abuse or maltreatment constitutes all forms of physical and/or emotional ill-treatment, sexual abuse, neglect or negligent treatment or commercial or other exploitation, resulting in actual or potential harm to the child's health, survival, development or dignity in the context of a relationship of responsibility, trust or power"*

World Health Organization [WHO] (1999) defined child neglect as" *Neglect is the failure to provide for the development of the child in all spheres: health, education, emotional development, nutrition, shelter, and safe living conditions, in the context of resources reasonably available to the family or caretakers and causes or has a high probability of causing harm to the child's health or physical, mental, spiritual, moral or social development. This includes the failure to properly supervise and protect children from harm as much as is feasible".*

Convention on the Rights of the child [CRC] (2011) defined Neglect or negligent treatment as *"neglect means the failure to meet children's physical and psychological needs, protect them from danger, or obtain medical, birth registration or other services when those responsible for children's care have the means, knowledge and access to services to do so".*

Child Abuse Prevention and Treatment Act [CAPTA] (2010) defines child abuse and neglect as: *Any recent act or failure to act on the part of a parent or caretaker, which results in death, serious physical or emotional harm, sexual abuse, or exploitation, or an act or failure to act which presents an imminent risk of serious harm.*

The Centers for Disease Control and Prevention [CDC] (2008) defines child maltreatment as any act or series of acts of commission or omission by a parent or other caregiver that results in harm, potential for harm, or threat of harm to a child from birth through age 17 years.

BACKGROUND

Child abuse and neglect has long history. Children have been abused and neglected since times immemorial. Child abuse and neglect has shattered the lives of millions of the children. Research has shown that child abuse and neglect is linked to number of development problems in children which includes poor self-esteem, sense of entitlement, post traumatic stress disorder, conduct disorder, anti-social behavior, difficulty with peers and authority figures, academic and achievement problems. The alarming trend in the child abuse and neglect has been highlighted in the research studies. Wihbey (2011) conducted a meta analysis study and analyzed 65 studies in 22 countries and estimated an "overall international figure of child sexual abuse and revealed that about 7.9% of males and 19.7% of females universally faced sexual abuse before they attain the age of 18 years. The highest prevalence rate of child sexual abuse [CSA] was found in Africa (34.4%). The findings further portrayed that Europe, America, and Asia had prevalence rate of 9.2%, 10.1%, and 23.9%, respectively. With respect to females, seven countries reported prevalence rates as being more than one fifth i.e., 37.8% in Australia, 32.2% in Costa Rica, 31% in Tanzania, 30.7% in Israel, 28.1% in Sweden, 25.3% in the US, and 24.2% in Switzerland, (Behere & Mulmule 2014; Wihbey 2011). Essabar, Khalqallah, and Dakhama, (2015) revealed that about approximately 15% of victims were between ages of 0 and 5 years, the percentage almost tripled (48%) between ages 6 and 10 years and children from ages 11 to 15 years accounted about (26%) of cases, with children 16 years and older accounting for the remaining 11% of cases. The results of the study further highlighted that before the age of 16 years boys were at about two times higher risk than girls, with a percentage of 68%. The victims who were 16 years and older were female in 82% of cases. Daral, Khokhar, and Pradhan, (2016) put forth that approximately 70% of the sample faced at least one form of maltreatment or other. The study further highlighted that 42.6% of the sample faced physical abuse, 26.6% faced sexual abuse, 37.9% faced emotional and last but not the least 40.1% faced neglect. Bala, Maji, Satapathy, and Routray, (2017), revealed that 61.69% of respondents report of having physical abuse, 17.17% report one of the major form of sexual abuse, whereas 55.22% faced one of the other form of sexual abuse.30.85% of children faced emotional abuse and 61.17% of girl child report of gender bias in the family. Radford, Corral, Bradley and Fisher, (2013) highlighted that 2.5% of children (under 11 years), 6% of children and young people (11 to 17 years) had one or more experiences of physical, sexual or emotional abuse, or neglect by a parent or caregiver in the past year and 8.9% of children (under 11 years), 21.9% of young people (11 to 17 years) and 24.5% of young adults had experienced this at least once during childhood. High rates of sexual victimization were found, 7.2% of females (11 to 17years) and 18.6% of females (18 to 24 years) reporting childhood experiences of sexual victimization by any adult or peer that involved physical contact. van der Kooij, et.al (2015) while studying the prevalence of child abuse and neglect found that 86.8% of adolescents and 95.8% of young adults reported having been exposed to at least one form of child maltreatment during their lives. May-Chahal, and Cawson, (2005), while exploring the prevalence of child abuse and neglect revealed that over 90% of respondents reported that they came from a warm and loving family background. The study further put forth that the maltreatment be it intra or extra familial was experienced by 16% of the sample and 7% of the respondents experienced serious maltreatment for physical abuse, 6% experienced emotional abuse, 6% experienced absence of care, 5% experienced absence of supervision, and 11% experienced sexual abuse involving contact. Catani and Sossalla, (2015) revealed that the frequency of traumatic experiences was very high, with physical and emotional child abuse being the most common trauma types. The study further highlighted that 87% of the persons reported at least one aversive experience on the family violence spectrum, and 50% of the sample reported a violent physical attack later in adulthood. 25% were having PTSD and 27% had a significant score on the depression scale. Kisely, Abajobir, Mills, Strathearn, Clavarino, and Najman, (2018) revealed that (4.5%) participants had a history of substantiated child maltreatment, most commonly emotional abuse (2.4%), followed by physical abuse (2.06%), neglect (1.93%) and sexual abuse (1.4%). Schudlich, et .el (2015) found that physical abuse was reported in 21%, sexual abuse in 20%, and both physical and sexual abuse in 11% of youths with bipolar spectrum disorders [BPSD]. The study further revealed that for youths without BPSD, physical abuse was reported in 16%, sexual abuse in 15%, and both physical and sexual abuse in 5% of youths. Taillieu, Brownridge, Sareen, and Afifi, (2016) concluded that Childhood the most prevalent form of emotional maltreatment was emotional neglect only (6.2%), followed by emotional abuse only (4.8%), and then both emotional abuse and neglect (3.1%). Deb and Walsh, (2012) revealed that (21.9%) students experienced physical, (20.9%) experienced psychological and (18.1%) experienced sexual violence at home, and 29.7% of the children had witnessed family violence. McCrann, (2017) while exploring child Sexual Abuse highlighted that the overall prevalence rate for child sexual abuse was 27.7%, with rates being higher for females than for males.

MAIN FOCUS OF THE CHAPTER

The main focus of the chapter is to provide insight into all the aspects associated with the child abuse and neglect i.e causes of child abuse and neglect, types of child abuse, different types of neglect, common physical and behavioural indicators of child abuse, impact of child abuse and neglect on children, risk and protective factors associated with child abuse and neglect, last but not the least prevention and intervention for child abuse and neglect which are discussed as below:

CAUSES OF CHILD ABUSE AND NEGLECT

Abuse of children can occur in several circumstances. Here are some scenarios where a child may be victimised to child abuse and neglect (Chitnis, 2018):

- **Domestic Violence:** Children who are part of households wherever there is frequent force or domestic violence are more vulnerable of becoming victims of abuse. Some men who abuse their woman partners are probably more accountable for abusing their children/youngsters in their homes too.
- **Alcohol and Drug Abuse:** Parents who used to abuse alcohol and drug is usually responsible for child abuse. Dependence of substance abuse is one among the key causes of child abuse and maltreatment which is often accompanied by physical abuse and intentional neglect.
- **Untreated Mental Illness:** The common cause of child abuse is parent's untreated mental illness. Manic depression or any other health problem associated with mind can become a major cause for the parents to be unavailable for the child. A mother might stay withdrawn from her children or in extreme cases suspect that the child plotting against her. A parent's suffering is commonly the cause of subjecting a child to abuse.
- **Lack of Parenting Skills:** Most of the parents have good parenting skills to take appropriate care for their children, but few may not be able to manage their physical and emotional needs adequately. Many parents would usually associate disciplining children with abusing them and often need counseling to understand the role of a parent in a enhanced manner.
- **Stress and Lack of Support:** Some children become more vulnerable of psychological mistreatment by their caregivers or parents when they are under stress. Parents often have difficulty to deal with the emotional needs of their children especially when they face some traumatic situations. Divorces and problems related to relationship, finance and job can lead to parents meting out abuse to their children.

TYPES OF CHILD ABUSE

According to the he Federal Child Abuse and Prevention Treatment Act (CAPTA), there are four types of child abuse which can be summed up as under:

- **Neglect:** Neglect is defined as the failure to provide child's basic needs, which may include physical, educational, or emotional needs.

- **Physical abuse:** Physical abuse may be defined as any physical injury as a result of any physical action that can cause harm to the child. The injury may range from minor bruises to severe fracture or death.
- **Sexual abuse:** It includes any sexual activity with a child, for example fondling, penetration, incest, rape, sodomy, indecent exposure, and commercial exploitation as a result of prostitution or the production of pornographic materials.
- **Emotional abuse:** Emotional abuse can be defined as any pattern of behavior that impairs a child's emotional development or sense of self-worth, which may include constant criticism, threats, rejection or withholding love and support.

UK Government guidance working Together to Safeguard Children (2006) have put forth following types of child abuse and neglect:

- **Physical abuse:** Physical abuse may involve burning, drowning, hitting, shaking, suffocating, throwing, poisoning, or causing physical harm to a child or failing to protect a child from that harm.
- **Emotional Abuse:** Emotional abuse may be defined as an unrelenting emotional maltreatment of a child such as to cause severe and persistent adverse effects on the child's emotional development. It may involve conveying to children that they are useless or unloved, inadequate, or valued only insofar as they meet the needs of another person. It may involve witnessing the maltreatment of another. It may involve serious bullying inflicting children frequently to feel frightened or in danger, or the exploitation or corruption of children. Some level of emotional abuse is concerned in all types of maltreatment of a child, though it may occur alone.
- **Sexual Abuse:** Sexual abuse involves forcing or tempting a child or young person to take part in sexual activities, including prostitution, whether or not the child is aware of what is happening. The activities may involve physical contact including either penetrative or non-penetrative acts such as kissing, touching or fondling the child's genitals or breasts, vaginal or anal intercourse or oral sex. It may also include non-contact activities such as involving children in looking at or in the production of, pornographic material or watching sexual activities, or encouraging children to behave in sexually inappropriate ways.
- **Neglect:** Neglect is the constant failure to fulfil a child's basic physical and/ or psychological needs, which in turn results in the serious impairment of the child's health or development. Neglect might occur throughout pregnancy as a result of maternal substance abuse. After the child is born, neglect may

involve a parent or caregiver failure to provide adequate food and clothing, shelter, including exclusion from home or abandonment; failing to protect a child from physical and emotional harm or danger, failure to ensure adequate supervision including the use of inadequate caretakers or the failure to ensure access to appropriate medical care or treatment. It may also include neglect of or unresponsiveness to a child's basic emotional needs.

- **Bullying:** Bullying may be defined as intentionally hurtful behaviour, usually repeated over a period of time, where it is difficult for those bullied to defend themselves. It may take several forms, but the three main types are physical which are hitting, kicking, theft, verbal that may include racist or homophobic remarks, threats, name calling and emotional i.e isolating an individual from the activities and social acceptance of their peer group.

The National Clearinghouse on Child Abuse and Neglect Information (2001) provides the following elaboration for clarification regarding the types of child abuse as under:

- **Physical abuse:** Physical abuse may be defined as an infliction of physical injury as a result of punching, kicking, biting, burning, shaking or otherwise harming a child. The parent or caretaker might have not have meant to hurt the child rather the injury might have resulted from over-discipline or physical punishment.
- **Child neglect:** Child neglect may be defined as a failure to provide the child's basic needs which may be physical, educational, or emotional. Physical neglect includes denial of or delay in seeking health care, abandonment, expulsion from the home or refusal to allow a runaway to return home and inadequate supervision. Educational neglect includes the allowance of chronic absence, failure to enrol a child of mandatory school age in school, and failure to attend to a special educational need of the child.
- **Emotional neglect:** It includes such behaviours as marked inattention to the child's needs for affection, rejection of or failure to provide needed psychological care, spouse abuse in the child's presence and permission of drug or alcohol use by the child.
- **Sexual abuse:** Sexual abuse includes the fondling of a child's genitals, intercourse, rape, sodomy, exhibitionism, and commercial exploitation through prostitution or the production of pornographic materials.
- **Emotional abuse:** It includes all those acts or omissions by the parents or other caregivers that have caused, or could cause, serious behavioral, cognitive, emotional, or mental disorders.

DIFFERENT TYPES OF NEGLECT

DePanfilis (2016) highlighted that while neglect may be harder to define or to detect than other forms of child maltreatment. The experts of child welfare have created universal categories of neglect which include physical neglect, medical neglect, inadequate supervision and educational neglect. The following types of neglect

Physical Neglect: It is one of the most commonly accepted forms of neglect. It includes:

1.   Abandonment
2.   Expulsion
3.   Shuttling
4.   Nutritional neglect
5.   Neglect of clothing

Medical neglect: It encompasses a parent or guardian's refusal of or delay in seeking required health care for a child as described below:

1.   Denial of health care
2.   Delay in health care

Emotional Neglect: Typically, emotional neglect is harder to assess than other types of neglect, but is thought to have more severe and long-lasting consequences than physical neglect. It usually occurs with other types of neglect or abuse, which may be easier to identify and includes:

1.   Inadequate nurturing or affection
2.   Chronic or extreme spouse abuse
3.   Permitted drug or alcohol abuse
4.   Other permitted maladaptive behavior
5.   Isolation

Educational Neglect: Both parents and schools are responsible for meeting certain requirements regarding the education of children Types of educational neglect include:

1.   Permitted chronic Truancy
2.   Failure to enrol or other Truancy
3.   Inattention to special education needs

Inadequate supervision: Inadequate supervision encompasses a number of behaviors that include:

1. Lack of appropriate supervision.
2. Exposure to hazards
3. Inappropriate caregivers.
4. Leaving a child without proper planning or consent with an appropriate caregiver.
5. Allowing or not keeping the child from engaging in risky, illegal, or harmful behaviors
6. Leaving the child with a caregiver who is not able to satisfactorily supervising the child.

COMMON INDICATORS OF CHILD ABUSE

PROTECT (2016) has put forth following physical and behavioral indicators of child abuse:

Common Physical Indicators of Child Abuse

- Burns, welts, bruises, cuts/grazes especially those on legs, bottom, back, arms and inner thighs or in unusual configurations and may resemble an object.
- Bone fractures and internal injuries not consistent with the explanation offered by the person.
- Any injury or harm to the genital or rectal area e.g. bleeding, swelling, bruising, infection or anything causing pain during toilet.
- Often wearing those clothes that are unsuitable for weather conditions in order to hide injuries.
- Sexually-transmitted diseases and/or frequent urinary tract infections
- Persistently appearing filthy and dirty.
- Being consistently hungry, tired and listless.
- Lack of routine medical care and checkups or having unattended health problems and internal injuries.
- Self destructive tendencies
- Aggression towards others
- Running away
- Bald patches

Common Behavioural Indicators of Child Abuse

- Revelation of abuse or portraying or writing something which depicts violence and abuse.
- Customary absences from school without realistic explanations.
- Inexplicable delays in mental, emotional or physical development
- Regressive or unusual changes to behaviour for example sudden decline in academic performance, nervousness, depression. Withdrawal, hyperactivity, aggression, bedwetting.
- Alcohol or drug abuse, suicide or self-harm, harm to others or animals.
- Unusual fear of physical contact with adults.
- Poor self-care or personal hygiene.

IMPACT OF CHILD ABUSE AND NEGLECT ON CHILDREN

Nyarko, Amissah, Addai, and Dedzo, (2014) while studying the effect of child abuse on children's psychological health on the victims of physical and psychological abuse revealed that both physical and psychological abuse leads to significant increase in children depression and anxiety. Vinnerljung, Hjern, and Lindblad, (2006) revealed that young adults maltreated as children are four to five times more likely than non-maltreated individuals to be hospitalized for suicide attempts or serious psychiatric disorders. Rostami, Abdi, and Heidari, (2014), while studying various types of abuse during childhood and mental health revealed that the less harassed or abused the individual, the better mental health they benefit from and the higher the measure of maltreatment in the individual, the more increase in their pathological symptoms and the more decrease in their mental health. Dlamini, and Makondo, (2017), while exploring the effects of child abuse on the academic performance concluded that child abuse adversely affects the academic performance of learners at primary school level. Hildyard and Wolfe, (2002) highlighted that neglected and physically abused children have more severe cognitive and academic deficits, limited peer interaction, social withdrawal and internalizing problems. Pollak, (2004) put forth that child maltreatment disrupts the normal course of children's emotional development and the maltreated children are at higher risk for a wide range of mental health-related problems, including anxiety, substance abuse depression, criminality and other forms of poorly regulated emotional behaviour. Sanchez, et.al (2017) found that compared to women with no childhood abuse, the odds of PTSD were increased 4.31 fold for those who reported physical abuse only 5.33 fold for sexual abuse only and 8.03 fold for those who reported physical and sexual abuse. Hsieh, et.al (2016) revealed that children who experience any kind of abuse be it psychological neglect, physical neglect, paternal physical violence or sexual violence were associated with increased risk among children of developing PTSD and Internet addiction in their later life. Riber, (2017), while studying trauma complexity and child abuse found that participants had personal impacts of child abuse in emotional, relational, and behavioral domains in their adult lives. Rehan, Antfolk, Johansson, Jern, and Santtila, (2017) found that women reported more childhood experiences of severe emotional, sexual abuse and emotional neglect than men. The study further revealed that in men, severe experiences of emotional and physical abuse as well as physical neglect were significantly associated with increases in the prevalence of depression and anxiety symptoms. Hayashi, et.al (2015) while studying the direct and indirect influences of childhood abuse on depression symptoms found that childhood abuse directly and indirectly predicted the severity of depression. Kisely, Abajobir, Mills, Strathearn, Clavarino, and Najman, (2018) studied Child maltreatment and mental health problems in adulthood and revealed that Child maltreatment, particularly neglect and emotional abuse, has serious adverse effects on early adult mental health. Kuo, Goldin, Werner, Heimberg, and Gross, (2011) highlighted that childhood emotional abuse and neglect, were associated with the severity of social anxiety, trait anxiety, depression, and self-esteem. Simon, et.al (2009) found that childhood maltreatment, specifically emotional abuse and neglect, are associated with greater severity and poorer function, resilience, and quality of life. Maniglio, (2013) revealed that child sexual abuse is a significant risk factor for anxiety disorders, especially posttraumatic stress disorder. Watson, Gallagher, Dougall, Porter, Moncrieff, Ferrier and Young, (2014) highlighted that childhood emotional neglect appears to be significantly associated with bipolar disorder. Daruy-Filho, Brietzke, Lafer, and Grassi-Oliveira, (2011) revealesd that the childhood abuse and neglect are risk factors associated with worsening clinical course of bi-polar disorder. Ngisa, Muriungi, and Mwenda, (2017) while studying the impact of child abuse on academic performance of pupils revealed that child abuse was found to affect school attendance, pupils' behaviour and learning disorders negatively. Apebende, Umoren, and Ukpepi, (2010) while exploring the influence of child abuse on the academic performance revealed that children that were not abused perform better than children who have been abused. Deb and Walsh, (2012) while investigating the impact of physical, psychological, and sexual violence on social adjustment of school children revealed that the social adjustment scores of school children who experienced violence, regardless of the nature of the violence, was significantly lower than those who had not experienced violence The study further highlighted that girls have poorer social adjustment than boys. Kendall-Tackett, (2002), highlighted that childhood abuse makes individual more prone to depression and post-traumatic stress disorder, participating in harmful activities, having difficulties in relationships, and having negative beliefs and attitudes towards others, which in turn increases the likelihood of health problems, and they are highly related to each other.

RISK FACTORS ASSOCIATED WITH CHILD ABUSE AND NEGLECT

Risk factors may be defined as the measureable characteristic/s of an individual or the community/society within which they reside that heightens the probability of a worse outcome in the future (Masten & Wright, 1998). As per Child and Family Services Reviews (2012) risk factors can be grouped into four domains:

1. **Parent or Caregiver**: It encompasses personality characteristics and psychological well-being, substance abuse, history of maltreatment and age
2. **Family**: It may include marital conflict, domestic violence, single parenthood and/or boyfriends in the home, financial stress, and social isolation.
3. **Child**: It may include child's age, development and special needs.
4. **Environmental**: It includes poverty, unemployment, and community characteristics including violent neighbourhoods.

As per National CASA volunteer manual (2015) the risk factors can be summed up as under:

1. **Child-Related Factors**. Chronological age of child, it is depicted that 50% of abused children are under the age of three; 90% of deaths are under one year of age; first-born children are most at risk.
   a. Physical or mental disabilities.
   b. Attachment problems or separation from parent during crucial periods or reduced positive relations between parent and child.
   c. Premature birth or illness at birth.
   d. The child who reminds parent of absent partner or spouse or unwanted child.
2. Parent/Caretaker-Related Factors
   a. Low self-esteem: Neglectful parents even often neglect themselves and see themselves as worthless people.
   b. Abuse as a child: Parents who have experienced neglect in their lives may often tend to repeat their own childhood experience if no intervention occurred in their case and no new or adaptive skills were learned during that time.

    c.   Depression: It may be related to any mental problems or as a result of having major problems and limited emotional resources to deal with them.

    d.   Impulsive: Abusive parents often have a noticeable incapability to channel anger or sexual feelings.

    e.   Substance abuse: The "high" resulting from drugs and/or alcohol serves as a temporary relief from overwhelming problems but, in fact, creates new and bigger problems.

    f.   Personality disorder or mental illness.

    g.   Lack of knowledge of child care, child development and unrealistic expectations.

    h.   Isolation: Neglectful and abusive families may tend to keep away from community contact and have few family ties to provide support, distance from, or disintegration of, an extended family that conventionally played a important role in child rearing may increase isolation.

    i.   Sense of entitlement: People often have belief that it's acceptable to use violence to ensure child's or partner's compliance.

    j.   Mental retardation or borderline mental functioning.

3.   **Social-Situational Factors** Abuse occurs in the family context. It is therefore necessary to understand the factors that may affect the family as a whole.

    a.   Structural or economic factors: The trauma of unemployment, poverty, little or no mobility, and poor housing can be instrumental in a parent's ability to adequately care for a child. The child needs to be shielding from separation from her or his family entirely because of stressed economic conditions.

    b.   Family violence: Children may be injured while trying to mediate to protect a battered parent or while in the arms or proximity of a parent being assaulted.

    c.   Devaluation of children and other dependents.

    d.   Overdrawn values of honor between men with intolerance of perceived disrespect.

    e.   Abnormal child-rearing practices which may include genital mutilation of female children or sexual abuse by intimate partner.

    f.   Cruelty in child-rearing practices for example putting hot peppers in child's mouth, depriving child of water, confining child to room for days, or taping mouth with duct etc.

4.   **Family Factors:** Family violence may indicate an inability of one parent to protect the child from another's abuse as a result of parent also being abused.

a.   Stepparent, or blended, families are at greater risk. There is some indication that adult partners who are not the parents of the child are more likely to maltreat them and also the changes in family structure create stress in the family.

b.   Single parents are extremely represented in abuse and neglect cases, economic status is typically lower in single-parent families, and the single parent is at a disadvantage in trying to perform the functions of two parents. Adolescent parents are at high risk because their own developmental growth has been disrupted as they are ill-prepared to respond to the needs of the child because their own needs have not been met.

c.   Child-rearing styles that are punishment-centred have greater risk of causing and promoting abuse.

d.   Late childhood adoptions, special needs, or with a temperamental mismatch.

5.   **Triggering situations:** Any of the factors that are mentioned above can contribute to a situation in which an abusive event occurs. Some of the possible triggering situations include:

a.   Sometimes baby will not stop crying.

b.   Sometimes parent is frustrated with toilet training.

c.   Sometimes an alcoholic is fired from a job.

d.   Sometimes mother, after being beaten by her partner, cannot make contact with her own family.

e.   Sometimes parent is served with an eviction notice.

f.   Sometimes prescription drug used to control mental illness is stopped.

g.   Sometimes a parent who was disrespected in the adult world later takes it out on his/her child

PROTECTIVE FACTORS ASSOCIATED WITH CHILD ABUSE AND NEGLECT

Protective factors are defined as a correlate of resilience that may reflect preventative or ameliorative influences, a positive moderator of risk or adversity (Masten & Wright, 1998,). Protective factors are those that may help protect families from vulnerabilities and help promote resilience (Child and Family Services Reviews, 2012). These include:

•   Nurturing and attachment i.e developing a bond with a caring adult.
•   Knowledge of parenting and child development i.e understanding how children grow and develop in all aspects.

- Parental resilience i.e having the ability to handle everyday stressors and recover from occasional crises.
- Social connections which includes having trusted and caring family and friends who provide emotional support.
- Tangible support for parents including accessing basic resources, such as food, clothing, housing, transportation and also the services that address family-specific needs which include child care, health care, social services for mental health and substance abuse treatment or domestic violence.
- Social and emotional competence of children i.e having the right tools for healthy emotional expression.

SOLUTIONS AND RECOMMENDATIONS

The term prevention has been derived from Latin word 'praevenire' which means 'anticipating', literally means 'to keep from happening or existing'. Prevention refers to the strategies that are taken to prevent child abuse and neglect even before it happens. Gross (2002) has suggested certain preventive measures for child abuse and neglect which can be summed up as under:

1. Every parent should take proper and good care of their children in all aspects.
2. Parents should always encourage the child if he/she is doing something right.
3. Parents should always encourage good person and condemn bad behaviour.
4. Parents should set fair, clear and explainable guidelines for children.
5. Parents should always try to make their children understand and recognise the bad touch.
6. Parents should not leave their children alone at home or in a park etc., until they have reached an age to take care of themselves.
7. The most important thing is parents should listen and talk to their child. It's important to inform children about child abuse and about what could happen.

James (1993) suggested that prevention of neglect requires action at three different levels which are as under:

1. **Primary Prevention**: Primary prevention is directed at the general population with the aim of stopping neglect from occurring. Primary prevention requires the services be available in the community that will provide support to the parents and will also provide adequate care for their children. When these services remain unavailable to parents their children are more at risk for neglect. The necessary services are as:

121

a. Affordable and accessible health care for mothers and children that includes prenatal and obstetric care, preventive paediatric care and treatment for illness, public health screening, health promotion, and immunization and other disease prevention services.

b. High-quality community education with curriculum that includes age-appropriate life skills training for children and parent, education for all older elementary and high school students and adults.

c. Recreational programs for children of all ages offered through public and private agencies to provide safe activities to enhance physical, intellectual, social, and emotional development and after school supervision for school-aged children.

2. **Secondary Prevention:** Secondary prevention involves targeting families at high risk of neglect and alleviating conditions associated with the problem. The targeting of high-risk groups to prevent the occurrence of neglect encompasses a range of strategies which can be summed up as under:

a. Remedying poverty.
b. Early childhood education.
c. Home health visitation.
d. Family planning.
e. Parent skill training.
f. Strengthening Social Network Supports.

3. **Tertiary Prevention:** Tertiary prevention includes targeting services to neglecting parents and their children to remedy the neglect and its consequences on the children and prevent its recurrence.

a. Any service or intervention selected for inclusion in the plan represents a tertiary prevention strategy.

b. Daro's review of demonstration programs aimed at helping neglectful families, underscores the importance of direct intervention with neglected children as a tertiary prevention strategy.

c. Another possible tertiary prevention result of direct intervention with neglected children revolves around the parents. The efforts of parents to improve their parenting abilities may be bolstered by evidence of improvement in their children.

INTERVENTION FOR CHILD ABUSE AND NEGLECT

Appropriate intervention must be customized to the type of neglect and the outcome of the assessment process.

James (1993) put forth following general guidelines for intervention

- Most neglectful parents want to be good parents but they lack the personal, financial, and/or supportive resources. Professional helpers must help the parents to improve the quality of care for their children. Interventions must be developed accordingly.
- All parents have inner strengths that can be channelized. The concealed strengths of the neglectful parent must be recognized during the assessment process, reinforced, and interventions planned to build upon those strengths. An act as simple as opening the door to the professional visiting the home suggests good will and positive intent.
- Helping interventions must be culturally sensitive. Professional helpers should intervene with information of and respect for the variations in life experiences, cultural and religious beliefs, child-rearing norms, and role expectations held by families.
- Neglectful parents are usually psychologically immature, usually as a result of their own lack of nurturing as children. They may have negative perception of themselves as parents and little confidence in their abilities to improve their parenting. They need to nurture themselves to enable them to nurture their children adequately.
- Intervention with negligent parents requires that the helper "parent the parent" and "begin where the client is." The professional helper must listen with full empathy and authenticate the concerns and feelings of family members, then prop up and encourage gradually more independent and accountable behavior.
- Nurturing dysfunctional reliance must be avoided by maintaining a balance between supportive counseling, enabling the family to use supportive formal and informal services, and communicating expectations for achievement of realistic, achievable goals that represent progressively more independent, responsible functioning.
- It is essential to set clearly stated, limited, achievable goals that are shared with and agreed upon by the parents and children. Goals should appear from the problems identified by the parents and the professional helper and from the causes or obstacles to remedying the problems and should be clearly expressed in a written service or treatment plan, which is developed with the family.
- Neglectful parents are empowered when the professional helper systematically reinforces the parent's limited, incremental achievements with tangible rewards and praise.

- The treatment or the service plan should be clearly outlined, with responsibilities for parent and professional helpers clearly identified.
- The exercise of legal authority by the professional helper is often necessary to overcome the initial denial and apathy of the neglectful parent. Confrontation with the reality of legal mandates and the possibility of legal intervention are sometimes necessary to disturb the dysfunctional family balance and mobilize the parent to change neglectful parenting practices.
- Neglectful families are typically poor and lack access to resources. Therefore, the intervention set up should include brokering and support to mobilize concrete formal and informal serving to resources. Case management of multiple services is necessary. Successful mobilization of out of doors resources to fulfil the family's identified priorities helps to beat the family's hopelessness, resistance, and distrust of professional helpers.

Community services that may need to be mobilized for neglectful families include the following:

- Emergency financial assistance
- Low-cost housing
- Emergency food bank
- Clothing bank
- Low-cost medical care
- Transportation
- Homemakers
- Parent aides
- Recreation programs
- Mental health assessment and treatment
- Temporary foster care or respite care
- Budget/credit counseling
- Job training and placement
- Parent support/skills training groups
- Low-cost child care.
- Treatment of chronic neglect is not a short-term project. Successful intervention with neglectful parents should last for twelve to eighteen months. When neglect isn't a chronic pattern, additional shorter term and more intensive intervention may be successful in this regard.

MULTICULTURAL PERSPECTIVE REGARDING CHILD ABUSE AND NEGLECT

As the population becomes more diverse, the need for multicultural counseling grows more apparent. Changing demographics of the population across countries demand for the development of multicultural competent counselors. The multicultural movement has highlighted the need for counsellors to be prepared for professional practice with clients from cultural backgrounds different from their own (Arthur, 1998). Both the Canadian Psychological Association (CPA) (1996) as well as the American Psychological Association (APA) (1993) has recognized the importance of multicultural counseling. The association for multicultural counseling and development [AMCD)] as put forth by Arredono (1996) had highlighted following competencies to achieve multicultural counselling i.e counselor's awareness of own cultural values and biases, Counselors Awareness of Client's Worldview and culturally appropriate intervention strategies which are discussed as below:

Counselors Awareness of Own Cultural Values and Biases

- Culturally skilled counselors should believe that cultural self-awareness and sensitivity to one's own cultural heritage is essential.
- Culturally skilled counselors should be aware of how their own cultural background and experiences have influenced attitudes, values, and biases about psychological processes.
- Culturally skilled counselors should be able recognize the limits of their multicultural competency and expertise.
- Culturally skilled counselors should recognize their sources of discomfort with differences that exist between themselves and clients in terms of race, ethnicity and culture.
- Culturally skilled counselors should have specific knowledge about their own racial and cultural heritage and how it personally and professionally affects their definitions and biases of normality/abnormality and the process of counseling
- Culturally skilled counselors should possess knowledge and understanding about how oppression, racism, discrimination, and stereotyping affect them personally and in their work.
- Culturally skilled counselors should possess knowledge about their social impact upon others

- Culturally skilled counselors should seek out educational, consultative, and training experiences to improve their understanding and effectiveness in working with culturally different populations.
- Culturally skilled counselors should constantly seek to understand themselves as racial and cultural beings and should actively seek a non racist identity.

Counselors Awareness of Client's Worldview

- Culturally skilled counselors should be aware of their negative and positive emotional reactions toward other racial and ethnic groups that may prove detrimental to the counseling relationship.
- Culturally skilled counselors should be aware of their stereotypes and preconceived notions that they may hold toward other racial and ethnic minority groups
- Culturally skilled counselors should possess specific knowledge and information about the particular group with which they are working.
- Culturally skilled counselors should understand how race, culture, ethnicity etc affect personality formation, vocational choices, manifestation of psychological disorders, help seeking behavior, and the appropriateness or inappropriateness of counseling approaches.
- Culturally skilled counselors should understand and have knowledge about socio political influences that impinge upon the life of racial and ethnic minorities.
- Culturally skilled counselors should familiarize themselves with relevant research and the latest findings regarding mental health and mental disorders that affect various ethnic and racial groups.
- They should actively seek out educational experiences that enrich their knowledge, understanding, and cross-cultural skills for more effective counseling behavior.

Culturally Appropriate Intervention Strategies

- Culturally skilled counselors should respect clients' religious and/ or spiritual beliefs and values, including attributions and taboos, because they affect worldview, psychosocial functioning, and expressions of distress.
- Culturally skilled counselors should respect indigenous helping practices and respect helpiving networks among communities of color.
- Culturally skilled counselors should value bilingualism and do not view another language as an impediment to counseling.

- Culturally skilled counselors should have a clear and explicit knowledge and understanding of the generic characteristics of counseling and therapy and how they may clash with the cultural values of various cultural groups.
- Culturally skilled counselors are aware of institutional barriers that prevent minorities from using mental health services.
- Culturally skilled counselors should have knowledge of the potential bias in assessment instruments and use procedures and interpret findings keeping in mind the cultural and linguistic characteristics of the clients.
- Culturally skilled counselors should have knowledge of family structures, hierarchies, values, and beliefs from various cultural perspectives. They should be knowledgeable about the community where a particular cultural group may reside and the resources in the community.
- Culturally skilled counselors should be aware of relevant discriminatory practices at the social and community level that may be affecting the psychological welfare of the population being served.
- Culturally skilled counselors should be able to engage in a variety of verbal and nonverbal helping responses.
- Culturally skilled counselors should be able to exercise institutional intervention
- Culturally skilled counselors should not averse to seek consultation with traditional healers or religious and spiritual leaders and practitioners in the treatment of culturally different clients when appropriate.
- Culturally skilled counselors should take responsibility for interacting in the language requested by the client and, if not feasible, make appropriate referrals or should seek a translator with cultural knowledge and appropriate professional background.
- Culturally skilled counselors should attend to as well as work to eliminate biases, prejudices, and discriminatory contexts in conducting evaluations and providing interventions, and should develop sensitivity to issues of oppression, sexism, heterosexism, elitism and racism.
- Culturally skilled counselors should take responsibility for educating their clients to the processes of psychological intervention, such as goals, expectations, legal rights, and the counselor's orientation.

FUTURE RESEARCH DIRECTIONS

The researchers have focused on the various issues related to both child abuse and neglect. However there is less documentation on the intervention and prevention part. Further the changing trends in the child abuse and neglect have not been publicized and widely known. There should be proper initiatives for the enforcement of the law regarding such issues, public awareness should be provided, and professional initiatives can be helpful in this regard. The present chapter by providing an insight into the issues related to child abuse and neglect will help the researchers to go a long way to better investigate the problem of child abuse. This can be made possible by many affirmative action's like recognition and understanding of the problem, knowing the reporting procedures and participating in available child abuse information programs. In sum, the researchers have ample opportunities to better highlight the problems associated with child abuse, by adhering to more appropriate research practices, this will largely help in putting an end to the menace of child abuse and neglect worldwide.

CONCLUSION

Child abuse and neglect existed in our societies from a long time and had adversely affected millions of children in all walks of life. The main focus of the present chapter was to provide an insight into the various dimensions of child abuse and neglect which include conceptualisation, prevalence, causes, physical and behavioural indicators, types, effects, risk and protective factors, prevention and interventions. The journey to prevent child abuse and neglect has been an ongoing struggle for many years. School counselors can play an important role in this regard. As put forward by the American School Counselor Association's [ASCA] Position Statement (ASCA, 2003) it is the absolute responsibility of professional school counselors to report suspected cases of child abuse/neglect to the proper authorities. Therefore the professional school counselors after gaining the basic theoretical information regarding child abuse and neglect can become instrumental in early detection of abuse and the treatment thereafter.

REFERENCES

American Psychological Association. (1993). Guidelines for psychological practice with ethnic, linguistic, and culturally diverse populations. *The American Psychologist, 48*(1), 45–48. doi:10.1037/0003-066X.48.1.45

American School Counselor Association. (2003). *Position statement: Child abuse/ neglect prevention: The professional school counselor and child abuse and neglect prevention.* Retrieved from http://www. schoolcounselor.org/content.asp?contentid

Apebende, E., Umoren, G., & Ukpepi, B. (2010). The Influence of Child Abuse on the Academic Performance of Primary School Pupils in Primary Sci333ence in Cross River State, Nigeria. *An International Multi-Disciplinary Journal, 3*(2), 49–51.

Arredondo, P., Toporek, R., Brown, S. P., Jones, J., Locke, D. C., Sanchez, J., & Stadler, H. (1996). Operationalization of the multicultural counseling competencies. *Journal of Multicultural Counseling and Development, 24*(1), 42–78. doi:10.1002/j.2161-1912.1996.tb00288.x

Arrhur, N. (1988). Counsellor education for diversity: Where do we go from here? *Canadian Journal of Counselling, 32,* 88–103.

Bala, D., Maji, B., Satapathy, J., & Routray, R. K. (2017). Prevalence of child abuse in eastern India: A tip of iceberg. *International Journal of Contemporary Pediatrics, 2*(4), 353–355.

Behere, P. B., & Mulmule, A. N. (2013). Sexual abuse in 8-year-old child: Where do we stand legally? *Indian Journal of Psychological Medicine, 35*(2), 203. doi:10.4103/0253-7176.116256 PMID:24049233

Butchart, A., Phinney, A., & Furness, T. (2006). *Preventing child maltreatment: A guide to taking action and generating evidence.* World Health Organization.

Canadian Psychological Association. (1990). *Guidelines for psychological practice with ethnic and culturally diverse populations.* Ottawa, Canada: Author.

Canadian Red Cross. (2019). Retrieved from https://www.redcross.ca/how-we-help/violence-bullying-and-abuse-prevention/educators/child-abuse-and-neglect-prevention/definitions-of-child-abuse-and-neglect

CAPTA Reauthorization Act of 2010 (P.L. 111-320), § 5101, Note (§ 3). (n.d.). Retrieved from https://www.childwelfare.gov/pubpdfs/whatiscan.pdf

Catani, C., & Sossalla, I. M. (2015). Child abuse predicts adult PTSD symptoms among individuals diagnosed with intellectual disabilities. *Frontiers in Psychology, 6,* 1600. doi:10.3389/fpsyg.2015.01600 PMID:26539143

Child and Family Services Reviews. (2012). Retrieved from https://training.cfsrportal.acf.hhs.gov/section-2-understanding-child-welfare-system/2984

Chitnis, R. (2018). *Causes of child abuse and neglect.* retrieved from https://parenting.firstcry.com/articles/child-abuse-a-guide-to-parents-caregivers/

Clement, M. E., Berube, A., & Chamberland, C. (2016). Prevalence and risk factors of child neglect in the general population. *Public Health*, *138*, 86–92. doi:10.1016/j. puhe.2016.03.018 PMID:27117500

Convention on the Rights of the Child (CRC). (2011). Retrieved from https://www. unicef-irc.org/portfolios/general_comments/CRC.C.GC.13_en.doc.html

Daral, S., Khokhar, A., & Pradhan, S. (2016). Prevalence and determinants of child maltreatment among school-going adolescent girls in a semi-urban area of Delhi, India. *Journal of Tropical Pediatrics*, *62*(3), 227–240. doi:10.1093/tropej/fmv106 PMID:26769624

Daruy-Filho, L., Brietzke, E., Lafer, B., & Grassi-Oliveira, R. (2011). Childhood maltreatment and clinical outcomes of bipolar disorder. *Acta Psychiatrica Scandinavica*, *124*(6), 427–434. doi:10.1111/j.1600-0447.2011.01756.x PMID:21848703

Deb, S., & Walsh, K. (2012). Impact of physical, psychological, and sexual violence on social adjustment of school children in India. *School Psychology International*, *33*(4), 391–415. doi:10.1177/0143034311425225

DePanfilis, D. (2006). Child neglect: A guide for prevention, assessment, and intervention. US Department of Health and Human Services, Administration for Children and Families, Administration on Children, Youth and Families, Children's Bureau, Office on Child Abuse and Neglect.

Dlamini, S. L., & Makondo, D. (2017). Effects of Child Abuse on the Academic Performance of Primary School Learners in the Manzini Region, Swaziland. *World Journal of Education*, *7*(5), 58. doi:10.5430/wje.v7n5p58

Essabar, L., Khalqallah, A., & Dakhama, B. S. B. (2015). Child sexual abuse: Report of 311 cases with review of literature. *The Pan African Medical Journal*, *20*(1). PMID:26090005

Gross, S. (2002). *Causes and Prevention of Child Abuse*. Munich: GRIN Verlag. Retrieved from https://www.grin.com/document/106157

Hayashi, Y., Okamoto, Y., Takagaki, K., Okada, G., Toki, S., Inoue, T., ... Yamawaki, S. (2015). Direct and indirect influences of childhood abuse on depression symptoms in patients with major depressive disorder. *BMC Psychiatry*, *15*(1), 244. doi:10.118612888-015-0636-1 PMID:26467656

Hildyard, K. L., & Wolfe, D. A. (2002). Child neglect: Developmental issues and outcomes. *Child Abuse & Neglect, 26*(6-7), 679–695. doi:10.1016/S0145-2134(02)00341-1 PMID:12201162

Hsieh, Y. P., Shen, A. C. T., Wei, H. S., Feng, J. Y., Huang, S. C. Y., & Hwa, H. L. (2016). Associations between child maltreatment, PTSD, and internet addiction among Taiwanese students. *Computers in Human Behavior, 56*, 209–214. doi:10.1016/j.chb.2015.11.048

James, M. (1993). Child neglect: A guide for intervention. U.S. Department of Health and Human Services Administration for Children and Families.

Kendall-Tackett, K. (2002). The health effects of childhood abuse: Four pathways by which abuse can influence health. *Child Abuse & Neglect, 26*(6-7), 715–729. doi:10.1016/S0145-2134(02)00343-5 PMID:12201164

Kisely, S., Abajobir, A. A., Mills, R., Strathearn, L., Clavarino, A., & Najman, J. M. (2018). Child maltreatment and mental health problems in adulthood: Birth cohort study. *The British Journal of Psychiatry, 213*(6), 698–703. doi:10.1192/bjp.2018.207 PMID:30475193

Kuo, J. R., Goldin, P. R., Werner, K., Heimberg, R. G., & Gross, J. J. (2011). Childhood trauma and current psychological functioning in adults with social anxiety disorder. *Journal of Anxiety Disorders, 25*(4), 467–473. doi:10.1016/j.janxdis.2010.11.011 PMID:21183310

Maniglio, R. (2013). Child sexual abuse in the etiology of anxiety disorders: A systematic review of reviews. *Trauma, Violence & Abuse, 14*(2), 96–112. doi:10.1177/1524838012470032 PMID:23262751

Masten, A. S., & Wright, M. O. (1998). Cumulative risk and protection models of child maltreatment. *Journal of Aggression, Maltreatment & Trauma, 2*(1), 7–30. doi:10.1300/J146v02n01_02

May-Chahal, C., & Cawson, P. (2005). Measuring child maltreatment in the United Kingdom: A study of the prevalence of child abuse and neglect. *Child Abuse & Neglect, 29*(9), 969–984. doi:10.1016/j.chiabu.2004.05.009 PMID:16165212

McCrann, D. (2017). *An Exploratory Study of Child Sexual Abuse in Tanzania*. Doctoral thesis.

National CASA Volunteer Manual. (2015). Retrieved from https://pgcasa.org/wp-content/uploads/2015/07/ch4.pdf

National Clearinghouse on Child Abuse and Neglect Information. (2001). *What is child maltreatment?* Washington, DC: National Clearinghouse on Child Abuse and Neglect.

Ngisa, F. S., Muriungi, P., & Mwenda, E. (2017). Impact of Child Abuse on Academic Performance of Pupils in Public Primary Schools in Kieni West Sub-County. *Nyeri County.*, *6*(9), 62–72.

Nyarko, K., Amissah, C. M., Addai, P., & Dedzo, B. Q. (2014). The effect of child abuse on children's psychological health. *Psychology and Behavioral Sciences*, *3*(4), 105–112. doi:10.11648/j.pbs.20140304.11

Pollak, S. (2004). The impact of child maltreatment on the psychosocial development of young children. In Encyclopedia on Early Childhood Development, (pp. 1-6). Academic Press.

PROTECT. (2016). *Indicators of child abuse and neglect.* Retrieved from https://www.education.vic.gov.au/Documents/about/programs/health/protect/ChildSafeStandard5_WarningSignsSchoolStaff.pdf

Raby, K. L., Roisman, G. I., Labella, M. H., Martin, J., Fraley, R. C., & Simpson, J. A. (2018). The legacy of early abuse and neglect for social and academic competence from childhood to adulthood. *Child Development*. doi:10.1111/cdev.13033 PMID:29336018

Radford, L., Corral, S., Bradley, C., & Fisher, H. L. (2013). The prevalence and impact of child maltreatment and other types of victimization in the UK: Findings from a population survey of caregivers, children and young people and young adults. *Child Abuse & Neglect*, *37*(10), 801–813. doi:10.1016/j.chiabu.2013.02.004 PMID:23522961

Rehan, W., Antfolk, J., Johansson, A., Jern, P., & Santtila, P. (2017). Experiences of severe childhood maltreatment, depression, anxiety and alcohol abuse among adults in Finland. *PLoS One*, *12*(5), e0177252. doi:10.1371/journal.pone.0177252 PMID:28481912

Riber, K. (2017). Trauma complexity and child abuse: A qualitative study of attachment narratives in adult refugees with PTSD. *Transcultural Psychiatry*, *54*(5-6), 840–869. doi:10.1177/1363461517737198 PMID:29130379

Risk and protective factors. (n.d.). Retrieved from http://www.prokids.org/wp-content/uploads/2017/01/Chap-9-Dec-2016.pdf

Rostami, M., Abdi, M., & Heidari, H. (2014). Study of Various Types of Abuse during Childhood and Mental Health. *Procedia: Social and Behavioral Sciences, 159*, 671–676. doi:10.1016/j.sbspro.2014.12.463

Sanchez, S. E., Pineda, O., Chaves, D. Z., Zhong, Q. Y., Gelaye, B., Simon, G. E., ... Williams, M. A. (2017). Childhood physical and sexual abuse experiences associated with post-traumatic stress disorder among pregnant women. *Annals of Epidemiology, 27*(11), 716–723. doi:10.1016/j.annepidem.2017.09.012 PMID:29079333

Schudlich, T. D. R., Youngstrom, E. A., & Martinez, M. (2015). Physical and sexual abuse and early-onset bipolar disorder in youths receiving outpatient services: Frequent, but not specific. *Journal of Abnormal Child Psychology, 43*(3), 453–463. doi:10.100710802-014-9924-3 PMID:25118660

Simon, N. M., Herlands, N. N., Marks, E. H., Mancini, C., Letamendi, A., Li, Z., ... Stein, M. B. (2009). Childhood maltreatment linked to greater symptom severity and poorer quality of life and function in social anxiety disorder. *Depression and Anxiety, 26*(11), 1027–1032. doi:10.1002/da.20604 PMID:19750554

Taillieu, T. L., Brownridge, D. A., Sareen, J., & Afifi, T. O. (2016). Childhood emotional maltreatment and mental disorders: Results from a nationally representative adult sample from the United States. *Child Abuse & Neglect, 59*, 1–12. doi:10.1016/j.chiabu.2016.07.005 PMID:27490515

Types of child abuse. (n.d.). Retrieved from http://www.childrenservices.org/cms/files/File/WearBlue2016definitions.pdf

UK types. (n.d.). Retrieved from https://www.ncl.ac.uk/studentambassadors/assets/documents/NSPCCDefinitionsandsignsofchildabuse.pdf

van der Kooij, I. W., Nieuwendam, J., Bipat, S., Boer, F., Lindauer, R. J., & Graafsma, T. L. (2015). A national study on the prevalence of child abuse and neglect in Suriname. *Child Abuse & Neglect, 47*, 153–161. doi:10.1016/j.chiabu.2015.03.019 PMID:25937450

Vinnerljung, B., Hjern, A., & Lindblad, F. (2006). Suicide attempts and severe psychiatric morbidity among former child welfare clients–a national cohort study. *Journal of Child Psychology and Psychiatry, and Allied Disciplines, 47*(7), 723–733. doi:10.1111/j.1469-7610.2005.01530.x PMID:16790007

Watson, S., Gallagher, P., Dougall, D., Porter, R., Moncrieff, J., Ferrier, I. N., & Young, A. H. (2014). Childhood trauma in bipolar disorder. *The Australian and New Zealand Journal of Psychiatry, 48*(6), 564–570. doi:10.1177/0004867413516681 PMID:24343193

WHO. (1999). *Definition of child abuse and neglect*. Retrieved from http://www. yesican.org/definitions/who.html

Wihbey, J. (2011). Global prevalence of child sexual abuse. Journalist Resource. Available from: Journalistsresource. org/studies/./global-prevalence-child-sexual-abuse

ADDITIONAL READING

Corby, B. (2006). *Child abuse*. McGraw-Hill International.

Hornor, G. (2014). Child neglect: Assessment and intervention. *Journal of Pediatric Health Care*, *28*(2), 186–192. doi:10.1016/j.pedhc.2013.10.002 PMID:24559807

Kumar, A., Pathak, A., Kumar, S., Rastogi, P., & Rastogi, P. (2012). The problem of child sexual abuse in India laws, legal lacuna and the bill–PCSOB-2011. *Journal of Indian Academy of Forensic Medicine*, *34*(2), 169–174.

McCoy, M. L., & Keen, S. M. (2013). *Child abuse and neglect*. Psychology Press.

O'Hagan, K. (2006). *Identifying Emotional And Psychological Abuse: A Guide For Childcare Professionals: A Guide for Childcare Professionals*. UK: McGraw-Hill Education.

Palusci, V. J., & Covington, T. M. (2014). Child maltreatment deaths in the US national child death review case reporting system. *Child Abuse & Neglect*, *38*(1), 25–36. doi:10.1016/j.chiabu.2013.08.014 PMID:24094272

Palusci, V. J., Greydanus, D. E., & Joav Merrick, M. D. (2017). Children, disability, and abuse. *International Journal of Child Health and Human Development*, *10*(3), 205–214.

Smith, M., & Fong, R. (2004). *Children of neglect: When no one cares*. Routledge. doi:10.4324/9780203493625

Wilkinson, J., Bowyer, S., & Research in Practice (Organization). (2017). The Impacts of Abuse and Neglect on Children: And Comparison of Different Placement Options: Evidence Review. Department for Education.

KEY TERMS AND DEFINITIONS

Bipolar Spectrum Disorder: Bipolar spectrum disorder is a term used to refer to the conditions of bipolar I disorder, bipolar II disorder, and Cyclothymic disorder.

Depression: It is a mood disorder characterized by constantly low mood and a feeling of sadness and loss of interest.

Domestic Violence: It is a violence or abuse by one family member to another in a family setting.

Entitlement: It is a belief that an individual inherently deserves better or more than the other.

Impulsive: A sort of behaviour in which an individual does things suddenly without even thinking of the consequences associated with it.

Post-Traumatic Stress Disorder: It is a mental health condition that's triggered by a traumatic event either experiencing it or witnessing it.

Substance Abuse: It can be defined as a pattern of harmful use of any psychoactive substance for mood altering purposes.

Chapter 7
Child Neglect:
The Role of School Counselors

Stephen Oluwaseun Emmanuel
(iD) https://orcid.org/0000-0002-6703-4796
Adeyemi College of Education, Ondo, Nigeria

ABSTRACT

This chapter provides a groundwork for school counselors. It amplifies their roles and responsibilities to neglected children and also discusses the issues that should be considered in the assessment and treatment of neglected children and their families. The chapter provides professional guides to therapists who specialize in the treatment of neglected children and school counselors who meet with the neglected children occasionally. The methodology adopted for the assessment and treatment of neglect in this chapter is child-centered, family-focused, and culturally receptive. The author posits that dealing with child neglect will be more effective when school counselors leave the four walls of the school to provide support for neglect children and thus integrating them into the school system.

INTRODUCTION

Even though child neglect has been reported as the most common type of maltreatment, its causes, effects, prevention, and treatment are not as explored and discussed frequently compared to physical or sexual abuse. Most sadly, counselors who are better equipped to tackle this menace are usually not recognized in discourses that centers on addressing child neglect. It is against this challenge that this chapter is presented. Child neglect is a form of child maltreatment that covers a range of behaviors which include educational, supervisory, administrative, physical, medical,

DOI: 10.4018/978-1-7998-0319-5.ch007

emotional neglect, and abandonment, often convoluted by cultural and contextual factors. Children who are victims of child neglect suffer physical, psychological and emotional abuse. Neglect is seen as a form of negligence from parents, guardians and the government. Child neglect is a social problem, that requires the intervention of school guidance counselors in assisting the affected students. However, this chapter extends the list to the abysmal societal neglect of children who are supposed to be cared for. Children who suffer child neglect are also predisposed to child abuse because it has been observed that a parent who exhibits neglecting behavior can also be abusive at the same time. This chapter looks into child neglect and its attendant effect on school-age children. The age group consists of children from infancy to eighteen.

Child neglect is avoidable and treatable, and as such if the recommendations put forward in this chapter are put to use by school guidance counselors and other mental health professionals the current problem will be put at bay. The objectives of this chapter are to: provide an understanding into the concept, forms, and factors that contribute to child neglect, provide a guide for the assessment of child neglect and most importantly, offer intervention strategies to put the problem at bay.

BACKGROUND

The term child neglect has been used alongside the term 'child abuse.' Although child neglect and child abuse vary in definitions, it should be noted that both are connected to the emotional and physical wellbeing of students. Both child neglect and child abuse are forms of child maltreatment. The World Health Organization defines child abuse as "all forms of physical and emotional ill-treatment, sexual abuse, neglect and exploitation that results in actual or potential harm to the child's health, development or dignity." While child neglect refers to failure from parents, guardians, government, society to give proper physical, medical and psychological care to the child. Child abuse refers to an action that causes harm to a child; this action could be physical, sexual, emotional, verbal, psychological, spiritual and financial. Neglect occurs when a child is deprived of the underlying physical and psychological needs which are needed for his/her health or overall development. Defining the concept, 'child neglect' has always been faced with difficulties across cultures and professions. Factors such as, social and cultural considerations that causes child neglect, how persistent the behavior is, environmental variables, the motive behind the neglect (whether it is intentional or not), what action or inaction can be categorized as child neglect, age and developmental level of the child, basic care that a child is entitled to, the situation of the family (poverty or parental neglect) among others have been factors affecting the definition of neglect. (Watson, 2005)

Suggests that narrower definitions are needed for legal and research purposes that are required for service provision purposes. Watson avows that a useful definition may be one that provides a broad understanding of the concept of neglect in combination with detailed descriptions of subcategories of neglectful behavior including physical, supervisory, emotional and educational neglect. Gaudin (1993) mentioned the Legal advocates in the United States of America suggesting that definitions of neglect which focus only on the behavior of the parent or caretaker are inadequate. They strongly advocate that the parents' behavior must result in some specific physical damage or impairment or some identifiable symptoms of emotional damage to a child resulting from the parents' behavior or failure to act. However, Zuravin (1991) disagrees with this, suggesting that the focus should be on the actions of the parents, not on the consequences of their behavior, nor their intent or culpability. (Gaudin, 1993) noted that parents who leave preschool-aged children without adult supervision for an hour or more are neglectful, regardless of their intent, or whether the child suffers serious injury or not. Interestingly, if some of the cases classified as child neglect in developed nations like the United States are applied in the Nigerian context, almost all the families in Nigeria will be charged for child neglect. This situation further confirms the complexity that is encountered in the definition of child neglect across cultures.

It should be noted that technical definitions of child neglect differ, relatively, subject to the purpose for which the definition is used. A child can be said to be neglected when the child's basic developmental needs have not been met either intentionally or unintentionally by the parents or a caregiver who is responsible for the child. The objective of this definition is not to blame any parent or caregiver but to protect children within this population and to improve their wellbeing. This definition is in line with the recommendation by the (Gaudin, 1993) that researchers interested in studying the long- and short-term consequences of neglect for the child, definitions of neglect would need to focus on parental behaviors that result in harm to the child. Polansky (1987) defines child neglect as a condition in which a caretaker responsible for the child, either deliberately or by extraordinary inattentiveness, permits the child to experience present avoidable suffering and/or fails to provide one or more of the ingredients generally deemed essential for developing a person's physical, intellectual, and emotional capacities. According to (Gaudin, 1993) this definition as a widely accepted conceptual definition of child neglect. The United States Center for Disease Control and Prevention defines Child neglect as the failure to meet a child's basic needs, including housing, food, clothing, education and access to medical care. Abamara (2017) defines child neglect as a failure to provide primary needed care for the child such as shelter, food, clothing, education, supervision, medical care and other necessities needed for the child physical intellectual and emotional development. It is a situation where the guardians or parents fail to perform tasks that are necessary for the well-being of the child which invariably can lead to the child's health and safety being endangered.

Child neglect is a common challenge in many cultures across the world ranging from developed economies to undeveloped economies. This postulation is represented in this definition of child neglect; neglect refers to failure by the parent or caregiver to provide a child, where they are in a position to do so, with the conditions that are culturally accepted as being essential for their physical and emotional development and wellbeing Broadbent and Bentley, World Health Organization cited in (Al-shail et al., 2012). It is excruciating that many of these nations, especially underdeveloped nations are yet to recognize the complex origins or the profound consequences of child neglect. Studies have shown forms of child neglect varies across cultures just as the punishment meted out to offenders also do. The 'acceptable' treatment of children varies across cultures, countries, and generations. Acceptable behavior in some countries, such as the use of corporal punishment, is no longer acceptable in others (Day, 2008). Policy and practice has so far been unable to develop a single definition of abuse or neglect which can be understood by all while taking into account the great variety of harms that children can experience, the possibility of both primary and secondary harm and how children's experiences of harm can vary throughout their childhood (Cawson et al., 2000).

The response of the government in many developing economies towards child neglect is not too good. Some studies have shown that neglect may be more detrimental to children's early brain development than physical or sexual abuse (Garbarino and Collins 1999). The Government is expected to provide the abused and neglected students the required services, which include medical care, family counseling, foster care, and specialized education such as; vocational education, aided education. The International Center for Assault Prevention reports that worldwide, approximately 40 million children below the age of 15 are subjected to child abuse each year. (World Health Organization (WHO) 2001) This chapter provides general information on the subject of Child Neglect among teenagers of school age as much as it is crucial that every student in the school system is given the required attention that will help them to improve in their academic. It is equally important to categorize the students who need special attention into a group. Such a group can be organized for students who are victims of child neglect because of the psychological challenges that they face which may impinge on their concentration in the classroom. It has been observed that many of the neglected children feel unworthy to interact with their colleagues and many of them encounter rejection from their colleagues. It is appalling that their counterparts are stigmatizing these students and some counselors are not helping in mitigating this anomaly. Many of the social workers in some parts of Nigeria are abetting to this crime as they support some of these destructive practices, either for economic benefits or on the guise of their religious commitment. It is, therefore, the aim of this chapter to empower parents, community leaders, stakeholders in the educational system and most importantly school counselors on the counseling techniques that can be adopted in dealing with child neglect and ultimately reducing the menace to the barest minimum in societies. This will result in due course foster a healthy academic engagement among neglected students without the fear of being bullied or ostracized by their colleagues.

Issues, Controversies, Problems

Sadly, the home which is presented as a place where children feel the safest, has gradually turned out to be a place where children are prone to a more sophisticated risk. Some studies conducted in Colorado and North Carolina estimated that 50 to 60 percent of deaths due to child maltreatment were not recorded and that child neglect is the most under-recorded form of fatal maltreatment (Child Welfare Information Gateway 2004; Crume, DiGuiseppi, Byers, Sirotnak, and Garrett, 2002; Herman-Giddens, Brown, Verbiest, Carlson, Hooten, Howell, and Butts, 1999). Child neglect requires urgent attention because the difference in the mortality rate between child neglect and child abuse is that deaths resulting from neglect is a failure to act by the parents or caregivers, while deaths from child abuse is a product of a physical act.

Sadly, one of the reasons for the increase in the cases of child neglect is because deaths are owing to child neglect, often are more difficult to investigate and take legal action. This difficulty is because records of death due to child neglect may offer a lesser amount of visible shreds of evidence as to who is guilty and how the death occurred than death toll due to abuse. Child neglect has led to many children becoming victims of child marriage, commercial sex workers, rape, child betrothal, hawking, some children have been led to take up offers to serve as domestic help outside their own homes or family environment, while some others are victims of some criminal activities.

FORMS OF CHILD NEGLECT

- **Physical Neglect:** This form of child neglect includes action or behavior by a parent or caregiver such as; desertion of the child without making provision for care or supervision. It also involves inadequate supervision; failure to provide food and health care, the expulsion of a child from home; inadequate nourishment, shelter, clothing, hygiene, negligence to avoidable vulnerabilities in the home; including; reckless disregard of a child's security and well-being. Physical neglect is the failure from the part of the caregiver's to provide basic physical necessities.

- **Educational Neglect:** Is considered as a parent's or caregiver's failure to provide the requisite resources, financial, academic and moral provision to carry on with various engagements at school. It involves the failure to provide supportive educational opportunities for the child, detaining a child to hawk goods at the expense of the child's academic pursuit, refusal to provide the compulsory primary education for the child, encouraging prolonged truancy. A child in a refugee camp who does not access schooling suffers educational neglect regardless of whether it is because there is no schooling available or because the parents permit the child not to attend (Watson, 2005). Educational neglect covers all forms of material, moral, financial and academic deprivation that a child could suffer in matters about their schooling or student needs at school (Onolemhenmhen and Osunde, 2018).

- **Psychological/Emotional Neglect**: Includes the refusal, or delay in providing, needed emotional/psychological care such as warmth, nurturance, encouragement and support and encouraging maladaptive actions such as chronic wrongdoing or physical attack. It involves withholding love or comfort or affection. Emotional neglect may also overlap to some extent with emotional abuse; however, the latter is usually considered to be more active (Tanner and Turney, 2003). Emotional neglect often emanates from parental unawareness and ignorance, depressive moods, chaotic lifestyles, poverty, lack of support and inappropriate child-rearing models (Sullivan, 2000). Therefore, psychological/emotional neglect refers to the unavailability of the parent to provide the required psychological/emotional warmth and care; it is also the absence of consistent interaction. Emotional or psychological neglect is characterized by a lack of parents' or caregivers' warmth, nurturance, encouragement, and support; it is noted here that emotional neglect is sometimes considered a form of emotional abuse or maltreatment(Al-shail et al., 2012). Moreover, it should be noted that Psychological neglect is different from psychological abuse; for example, neglecting a person means deferring or refusing to provide physiological care to a child and permitting abusive deeds.

- **Medical Neglect**: A parent/caregiver's failure to provide for the appropriate healthcare of a child, it could also be the act of withholding medical care from the child which may be due to obnoxious practices or unhealthy religious beliefs. A neglected child may exhibit signs of poor health such as fatigue, infected cuts, and constant itching or scratching of the skin. Although, the USDHHS, 2012 revealed that medical is the lowest form of child maltreatment in the United States from Oct. 1, 2010–Sept. 30, 2011(Mcmahon, 2013). This report should not be a reason to underestimate the overwhelming effect of child neglect in the developing nations where access to quality medical treatment may be considered a life goal. Dental neglect which is the failure to provide a child the adequate dental care or treatment is also classified as medical neglect.

- **Environmental Neglect**: This form of child neglect occurs when the parent or caregiver fails to ensure environmental safety, opportunities, and resources. The environment could be the immediate environment at the child's home or other external environments. A child must not be neglected to loaf around the streets, thereby exposing him or her to the hazards in the environment. It can also be referred to like all forms of victimization, marginalization or alienation that a child may suffer from parents, teachers, peers, siblings or significant others within his immediate environment (Akoloh, Okenjom and Obiahu 2016)

Factors Which Contribute to Child Neglect

Since child neglect is a complex phenomenon with multiple factors contributing to its occurrence. Understanding the factors which may contribute to child neglect is critical to addressing the problem.

1. **Socioeconomic Factors:** Family members experiencing financial difficulties can project their troubles on their relationships with each other. Although, neglect and abuse are considered to be more frequent in low socioeconomic level families, while the upper socioeconomic level families conceal such incidents (Bilge 2006). It has been observed that many low-income families force their children to work at a tender age. Several children are engaged in heavy labor, which is physically and mentally unsafe for them. Some are also forced into participating in illegal activities, such as begging, theft or prostitution, whereas middle and upper economic level families exhibit attitudes, which are emotionally traumatic for the child, such as expressing disappointment or accusation. Low family status could serve as a socioeconomic factor that may necessitate neglectful behavior among some caregivers.

2. **Childhood Experiences**: Childhood experiences could also be a factor that contributes to child neglect. Parents who experience poor, caring behaviors in their childhood may tend to child neglect. Parents who experience physical and emotional deprivation as part of their childhood experience may exhibit neglect behavior. Parents who experience physical, emotional and possibly sexual abuse as part of their childhood experience may themselves be neglectful in their parenting roles. Weinstein and Weinstein (2000) study estimate that approximately one-third of neglected children will maltreat their children.

3. **Search for Greener Pastures by Parents**: This is one of the primary cause of child neglect in the 21ˢᵗ century. Parents' rural to urban migration in search of greener pastures such as more comfortable working conditions, among other factors may result in the child becoming neglected. This is because parents may become too busy to find any spare time with the children and supervise them. Such parents leave their children with inexperienced caregivers, neighbors while some leave the children to fend for themselves. Some parents in their bid of making more money, travel outside the country neglecting their children. Some of these neglected children are found to be involved in crimes and drugs. This factor takes another shape among the Almajairis of Nigeria (Ede, 2018).

4. **Characteristics of the Perpetrator**: It can be said that characteristics, such as young age, low level of education, being a victim of neglect and abuse in childhood, aggressive personality, addiction to alcohol, medication or drugs, unemployment, underdeveloped sense of responsibility and justice, immature personality and having a personality disorder can cause the parents or the caregiver to commit child neglect and abuse. Kutlu, Batmaz, Bozkurt, Gencturk, and Gul (2007) reported that mothers whom themselves were subjected to punishment as they were growing up, also considered punishment to be a useful method, and therefore, punished their children more often.

5. **Stress in the Family**: Stress in the family is one of the causes of child neglect and abuse. Solutions for coping with family stress can be better and easily proposed after identifying whether stress is economic or social. Training activities for neglect and abuse prevention involve the identification of people at risk, provision of counseling and protective services, in addition to conflict and stress management training (Bildik, 2002; Keskin and Cam, 2005).

Other factors include Family violence, modeling of inappropriate behavior, multiple co-habitation, and change of partner, alcohol and substance abuse, maternal low self-esteem and self-confidence, social and emotional immaturity, health problems during pregnancy, single parenting and teenage pregnancy.

Effect of Child Neglect

The effect of child neglect differs by its severity, frequency, duration, the relationship between the child and the parent and the child's age. The effect of child neglect if not appropriately managed may pass from the victim to their offspring. Weinstein and Weinstein (2000) confirm this in their estimate that approximately one-third of neglected children will maltreat their children. Fundamentally, Child neglect is one of the most common forms of child maltreatment, has remained a severe problem for many children. The precipitating effect of child neglect on children cannot be overemphasized. Feit, Joseph, Petersen, and Anne (2014) while commenting on the consequences of child abuse asserts that child neglect tremendously affects the physical development, mental development, and emotional development of a child causing long term consequences, such as poor academic achievement, depression (mood), and personality disorders. They admit that these consequences also impact society since it is more likely that children who suffered from child neglect will have drug abuse problems and educational failure when they grow up.

Physical Abuse

Child neglect in some cases lead to both physical abuse and sometimes extends to sexual abuse. Physical abuse involves physical violence, such as hitting with the hand or an object, pushing, shaking, burning or biting, directed towards the child by the parents or an adult responsible for the child's care (Yucel, 1993). Children who are subjects of frequent physical abuse constantly fear their parents, can easily lie to avoid a beating and can be overly aggressive or overly withdrawn and diffident shying away from physical contact and proximity of an adult (Lewis 1992; Livingston 1987). Many of the victims of child neglect are predisposed to sexual harassment. Goddard and Hiller (1993) in their study, revealed that fifty-five percent of the children were subjected to physical abuse, forty percent of the children experienced sexual abuse, and the majority of these children were placed under protection. A summary of the Report of the Independent Expert for the United Nations Study on Violence against Children (2008) reveals that annually, 150 million girls and 73 million boys experience rape or other forms of sexual violence throughout the world and that perpetrators are usually family members of the children. The report stated that annually, more than fifty thousand children fall victim to murder, approximately one or two million children were hospitalized for physical injuries due to violence, whereas only sixteen countries prohibited violence against children, thereby, leaving the vast majority of the children in the world deprived of adequate legal protection (Waterston and Mok 2008).

McGuigan and Pratt cited in Biçakçi, Er, and Aral (2016) emphasized that the majority of children aged between six months and five years old were subjected to emotional violence by their parents. Physically abused children experience various undesired consequences, ranging from soft tissue injuries to deaths with unknown causes. Loss of memory, growth retardation, speech delay, social withdrawal, limited friends and peer relationships, academic failure and suicidal tendencies, as well as, interpersonal, cognitive, emotional and behavioral problems, are observed in these children. Besides, impairment in cognitive skills and academic failure is frequently observed in these children (Kaplan, Pelcovitz and Labruna 1999; Gokler 2002). Furthermore, suicidal ideation and suicide attempts are more common in physically abused children (Tackett, 2002). Sexual abuse is a form of child abuse, in which an adult uses a child as a means to satisfy his/her sexual needs and desires (Green, 1996). According to the National sexual violence resource center report (2015), one in four girls and one in six boys will be sexually abused before they turn 18 years. 12.3 percent of women and 27.8 percent of men were age 10 or younger at the time of their first rape or victimization (Beitchman, et. al. 1992).

Sexual Abuse

Sexual abuse was described to be more frequent in families with divorced parents, domestic violence, alcohol and substance use, but can be experienced at any socioeconomic level (Hedin, 2000). Most of the time, there is no physical indication of sexual abuse. However, in some cases, a medical examination can reveal specific indications. In sexually abused children, symptoms include abnormal or complete lack of interest in sexual activities, sleep disorders or nightmares, phobias, bedwetting, depression or estrangement from family members or friends, behavioral problems, attention deficit and hyperactivity disorder, lack of appetite and weight loss, being frequently ill, believing their bodies are dirty, or there is something wrong with their genitals, not wanting to attend school, abnormal misbehavior and disobedience, overly aggressive behavior, and the avoidance of drawings or games expressive of sexual abuse (Green 1996). Sexually abused children experience higher rates of depression and significantly low self-esteem. Therefore, suicidal ideation and suicide attempts in sexually abused children are more frequently observed with increasing age (Livingston 1987). Sexually abused individuals either avoid establishing relationships or have a tendency to show excessive closeness and have numerous, overly demanding and controlling relationships. Both styles are dysfunctional and are likely to result in loneliness (Tackett, 2002). The child is forced to quit school due to economic difficulties the family faces, and to find employment in order to survive in the time of economic poverty and to support his/her family in their struggle against poverty. The environment and type of work are generally, physically, and mentally unsuitable for children and endangers their physical and psychological wellbeing. Children are deprived of their childhood and their right to play and receive education, as well as, have health problems due to economic abuse and unhealthy working conditions (Yagci, 2006). Emotionally neglected and abused children are exposed to attitudes and behaviors that have negative impacts or are deprived of the attention, love, and care they need, and therefore, they are psychologically traumatized according to social and scientific standards (Kara, Bicer, Gokalp, 2004). Kent and Waller (1998) revealed that children's anxiety and depression levels were adversely affected by emotional abuse. In their studies investigating emotional abuse in adolescents, Mullen et al. (1996) and Savi (1999) emphasized that a sense of self in adolescents was negatively affected by increasing degrees of emotional abuse. Children, who experience emotional neglect and abuse become estranged from their families, are stressful, feel worthless, develop a dependent personality, and display maladjusted and aggressive behavior. These children have mixed emotions for their parents, such as having the feeling of love and hatred simultaneously, fear of abandonment, fear of expressing emotions, fear of injury, feeling angry for the violence and disorder in their lives, depression, feel- ing helpless and powerless, and feeling ashamed of domestic incidents. Ozturk (2007) reported that emotional abuse adversely affected children's personality development. Traumas resulting from emotional neglect and abuse are as harmful as those of physical abuse, yet their symptoms cannot be readily observed (Polat, 2002; Jain, 1999).

Recent studies have revealed the negative impacts of child neglect on children. Research on juvenile delinquency reported higher criminal tendencies in children neglected by their families. According to the results of the review article by Smith and Walters cited in (Ulugtekin 1991) on fathers and their role in the family, fathers contribute more to delinquency in male children than the mothers. Furthermore, neglected children also experience difficulties concerning food, accommodation, clothing, hygiene, play, education, safety, and medical care.

Difficulty in Building Interpersonal Relationship

Neglected children are usually having difficulty in their interpersonal relationship. Neglected children often exhibit withdrawal behaviors while interacting with peers. Sadly, these behaviors are exhibited in a confused and aggressive way. Child neglect presents more difficulty in peer relationship than any other form of child maltreatment. This is supported by Hoffman-Plotkin and Twentyman (1984) report that neglected children tend to be more withdrawn than physically abused children and nonmaltreated children.

Furthermore, their research report suggests that both physically abused and neglected children exhibit less prosocial behavior than non-maltreated children. (Urquiza and Winn, 1994) found other findings that are consistent with research reports on neglected children directing fewer positive behaviors toward their peers, initiating fewer interactions, and involving in more straightforward forms of play.

The excruciating effect of child neglect is that it is sometimes passed on to the next generation. This implies that neglect behaviors may unconsciously turn out to become a behavior that is passed on from parents to their children. Kutlu, Batmaz, Bozkurt, Gencturk, and Gul (2007) reported that mothers whom themselves were subjected to punishment as they were growing up, also considered punishment to be a useful method, and therefore, punished their children more often. Sroufe and Fleeson argued that many neglectful mothers have difficulty providing adequate care for their children because of their past histories of maltreatment. It is reported that these mothers have difficulty coping with the demands of an intimate relationship, and they may not understand the critical cues and interactions because of their emotional instability. Therefore, because of their inability to function effectively as well as their impaired relationships, these mothers cannot engage in healthy attachment relationships with their children. Consequently, their children never acquire basic interpersonal skills and may grow up to perpetuate an intergenerational transmission of relationship dysfunction.

Physical Consequences

Neglected children suffer malnutrition and delay in their physical growth. The effect of child neglect may be evident at an early stage while in some cases it may be manifested later as the child grows to maturity. Child development is significantly affected by neglect. Retardation in mental growth resulting in the academic problem, difficulty in developing language abilities, delay in physical growth and development along with intellectual and psychological dysfunctioning are some of the physical consequences of child neglect. Sexual harassment and abuse are equally products of child neglect.

ASSESSMENT OF CHILD NEGLECT

While assessing child neglect, it is beneficial to approach neglect as a symptom, rather than a disease or disorder. Assessment of child neglect involves investigating into whether or not neglect has occurred, its nature, severity, and chronicity. Therefore, it involves cultural awareness and professional competencies. Since the school counselor is not all-knowing, the assessment process will require assistance from other specialists, such as law enforcement officers, child protective services (CPS) caseworkers, health care providers, child development specialists, mental health counselors, and other social service professionals. If there happen to be a cultural difference, it is crucial that the school counselor becomes knowledgeable about the culture.

It should be noted that the assessment process presented in this chapter is to be effected after the counselor has conducted an initial assessment and confirmed that neglect occurred, which involves the counselor contacting the child's family to collect information on whether neglect has occurred and evaluating the risk of possible neglect in the future. During assessment and intervention, the counselor should ensure that the neglected children and their families are orientated on the need to feel free to confide information, trust the counselors, and feel comfortable exploring difficult issues and subject matter. The counselor should uphold the principles of confidentiality as this will facilitate the children and their family's understanding of the scope and purpose of the counseling services.

Family Assessment

Assessment of child neglect begins from the family; the family members, especially the parents or the caregivers provides one of the most important sources of information about a child. Family assessment is an investigative approach to assessment. Urquiza and Winn (1994) established that for a comprehensive assessment of a child, it is essential to interview each parent and obtain information about the child's functioning in a variety of settings (e.g., home, neighborhood, school, or church). They explained further that without a clear understanding of the problems, capacities, and abilities of the entire family, it is difficult to determine a treatment plan for the child. It is critical that, school counselors understand family dynamics as a first step in the assessment process. The family is presented as the microsystem where life starts for the child; therefore it is crucial to handle family issues with care. Counselors should maintain unconditional positive regard for the family under assessment. The goal of the alliance with the families where neglected children come from is to understand the cause of the neglect, and thus develop a plan tailored to the individual needs of the child and family. Strauss and Kantor cited in (Watson, 2005) suggest that the use of terms such as abuse, neglect, violence, injury or harm during assessment should be avoided. They suggest prefacing a question with a phrase such as 'Many parents find it difficult to provide nutritious meals for their children' and then ask 'How many times has this happened to your family in the past referent time frame?' Rather than asking for a 'yes' or 'no' answer which has greater social desirability demand characteristics. Collaboration with families is key towards addressing child neglect. (Gaudin, 1993) Argued that All parents have strengths that can be mobilized. The hidden strengths of the neglectful parent must be identified during the assessment process, reinforced, and interventions planned to build upon those strengths. If proper regard is not given to these diversities, the result of the assessment may be weak and, consecutively, affect decision making. The counselor's access to family assessment measures will foster the assessment of families. Family Adaptability and Cohesion Evaluation Scales (FACES), The Family Assessment Measure (FAM) and the Family Environment Scale (FES) are examples of some common assessment measures.

Most importantly, it is essential to evaluate both the information provided by the family members and their capacity along with their willingness to provide valid and reliable information regarding the child.

Furthermore, in order to gain more insight into the origin of the neglect from the family standpoint, the counselor can schedule a discussion in the form of a clinical interview in order to observe each member of the family separately in addition to the observation of the family as a mutual entity. The family assessment helps the counselor to determine whether the case can be termed neglect or rendered inconsequential. Therefore, the essence of family assessment is that it promotes an understanding of the neglect and it is the basis for its prevention and intervention. (Watson, 2005) Argued that neglectful behavior and the causes or correlates of neglectful behavior should be measured separately. For instance, if parents live in poverty and are unable to provide, their child is still neglected, regardless of the cause. The intervention adapted to overcome the neglect will be different, but the child is suffering neglect regardless of cause.

School Personnel

Children spend much time within the school setting; this gives the school personnel, especially teachers the opportunity to observe them. Interviewing teachers about a specific child often yields information about social skills, peer relations, intellectual ability, cooperative skills, behavior management techniques, attentiveness, emotional stability, and response to authority (Urquiza and Winn, 1994). Teachers can provide information about their observations of a child within a classroom setting, on the playground, at the cafeteria, and before and after school. Useful data regarding the child's habits, for example, personal hygiene and eating habits can be provided by the teachers and other school personnel. Urquiza and Winn (1994) explain further that because schools typically attempt to maintain regular contact with parents, teachers are often able to provide supplemental information about their interactions with the child's parents. This may include an assessment of the parents' level of involvement, concern about parenting ability, and overall stability of the parents.

Use of Standardized Clinical Assessment

Standardized instruments are beneficial for assessing the presence or the extent of neglect. Standardized instruments provide a detailed clinical report to confirm or repudiate the observation by the counselor. Using standardized assessment techniques and combining these techniques with sound judgment based on clinical experience and training is the best approach. Therefore, the clinician must become familiar with assessment instruments, their development, applicability to different populations, psychometric properties, and limitations (Urquiza and Winn, 1994). The counselor conducts a family assessment for members of the family (especially parents' report), direct assessment of the child which include, projective assessment, cognitive assessment, behavioral reports and projective drawings, and clinical interviews with the child. (Watson, 2005) Reports that the behaviorally-anchored scales had stronger associations with neglect. The Child Well-Being Scales (Magura and Moses, 1986) have been shown to discriminate between neglecting (79 percent accuracy) and non-neglecting (81 percent accuracy) families. The strongest discriminating factors have been household adequacy (Gaudin, 1993) and to a lesser extent health care, diet, clothing, hygiene sanitation, child supervision and utilities. A neglect scale is an assessment tool that shows promise for determining the possible existence of neglect. It is an easy-to-administer, retrospective, self-report measure that can be administered to diverse client populations (Schetky and Green). Other measures include observational measures (Family Assessment Form, Child Well-being Scales, Home Observation for Measure of the Environment) and self-report measures (Family Functioning Style Scale, Family Needs Scale, Support Functions Scale (Diane DePanfilis, 2006).

Working with other Professionals

As stated in the introduction to the assessment of neglect, school counselors cannot assess child neglect all alone. Therefore, it is essential that the counselor works with other professionals in the assessment of child neglect. In conducting physical neglect, the counselor works with medical personnel in the assessment of physical neglect. In countries where there are Child Welfare Caseworkers, the counselor needs to work with them to obtain appropriate data about children in their caseload. Caseworkers may not be able to provide sufficient direct information about a child, but be an excellent source of indirect information(Urquiza and Winn, 1994). Community and religious leaders can offer supports and services to tackle problems contributing to neglect.

Cultural Competence in Assessment:

The counselor must possess a rich understanding of the cultural, ethnical and socio-economic background of the family. This includes the language of the population, patterns of behavior, belief system, values, tradition and other peculiarities that are connected with the environment. A problem results when assessing a child for the presence of a behavioral, emotional, or psychological problem. By failing to be culturally sensitive to the specific behaviors exhibited by a specific ethnic group (or child of a specific cultural heritage), the clinician may erroneously identify the presence of a problem when one does not exist. (Urquiza and Winn, 1994).

Therefore, the counselor must ensure that any form of labeling, resentment, and anger is avoided. As stated earlier, parental intentions cannot just be categorized as deliberate or not; it must also be considered in a cultural context.

In deciding whether a cultural practice is potentially harmful to a child, the following questions can foster a culturally sensitive consideration of the issue of neglect:

- *What exactly is the practice?*
- *Is it safe?*
- *Is actual or potential harm involved?*
- *Is there a significantly better option?*
- *Are there potentially harmful implications of deviating from the cultural practice?*
- *Have the child's basic needs not been met? Is it against the law?* DePanfilis, (2004).

Risk Assessment

Risk assessment is essential to preclude future cases of neglect. Structured risk assessment instruments are primarily focused on whether a child will be maltreated in the future, either by identifying unreported families before they neglect their children or assessing the likelihood of recurrence of neglect in already reported families (Stowman and Donohue, 2005). Where parents have not been reported, structured risk assessments are usually based on general correlates of neglectful parenting. The more traditional risk assessment instruments have placed reliance on the mothers' childhood history to see if she has suffered abuse or been fostered as a child (Watson, 2005). He explained further that these risk assessment instruments investigate her level of useful social support and her current and past mental health and substance abuse record. Parents selected through this assessment process are likely to be parents who are parenting under challenging circumstances, but most will not be neglectful. This is the case of many parents from an African background.

Parent's levels of resentment towards the counselor, or contrariwise their enthusiasm to alteration of the neglect behavior, can be recognized as important indicators of change. Most risk assessments often take the child's age, the number, and ages of other children in the family, and the family's previous contact with child protection into account, as these factors are associated with heightened vulnerability(Watson, 2005).

INTERVENTION STRATEGIES

The outcome of the assessment process and the type of neglect identified serves as the basis for the approach to be taken in the intervention process. After the assessment process, the counselor has to design a framework that outlines the goals and objectives of intervention, including the methods that will be used to address the indicators of neglect. Treatment objectives should focus on increasing positive behaviors more willingly than decreasing negative behaviors. It must include autonomy, building feelings of hope and self-esteem. Intervention programmes are custom-made to prevent the occurrence and recurrence of child neglect. A school counselor's understanding of what may contribute to neglect is critical in developing intervention programmes. Therefore, while planning for the appropriate intervention programmes to adopt in child neglect, it is critical to note that not all cases in which a parent or caregiver fails to make available the basic needs for a child can be considered neglect. Gaudin(1993) argued that the treatment/service plan should be clearly outlined, with responsibilities for parent and professional helpers identified. The plan should be viewed as a contract between the neglecting family and the professional helper.

Therefore, factors involving the parent or caregiver's health and well-being, such as domestic violence and psychological challenges often contribute to neglect. The counselor must be aware that intervention is different when neglect is primarily a result of individual and family factors than when it is a matter of environment or community conditions.

Interventions to child neglect may take three socio-ecological approaches which include;

- Family approach
- Community approach
- Systems approach.

School counselors in their intervention programmes on child neglect should involve stakeholders such as parents, community leaders, legislators, faith-based bodies, researchers, and other practitioners who are directly involved with children. The community must be inclusive in the intervention programmes because child neglect is not only a family or an individual problem but also a severe problem to the communities. As such, all stakeholders must work collaboratively in mitigating this recurring problem. School counselors are expected to exhibit multicultural traits that will foster their relationship with the parents and other stakeholders that are required in combating child neglect. Owing to the reality that child neglect is prevalent across various cultures. Students who are faced with child neglect emanate from various cultures and backgrounds. Therefore, school counselors should develop their multicultural competence in understanding the perspective of these groups. Cultural competency requires acceptance of and respect for differences, diversity of knowledge and skills, and adaptation of services to fit the target population's culture, situation, and perceived needs. U.S. Department of Health and Human Services, NCCAN cited in (Diane DePanfilis, 2006). Professional school counselors should possess the competencies necessary to develop and implement culturally responsive school counseling programs and to promote inclusive environments in their schools (Park-Taylor, Walsh, and Ventura, 2007). The assessment of child neglect requires consideration of cultural values and standards of care as well as recognition that the failure to provide the necessities of life may be related to poverty. Therapeutic interventions should be culturally sensitive. School counselors should respect the differences in the customs, cultural and religious beliefs, role expectations and parenting customs held by families. Helpers should, for example, make use of respected elders as role models and key resources, involve extended family members in child caring, respect and affirm religious/spiritual values and beliefs that support responsible parenting, and seek to involve males in child-caring tasks (Holtin, 1990).

School counselors in the process of developing intervention strategies should ensure that they put into consideration the developmental needs of the children. This consideration is because children whose physical, medical and emotional needs have been neglected often will suffer significant developmental delays. The counselor in his intervention strategy will have to work closely with the families of neglected children by playing a multiple role of a mentor, coach, advocate, mediator and ultimately maintains his/her role as a guidance counselor, thereby teaching them how to cope effectively with the multiple pressures and circumstances that they encounter in their lives. This is very important in the intervention programmes of counselors. This strategy will assist some of the families in learning how to solve their problems uniquely and thus curtailing the culture of overdependence on the government. Some neglectful parents want to be good parents, however, they are limited due to lack of personal, financial, and adequate supportive resources. Therefore, school counselors should develop intervention strategies that will help parents to improve the quality of care for their children. Intervention programmes should promote a positive and responsive parent-child relationship. School counselors must be poised of their skills in providing necessary support to neglected students in their adjustment process.

Counselors as Advocates

Since most families whose children are faced with neglect tend to suffer from poverty, social isolation, and lacks access to resources. Accordingly, the role of school counselors extends to encouraging the government to provide both formal and informal helping resources such as an all-encompassing drug prevention and treatment programmes, enough affordable child care initiatives, advocacy to mobilize concrete formal and informal helping resources quality education and employment opportunities, and accessible low-income housing.

Mandated Reporting

When addressing neglect, school counselors are reminded that they are obliged to report cases of neglect to child welfare services, especially in severe cases of neglect. This is very important in cases when initial interventions have failed and when other forms of maltreatment are assumed to be present. The counselor may in rare cases apply legal authority in order to repress the initial denial and apathy of the neglectful parent. However, (Gaudin, 1993) argued that the threat of legal action should be used only as a last resort after efforts to obtain cooperation have been tried.

Continuous Observation

It is essential that adequacy of care and factors in the environment contributing to disease or injury be considered in children and families presenting for health care. In families with a history of neglect, the use of case management, patient management contracts, and the provision of additional resources may be indicated for monitoring medical, developmental, psychological, educational or safety concerns. Treatment of chronic neglect is not a short-term project. Successful intervention with neglectful parents should last for 12 to 18 months. When neglect is not a recurring pattern, shorter term, more intensive intervention may be successful.

As part of the intervention programme, the counselor could suggest to the government to provide the following services for neglectful families:

- Momentary foster care
- Emergency financial assistance
- low-cost child care, housing, and medical care
- job training and placement,
- effective transportation
- parent support/skills training groups
- regular mental health assessment and treatment.

It is important that the counselor provides ongoing support to the child throughout and after the intervention process.

SOLUTIONS AND RECOMMENDATIONS

The author posits that dealing with child neglect will be more effective when school counselors leave the four walls of the school to provide support for educational neglected children and thus integrating them into the school system. The government should also provide preventive services that will help forestall the occurrence of neglect or the stemming it before it becomes severe. A review of the literature on child neglect revealed that the dearth of consistent research definitions on child neglect had hampered the development of a cohesive research base on the subject. Therefore, the author suggests that multidisciplinary panels of proven experts, including the field's best-known contributors, should be organized to review existing works, thereby developing a harmony on the research definition of child neglect. It is equally put forward that more studies on the recurring problem of child neglect are required as extant literature has revealed that child neglect is so closely linked with low education and low income. Furthermore, it is imperative to tell the difference in the acceptable way to make a distinction of neglect by parents from deprivation through poverty.

Parents with large family size should be sensitized on the need for birth control as most of the cases of child neglect stem from families with a large number of children. School counselors have a duty to pool resources with Not for profit Organizations especially media organizations on revitalizing their efforts on a colossal crusade against child neglect and any other form of maltreatment. School counselors and other mental health professionals are encouraged to be advocates for neglected children since they are very much aware of the ubiquitous nature of child neglect. Advocacy can start at the community level before it grows to the global stance, this is hoped to minimize the ripple effect of neglect on the children in this population.

FUTURE RESEARCH DIRECTIONS

Future research should concentrate on using parents as participants in experimental studies in offering a lasting solution to child neglect. This is pictured in the report from Chen and Chan (2016) who reported that studies that looked at the number of official reports of maltreatment and self-reported reductions in harsh parenting and neglect showed significantly lower rates of those behaviors in parents who participated compared to parents in control groups. Future research should extend to the continent of Africa, as it is observed that there is a paucity of studies on child neglect on the black continent. Researches of this caliber will provide insights that the current challenge of child neglect in many developing countries of the world can be treated and as such bringing a solution can be brought to it. Researches addressing the challenge of child neglect from a multicultural lens is envisaged in the future.

CONCLUSION

Children are believed to be the hope of the coming generation. Twenty-six percent of the world's population consists of children under the age of fifteen with a significant number of them faced with maltreatment with child neglect being the most frequent. This reality should raise a need for awareness of the need to combat the pervasive manifestation of child neglect. Child neglect should be addressed as a communal subject requiring the concerted efforts of everyone in the community and not just as an individual or a family problem. Child-focused social welfare and economic supports programmes should be provided to families with records of child neglect. This study is limited in not providing a detailed explanation of the assorted types of child neglect, such as abandonment, lack of food, lack of attention to health care needs among others. Most importantly, School counselors should not renege on their efforts to help neglected children, consistent follow-up sessions should be made available after therapy.

ACKNOWLEDGMENT

This research received no specific grant from any funding agency in the public, commercial, or not-for-profit sectors.

REFERENCES

Abamara, N. (2017). *Factors Precipitating Child Abuse and Neglect Among Nigerians*. Unpublished Thesis.

Akoloh, L., Okenjom, G. P., & Obiahu, C. L. (2016). The effect of child abuse on youths and their academic performance in secondary schools in Bayelsa State, Nigeria. *Greener Journal of Educational Research*, 6(4), 170–176. doi:10.15580/GJER.2016.4.040916075

Al-shail, E., Hassan, A., Aldowaish, A., Kattan, H., Lazenbatt, A., Cyr, C., & Lutya, T. M. (2012). *Child Abuse and Neglect – – A Multidimensional Approach*. InTech; doi:10.5772/3035

Beitchman, J. H., Zucker, K. J., Hood, J. E., DaCosta, G. A., Akman, D., & Cassavia, E. (1992). A review of the long- term effects of child sexual abuse. *Child Abuse & Neglect*, 16(1), 101–118. doi:10.1016/0145-2134(92)90011-F PMID:1544021

Bildik, T. (2002). School period emotional abuse [in Turkish]. *Journal of Children's Forum*, *5*, 9–13.

Bilge, F. (2006). Child neglect and abuse, violence in schools and juvenile delinquency. In S. Ercetin (Ed.), *Education and Violence* (pp. 219–260). Ankara: Pegem Publications.

Blumenthal, A. (2015). *Child Neglect II : Prevention and Intervention*. Academic Press.

Cawson, P., Wattam, C., Brooker, S., & Kelly, G. (2000). *Child maltreatment in the United Kingdom: a study of the prevalence of abuse and neglect.* London: NSPCC.

Child Welfare Information Gateway. (2004). *Child abuse and neglect fatalities: Statistics and interventions.* Available: http://www.childwelfare.gov/ pubs/factsheets/ fatality.pdf

Crume, T., DiGuiseppi, C., Byers, T. L., Sirotnak, A. P., & Garrett, C. (2002). *Under ascertainment of child maltreatment fatalities by death certificates, 1990–1998.* Available: http://pediatrics.appublications.org/cgi/reprint/110/2/e18.pdf

Day, C. (2008). *A Literature Review into Children Abused and / or Neglected Prior Custody*. Academic Press.

DePanfilis, D. (2004). *Child neglect: Working to increase safety and well-being.* Presented at the Family Advocacy Training Section, Soldier & Family Support Branch, Department of Preventive Health Services, Army Medical Department Center & School, San Antonio, TX.

DePanfilis, D. (2006). *Child Abuse And Neglect Child Neglect: A Guide for Prevention, Assessment, and (Child Abuse)*. Washington, DC: Child Welfare Information Gateway. Retrieved from http://www.childwelfare.gov/pubs/usermanual.cfm

Garbarino, J., & Collins, C. C. (1999). Child neglect: The family with a hole in the middle. In H. Dubowitz (Ed.), *Neglected children: Research, practice, and policy* (pp. 1–23). Thousand Oaks, CA: Sage. doi:10.4135/9781452225586.n1

Gaudin, J. (1993). Child neglect: A guide for intervention. Westover Consultants, Inc.

Gokler, I. (2002). Child neglect and abuse: The effect of stress on neurobiological development [in Turkish]. *Journal of Child and Youth Mental Health.*, *9*, 47–57.

Green, A. (1996). Child sexual abuse and incest. In M. Lewis (Ed.), *Child and Adolescent Psychiatry* (pp. 41–48). Williams & Wilkins.

Hedin, L. W. (2000). Physical and sexual abuse against women and children. *Current Opinion in Obstetrics & Gynecology, 12*(5), 349–355. doi:10.1097/00001703-200010000-00003 PMID:11111876

Helfer, R. E., & Kempe, C. H. (Eds.). (1987). *The Battered Child* (4th ed.). Chicago: University of Chicago Press.

Herman-Giddens, M., Brown, G., Verbiest, S., Carlson, P., Hooten, E., Howell, E., & Butts, J. (1999). Under-ascertainment of child abuse mortality in the United States. *Journal of the American Medical Association, 282*(5), 463–467. doi:10.1001/jama.282.5.463 PMID:10442662

Hoffman-Plotkin, D., & Twentyman, C. (1984). A Multimodal Assessment of Behavioral and Cognitive Deficits in Abused and Neglected Preschoolers. *Child Development, 55*(3), 794–802. doi:10.2307/1130130 PMID:6734318

Holtin, J. K. (1990). *Black Families and Child Abuse Prevention: An African American Perspective and Approach.* Working Paper No. 852. Chicago: National Committee for Prevention of Child Abuse.

Jain, A. M. (1999). Emergency department evaluation of child abuse. *Emergency Medicine Clinics of North America, 17*(3), 575–593. doi:10.1016/S0733-8627(05)70083-3 PMID:10516839

Kaplan, S., Pelcovitz, D., & Labruna, V. (1999). Child and adolescent abuse and neglect research: A review of the past 10 years. Part I: Physical and emotional abuse and neglect. *American Academy Child Adolescence Psychiatry, 38*(10), 1214–1222. doi:10.1097/00004583-199910000-00009 PMID:10517053

Kara, B., Bicer, U., & Gokalp, A. S. (2004). Child abuse [in Turkish]. *Journal of Child Health and Diseases, 47*, 140–151.

Kent, A., & Waller, G. (1998). The impact of childhood emotional abuse: An extension of the child abuse and trauma scale. *Child Abuse & Neglect, 22*(5), 393–399. doi:10.1016/S0145-2134(98)00007-6 PMID:9631251

Keskin, G., & Cam, O. (2005). Psychodynamic nurse approach towards child sexual abuse (in Turkish). *New Symposium, 43*(3), 118-125.

Kutlu, L., Batmaz, M., Bozkurt, G., Gencturk, N., & Gul, A. (2007). Punishment methods towards mothers in their childhood and their own punishment methods towards their children [in Turkish]. *Anatolian Journal of Psychiatry, 8*, 22–29.

Lewis, D. O. (1992). From abuse to violence: Psychophysiological consequences of maltreatment. *J American Child Adolescence Psychiatry, 31*, 383–391.

Livingston, R. (1987). Sexually and physically abused children. *Journal of the American Academy of Child and Adolescent Psychiatry*, 26(3), 413–415. doi:10.1097/00004583-198705000-00023 PMID:3597298

Magura, S., & Moses, B. S. (1986). Outcome measures for child welfare services. Washington, DC: Child Welfare League of America.

Mcmahon, J. (2013). Child Neglect. *Impact and Interventions Impact of Neglect on Brain Development and Attachment*, 18(1), 1–9.

Mullen, P. E., Martin, J. L., Anderson, J. C., Romans, S. E., & Her-bison, G. P. (1996). The long-term impact of the physical, emotional, and sexual abuse of children: A community study. *Child Abuse & Neglect*, 20(1), 7–21. doi:10.1016/0145-2134(95)00112-3 PMID:8640429

National Research Council. (1993). *Understanding Child Abuse and Neglect*. Washington, DC: The National Academies Press; doi:10.17226/2117

Onolemhenmhen,, P. E., & Osunde, Y. (2018). Child Neglect as Predictor of Academic Performance among Senior Secondary School Students in Edo State, Nigeria. *International Journal of Humanities and Social Science*, 7(4), 75–84.

Ozturk, S. (2007). *Psychological Abuse Towards Children* (in Turkish) (MA Thesis). Elazig: Firt University.

Park-Taylor, J., Walsh, M. E., & Ventura, A. B. (2007). Creating healthy acculturation pathways: Integrating theory and research to inform counselors' work with immigrant children. *Professional School Counseling*, 11(1), 25–34. doi:10.5330/PSC.n.2010-11.25

Polansky, N. L. (1979). The Absent Father in Child Neglect. *The Social Service Review*, 63–74.

Polat, O. (2002). *Children and Violence*. Istanbul: Der Publications. (in Turkish)

Prevent Child Abuse America. (2001). *Child maltreatment*. Available from: http://www.who.int/topics/childabuse/en/2007

Savi, F. (1999). *Psychological Abuse Towards Adoles- cents and its Relationship Between Sense of Self and Anxiety Level* (in Turkish) (MA Thesis). Bursa: Uludag University.

Schetky, D. H., & Green, A. H. (1988). *Child Sexual Abuse: A Handbook for Health Care and Legal Professional*. New York: Brunner/Mazel.

Sroufe, L. A., & Fleeson, J. (1986). Attachment and the Construction of Relationships. In W. W. Hartup & Z. Rubin (Eds.), *Relationships and Development*. New York: Cambridge University Press.

Stowman, S. A., & Donohue, B. (2005). Assessing child neglect; *A review of standardized measures. Aggression and Violent Behavior, 10*(4), 491–512. doi:10.1016/j.avb.2004.08.001

Sullivan, S. (2000). *Child neglect: Current definitions and models—A review of child neglect research, 1993-1998*. Ottawa, Canada: National Clearinghouse on Family Violence.

Tackett, K. K. (2002). The health effects of child abuse: Four pathways by which abuse can influence health. *Child Abuse & Neglect, 26*(6-7), 715–729. doi:10.1016/S0145-2134(02)00343-5 PMID:12201164

Ulugtekin, S. (1991). *Hükümlü Çocuk ve Yeniden Toplum- sallasma*. Ankara: Bizim Büro.

Urquiza, A. J., & Winn, C. (1994). *Treatment for Abused and Neglected Children: Infancy to Age 18*. U.S. Department of Health and Human Services; doi:10.1042/BJ20021886\nBJ20021886

U.S. Department of Health and Human Services (NCCAN). (1996). Child maltreatment, 1994: Report from the states to the National Center on Child Abuse and Neglect. Washington, DC: Government Printing Office.

Waterston, T., & Mok, J. (2008). Violence Against Children. The UN Report. *Archives of Disease in Childhood*, 93–85. PMID:17804588

Watson, J. (2005). Child neglect Literature review. Centre for Parenting & Research NSW Department of Community Services.

Yagci, E. (2006). Positive Learning Environments and the Child. In S. Ercetin (Ed.), *Education and Violence* (pp. 139–175). Ankara: Pegem Publications.

Yucel, M. (1993). *Prevention of Child Neglect and Abuse*. Academic Press. (in Turkish)

Zuravin, S. J. (1991). Suggestions for Operationally Defining Child Physical Abuse and Physical Neglect. In R. H. Starr & D. A. Wolfe (Eds.), *The Effects of Child Abuse & Neglect New York*. Guilford Press.

ADDITIONAL READING

Anthony, J. U., & Cynthia, W. (2004). *Treatment for Abused and Neglected Children: Infancy to Age 18 - User Manual Series.* DIANE Publishing.

David, K., Cindy, C. S., & Cynthia, C. S. (2002). Assessing and Treating Physically Abused Children and Their Families: A Cognitive-Behavioral Approach. *Sage (Atlanta, Ga.).*

De Bellis, M. D. (2005). The psychobiology of neglect. *Child Maltreatment, 10*(2), 150–172. doi:10.1177/1077559505275116 PMID:15798010

Forrest, P. T. (2005). *Handbook for the Treatment of Abused and Neglected Children.* Haworth Social Work Practice Press.

Howard, D. (1999). Neglected Children: Research, Practice, and Policy. *Sage (Atlanta, Ga.).*

Isabella, A., & Okagbue, E. (1996). *The Rights of the Child in Nigeria. Nigerian Institute of Advanced Legal Studies James, M. G. (1995). Child Neglect: A Guide for Intervention.* Diane Publishing.

Jan, H. (2007). *Child Neglect: Identification and Assessment.* Palgrave Macmillan.

Jenny, C. (2007). American Academy of Pediatrics, Committee on Child Abuse and Neglect Recognizing and responding to medical neglect. *Pediatrics, 120*(6), 1385–1389. doi:10.1542/peds.2007-2903 PMID:18055690

KEY TERMS AND DEFINITIONS

Child Abuse: Failure to act on the part of a parent or caregiver which may lead to an impending danger such as; physical severe or emotional harm, sexual abuse or death.

Child Neglect: The failure to provide for the basic needs of a child. It could be physical, educational, emotional/psychological, medical or environmental.

Cultural Competence: A set of attitudes, behaviors, and policies that helps school counselors in working with students from different cultures and ethnic groups to implement strategies to achieve their educational goals.

Group Counselling: A counseling session where a group of clients with similar issues or concerns meet with one or more counselors/therapists, to discuss those concerns, learn about and share information and solutions about those concerns.

Individual Counselling: A one on one counseling session between a school counselor and a client.

Parent/Caretaker: A person whose responsibility is to care for the child.

School Counselors: A professional trained in counseling who works in elementary and middle schools and secondary schools who provide academic, career, social-emotional competencies to students through a school counseling program.

Support Systems: Individuals such as family, friends, and professionals (counselors, social worker or members of the same group counseling) who are quick to respond and are ready to lend a hand to the neglected child.

Symptoms: Emotional or behavioral responses to the presence of neglect.

Treatment: The therapeutic stage whereby particular treatment services targeted towards the reduction of risk of maltreatment are provided by school counselors or mental health professionals.

Chapter 8

Attentiveness to the Voiceless:
A Closer Valuation of Child Abuse and Neglect in the Early Childhood Years

Joyce Mathwasa
University of Fort Hare, South Africa

Zoleka Ntshuntshe
University of Fort Hare, South Africa

ABSTRACT

Children worldwide begin life with greater vulnerability as they suffer from various forms of mistreatment, discrimination, and exploitation at the hands of those who are supposed to protect and provide for them. This chapter focuses on how the rights of the child are violated through child abuse and neglect based on socioeconomic status in multi-religious and multi-cultural societies. Child abuse and neglect are social ills that threaten to diminish the social and moral obligation of every parent causing moral decay in the youth populace. While neglect may be viewed as parental behaviour of failure to nurture children, children suffer various forms of abuse from trusted relatives, caregivers, and strangers. Factors such as political instability, famine, and poverty have robbed children of their right to normal life. The chapter will also explore the criticisms or loopholes in the children's rights so that parents and caregivers can infuse them in their nurturing of the child.

DOI: 10.4018/978-1-7998-0319-5.ch008

OUTCOMES

By the end of this chapter you should be able to:

- Define child abuse and explain how it affects children in the Early Childhood Development (ECD) phase.
- Define child neglect and explain how it affects children in the ECD phase.
- Identify types of abuse and neglect, and how that affects quality of learning in ECD.
- Identify intervention stratagems for dealing with child abuse and neglect in institutions of learning.
- Assess the efficacy and effectiveness of victim friendly courts, legislative structures and human rights drives in alleviating suffering to the children.
- Engage in discussions on child abuse and neglect with the aim of making awareness to influence legislative attention and action.

INTRODUCTION

According to The United Nations Convention on The Rights of the Child (UNCRC), any human being who has not attained the age of 18 years is defined as a child and should still be living under the protection of parents or legal guardians. These human rights also state that children have the right to life, education, food, health, water, identity, freedom, and protection (UNCRC, 1989). The original legitimately binding international instrument is the United Nations' 1989 Convention on the Rights of the Child (CRC), which ensures that the full range of human rights; civil, cultural, economic, political and social rights are observed. Worldwide, governments have endorsed commitment to the protection and guarantee that children's rights are observed and at the same time holding themselves accountable for this commitment before the international community. Despite the existence of the strong and legal statutes, constitutional, legislative and civic environment meant to protect children's rights, media is amassed with child abuse and neglect globally. Hence, this chapter intends to highlight the magnitude of detrimental child abuse and neglect. For example, the IOL News reporter Charles informed the public on the 18th May 2018 that forty-one percent of rapes committed in South Africa were against very young children (www.iol.co.za/news). On the 31st May 2018, Pitt of New24 also reported a similar incident where a 9-month-old was allegedly sexually abused (www.news24. com/SouthAfrica). These stories confirmed earlier reports by Richter (2003) and Bird and Spurr (2004) that abuse and maltreatment of children in South Africa was outrageously high as established by extensively described rape of numerous infants and toddlers in 2001. In Latin America, watchdogs on the prevalence of violence against children estimate that thirty percent of children experienced violence (in the past 12 months) (Hillis, Mercy, Amobi & Kress, 2016). UNICEF (2019:6) in their Humanitarian Action for Children overview gave details of numerous types of violence against children in various countries in need of humanitarian aid:

Five hundred thousand children in eastern Ukraine affected by conflict are in urgent need of protection.

Two hundred and forty-one thousand children in Libya require humanitarian assistance due to protracted conflict, political instability, deteriorating public services and a dysfunctional economy.

In Cameroon, Central African Republic, Chad, the Niger and Nigeria, 1.5 million children will require humanitarian assistance due to political violence causing economic instability.

More than 2.5 million Syrian children are living as refugees in Egypt, Iraq, Jordan, Lebanon and Turkey, where demand for basic services such as health and education continues to outstrip the capacity of institutions and infrastructure to respond.

Four hundred thousand Rohingya children, have fled violence in Myanmar and settled in Cox's Bazar District, Bangladesh.

Children who survive these horrific incidences are scared for life where very few of them receive healing later through their spiritual faith.

Early childhood is an important phase which forms the foundation of long-term cognitive learning, emotional stability and social interaction (Phillips & Shonkoff, 2000). Neuroscience has established and documented that adverse experiences in the early childhood have long-lasting effects on children's brain structures and stress or trauma responses (Crowe & Blair, 2008; De Bellis & Van Dillen, 2005). Significant evidence suggests that exposure to trauma early in life distinctly upsurges the danger for syndromes such as bipolar disorder, depression, post traumatic stress disorder (PTSD) and schizophrenia, which are all categorised by cognitive dysfunction. Numerous studies such as those by McClintock, Husain, Greer and Cullum (2010) and Nebes, Butters, Mulsant, Pollock, Zmuda and Houck, et al. (2000) found discrepancies in active functioning, attentiveness and concentration, memory and processing speed in patients with depression. Such impairment seems to be common to people with severe depression (Porter et al., 2007), and early exposure to trauma could clearly explain the variability in these findings. The above scholars concur that child abuse is detrimental to the young brain especially in early stages of development. Manifestation of the effect happens at different stages of growth depending on the resilience of the child. Although children are physically visible in many African cultures their voices are silent as culture does not allow children to voice their concerns, ideas or dislikes because it is considered disrespectful.

BACKGROUND

Child abuse and neglect are social ills that have received less attention because mostly those who suffer are defenceless, voiceless and dependent on the perpetrators. Child abuse and neglect are subjects rarely discussed in family or legislative fora in Sub-Sahara countries due to traditional, religious and cultural beliefs hence children continue suffering in the hands of protectors. Children never decide who gives birth to them or where they are born. They are a gift from God; therefore, they deserve to be treated as such with love and respect. Despite them being individuals that come as a blessing, they have full rights to safe living with all life's benefits. On the 20th November 1989, the General Assembly adopted the Convention on the Rights of the Child through resolution 44/25. However, these rights came into full force on 2nd September 1990 in accordance with article 49 (Detrick,1999). It is clearly stated that children have the right to protection from abuse, exploitation and harmful substances. The responsibility lies with the government of any country to ensure the child has the right to protection by helping families to protect the child's rights and by creating an environment where the child can grow and reach their potential.

Worldwide, this right to protection has been violated due to political conflicts, spousal conflicts, poverty, famines and many circumstances hence, children are subjected to various forms of abuse and neglect (O'Donnell et al., 2010; Hillis, Mercy, Amobi & Kress, 2016). Governments in different countries have paid lip service to the Rights of the children and parents have intentionally or inadvertently dishonoured the children's right to protection. Child abuse tends to be a vicious cycle where the abused grow up to be abusers. In some communities, child abuse has become the accepted norm such that the abused think it is the normal way of life. Child neglect is a type of child abuse which can be defined as failure to meet the basic needs of a child where the first offenders are parents (McSherry, 2007; Mennen, Kim, Sang & Trickett, 2010). Child neglect includes failure to adequately provide nutrition, shelter, health care, supervision, clothing, as well as their physical, emotional, social, educational and safety needs (Stoltenborgh, Bakermans-Kranenburg, & van Ijzendoorn, 2013; Hornor, 2014). While there are varied sources of Child neglect parental conflicts are the worst as children are caught up in a war and sometimes used as weapons to settle scores in estranged partners. As the famous statement expressed in African says 'it takes a community to raise a child' it equally takes a community to destroy childhood innocence creating a maladjusted individual. Sometimes communities take time before they intervene in child abuse or neglect cases until the child is broken beyond repair. This chapter is an awareness campaign to highlight the gravity of child abuse and child neglect in the early years of the child to provoke policy implication and the design to child friendly programmes that reduce child suffering and enact healing to victims.

CHILD ABUSE

Savagery against women and children is a global public health concern and human rights violation. Child abuse as pronounced by Al Dosari, Ferwana, Abdulmajeed, Aldossari and Al-Zahrani (2017:80) is "an act or failure to act on the part of a parent or caretaker that results in death, serious physical or emotional harm, sexual abuse or exploitation; or an act or failure to act which introduces an avoidable danger or substantial damage to anyone under the age of 18." Child abuse is defined in various way by different professional depending on the forms of abuse. Generally, child abuse includes any action by a parent, a caregiver or any person responsible for the child's welfare, that results in physical, mental or social harm, or risk of harm, to a child's health and welfare (Dubowitz & Bennett, 2007). The definitions of abuse and neglect as across-the-board are perceived to be in response to various cultural beliefs, norms, and values where not all maltreatment is seen as abuse and defined child maltreatment as the portion of harm to children that results from human action that is proscribed, proximate and preventable (Norman et al., 2012; Mennen, Kim, Sang & Trickett, 2010). Comprehensively, the World Health Organisation (WHO) (2014) defines child abuse and child maltreatment as all forms of physical and/or emotional ill-treatment, sexual abuse, neglect or negligent treatment or commercial or other exploitation, resulting in actual or potential harm to the child's health, survival, development or dignity in the context of a relationship of responsibility, trust or power. Children are exposed to abuse, mistreatment or neglect from their homes which would be considered a safe haven for them. Child abuse can happen in child care centres or schools where parents expect safety for their children.

Child abuse has been defined as a societal problem (Qiao & Chan, 2005; Qiao & Xie, 2017) which influences the labeling of interaction between parents and their children as intricately knotted to culture (Saluja, Kotch & Lee, 2003) even though recently, those working passionately with child maltreatment cases have instigated the comparison of how abuse and neglect is considered an urgent matter in countries with diverse cultures. Finkelhor and Korbin (1988) cited in Pierce and Bozalek (2004) have acknowledged the existence of six dimensions of child maltreatment that appear to influence the application of the notion of child abuse in an international framework. For the infringement to be considered as maltreatment, it must be (1) premeditated; (2) socially criticised in the location in which it has happened; (3) abusive according to universal agreement; (4) perpetrated by an individual, although governmental, economic, and religious actions have been known to constitute child abuse; (5) be more harmful to the children more than everyone in the society; and (6) be perpetrated against a child who is considered a person by that society. A closer look at this framework one can deduce a multiplicity of wrongs fall into deaf adult ears. It means in a location where the society has normalised abuse children suffer the most as they cannot defend themselves.

Domestic Violence

Domestic violence which is also known as intimate partner violence (IPV), is a pattern of assaultive and coercive behaviours including physical, sexual and psychological attacks, as well as economic coercion used by adults or adolescents against their current or former intimate partners (Ellsberg & Heise, 2005; Home Office, 2015). The usual trend in domestic abuse is when the perpetrator alternates between violent, abusive behaviour and remorseful behaviour with deceptively heartfelt promises to change. The abuser may be very pleasant most of the time and without significant provocation be very violent. Within no time, the perpetual appeals to the abused partner and that is why many people are unable to leave the abusive relationship. Trapped in this web of domestic violence are defenceless children.

Suspicion, fear and confusion are common among children who have endured violence in their homes (Ferrato, 2000:53). What makes domestic violence a distinct type of trauma is that the perpetrator lives in the same house as the child and often is the child's father or can be the mother or an uncle. Children exposed to this type of violence often feel betrayed, harbour a sense of worthless or blame themselves. They feel unwanted as they receive blows or are hit by objects meant to hurt the other partner. Their perceptions of home as a place of safety and security are seriously tarnished. Children exposed to domestic violence are at increased risk of multiple behavioural and emotional difficulties evidenced by low self-esteem, anxiety attacks, aggressive behaviour, withdrawal and suicidal thoughts (Danis & Lockheart, 2004:34). These behaviours and emotional thoughts manifest at adolescent stage if they remain unaddressed. Long-term effect of domestic abuse is that when children normalise the mistreatment, they also become the culprits of abuse.

Parental Depression

At some point, everyone feels low, uninterested in social activities, but the feeling lasts for a short time. However, when the feeling of sadness lingers on for longer periods it turns to be depression. Depression or major depressive disorder is a familiar and solemn medical ailment that presents a negative effect on how one feels, thinks and acts (Bosmans, 2016). The good thing about depression is that it can be treated. When one is depressed they have that heavy sadness which causes them to lose interest in activities once enjoyed. Depression can lead to a diversity of emotional and physical complications and can diminish a person's ability to function at work and at home.

Studies indicate that when a mother is depressed children are more likely to have cognitive, behavioural and attachment challenges (Ali, Mahmud, Khan & Ali, 2013; Brito et al., 2015). Furthermore, these children are also at high risk of decreased physical development (O'Brien, Heycock, Hanna, Jones & Cox, 2004). Research on the impact of parental depression on the development of the child has remained in the periphery (Goodman, 2004) even though such children usually exhibit more problematic unpredictable characteristics (Beck, 1996; Bruder-Costello et al., 2007). Parents especially mothers who are depressed tend to neglect nurturing their children they may become undernourished making them susceptible to various diseases and unwarranted behaviours. When a parent is not happy the sadness usually spills over to the children. Research suggests that difficult child temperament and behavioural apathy are linked with depression in both childhood and adulthood.

Parental History of Childhood Abuse

Physical abuse tends to be cyclic in nature leading someone into becoming a perpetrator of abuse (Romero-Martínez, Figueiredo & Moya-Albiol, 2014). When physical abuse becomes a way of life at an early age, the victim assumes that as normal. From an early age, victims of abuse become bullies or engage in gangsterism later in life. Furthermore, the early social learning theories have enlightened on the intergenerational transmission of abusive parent behaviour (Muller, Hunte & Stollak, 1995) which is partially clarified by mechanical and functional brain anomalies common in maltreated children (Mesa-Gresa & Moya-Albiol, 2011). Some parents abuse or neglect their children because they emulate their own upbringing. Sexually abused boys tend to become paedophiles. Research has established that child abuse and violence are more prevalent in poverty-stricken communities where high incidences of anti-social behaviour, aggressive behaviour, anger outbursts and insecure attachments are common (Kithakye et al., 2010; Thabet, Karim & Vostanis, 2006).

Civil Unrest

Civil unrest is violence, a clash or fighting of different groups of people within the same country. Civil unrest violates every human right of the children, including their right to live with their families and within their communities, to be nurtured and protected (Machel & Sowa, 2001). When countries engage in political or tribal wars there is a generation of children deprived of their human rights. In war-torn countries, life is increasingly becoming dangerous for children who are involved in conflict. According to Young (1990), children are frequently recruited, trained and used due to their lack of fear and that they can be indoctrinated easily. Recent research has revealed that worldwide approximately 250,000 child soldiers were used, and that number continues to grow (Courtney, 2010; Miller 2016). Furthermore, it was noted that the older boys who tended to be physically larger, economically impoverished, or are orphans are the most vulnerable group for recruitment (Courtney, 2010; Miller 2016). While international laws prohibit the recruitment of under-age children, most of them are still found in the forefront of battles regarded as civilians. As children actively participate in wars they the probability of prosecution yet they are victims who need assistance in dealing with the trauma caused by the battlefield experience. Authorities need to realise that such children need counseling that will integrate them into the society and not prosecution.

Figures 1 and 2 are sample images of the effects of civil unrest.

CHILD NEGLECT

Child abuse and neglect is a social problem as well as an infringement of the rights of the child. Neglect is another form of abuse and can lead to a wide range of adverse consequences for children and young people. Hence it is proper to clearly define what neglect is. Child neglect in general, is considered the failure of parents or caregivers to meet the needs that are necessary for the mental, physical, and emotional development of a child. Child neglect is one of the most common forms of child maltreatment, and it continues to be a serious problem for many children. This means that a child may be left hungry or dirty, without adequate clothing, shelter, supervision, medical or health care. A child may be put in danger or not protected from physical or emotional harm. Thus, child neglect refers to any behaviour by parents, caregivers, other adults or older children/adolescents that is outside the norms

Figure 1. A girl who was burned during religious violence in Orissa, India (adapted from Wikipedia.org)

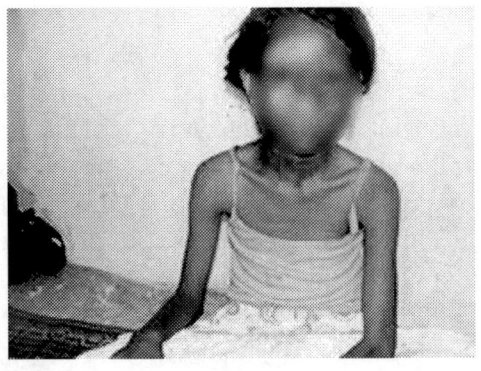

Figure 2. A child soldier in El Salvador 1990 (Adapted from Wikipedia.org)

of conduct that is expected of an adult. Abuse and neglect come in different forms and these different types of maltreatment can be associated with specific adverse consequences in childhood and adolescence and even spilling over into adulthood.

The Types and Effects of Neglect

There are different types of child neglect that affect children in various ways. However, varied the neglect is the outcomes are usually the same. Children who are neglected develop at a lower pace than those who are nurtured. The types of neglect are outlined below.

Abandonment

The term 'child abandonment' is largely characterised to describe a diversity of behaviours such as foundling, baby dumping and rehoming. Child abandonment is when a parent surrenders the welfares and entitlements over their own offspring in an extralegal manner without intention of ever again resuming or reaffirming guardianship over them. Parental abandonment tends to have grave consequences and is classifiable as a severe form of child neglect and abuse, whereby parents refrain from taking proper care and protection for their child[ren]. Child abandonment is a form of neglect when a parent, guardian, or person in charge of a child either fails to provide for basic needs for a child living under their roof or deserts the child without any formal arrangements for their health welfare or safety. In some occurrences, the parent disconnects from the children completely. Children experience various forms of abandonment such as physical, medical, educational and emotional abandonment.

Failure to provide food, appropriate clothing, supervision, a safe and clean home is the reason why most of the children to running away from home (Finkelhor et al., 2005). Some researchers note that many children who run away are not running toward something but rather are running away from something, and that is, a home life where they are subjected to abuse and neglect. Homelessness and poverty are root causes for child abandonment. Children born outside wedlock are at high risk of being abandoned to avert shame that the family may experience in the society. Although not of their making, some children born with congenital disorders or health complications are abandoned by their parents because they feel overwhelmed and cannot handle the situation. Fathers usually abandon their wives after giving birth to a child with health disorders. Abandoned children are at high risk of abuse and neglect, physical disability, mental illness and substance abuse and maladjusted tendencies in social interaction may be detected with reactive attachment disorder or disinhibited social engagement disorder Child Welfare Information Gateway. (2017).

Parental abandonment is alarmingly high in South Africa due to unemployment, poverty, unwanted pregnancies, HIV/Aids pandemic and unawareness of the helpful mechanisms accessible to assist parents. Labour migration is another phenomenon in which parents have to travel and live away from home for protracted periods of time to be able to provide financial support to the family. However, the arrangement often fails the children as the adult tends to forget their way back home contributing to abandonment neglect and abuse. In most cases children are also ignorant on the existence of organisations that aid children such as Childline, Nelson Mandela Foundation, Grassroot Soccer, Save the Children, Love Life South Africa Solidarity Center and many others. The most affected are the young ones who cannot easily escape from the perpetrators of abuse because they are voiceless, defenceless and yet too trusting.

Some parents may permanently lose their parental rights through an involuntary termination by the state because of child abandonment. That is why many children find themselves in foster homes because of the intervention by the child welfare system. In such cases parents may require legal assistance to avert the termination of their rights if they still want to parent their children.

Child Marriages

Detrimental traditional practices such as child marriage, using children to appease avenging spirits are still predominant in parts of Africa. Child marriage is when a formal or informal union is arranged for a boy or girl below the age of 18 to live with a partner in a marriage relationship. Child marriages are arranged by parents without the consent of the children who rarely meet their spouse before the union. Children are not given the chance to make their own choice and they cannot complain but suffer silently. Besides violating the human rights, child marriage continues to significantly hinder development in Africa and making the children vulnerable to violence, exploitation, and abuse. Although perceived to be an ancient practice, child marriage continues to be a worldwide custom which is driven by poverty, culture and traditional values. Besides violating the United Nations 1948 Declaration on Human Rights, child marriage is a harmful and traditional practice that is infringes on the physical, cognitive and emotional development of the child and deprives the empowerment and participation of girls and women in development. In child marriages, the girl's education is abruptly terminated, and they face a diversity of risks such as early child birth, high chances of being infected with HIV and living in poverty.

The Universal Declaration of Human Rights (1948) states that individuals must enter marriage freely with full consent and must be at full age. In line with this Declaration, many countries have passed a law that make marriages under the age of 18 are illegal. Despite the adoption of these declarations, enforcement of these laws, and of laws requiring marriages to be registered, is weak in many countries (Nour, 2006; Walker, 2012). Cases of child marriage are often diverted from the state legal system and they frequently occur under customary or religious laws.

A report on child marriage in Africa (2018:8 – 10) tabulated efforts by different high-ranking offices to eradicate child marriages in various countries as follows:

In 2013, the United Nations Human Rights Council approved a resolution intended at solidifying efforts to prevent and eradicate child marriage (United Nations Office of the High Commissioner on Human Rights, (OHCHR) 2014).

In 2014, the same office (OHCHR) issued a global report on preventing and eliminating child, early and forced marriage. Complementing the global effort on eradicating child marriage a number of African mechanisms and institutions that have recognised and taken measures to address the harmful impact of child marriage.

In May 2014, the African Union (AU) launched a campaign to end child marriage in Africa, by enhancing continental awareness of its harmful impacts and requiring states to take appropriate legal, social and economic measures to address child marriage. Also, in 2014, the AU appointed a Goodwill Ambassador for Ending Child Marriage and the African Committee of Experts on the Rights and Welfare of the Child (Committee) appointed a Special Rapporteur.

In 2015, the Heads of State and Governments of the AU announced that they had formally adopted an African common position on the AU Campaign to End Child Marriage in Africa.

Drug/Substance Abuse

Drug or substance abuse is a social ill that is synonymous with child maltreatment. Substance abuse is a broad term that embraces legal or illegal intoxicating substance. Substance abuse can simply be defined as a pattern of consuming or smocking harmful substances for mood-altering purposes. Research has established that children whose parents are addicted to substance abuse are more likely to endure physical, sexual, or emotional abuse, neglect than children in non-substance abusing households (DeBellis, Broussard, Herring, Wexler, Moritz & Benitez, 2001; Dube, Anda, Felitti, Croft, Edwards & Giles, 2001). When parents abuse substances are less likely to be able to function effectively in a parental role. They spend the family income on alcohol and other drugs, spend less time with them and, hence, nutrition, supervision and nurturing needs are not met.

In addition, in families where one or both parents are addicted to substance abuse, often face numerous challenges such as unemployment, poverty, high levels of stress, mental illness, and impaired family operational, putting children at risk for abuse abandonment and neglect. There is a variation in statistics from country to country, but research indicates that between one-third and two-thirds of child maltreatment cases are due to substance abuse (U.S. Department of Health and Human Services, 2011). Parental substance abuse continues to be a social menace compelling child welfare system to rescue children and place them in Foster care. However, it does not always go well for the rescued child because the extent of the damage may not be visible at the time of liberation. Some children may fail to conform to the new home while others are subjected to a different form of abuse experienced in their homes.

Parental Conflict

High rate of divorce and less people willing to solemnise their union causes more children to experience neglect. Failure to provide a child love results in emotional neglect. Emotional neglect like the other forms of neglect can have devastating results. Some studies have shown a link between parental behaviours to have emotionally or psychologically destructive consequences on children. Children receive love and attention from parents but when there is parental conflict, the home harbours verbal abuse and symbolically abusive acts that deliberately or inadvertently scare and terrorise a child. This includes intimidation, which can be in the form of constant belittling, destruction of a favourite toy or object, which can be associated with lasting adverse effects. The failure to provide age-appropriate care, such as parental availability and nurturance, can have profound psychological consequences especially during critical stages of child development and adolescence. For infants, the absence of a parent/caregiver can result in the absence of cognitive stimulation, which may even delay milestone expectations.

Consequently, there may be deficiencies in the development of stable attachments to an adult caregiver where there is parental conflict. Thus, making poorly attached children to be at risk of having a lowered self-esteem, and a negative self-concept compared to children exposed to love and attention. The consequences of neglect by an adult caregiver can seriously affect a child's development. Studies have noted that maternal neglect, detachment and absence may harm the development of bonding and affect attachment between a child and a parent. This can seriously affect the child's expectations of an adult being available to care for him/her, affecting a child's problem-solving abilities, as well as social relationships and failure to cope with stressful situations.

The effect of parental conflict usually surfaces later in the form of suicide attempts and self-mutilation in young adolescents. There are also higher levels of depression, hopelessness and lowered self-esteem. This is because a parent or caregiver's behaviour has a big impact on a child. It can also affect the relationship between a parent and a child. When a child is neglected normally there isn't a good relationship or a bond between them. Poor attachment has the potential to affect the relationships people have throughout their lives, including how they interact with their own children (Howe, 2011). If a child has a poor attachment or very little interaction with a parent in their early years, then it can change how their brain develops emotional and verbal pathways. Changes to the brain caused by neglect have also been linked to panic disorder, post-traumatic stress disorder (PTSD) and attention deficit and hyperactivity disorder (ADHD) (Child Welfare Information Gateway, 2009).

Poverty

Poverty, lack of education, drug and substance abuse contribute significantly to child abuse and neglect. In 2004, the then President of South Africa, Thabo Mbeki, echoed these sentiments 'Endemic and widespread poverty continues to disfigure the face of our country. It will always be impossible for us to say that we have fully restored the dignity of all our people as long as this situation persists. For this reason, the struggle to eradicate poverty has been and will continue to be a cornerstone of the national effort to build the new South Africa'. Poverty is a global phenomenon that has been the agenda in international forums about the quality of humanity in different countries. Poverty is a multidimensional concept that can be understood as absolute or as relative and embraces economic, social and political elements (Anderson, Butcher & Levine, 2003). Poverty is the scarcity or the lack of various amount of material things such as lack of income or with failure to attain capabilities. Absolute, extreme poverty or destitution are terms used interchangeably to describe complete absence of earnings essential to provide basic personal needs such as food, clothing and shelter. According to Lok-Dessallien (2000), poverty can either be chronic or temporary and is occasionally closely related with inequality. Along similar thinking Atkinson (1998) explained that poverty is often associated with vulnerability and social exclusion. It has been established that people rarely escape from chronic poverty because it brings very few opportunities for survival (Helton et al., 2018).

Poverty causes nutritional insufficiency in infants which may be associated with non-organic failure to thrive. This is explained as the absence of physical growth which can be measured by objective scales of height and weight (Hussey, Chang & Kotch, 2006). Poverty is the root cause of diverse ailments and conditions found in children such as dwarfism, is a medical term that applies to children of small stature whose physical growth is impaired by nutritional deficiency. In addition, symptoms of nonorganic failure to thrive include lack of smiling, an expressionless face, gaze aversion, self-stimulating behaviour, intolerance of changes in routine, low activity level and flexed hips.

Abuse and neglect may cause serious health problems which can seriously affect a child's development resulting in irreversible consequences. Furthermore, if a baby is malnourished, neural cells can become weak or damaged leading to lowered brain function (Child Welfare Information Gateway, 2009). There is a link between physical neglect and nutritional neglect as lack of proper nutrition may lead to neuromotor handicaps, including central nervous system damage, physical defects, growth and mental retardation and serious speech problems. Poverty has equally proved to be detrimental to educational development of the child. There can be psychological consequences associated with emotional neglect which is related to defiant and hostile behaviour exhibited by young adolescents.

Vulnerability

In literature, vulnerability is described as a multifaceted concept that is frequently associated with economic hardship and social exclusion. Vulnerability may be perceived differently in various circles. Brown (2011) assumed that vulnerability is a variable as social protection and refers to it as a state of weakness. Specifically, children are well thought-out as vulnerable if their emotional, physical and social needs are not satisfied (Radcliff, Racine, Brunner, Huber & Whitaker, 2012). It is a known fact that economic poverty is a central facet of vulnerability. In such instances, it is predictable that a family becomes vulnerable when parents are not gainfully employed and cannot afford to provide for their family. Barrientos (2011:242) opined vulnerability means the "probability that a person, household or community will be in poverty in future". Children are at risk of being vulnerable when faced with a set of conditions such as illness or having to live with a chronically ill parent, suffering, poverty and infringement on rights. When their rights are infringed basic needs such as food, shelter and education are susceptible because of social and programmatic factors (Ayres, Paiva & França, 2011). However, children are likely to be vulnerable due to some eventualities such as natural disasters that might plummet on individuals, households or communities into poverty, either temporarily or permanently like cyclones, draught or wars.

THE RIGHTS OF THE CHILD

Recognition of the need to protect the child started in the 19th century with Europe passing laws governing child labour. A league of Nations formed a committee in 1919 to deliberate on the protection of the child from which the Declaration of the Rights of the Child was adopted on September 16, 1924. This led to the Geneva Declaration, the first international treaty on the rights of the child which was influenced by the Polish physician Janusz Korczak. The rights of the child gained momentum leading to the creation of the United Nations declarations as follows:

1948: Universal Declaration of Human Rights,
1959: The UN adopted the Declaration of the Rights of the Child
1979: International Year of the Child
1979-1989: Defence for Children International (piloted by a group of NGOs)
1989: On November 20, the Convention on the Rights of the Child (CRC) was unanimously adopted by the United Nations General Assembly. Globally, countries are signatories to this convention.

Based on these Rights, member states have their own Acts, Statutory Instruments and declarations to safeguard the Rights of the Child. In South Africa relevant legislation includes the Children's Act 38 of 2005; the Child Justice Act 75 of 2008, and the Criminal Law (Sexual Offences and Related Matters) Amendment Act 32 of 2007 and Regulations thereto. While governments have shown commitment to adhering to the Rights formulated their implementation has been floated.

Loopholes/ Criticism of The Child Rights

Chapter 9 of the Children's Act.16 Section 150(1)(a) of the Children's Act stipulates that a child who "has been abandoned or orphaned and is without any visible means of support" needs care and protection. However, the current form of the Children's

Act does not have adequate detail and clarity. In abandonment cases, the law usually places children in alternative care and yet those who violate their parental care duties are let to live free from their responsibility. By so doing, the right of parents as primary caregivers of their children is violated.

In certain countries, specific age limits are not fixed leaving children open to abuse. For instance, the African Charter on the Rights and Welfare of the Child forbids the enlistment of children for armed conflict but fails to stipulate the age at which this rule applies (Bosch, 2012). The desire to secure a position in armed conflict, 11-year-old 'adults' are enlisted without considering the Rights and Welfare of the Child. In the International Convention on the Rights of the Child, Article 4 states that member states should undertake to implement children's rights as set out in the text. Despite the clarity of this Article some countries continue to violate human rights, including children's rights. In fact, in spite of the obligatory nature of the international law, many states still do not consider children's rights as anything more than moral principles.

The existence of children's rights in some countries is sheer mockery of the legislation and cases of abuse still go with impunity. In spite of having the rights a child cannot lodge a complaint himself without being accompanied by an adult to be heard. Similarly, international law promotes principles of equality and non-discrimination, but that remains purely theoretical because children still remain voiceless. Forms of child abuse and neglect in homes have continued unabated due to several reasons such as, a) indistinctive policies and procedures relating to domestic violence, b) indication of discrepancies in decision-making and recording in domestic violence cases, c) unclear classification into family support or child protection cases (Nicholl 2001). Some law enforcement agencies are reluctant to swiftly act on domestic violence because fighting partners often reconcile yet children are still caught up in the violent episodes.

IMPLICATIONS FOR COUNSELING

This chapter has identified loopholes in adhering to the rights of the child and how these rights are violated in different countries hence the need to find ways to strengthen counseling to alleviate the pain children endure due to abuse and neglect. Family friendly or victim friendly units/courts have not comprehensively understood or assessed abuse and neglect to effectively curb the scourge. Law enforcement agents in some countries are slow to respond when children present their cases of abuse and neglect while every minute counts towards the safety of the child. This calls for concerted efforts by school personnel, health workers as well as the community to be sensitive to children in abusive situations and engage counseling services to victims as well as perpetrators who need help to stop abuse and neglect to children.

SOLUTIONS AND RECOMMENDATIONS

Even though it has been established that child abuse and neglect are devastating social ills world- wide, but they still continue to plague our societies and have detrimental effects to young children who fall victim to this scourge. In addition, it has the potential to seriously affect children's psychological health as its scars are deep and continue to affect a child right through to adulthood.

- The chapter strongly urges that children, teachers, and society at large engage in open discussions on abuse and neglect topics and not treat them as taboo subjects to be avoided.
- Teachers in particular should be taught how to identify "affected children" and "children at risk", so that the necessary steps like "referral to social workers, psychologists and the police" can be done promptly. In short, a multidisciplinary approach is needed to support the victims, which will yield better results than fragmented efforts.
- Places where children can get help like "Childline" or "Love life" should be made more visible and accessible to children and the general public so that children do not suffer unnecessarily due to a lack of knowledge.
- Data for all reported cases should be created to enable the tracking of all cases so that there is no gap in the chain of help.
- A database for all abusers be created and made open for public scrutiny as no perpetrator should be hidden to come back and repeat the crimes.
- On-going psychosocial support for all victims as they will need support throughout their childhood. Social workers and teachers to meet regularly to monitor and support victims.
- There is a need to strengthen learning areas like Life Orientation where children get a chance to learn more about where and how to access protection.
- Stricter laws need to be put in place for abusers/perpetrators.

FUTURE RESEARCH DIRECTIONS

There is need for research and training on the impact of domestic violence, parental conflict and divorce on children.

CONCLUSION

The above discussion has shown how child abuse and neglect can have serious and long-lasting consequences. It has shown that abuse and neglect come in different forms and can range from denying a child love and attention, malnutrition, denying the child the care that they need, which can cause serious and permanent damage and even death in cases of severe abuse. Sometimes, neglect can be hard to identify making it difficult for professionals to take early action in order to protect and rescue the child. Children who are neglected may present with some signs and indicators of neglect such as poor appearance and hygiene; health and development problems and family issues.

It is every child's right to grow and thrive until they reach adulthood and it is everybody's responsibility to keep our children safe from neglect. That is why we need to make sure that every child has a place to turn to if ever the need arises, be it day or night. That is why every government should ensure that child helplines are set up and running twenty-four hours a day. They should also ensure that child protection registers (which include all categories of maltreatment) are there to register all those children who have been identified and assessed as being in ongoing risk of significant harm from neglect

REFERENCES

Al Dosari, M. N., Ferwana, M., Abdulmajeed, I., Aldossari, K. K., & Al-Zahrani, J. M. (2017). Parents' perceptions about child abuse and their impact on physical and emotional child abuse: A study from primary health care centers in Riyadh, Saudi Arabia. *Journal of Family & Community Medicine*, 24(2), 79–85. PMID:28566970

Ali, N. S., Mahmud, S., Khan, A., & Ali, B. S. (2013). Impact of postpartum anxiety and depression on child's mental development from two peri-urban communities of Karachi, Pakistan: A quasi-experimental study. *BMC Psychiatry*, 13(1), 274. doi:10.1186/1471-244X-13-274 PMID:24148567

Anderson, P. M., Butcher, K. F., & Levine, P. B. (2003). Maternal Employment and Overweight Children. *Journal of Health Economics*, 22(3), 477–504. doi:10.1016/S0167-6296(03)00022-5 PMID:12683963

Assembly, U. G. (1948). *Universal declaration of human rights*. UN General Assembly.

Atkinson, A. B. (1998). *Exclusion, Employment and Opportunity. In Exclusion, Employment and Opportunity. CASE Paper 4*. Centre for Analysis of Social Exclusion, London School of Economics.

Ayres, J. R. C. M., Paiva, V., & França, I. Junior. (2011). From natural history of disease to vulnerability. In R. Parker & M. Sommer (Eds.), *Routledge handbook in global public health* (pp. 98–107). New York: Routledge.

Barrientos, A. (2011). Social protection and poverty. *International Journal of Social Welfare*, *20*(3), 240–249. doi:10.1111/j.1468-2397.2011.00783.x

Beck, C. T. (1996). A meta-analysis of the relationship between postpartum depression and infant temperament. *Nursing Research*, *45*(4), 225–230. doi:10.1097/00006199-199607000-00006 PMID:8700656

Bernstein, M., & Munoz, N. (2012). Position of the Academy of Nutrition and Dietetics: food and nutrition for older adults: promoting health and wellness. *Journal of the Academy of Nutrition and Dietetics*, *112*(8), 1255–1277. doi:10.1016/j.jand.2012.06.015 PMID:22818734

Bird, W., & Spurr, N. (2004). Media representations of baby rape: The case of 'Baby Tshepang'. The rape of young children in Southern Africa, 36-52.

Bosch, S. (2012). Targeting and prosecuting 'under-aged' child soldiers in international armed conflicts, in light of the international humanitarian law prohibition against civilian direct participation in hostilities. *The Comparative and International Law Journal of Southern Africa*, *45*(3), 324–364.

Brito, C. N. D. O., Alves, S. V., Ludermir, A. B., & Araújo, T. V. B. D. (2015). Postpartum depression among women with unintended pregnancy. *Revista de Saude Publica*, *49*(0), 33. doi:10.1590/S0034-8910.2015049005257 PMID:26083941

Brown, K. (2011). Vulnerability: Handle with care. *Ethics & Social Welfare*, *5*(3), 313–321. doi:10.1080/17496535.2011.597165

Bruder-Costello, B., Warner, V., Talati, A., Nomura, Y., Bruder, G., & Weissman, M. (2007). Temperament among offspring at high and low risk for depression. *Psychiatry Research*, *153*(2), 145–151. doi:10.1016/j.psychres.2007.02.013 PMID:17651814

Child Welfare Information Gateway. (2017). *Foster care statistics 2015*. Washington, DC: U.S. Department of Health and Human Services, Children's Bureau.

Courtney, J. (2010). The Civil War That Was Fought by Children: Understanding the Role of Child Combatants in El Salvador's Civil War 1980-1992. *The Journal of Military History*, *74*(2), 525.

Crowe, S. L., & Blair, R. J. R. (2008). The development of antisocial behavior: What can we learn from functional neuroimaging studies? *Development and Psychopathology*, *20*(4), 1145–1159. doi:10.1017/S0954579408000540 PMID:18838035

Danis, F. S., & Lockheart, L. (2004). *Breaking the silence in social work education. Domestic violence modules for foundation courses*. Alexandria: Council of Social Work Education.

Daro, D., & Benedetti, G. (2014). Sustaining progress in preventing child maltreatment: A transformative challenge. In *Handbook of child maltreatment* (pp. 281–300). Dordrecht: Springer. doi:10.1007/978-94-007-7208-3_14

De Bellis, M. D., & Van Dillen, T. (2005). Childhood post-traumatic stress disorder: An overview. *Child and Adolescent Psychiatric Clinics of North America*, *14*(4), 745–772. doi:10.1016/j.chc.2005.05.006 PMID:16171701

DeBellis, M. D., Broussard, E. R., Herring, D. J., Wexler, S., Moritz, G., & Benitez, J. G. (2001). Psychiatric co-morbidity in caregivers and children involved in maltreatment: A pilot research study with policy implications. *Child Abuse & Neglect*, *25*(7), 923–944. doi:10.1016/S0145-2134(01)00247-2 PMID:11523869

Detrick, S. (1999). *A Commentary on the United Nations Convention on the Rights of the Child*. Martinus Nijhoff Publishers.

Dube, S. R., Anda, R. F., Felitti, V. J., Croft, J. B., Edwards, V. J., & Giles, W. H. (2001). Growing up with parental alcohol abuse: Exposure to childhood abuse, neglect, and household dysfunction. *Child Abuse & Neglect*, *25*(12), 1627–1640. doi:10.1016/S0145-2134(01)00293-9 PMID:11814159

Dubowitz, H., & Bennett, S. (2007). Physical abuse and neglect of children. *Lancet*, *369*(9576), 1891–1899. doi:10.1016/S0140-6736(07)60856-3 PMID:17544770

Ellsberg, M., & Heise, L. (2005). *Researching Violence against Women. A Practical Guide for Researchers and Activists*. Washington, DC: World Health Organization, PATH.

Ferrato, D. (2000). *Living with the enemy*. New York: Aperture Foundation.

Finkelhor, D., & Korbin, J. (1988). Child abuse as an international issue. *Child Abuse & Neglect*, *12*(1), 3–23. doi:10.1016/0145-2134(88)90003-8 PMID:3284612

Finkelhor, D., Ormrod, R. K., Turner, H. A., & Hamby, S. L. (2005). Measuring poly-victimization using the Juvenile Victimization Questionnaire. *Child Abuse & Neglect*, *29*(11), 1297–1312. doi:10.1016/j.chiabu.2005.06.005 PMID:16274741

Goodman, J. H. (2004). Paternal postpartum depression, its relationship to maternal postpartum depression, and implications for family health. *Journal of Advanced Nursing*, *45*(1), 26–35. doi:10.1046/j.1365-2648.2003.02857.x PMID:14675298

Helton, J. J., Jackson, D. B., Boutwell, B. B., & Vaughn, M. G. (2018). Household Food Insecurity and Parent-to-Child Aggression. *Child Maltreatment, Volume, 24*(2), 213–221. doi:10.1177/1077559518819141 PMID:31094579

Hillis, S., Mercy, J., Amobi, A., & Kress, H. (2016). Global prevalence of past-year violence against children: A systematic review and minimum estimates. *Pediatrics, 137*(3), 1–13. doi:10.1542/peds.2015-4079 PMID:26810785

Home Office. (2015). *Definition of domestic abuse.* Retrieved from https://www.gov.uk

Hornor, G. (2014). Child neglect: Assessment and intervention. *Journal of Pediatric Health Care, 28*(2), 186–192. doi:10.1016/j.pedhc.2013.10.002 PMID:24559807

Howe, D. (2011). *Attachment across the life course: a brief introduction.* Basingstoke, UK: Palgrave Macmillan. doi:10.1007/978-0-230-34601-7

Hussey, J., Chang, J., & Kotch, J. (2006). Child maltreatment in the United States: Prevalence, risk factors, and adolescent health consequences. *Paediatrics, 118*(3), 933–942. doi:10.1542/peds.2005-2452 PMID:16950983

Kithakye, M., Morris, A. S., Terranova, A. M., & Myers, S. S. (2010). The Kenyan political conflict and children's adjustment. *Child Development, 81*(4), 1114–1128. doi:10.1111/j.1467-8624.2010.01457.x PMID:20636685

Koski, A., Clark, S., & Nandi, A. (2017). Has child marriage declined in sub-Saharan Africa? An analysis of trends in 31 countries. *Population and Development Review, 43*(1), 7–29. doi:10.1111/padr.12035

Lok-Dessallien, R. (2000). *Review of Poverty Concepts and Indicators.* New York: United Nations Development Programme.

McClintock, S. M., Husain, M. M., Greer, T. L., & Cullum, C. M. (2010). Association between depression severity and neurocognitive function in major depressive disorder: A review and synthesis. *Neuropsychology, 24*(1), 9–34. doi:10.1037/a0017336 PMID:20063944

McSherry, D. (2007). Commentary: Understanding and addressing the "neglect of neglect": Why are we making a mole-hill out of a mountain? *Child Abuse & Neglect, 31*(6), 607–614. doi:10.1016/j.chiabu.2006.08.011 PMID:17602743

Mennen, F. E., Kim, K., Sang, J., & Trickett, P. K. (2010). Child neglect: Definition and identification of youth's experiences in official reports of maltreatment. *Child Abuse & Neglect, 34*(9), 647–658. doi:10.1016/j.chiabu.2010.02.007 PMID:20643482

Mesa-Gresa, P., & Moya-Albiol, L. (2011). Neurobiología del maltrato infantil: El ciclo de la violencia [Neurobiology of child abuse: The 'cycle of violence']. *Revista de Neurología, 52*(8), 489–503. doi:10.33588/rn.5208.2009256 PMID:21425102

Miller, S. (2016). Child Soldiers in the Salvadoran Civil War. *Xavier Journal of Undergraduate Research, 4*(2). Available at: https://www.exhibit.xavier.edu/xjur/vol4/iss1/2

Muller, R. T., Hunter, J. E., & Stollak, G. (1995). The intergenerational transmission of corporal punishment: A comparison of social learning and temperament models. *Child Abuse & Neglect, 19*(11), 1323–1335. doi:10.1016/0145-2134(95)00103-F PMID:8591089

Nebes, R. D., Butters, R. D., Mulsant, B. H., Pollock, B. G., Zmuda, M. D., Houck, P. R., & Reynolds, C. F. (2000). Decreased working memory and processing speed mediate cognitive impairment in geriatric depression. *Psychological Medicine, 30*(3), 679–691. doi:10.1017/S0033291799001968 PMID:10883722

Nicholl, P (2001). An exploration of the social work response to police referred cases of domestic violence within the four community Health and Social Services Trusts in the Eastern Health and Social Services Board area. (unpublished)

Norman, R. E., Byambaa, M., De, R., Butchart, A., Scott, J., & Vos, T. (2012). The long-term health consequences of child physical abuse, emotional abuse, and neglect: A systematic review and meta-analysis. *PLoS Medicine, 9*(11), e1001349. doi:10.1371/journal.pmed.1001349 PMID:23209385

Nour, N. M. (2006). Health consequences of child marriage in Africa. *Emerging Infectious Diseases, 12*(11), 1644–1649. doi:10.3201/eid1211.060510 PMID:17283612

O'Brien, L. M., Heycock, E. G., Hanna, M., Jones, P. W., & Cox, J. L. (2004). Postnatal depression and faltering growth: A community study. *Pediatrics, 113*(5), 1242–1247. doi:10.1542/peds.113.5.1242 PMID:15121936

O'Donnell, M., Nassar, N., Leonard, H., Mathews, R., Patterson, Y., & Stanley, F. (2010). Monitoring child abuse and neglect at a population level: Patterns of hospital admissions for maltreatment and assault. *Child Abuse & Neglect, 34*(11), 823–832. doi:10.1016/j.chiabu.2010.04.003 PMID:20888637

Office of the United Nations High Commissioner for Human Rights. Convention on the Rights of the Child: Adopted and opened for signature, ratification and accession by General Assembly resolution 44/25 of 20 November 1989. Geneva: UN; c1997–2003 [cited 2008 Oct 24]. (n.d.). Available from: http://www. unhchr. ch/html/menu3/b/k2crc.htm

Patterson, M. (2013). *Vulnerability: A short review* (ICR Working Paper No. 3). Retrieved from Vancouver Island University website: www2.viu.ca/icr/files/2012/06/ VulnerabilityLiterature-review-SSHRC-partnership-grant.pdf

Phillips, D. A., & Shonkoff, J. P. (Eds.). (2000). *From neurons to neighborhoods: The science of early childhood development*. National Academies Press.

Pierce, L., & Bozalek, V. (2008). Child Abuse in South Africa: An examination of how child abuse and neglect are defined. *Child Abuse & Neglect*, *28*(8), 817–832. doi:10.1016/j.chiabu.2003.09.022 PMID:15350767

Porter, R. J., Bourke, C., & Gallagher, P. (2007). Neuropsychological impairment in major depression: Its nature, origin and clinical significance. *The Australian and New Zealand Journal of Psychiatry*, *41*(2), 115–128. doi:10.1080/00048670601109881 PMID:17464689

Qiao, D. P., & Chan, Y. C. (2005). Child abuse in China: A yet-to-be-acknowledged 'social problem' in the Chinese Mainland. *Child & Family Social Work*, *10*(1), 21–27. doi:10.1111/j.1365-2206.2005.00347.x

Qiao, D. P., & Xie, Q. W. (2017). Public perceptions of child physical abuse in Beijing. *Child & Family Social Work*, *22*(1), 213–225. doi:10.1111/cfs.12221

Radcliff, E., Racine, E., Brunner Huber, L., & Whitaker, B. E. (2012). Association between family composition and the well-being of vulnerable children in Nairobi, Kenya. *Maternal and Child Health Journal*, *16*(6), 1232–1240. doi:10.100710995-011-0849-y PMID:21750894

Richter, L. M. (2003). Baby rape in South Africa. *Child Abuse Review*, *12*(6), 392–400. doi:10.1002/car.824

Romero-Martínez, A., Figueiredo, B., & Moya-Albiol, L. (2014). Childhood history of abuse and child abuse potential: The role of parent's gender and timing of childhood abuse. *Child Abuse & Neglect*, *38*(3), 510–516. doi:10.1016/j.chiabu.2013.09.010 PMID:24269330

Saluja, G., Kotch, J., & Lee, L. C. (2003). Effects of child abuse and neglect: Does social capital really matter? *Archives of Pediatrics & Adolescent Medicine, 157*(7), 681–686. doi:10.1001/archpedi.157.7.681 PMID:12860791

Sternberg, K. (1993). Child maltreatment: Implications for policy from cross-cultural research. In D. Cichette & S. Roth (Eds.), *Child abuse, child development and social policy* (pp. 192–212). Norwood, NJ: Ablex Publishers.

Stoltenborgh, M., Bakermans-Kranenburg, M. J., & van Ijzendoorn, M. H. (2013). The neglect of child neglect: A meta-analytic review of the prevalence of neglect. *Social Psychiatry and Psychiatric Epidemiology, 48*(3), 345–355. doi:10.100700127-012-0549-y PMID:22797133

Thabet, A. A. M., Karim, K., & Vostanis, P. (2006). Trauma exposure in pre-school children in a war zone. *The British Journal of Psychiatry, 188*(2), 154–158. doi:10.1192/bjp.188.2.154 PMID:16449703

UNICEF. (1989). *Convention on the Rights of the Child.* UNICEF.

UNICEF. (2019). UNICEF Humanitarian. *Action for Children.*

United Nations Children's Fund. (2014). *Ending Child Marriage: Progress and Prospects.* New York: UNICEF.

United Nations Office of the High Commissioner on Human Rights. (2014). *Preventing and eliminating child, early and forced marriage.* Available at http://www.ohchr.org/EN/HRBodies/HRC/RegularSessions/Session26/Documents/A-HRC-26-22_en.doc

U.S. Department of Health and Human Services. Administration for Children and Families, Administration on Children, Youth and Families, & Children's Bureau. (2011). *Child Maltreatment 2010.* Washington, DC: Author. Retrieved from http://archive.acf.hhs.gov/programs/cb/pubs/cm10/cm10.pdf

Vogelstein, R. B. (2013). *Ending Child Marriage: How Elevating the Status of Girls Advances U.S. Foreign Policy Objectives.* New York: Council of Foreign Relations.

Walker, J. A. (2012). Early marriage in Africa: Trends, harmful effects and interventions. *African Journal of Reproductive Health, 16*(2), 231–240.

Weinstein, D., Staffelbach, D., & Biaggio, M. (2000). Attention deficit hyperactivity disorder and posttraumatic stress disorder: Differential diagnosis in childhood sexual abuse. *Clinical Psychology Review, 20*(3), 359–378. doi:10.1016/S0272-7358(98)00107-X PMID:10779899

World Health Organization (WHO). (2014). *Child maltreatment*. Geneva: WHO. Available at: http://www.who.int/mediacentre/factsheets/fs 150/en/

Young, J. (1990, July 15). Child Soldiers. Sunday Herald Sun, p. 1.

KEY TERMS AND DEFINITIONS

Abuse: The inappropriate treatment of a child, an unfair treatment or indecorously gain benefit or satisfaction from the horrific act. Abuse comes in numerous forms, such as: physical or verbal maltreatment, assault causing injury, defilement or rape, unjust practices, criminal acts, or other types of hostility.

Abandonment: When a parent surrenders the welfares and entitlements over their own children in an extralegal manner without intention of ever again resuming or reaffirming guardianship over them. Abandonment can also mean that whosoever has the responsibility of taking care of the child[ren] deprives them of basic needs such as food health shelter security and education. Abandonment is considered a form of abuse and neglect.

Antisocial Behaviour: A personality disorder categorised by immorality, capable of being violent, and the individual has no respect for authority.

Civil Unrest: Fighting between different groups of people living in the same country.

Exploitation: The action of treating someone unfairly in order to benefit from their work. This usually happens to children who are used without compensation or to immigrants who are paid below the expected renumeration scale.

Neglect: A passive form of abuse in which a caregiver responsible for providing care for the child, fails to provide adequate care to the detriment of the child.

Parental Conflict: Can be articulated through verbal abuse, taciturn wars, repudiating affection, denying a spouse indispensable resources and frequently there is physical violence.

Protection: A legal or other formal measure intended to preserve civil privileges and constitutional rights.

Social Disorganisation: A state of society characterized by lawlessness, the breakdown of effective social control resulting in a lack of functional integration between groups, conflicting social attitudes, and personal maladjustment This disorganization can take the form of crime and other disruptions that can affect a segment of society.

Section 5
Stress

Chapter 9
Parent–Child Stress on School Mathematics Homework in a Multicultural Society

Daya Weerasinghe
ⓘ https://orcid.org/0000-0002-9449-1052
Federation University Australia, Australia

ABSTRACT

The aim of this chapter is to discuss parent-child stress among different cultures in relation to parents' perceptions and their involvement in mathematics homework and children's academic achievement. Several decades of research have demonstrated that parental involvement in children's achievement is associated with a variety of positive and negative academic and motivational outcomes. It is argued that parents' involvement may matter more for some children than for others and parents are active participants rather than passive observers in children's education. This chapter provides insights on how parental involvement in homework can make a difference and why excessive involvement of parents can cause stress for both parents and children. Further, it is discussed how the cultural differences between Asian and European groups appear to narrow down with acculturation over the years.

INTRODUCTION

Parents of different cultures have different intervention strategies and act differently when they are involved in education of their children (Hong & Ho, 2005; Phillipson & Phillipson, 2007). Attitudes towards completing students' homework may be no different. At present the amount of homework assigned to students in any subject

DOI: 10.4018/978-1-7998-0319-5.ch009

seems to be a concern in most families. It is observed that some parents prefer more homework to keep their children busy with their studies while some parents prefer their children to do extra-curricular activities after school. Given the discrepancies in findings in literature, it seems important to explore the parent–child stress in mathematics homework as well as the influence of culture and context. This chapter provides details of how parents' perceptions and involvement affect their children and the ways of such interaction take place in the home environment of different cultures.

While involving parents in school activities has an important social and community function, the engagement of parents with their children at home is most likely to result in a positive difference to academic outcomes. Harris and Goodall (2008) argued that parental engagement in children's learning in the home makes the greatest difference to student achievement. Parents' involvement in children's education at home differs with subjects as described by Fan and Williams (2010). Their studies have implied the necessity for further investigation of the factors that contribute to the development of parent–child relationship in education. However, this seems to create parent–child stress in some families through which children's academic and cognitive outcomes can be affected.

It is noticed that there are extreme cases of parenting among Asian groups. Some parents complained about their children's carelessness when they had achieved a mark around 97% for a test. They wanted their children to be perfect and they seemed to inquire about the 3% lost. Sometimes they blamed their children for playing too much and confiscated items such as laptops, iPads, and mobile phones, not allowing any entertainment. It is important to realise that these parents might not have achieved perfect scores for every subject when they were young. Unfortunately it seems that they expect too much from their children. Certain parents preferred teachers to give more homework just because they thought that these children played too much. Such parental attitudes seem to be varied among different cultures but cause parent–child stress within families.

Background

Mathematics learning, like other subject areas, is embedded in cultural contexts. In fact, there are many variables within a country or culture that impact on student achievement (Leung, 2012). One such variable is where parents can teach their children to love challenges, be intrigued by mistakes, enjoy effort, and keep on learning (Dweck, 2006). However, the process through which parental involvement influences student performance is not well understood (Hong & Ho, 2005). Parental involvement factors may not be able to stand alone as they are inter-related. Although the importance of parental involvement in students' education is not debatable, the kind of parental roles that are most effective is still not clear enough. According to findings of Dandy and Nettelbeck (2002) the relationship between the academic achievement of children and parental involvement across ethnic groups is complex and varies across different cultures.

Parental support in homework seems to be an important aspect of learning within certain cultural groups. As previous researchers have found one of the most common, dominant, and controversial ways parents involve themselves with their children at home is by helping them with homework (Moroni et al., 2015; Phillipson, 2013). Homework is an important part of the daily lives of students and parents and can be viewed as a link between home and school (Moroni et al., 2015). Those parents who valued homework were more involved in their children's education than other parents. As McNeal (2012) revealed, the lower achievement of students who have difficulties in academic attainment may result in their parents becoming more involved.

In a study with three Grade 8 teachers and 115 of their students in Singapore, Kaur (2011) found six functions of homework from the perspectives of children. Kaur describes that these functions can be of importance to a parent who strives for his/her children's academic achievement. They are: improving/enhancing understanding of mathematics concepts, revising/practising the topic taught, improving problem-solving skills, preparing for test/examination, assessing understanding/learning from mistakes and extending mathematical knowledge (p. 187). While homework provides an opportunity for students to consolidate and expand what they have learned at school (Kaur, 2011), it also helps parents to monitor and be involved in the education of their children.

Parents' involvement in their children's homework may affect positively or negatively on children. Phillipson (2013) argued that direct help with homework and setting rules about homework completion improve academic achievement while homework assistance can exert excessive pressure on children, interfering with their autonomy and negatively affecting academic performance. Further, in a study conducted by Fan and Williams (2010), the findings pertaining to parents' involvement at home differ in accordance with the subjects. While there were no significant links between parental advice and self-efficacy towards mathematics or intrinsic motivation for mathematics, they found parental advice at home was positively associated with improved sense of self-efficacy towards English, intrinsic motivation in English, and academic engagement. These studies imply the need to further identify factors which contribute to the parent–child homework involvement through which students' academic and cognitive outcomes can be affected.

Previous studies have found that parents developed an understanding of what their children were experiencing in mathematics learning at school by communicating and collaborating with schools (Zhao & Akiba, 2009). However, it was argued that many parents simply did not recognise the mathematics that their children were learning, while some parents thought that their children were not getting enough homework. When children brought home mathematics assignments in which the mathematical context was not clear, or large amounts of traditional mathematics was not required, many parents were dismayed and did not realise the significance of these assignments. In addition, parents were unsure of the consequences that current mathematics education would have for their children, and as a result, the tension that parents experienced in watching their children learn mathematics increased. This may be one of the reasons why some parents tend to provide supplemental education such as tutoring for their children, which is another form of parental support that may differ among cultures.

In most cultures, it is common practice for students to seek support from their parents for their homework. Katz, Kaplan, and Buzukashvily (2011) described homework as a unique academic activity that is administered at school but is expected to undertake at home. In the home learning environments, parents can engage in supervision while providing support with homework (Harris & Goodall, 2008). However, the links between parental attitudes, students' homework and students' achievement are complex and often debated. Several studies have identified and investigated factors related to parental involvement in students' homework.

One such study on parent–child discussion about homework in the USA and Sweden, conducted by Wingard and Forsberg (2009) found that parents became involved in their children's homework in two ways, namely, involvement through anticipating and planning the activity of homework, and involvement by directly participating in the accomplishment of the homework task itself. Wingard and Forsberg (2009) also explained that every family with schoolchildren was affected by a complex set of variables with regard to parental involvement in homework on a daily basis. These variables include a child's own willingness and orientation to do homework, the amount and type of homework the child receives, and the child's needs and expectations for homework help. Thus, the factors related to involvement in homework that could affect both parents and children were further investigated.

Based on a survey with 709 parents in the USA, Cooper, Lindsay, and Nye (2000) described three dimensions of parental involvement in students' homework. These were autonomy support, direct involvement, and elimination of distractions. All these dimensions were related to different parenting styles such as authoritative, authoritarian, permissive-indulgent, and permissive-uninvolved (Maccoby & Martin, 1983). In addition, Cooper et al. found a fourth dimension, parental interference, for students in higher grades. In another study drawing data from two large scale studies ($N = 1274$ and $N = 1911$) in Germany, Dumont et al. (2012) viewed parental homework involvement as a multidimensional construct. Three dimensions identified by them were perceived support, conflict, and parental competence. Their research found that perceived parental support and perceived parental competence to help with homework were positively related to the academic achievement of students, while perceived parental homework interference and perceived homework-related conflict were negatively related to academic outcomes.

There are other parental involvement factors that have been positively or negatively associated with students' homework. With the data collected from 165 mother–child dyads in the USA, Hyde, Else-Quest, Alibali, Knuth, and Romberg (2006) argued that frequency of homework had a positive effect on mathematics achievement while length of homework had a negative effect for some students. These findings on frequency of homework were supported by Trautwein (2007) in a study on homework variables and achievement with 24,273 (Study 1) and 2,216 (Study 2) year 9 students in Germany. The study by Kashahu et al. (2014) found parental involvement with homework in both mathematics and native language studies had moderate positive effects on children's academic performance. Based on a study with 709 students and 82 teachers in the USA, Cooper, Lindsay, Nye, and Greathouse (1998) found weak relations between the amount of homework assigned and students' achievement. They also found positive relations between the amount of homework students completed and students' achievement, especially at Grades 6 to 12. Further, the time parents spent helping their children with mathematics homework (Pezdek, Berry, & Renno, 2002) or the time students spent on homework (Trautwein, 2007) was unrelated to students' achievement. Even though direct involvement and guidance were positively related to students' achievement (Xu, 2004), monitoring of homework by parents was negatively related (Bempechat & Shernoff, 2012; Patall et al., 2008). There was a lower homework effort in higher grades (Trautwein et al., 2006) and the effect of parental involvement varied with the student's age (Patall et al., 2008).

In contrast, few studies found no relation between parental involvement in homework and academic achievement of their children. In a meta-analysis of 50 studies, Hill and Tyson (2009) argued that the involvement pertaining to homework was not consistently related with achievement. However, they found that assisting with homework was the only type of involvement that demonstrated an association with achievement but that was also weak. In another meta-analysis of 14 studies, Patall et al. (2008) argued that the overall effect of parental involvement in homework was small and often not significant. They also explained that homework involvement was not equal across all circumstances. Also, the type of homework involvement provided by parents and the subject matter were other important moderators. Overall, there are differences and inconsistences in the above studies. Hence, it emerges the necessity and provides foundation to further research in the area of parental involvement in the homework of their children and the stress that accompanies.

MAIN FOCUS OF THE CHAPTER

This chapter is focused on gaining insights into parents' perceptions and their involvement in mathematics homework of their children and how such perceptions and involvement can be supportive for, or a pressure on, children. Hence, it is of interest to study the parent–child interaction or relationship in mathematics homework within different cultures. While reviewing research on parental involvement factors and parenting styles, it was found that the theories and concepts employed in previous studies are inter-related and parental involvement factors are directly or indirectly related to the academic achievement of the parents' children. The motivation to explore parents' perceptions and their involvement in the mathematics homework of children followed the exploration of concepts related to parents' influence once it was decided to conduct the research. Firstly, this study aimed to explore homework involvement which positively or negatively affect secondary school children and influence their mathematics education due to parental attributes such as attitudes, beliefs, expectations, aspirations, values, and academic standards which were collectively considered as parental perceptions. Secondly, the differences in parental involvement in homework due to cultural background were investigated in the Australian context.

Quantitative data were collected through parent and child participants in Melbourne, Australia. They responded to similar questionnaires available online. According to demographics of the participants two groups were defined as follows:

Asian–Australian - Asian background parents who live in Australia and their children who live and study in Australia were grouped as Asian–Australians. According to world regions, this study had participants from East and South Asian backgrounds. Four dyads of those parents and their children participated in the qualitative aspects of study providing more details. Both parents and children were born overseas and migrated to Australia within the last five years at the time of the interviews.

European–Australian - European background parents who live in Australia and their children who live and study in Australia were considered as European–Australians. Those participants were from both European Union and other European backgrounds. Four parent–child dyads were willing to participate in the interviews. Two of those parents were born overseas and migrated to Australia with their parents when they were young, that is, about 40 to 50 years ago. The other two parents were born in Australia. The four European–Australian children were born in Australia belonging to the first or second generation of their family tree.

Accordingly, Asian–Australian participants could be considered as recent migrants while European–Australian participants were more established in the country. This was purposefully done in order to make sure that Asian participants still have their own perceptions such as attitudes, beliefs, expectations, aspirations, values, and academic standards due to the recency of their migration. The differences between groups according to years of stay in the country are excluded as a variable in this study to narrow it down to a feasible level. The two groups consist of a mix of male and female children across Year 7 to Year 12 and their male and female parents.

The goal of this chapter is to discuss parents' perceptions and involvement in mathematics homework of secondary school children. Cultural differences in parent–child stress with regard to mathematics achievement were also investigated. The study involved a mix of both quantitative and qualitative research inquiry, which suggested mixed methods research design. Using the information in literature, general beliefs, and the researcher's experience as a student, parent, teacher, and tutor a conceptual framework was developed to guide and clarify the research process. Hence, the design of the following framework was a combination of prior research and experiential knowledge. The possible connections among parents' perceptions and homework involvement together with children's achievement are displayed in the conceptual framework, which shows how these factors may be related. As shown in Figure 1, parental attributes may influence parental involvement in homework and children's perceptions. Children's perceptions due to parental involvement in homework may also be divided into positives and negatives depending on how this factor influence children.

In this study, which is primarily quantitative, there are aspects of the phenomenon that cannot be measured. That is why the study began with a survey and in a second phase, focused on qualitative, open-ended, and face-to-face interviews to collect detailed views from participants, and observations. Responses from parents and children were gathered using two questionnaires which were similar to each other. Interview questions for parents and children were also similar. There were different

Figure 1. Conceptual framework of parental involvement in homework and academic achievement of children

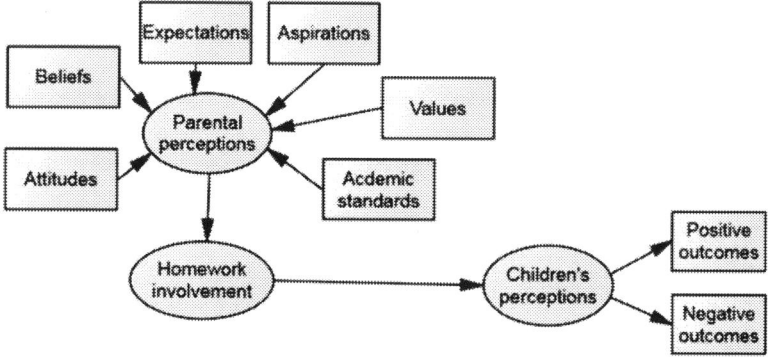

groups or clusters of participants in the probability sample of this study. They were both male or female secondary students from Year 7 to Year 12 and their male or female parents from the sets of Asian and European backgrounds who live in Australia. However, the purposive sample selected from the probability sample included senior secondary students from Years 10, 11, or 12 only. They were students and their parents from the two sets of ethnic backgrounds.

Quantitative analyses in this study describe the processes involved in finding possible answers to research questions using data from parents' and children's questionnaires. To begin, correlations among items related to parental perceptions, homework involvement, and children's perceptions were found. Each of the above factors with items of appropriate correlations were involved in the processes of determining emerging relationships. Then, several statistical techniques were used to analyse data with respect to ethnic background of students. The analyses include both parents' and children's data because they represent different perspectives.

Homework Involvement and Ethnic Groups

Use of independent samples t-tests enable comparisons in parents' data between European–Australian and Asian–Australian cultural groups in relation to parental perceptions, homework involvement, and children's perceptions as shown in the table 1 below.

Out of the three factors above none of the factors show a significant difference ($p > 0.05$) between the two ethnic groups. Effect size statistics show that the magnitude of this difference is small in homework involvement between the two groups and there is a small difference in parental perceptions and almost no effect in children's perceptions. This can be observed by the composite bar graphs in Figure 2. Homework involvement indicates a lower mean value for the European–Australian group than Asian–Australian counterparts. A lower mean value means stronger agreement with

Table 1. Comparison of ethnic group differences in homework involvement

	European–Australian ($n = 30$)		Asian–Australian ($n = 55$)				
	M	SD	M	SD	$t(83)$	p	η_i^2
Parental perceptions	1.758	.489	1.853	.442	-.907	.367	.010
Homework involvement	2.117	.556	2.291	.631	1.268	.208	.019
Children's perceptions	1.890	.568	1.936	.549	-.359	.720	.002

Figure 2. Graphical representation of parental perceptions, homework involvement, and children's perceptions between the two ethnic groups

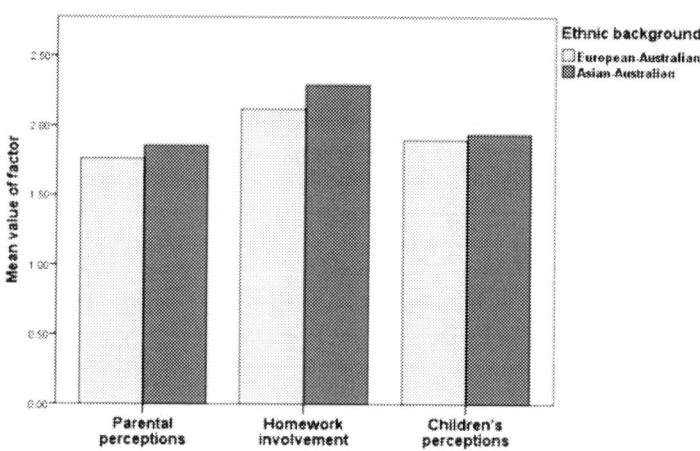

the questions in the survey. Hence, it appears that European–Australian parents involved themselves more with their children's homework than Asian–Australian participants. However, it was impossible to make a conclusion because the difference was not statistically significant.

According to similar analysis with children's data both Asian–Australian and European–Australian parents seem to have similar perceptions about homework involvement in mathematics education as data comparisons show no significant difference in terms of their perceptions. Further, the two sets of cultures do not appear to be significantly different in parental involvement in homework. However, children's perceptions in homework involvement between the two cultural groups are significantly different with a medium effect size in contrast to the analysis in parents' data.

Even though Asian–Australian parents involved less with their children's homework, interestingly, data comparisons found that Asian–Australian parents checked their children's mathematics work more often than European–Australian parents. About 64% of Asian–Australian parents and 37% of European–Australian parents reported that they checked mathematics work of their children at least once a week. About 15% of Asian–Australian and 20% of European–Australian parents never checked mathematics work of their children.

The following are based on the findings from parents' and children's interviews and the notes from survey participants. Note that all of the four European–Australian children were born in Australia, and all four of Asian–Australian parents and their four children were born overseas and they were recent migrants. As described by both parents and children homework involvement can be divided into sub categories, which are parental activities that can support children's academic achievement. When parents were involved they sometimes helped with homework, perhaps checking the workbook, or monitoring children from a distance while children were engaging in homework. Although some parents saw the importance of homework, others thought homework was work to be done by the child. Parental involvement in homework seemed to decline with the advancement of the year level of students.

Helping With Homework

While the majority of interviewed parents showed interest in helping their children with homework, there were others who were not able to help because they had forgotten their high school mathematics or did not have enough knowledge in mathematics to help their children. Even though one of the European–Australian parents found it difficult to help his daughter with senior mathematics, he described parental assistance as a great resource. A European–Australian child preferred working independently without support from her parents. Her mother wanted to get the children to think for themselves, and to do the homework so that it was their own work. However, the child commented that she sometimes needed assistance with her homework. The person she would look for in such situations was her father. Expressing her ideas about homework, another European–Australian child said, "If parents help all the time then you're not really being independent, you're not trying to solve problem by yourself". She added that she would first try the question a few ways herself, and if she was not sure at all how to continue she would ask for help. Moreover, she said, "Obviously it is good to ask for help when you are really stuck with something and have no idea how to continue with it". When this student needed help with homework she would ask her father who was a secondary school mathematics teacher. This parent also added, "I help [my daughter] and she wants to be helped and we work pretty well together, which is unusual because a lot of students say to me that it is very hard to learn from parents". He emphasised the importance of discussions between parents and children to find out the difficulties faced by children in their studies or in daily life as senior secondary students. Further, he pointed out a problem that might arise when parents try to help their children with homework. If the method the student learnt at school and the method the parent tried to teach were different, there could be arguments between parent and child and this could cause disappointment. Hence, the child might refuse help from the parent and both of them could be stressed.

Some survey responses from parents commented that those parents found mathematics at school challenging and hard to decipher, being different from what they had learnt a long time ago or different from what they had learnt overseas.

Another parent mentioned that parents' educational levels could be different and not all parents could be involved with their children's mathematics education at home. Those parents believed that teachers should be more responsible to develop students' mathematical knowledge, skills, and techniques at school than are the parents. Especially, one European–Australian parent said, "I know a lot of parents say they can't help their children with mathematics because they don't remember those particular concepts from their own schooling". She thought it was normal for parents not to get involved in the mathematics education of their children due to lack of capabilities.

An Asian–Australian child believed that children would not listen to their parents and she added that she would not get much help from her parents even if she asked them. She admitted that her father had helped her more than her mother when she was in lower secondary year levels. Later, she realised that she could get more help from her elder brother than her father because her brother was able to answer questions and explain faster than her father. Hence, she continued to ask her brother for help when she needed it. Mother of this student mentioned that the reluctance to get help from her father seemed to be a matter of the time taken when explaining a particular question. Further, this mother added that her husband kept trying to teach their child but she refused to have father's support. However, another Asian–Australian student had faith in his father's competence in mathematics and said he could ask him for help when required. Conversely, this particular father had a different thought about his knowledge of mathematics. He said that he would not be capable of helping his son with his senior secondary mathematics. The child was just starting his senior secondary education and it seemed that he had not realised his father's concerns about helping with senior mathematics.

A child participant in the survey mentioned, "Parents become annoying when trying to explain maths problems that I don't understand". One of the survey responses from a parent claimed that their child did not want or seek help because the child felt that it was enough to learn from school only. Similarly, another Asian–Australian student showed self-confidence in his performance in mathematics and said that he did not require help from parents. When asked about a person who could help him if necessary, he said he would prefer to ask his father. He added that he preferred parental advice but not their involvement in his work. A survey response from an Asian–Australian child implied a different idea about parental support. The child mentioned, "I believe parents' involvement in my mathematics education is very helpful and motivating. They always help me with my homework ... Therefore, I like their involvement in my education".

Based on the ideas of above parents and children, there are four types of relations existing in parent–child homework help in mathematics: Parent wants to help and child wants to be helped, Parent wants to help and child does not want to be helped,

Parent cannot help and child wants to be helped, and Parent cannot help and child does not want to be helped. In addition to helping or assisting, some parents used to check their children's homework, especially when they were young. Wanting to make their parents happy, the children seemed to do their work. That might be a method parents adhered to in order to involve children in educational activities while at home.

Checking Homework

While some parents were interested in checking their children's homework, others said that they would not check homework because they were not able to help with secondary school mathematics. Regardless, they would remind their children about homework or they would ask whether the children were up-to-date. When asked about mathematics homework one Asian–Australian child said "I feel confident in maths and I just can do it myself. I do all my homework". A few years earlier he had allowed his parents to check his homework but he did not like it later. Though he was not happy to show his homework to parents, his mother wanted to check her son's work. However, she found it impossible to check his homework because she was not able to access his electronic textbook which was password protected by the child.

While some parents were keen to check their children's homework, others had given up on checking with the growth of children. One European–Australian child said that her parents would not check her homework but they would expect her to get her work done. However, if they came to know that she was behind, her parents would encourage her to catch up as they knew the importance of mathematics for her future career plans. They did not seem serious when answering the question about checking homework, probably because it seemed not to be common practice for those parents and children. Hence, it appeared that some parents were not comfortable or did not want to check the homework of their senior secondary school children. Another European–Australian child said that she did not want her parents to be involved too much. She added "I guess if they were always on my back about everything I was doing, it would probably stress me out even more. That would probably make it a lot harder for me to do well at school if my parents were always really hard and wanted me to do really well… It would stress me out a lot more than just knowing that I can do it at my own pace. It'd be a lot easier, I think". Similarly, one of the child participants of the survey mentioned that parental aspirations had put pressure on children because parents would not be able to understand children's thoughts. Discussing the checking of homework the participant added "My parents do not check my homework because I always do it to the best of my ability. So there is no need. I sometimes feel pressure from my parents to do well, especially from my dad, but they don't realise that they are".

As has been noted, most of the parents checked their children's homework and helped them when the children were at primary school. Eventually, parents found it unnecessary to check their children's homework as they grew up. Checking the mathematics homework of children showed a decreasing trend with the increase of age of children due to following reasons. Firstly, many parents could not remember high school mathematics. Secondly, many parents thought the curriculum and teaching methods were different from what they had experienced. Thirdly, when parents helped children, either parents or children could be annoyed and disrupt the partnership. Finally, children find it easier to do homework by themselves or to get help from a friend, sibling, tutor, or their teacher than to work with parents.

Monitoring From a Distance

Although some parents did not involve themselves in checking senior secondary students' school work it seemed that they were monitoring what their children were doing, from a distance. The purpose of such observations were to guide their children in the right direction and to remind them to be on task without wasting time or procrastinating.

Despite the children being engaging in their homework independently, parents did have concerns about their children. One child participant from European–Australian background said that her parents would not be happy if she was staying up late at night doing homework. She thought that they would say, "Hey, you should have done this earlier." or "You should be going to bed earlier." Therefore, she always tried to finish her homework before everything else. Another child agreed that parents should know what was happening with children's education and their homework and should keep up to date to a certain extent. However, she said if the parents wanted to "look over your shoulder" and monitor everything you do every five minutes, it would be annoying.

Having an Opinion About Homework

As explained by one of the European–Australian background parents, homework could be an important way of building on skills and engaging with the content learned during the day. He also said that he would not be able to imagine doing well in mathematics without actually doing homework. Another parent had the following opinion:

I'm not a big believer in homework for children until they reach about year 10 unless it's something authentic type learning. Real life learning. I don't believe in photocopied work sheets that teachers give children to do as homework. I've always had the attitude that it's not my homework, and I have never helped my son with his homework.

Parents have different attitudes about homework and they act differently with their children. One of the Asian–Australian parents considered homework as an extension to school work which could help children reflect on what they learned in class. If his son did not attempt his homework this particular parent believed that his son would be missing out on the opportunity to enhance his skills.

Hence, the data in the study show that when parents want to be involved in homework they seemed to help. Some parents checked to see if the homework was done and submitted before the deadlines. Another group of parents did not directly help with homework but monitored their children from a distance and provided guidance. Sometimes these parents asked about the homework and kept an eye on their children to check if they were engaging in those activities. While some parents believed that homework can be important to understand the learning at school, some other parents did not see homework as important. It also seems that there were parents who could not help their children with homework because they had forgotten what they had learnt in high school or due to lack of knowledge in mathematics.

A further implication of parents' and children's perceptions in achievement was the bidirectional interaction of these factors. As shown in table 2, on the one hand, when parental perceptions of education were high, the way children thought about academic achievement could also be highly positive. On the other hand, if children had high perceptions of their likelihood of achievement, this in turn, can increase parents' perceptions in supporting their children, which is a positive bidirectional relation implied by the strong association between parents' and children's perceptions. It appeared to be a circular pathway where parental perceptions affected children's perceptions and that meant they sought further parental involvement, which in turn fostered positive perceptions of the likelihood of achievement. This is a mutually supportive environment where both parents and children can achieve their academic goals. This finding was consistent with other studies (Briley et al., 2014; Gonzalez-DeHass et al., 2005; Murayama et al., 2016; Zhang et al., 2011) which provided insights into the reciprocal relationship between parents' and children's expectations in academic achievement.

Table 2. Correlations among parental perceptions, homework involvement, and children's perceptions

	M	*SD*	Parental perceptions	Homework involvement	Children's perceptions
Parental perceptions	1.820	.459	-		
Homework involvement	2.229	.608	.426**	-	
Children's perceptions	1.920	.553	.640**	.332**	-
**. Correlation is significant at the 0.01 level (2-tailed).					

In agreement with the current study, while Murayama et al. (2016) found a mutual influence between parental aspirations and children's academic achievement, Briley et al. (2014) found a similar relation between parental expectations and achievement. Moreover, parental expectations as an attribute of parental perceptions were consistent with expectancy-value theory (Wigfield & Eccles, 2002) which supports the conception of a circular pathway, whereby children's previous achievement affects parental expectations, which again affect children's expectations. In addition to expectations and aspirations, this study extended previous studies by considering other attributes such as attitudes, beliefs, values, and academic standards. As Kirk et al. (2011) noted, parental perceptions do not account for all the variations in children's perceptions. There may be other factors such as parent-school participation, parent-teacher communication, parents' education level, socio-economic status (SES), and students' prior knowledge, which were not taken into account in the research design of this study.

Many studies in the field reported that parents sought to support their children in achieving better academic outcomes (e.g., Harris & Goodall, 2008; Ule et al., 2015). The current study found moderate and significant correlations between parents' perceptions and homework involvement according to perceptions of parents. The same factors showed large and positive correlations according to children's reports.

In this study, parents' homework involvement and children's perceptions of academic achievement showed medium and large positive correlations between the two factors according to parents' and children's data respectively. This was consistent with previous findings that suggested when parents were involved, children reported more effort, concentration, and attention, resulting in cognitive competence (Gonzalez-DeHass et al., 2005; Phillipson, 2010; Phillipson & Phillipson, 2012; Sirvani, 2007; Spera, 2005; Topor et al., 2010; Vellymalay, 2012; Wilder, 2014; Xu, 2004). However, these results may well vary in a replicated study with different participants from other areas of the country.

Parental support exhibited bidirectional relations with children's achievement to a certain level only. It seemed that excessive involvement in homework could hinder children's achievement. These findings from interview data were in agreement of the results of previous studies although some researchers have found not only positive effects of parental homework help but also detrimental effects on the academic success of children (Bempechat & Shernoff, 2012; Fan et al., 2012; Hill & Tyson, 2009; Pomerantz et al., 2007; Xu, 2004). After investigating the quality of parental homework help as perceived by children, Moroni et al. (2015) revealed differentiated results. As they explained, parents' homework involvement was positively associated with children's achievement when it was perceived as supportive, but their help was negatively associated with children's achievement when parents were perceived as intrusive and controlling in the process. In these circumstances, the relationship between parental support and children's perceptions cannot be considered as positive and bidirectional. The current study was consistent with the above results and also in line with the self-determination theory (Deci & Ryan, 1987), which states that children's innate needs for competence, autonomy, and relatedness are undermined when parents are intrusive and controlling.

Comparisons of Culture and Homework

As parental involvement is multidimensional in nature, parental perceptions across cultural groups can vary depending on how the perceptions are conceptualised (Hall et al., 1999; Phillipson & Phillipson, 2007). For example, while Fan et al. (2012) found cultural differences in parental aspirations and students' intrinsic motivation, Hong and Ho (2005) could not carry out such comparisons due to the way they conceptualised their model, because intrinsic motivation was not considered in their study. The current study conceptualised parental perceptions as a set of attributes and parental involvement as parents–child interactions related to education at home.

For the sample of parents in this study, parental perceptions in homework involvement of both Asian–Australian and European–Australian parents seemed to have similar perceptions in mathematics education because the data comparisons found no significant difference between the two groups. Further, data triangulation showed that the way parents thought about their own perceptions in supporting their children and the way children thought about their parents' perceptions were similar between the two culture sets.

Further, this research was informed by the theory of relative functionalism (Sue & Okazaki, 1990) which has been used to describe the educational achievements of Asian–American students. They argued that the academic achievement of children of Asian–American migrants can not only be solely attributed to Asian cultural values but also to their migrant status. Thus, as Asian participants this study involved recent migrants who were believed to have their own cultural values of education. European participants who lived in Australia longer than Asian participants did, were expected to have more Australian perceptions of education and were purposefully selected. Extending the current study further, it seemed possible to investigate Sue and Okazaki's theory of relative functionalism in relation to Asian–Australian and European–Australian parents' perceptions of education. However, the above quantitative finding, which did not show differences between cultures in parental perceptions regarding parental involvement in homework in the Australian context, was inconsistent with Sue and Okazaki's theory of relative functionalism, though this theory had been originally supported by other studies (e.g., Dandy & Nettelbeck, 2002; Henry et al., 2008). Dandy and Nettelbeck (2002) note that, in particular, migrant parents who believed in education as the only way to exploit opportunities not available in their homelands were likely to be more involved in their children's education than others. Their explanation was informed by the theory of relative functionalism (Sue & Okazaki, 1990), which was used by the authors to describe the achievements of Asian–American students. The theory of relative functionalism explored the extent to which migrants adopt the cultural traits or social patterns of another country. Sue and Okazaki (1990) argued that the academic achievement of children of Asian–American migrants could not be solely attributed to Asian cultural values but also to their migrant status.

According to parents and children in this study parental involvement in homework is not significantly different between the two cultures. Even so, the findings extended the study of Spera (2005), which suggested that parental aspirations, values, and goals for their children do not vary dramatically by ethnicity. Even though there were no variations found in parental perceptions when considered as a combination of several attributes, as a single factor, there were deviations in parental expectations between the two sets of cultures in this study. Most of the European–Australian parents seemed to be happy if their child was a good student but the majority of Asian–Australian parents expected their child to be one of the best students in class and these variations in parental expectations were consistent with the theory of relative functionalism. Further, these findings were in agreement with Vartanian et al. (2007) who found significant differences in parental expectations between Asian– and non-Asian–Americans due to immigrant status. Also, Yamamoto and Holloway (2010) suggested that there was variability in academic expectations held by minority groups other than Asian–Americans. These parents were less likely than Asian–American parents to value education or to hold high expectations for their children.

Children's perceptions of parental support in homework were significantly different between Asian and European background parents according to data gathered from children. However, those differences were not significant in the parents' data. This is an unprecedented finding which needs further exploration.

SOLUTIONS AND RECOMMENDATIONS

In this study, it was found that when parents had higher perceptions of being involved in children's homework, children had higher perceptions of academic achievement as indicated by the positive relationship between the two factors. In addition to comparisons between homework involvement and children's achievement, this research extended previous studies (Dumont et al., 2012; Fan & Williams, 2010) by comparing parents' perceptions in homework involvement, parental involvement in homework, and children's perceptions in mathematics achievement. The results did not support a finding from Pezdek et al. (2002) who reported that parents overestimated their children's mathematical abilities and the time parents spent helping their children with mathematics homework was unrelated to children's performance in the subject. This study, however, found that parental perceptions in supporting their children's homework can be a positive outcome of parent–child involvement if the parent wants to help and the child wants to be helped. It is important to note that greater amounts of parental help may be perceived as more controlling and intrusive by children.

With the findings of this study, several important implications, public policy recommendations, and initiatives follow. Parents, policy makers, school administrators, and teachers should continue to investigate ways to increase parental involvement in mathematics education of their children to improve the children's academic performance as well as their cognitive competence. Of course teachers and parents are the most influential in children's education, but their responsibilities are different. Australian teachers could focus on providing variety in the tasks and choosing illustrative examples in their lesson plans to keep students attentive in class (Sullivan, 2011) while parents could support their children at home to achieve academic success.

Usually, parents convey their perceptions about education by being involved with their children during out-of-school hours. This involvement consists of several actions, which may positively or negatively contribute to the mathematics achievement of children. Parental involvement in homework can result in positive outcomes if children are happy to have such support. Also, it was found that parental involvement seemed to reduce across secondary year levels due to autonomy grant and inability to provide support with higher level mathematics.

Therefore, future policy, educational reforms, and initiatives should focus on developing and promoting in-school and out-of-school programs that enable parents to become more involved and spend more time with their offspring, supporting them to improve their academic achievement. Even though some parental control is necessary, it is advisable for parents to bear in mind the need to provide support in developing autonomy to their adolescent children, at least to an appropriate level. This in turn is helpful to reduce the stress of both parents and children.

FUTURE RESEARCH DIRECTIONS

Even though this study has many interesting findings to contribute to the literature, there are features that limit the generalisability of these findings. Firstly, future research needs clear definitions of demographics, especially regarding culture, to select more groups for comparison (e.g., East Asian–Australian, South Asian–Australian, African-

Australian, and European–Australian). According to international comparative studies such as Trends in Mathematics and Science Studies (TIMSS) and Programme for International Student Assessment (PISA), it is observed that not all Asian countries or all European countries have performed in mathematics at the same levels. There are Asian countries as well as European countries which perform at varying levels achieving highest to lowest rankings. Hence, the categorisation of Asian–Australian and European–Australian groups needed more attention and might be sub-divided in a larger study for better results in future. Secondly, it is advisable to keep track of parent–child dyads, even for quantitative data, as it helps to relate the study to other existing theories. Thirdly, it is important to take into account the number of years participants had lived in Australia. Grouping participants accordingly may be another aspect that needs attention. In this case, a longitudinal study may be an appropriate option rather than this cross-sectional study. Further, in order to demonstrate the robustness and generalisability of findings, it is advisable to replicate the study with larger samples from Australia and also preferably from other countries to improve this research to the level of an international comparative study. Finally, a future study would need to represent the country as a whole including metropolitan and country schools as well as public, private, and independent schools when inviting participants. This inclusion should facilitate analyses according to socioeconomic status, parents' education level, and parental engagement in schools.

During the analysis stage it was realised that there were several methodological limitations in this study that needed to be noted. Firstly, one of the strongest limitations attributable to the results is the nature of the sample which is skewed towards volunteered parents who seemed to be highly motivated to support their children. Also, children were asked to participate if they wished and the participated volunteers could be some of the better students in a classroom, leading the study towards skewness. However, it was impracticable to gather responses from all the children and their parents in a school. Secondly, only four schools in Melbourne, Australia were approached to participate in the study and only three principals consented to involve students and their parents. As a result, this research was conducted in three schools, and this chapter is based on a study with only 128 secondary school children and 85 of their parents. Hence, it must be acknowledged that the sample is not representative of the population in the country. While the results from the sample of participants used in this study provide some interesting insights, it would be ideal if a larger number of participants could be studied across all year levels from both urban and country schools in all states of Australia. The results would then enable generalisability and be more significant. Thirdly, it would be more meaningful to divide secondary school students into lower, middle, and upper secondary school students to find any differences as the age differences could be an issue in data analysis. Fourthly, it was impossible to track a child and the parent from the same family unless they had provided contact details in the online questionnaires. Consequently, the study lost the opportunity to incorporate some of the important theories in educational psychology. Finally, the non-homogeneity of the Asian–Australian or European–Australian groups would be an issue and a limitation in this study.

CONCLUSION

This chapter aimed to provide insights on how parental involvement in homework can make a difference and why excessive involvement of parents is not always better for children. There is no universal pattern of parental involvement that results in higher achievement, nor do all forms of involvement enhance learning outcomes (Jeynes, 2011; Pomerantz et al., 2007). It is argued as well that parents' involvement may matter more for some children than for others.

As described by both parents and children in this study, homework involvement can be divided into sub categories, which are parental activities that can support children's academic achievement. The data in the study show that when parents want to be involved in homework most of them seemed to try and help their children. Some parents checked to see if the homework was done and submitted before the deadlines. Another group of parents did not directly help with homework but monitored their children from a distance. Sometimes these parents asked about the homework and kept an eye on their children to check if they were engaging in those activities. While some parents believed that homework can be important to understand the learning at school, some other parents did not see homework as important and they thought homework was work to be done by the child. It was found that there were parents who could not help their children with homework because they had forgotten what they had learnt in high school or due to lack of knowledge in mathematics.

The study has been able to confirm that children are differentially responsive to how parents become involved in homework and the benefits of such involvement depend on what children themselves bring to their interactions with parents. However, it was an onerous task to attempt to categorise parental involvement as positive or negative outcomes because even homework help can be inverted to a negative pressure if there are no limitations to the activity. Hence, parents need to be mindful of becoming involved with their children's education to an appropriate level only. According to participants in this study it was not the cultural differences that created parent–child stress in homework involvement but the frequency of involvement or the number of times per day or week and the duration of such interaction.

By inviting children's own accounts of their everyday lives and also combining these with adult accounts of children's lives, this study has shed some light on other findings through a conceptual understanding and methodological contribution to the field of parents' homework involvement and children's mathematics achievement. The present study extends prior work on parental involvement in homework by examining cultural differences among Asian–Australian and European–Australian parents and children. One of the commonly offered explanations of the differences is based on people from different ethnic backgrounds having different perceptions regarding the parental role in children's education (Wilder, 2014). However, in this study, according to both parents and children there was no difference in parents' homework involvement between cultures. The similarities between ethnic groups can be explained by the process of acculturation as explained by Sue and Okazaki (1990) in theory of relative functionalism. Hence, the longer the period of stay in a foreign country the lesser the cultural differences within a multicultural society.

REFERENCES

Bempechat, J., & Shernoff, D. J. (2012). Parental influences on achievement motivation and student engagement. In S. L. Christenson, A. L. Reschly, & C. Wylie (Eds.), *Handbook of research on student engagement* (pp. 315–342). New York: Springer US. doi:10.1007/978-1-4614-2018-7_15

Briley, D. A., Harden, K. P., & Tucker-Drob, E. M. (2014). Child characteristics and parental educational expectations: Evidence for transmission with transaction. *Developmental Psychology*, *50*(12), 2614–2632. doi:10.1037/a0038094 PMID:25285965

Cooper, H., Lindsay, J. J., Nye, B., & Greathouse, S. (1998). Relationships among attitudes about homework, amount of homework assigned and completed, and student achievement. *Journal of Educational Psychology*, *90*(1), 70–83. doi:10.1037/0022-0663.90.1.70

Cooper, H. M., Lindsay, J. J., & Nye, B. (2000). Homework in the home: How student, family and parenting style differences relate to the homework process. *Contemporary Educational Psychology*, *25*(4), 464–487. doi:10.1006/ceps.1999.1036 PMID:11001787

Dandy, J., & Nettelbeck, T. (2002). Research note: A cross-cultural study of parents' academic standards and educational aspirations for their children. *Educational Psychology: An International Journal of Experimental and Educational Psychology*, *22*(5), 621–627.

Deci, E. L., & Ryan, R. M. (1987). The support of autonomy and the control of behavior. *Journal of Personality and Social Psychology*, *53*(6), 1024–1037. doi:10.1037/0022-3514.53.6.1024 PMID:3320334

Dumont, H., Trautwein, U., Lüdtke, O., Neumann, M., Niggli, A., & Schnyder, I. (2012). Does parental homework involvement mediate the relationship between family background and educational outcomes? *Contemporary Educational Psychology*, *37*(1), 55–69. doi:10.1016/j.cedpsych.2011.09.004

Dweck, C. S. (2008). *Mindset – The new psychology of success*. Ballantine Books.

Fan, W., & Williams, C. M. (2010). The effects of parental involvement on students' academic self-efficacy, engagement and intrinsic motivation. *Educational Psychology*, *30*(1), 53–74. doi:10.1080/01443410903353302

Fan, W., Williams, C. M., & Wolters, C. A. (2012). Parental involvement in predicting school motivation: Similar and differential effects across ethnic groups. *The Journal of Educational Research*, *105*(1), 21–35. doi:10.1080/00220671.2010.515625

Gonzalez-DeHass, A. R., Willems, P. P., & Holbein, M. F. D. (2005). Examining the relationship between parental involvement and student motivation. *Educational Psychology Review*, *17*(2), 99–123. doi:10.100710648-005-3949-7

Hall, C. W., Davis, N. B., Bolen, L. M., & Chia, R. (1999). Gender and racial differences in mathematical performance. *The Journal of Social Psychology*, *139*(6), 677–689. doi:10.1080/00224549909598248 PMID:10646303

Harris, A., & Goodall, J. (2008). Do parents know they matter? Engaging all parents in learning. *Educational Research*, *50*(3), 277–289. doi:10.1080/00131880802309424

Henry, C. S., Merten, M. J., Plunkett, S. W., & Sands, T. (2008). Neighborhood, parenting, and adolescent factors and academic achievement in Latino adolescents from immigrant families. *Family Relations*, *57*(5), 579–590. doi:10.1111/j.1741-3729.2008.00524.x

Hill, N. E., & Tyson, D. F. (2009). Parental involvement in middle school: A meta-analytic assessment of the strategies that promote achievement. *Developmental Psychology*, *45*(3), 740–763. doi:10.1037/a0015362 PMID:19413429

Hong, S., & Ho, H. (2005). Direct and indirect longitudinal effects of parental involvement on student achievement: Second-order latent growth modelling across ethnic groups. *Journal of Educational Psychology*, *97*(1), 32–42. doi:10.1037/0022-0663.97.1.32

Hyde, J. S., Else-Quest, N. M., Alibali, M. W., Knuth, E., & Romberg, T. (2006). Mathematics in the home: Homework practices and mother–child interactions doing mathematics. *The Journal of Mathematical Behavior, 25*(2), 136–152. doi:10.1016/j.jmathb.2006.02.003

Jeynes, W. H. (2011). Aspiration and expectations: Providing pathways to tomorrow. In S. Redding, M. Murphy, & P. Sheley (Eds.), *Handbook on family and community engagement* (pp. 57–59). Lincoln, IL: Academic Development Institute.

Kashahu, L., Bushati, J., Dibra, G., & Priku, M. (2014). Parental involvement in a teenager's academic achievements in mathematics and native language courses. *European Scientific Journal, 10*(13), 8–26.

Katz, I., Kaplan, A., & Buzukashvily, T. (2011). The role of parents' motivation in students' autonomous motivation for doing homework. *Learning and Individual Differences, 21*(4), 376–386. doi:10.1016/j.lindif.2011.04.001

Kaur, B. (2011). Mathematics homework: A study of three grade eight classrooms in Singapore. *International Journal of Science and Mathematics Education, 9*(9), 187–206. doi:10.100710763-010-9237-0

Kirk, C. M., Lewis-Moss, R. K., Nilsen, C., & Colvin, D. Q. (2011). The role of parent expectations on adolescent educational aspirations. *Educational Studies, 37*(1), 89–99. doi:10.1080/03055691003728965

Leung, F. K. S. (2012). What can and should we learn from international studies of mathematics achievement? In J. Dindyal, L. P. Cheng & S. F. Ng (Eds.), *Mathematics education: Expanding horizons. 35th Annual Conference of the Mathematics Education Research Group of Australasia Inc*. (pp. 34–60). Singapore: MERGA.

Maccoby, E. E., & Martin, J. A. (1983). Socialization in the context of the family: Parent–child interaction. In P. H. Mussen & E. M. Hetherington (Eds.), Handbook of child psychology (Vol. 4, pp. 1–101). New York: John Wiley and Sons.

McNeal, R. B. Jr. (2012). Checking in or checking out? Investigating the parent involvement reactive hypothesis. *The Journal of Educational Research, 105*(2), 79–89. doi:10.1080/00220671.2010.519410

Moroni, S., Dumont, H., Trautwein, U., Niggli, A., & Baeriswyl, F. (2015). The need to distinguish between quantity and quality in research on parental involvement: The example of parental help with homework. *The Journal of Educational Research, 2015*, 1–15. doi:10.1080/00220671.2014.901283

Murayama, K., Pekrun, R., Suzuki, M., Marsh, H. W., & Lichtenfeld, S. (2016). Don't aim too high for your kids: Parental overaspiration undermines students' learning in mathematics. *Journal of Personality and Social Psychology*, *111*(5), 766–779. doi:10.1037/pspp0000079 PMID:26595715

Patall, E. A., Cooper, H., & Robinson, J. C. (2008). Parent involvement in homework: A research synthesis. *Review of Educational Research*, *78*(4), 1039–1101. doi:10.3102/0034654308325185

Pezdek, K., Berry, T., & Renno, P. A. (2002). Children's mathematics achievement: The role of parents' perceptions and their involvement in homework. *Journal of Educational Psychology*, *94*(4), 771–777. doi:10.1037/0022-0663.94.4.771

Phillipson, S. (2010). Parental role in relation to students' cognitive ability towards academic achievement in Hong Kong. *The Asia-Pacific Education Researcher*, *19*(2), 229–250. doi:10.3860/taper.v19i2.1594

Phillipson, S. (2013). Parental expectations: The influence of the significant other on school achievement. In S. Phillipson, K. Y. L. Ku, & S. N. Phillipson (Eds.), *Constructing educational achievement: A sociocultural perspective* (pp. 87–104). Routledge.

Phillipson, S., & Phillipson, S. N. (2007). Academic expectations, belief of ability, and involvement by parents as predictors of child achievement: A cross-cultural comparison. *International Journal of Experimental and Educational Psychology*, *27*(3), 329–348. doi:10.1080/01443410601104130

Phillipson, S., & Phillipson, S. N. (2012). Children's cognitive ability and their academic achievement: The mediation effects of parental expectations. *Asia Pacific Education Review*, *13*(3), 495–508. doi:10.100712564-011-9198-1

Pomerantz, E. M., Moorman, E. A., & Litwack, S. D. (2007). The how, whom and why of parents' involvement in children's academic lives: More is not always better. *Review of Educational Research*, *77*(3), 373–410. doi:10.3102/003465430305567

Sirvani, H. (2007). The effect of teacher communication with parents on students' mathematics achievement. *American Secondary Education*, *36*(1), 31–46.

Spera, C. (2005). A review of the relationship among parenting practices, parenting styles, and adolescent school achievement. *Educational Psychology Review*, *17*(2), 125–146. doi:10.100710648-005-3950-1

Sue, S., & Okazaki, S. (1990). Asian-American educational experience. *The American Psychologist*, *45*(8), 913–920. doi:10.1037/0003-066X.45.8.913 PMID:2221563

Sullivan, P. (2011). *Teaching Mathematics: Using research-informed strategies. Australian Education Review*, 59.

Topor, D. R., Keane, S. P., Shelton, T. L., & Calkins, S. D. (2010). Parent involvement and student academic performance: A multiple mediational analysis. *Journal of Prevention & Intervention in the Community, 38*(3), 183–197. doi:10.1080/10852 352.2010.486297 PMID:20603757

Trautwein, U. (2007). The homework–achievement relation reconsidered: Differentiating homework time, homework frequency, and homework effort. *Learning and Instruction, 17*(3), 372–388. doi:10.1016/j.learninstruc.2007.02.009

Trautwein, U., Lüdtke, O., Kastens, C., & Köller, O. (2006). Effort on homework in grades 5 through 9: Development, motivational antecedents, and the association with effort on classwork. *Child Development, 77*(4), 1094–1111. doi:10.1111/j.1467-8624.2006.00921.x PMID:16942508

Ule, M., Zivoder, A., & du Bios-Reymond, M. (2015). 'Simply the best for my children': Patterns of parental involvement in education. *International Journal of Qualitative Studies in Education: QSE, 28*(3), 329–348. doi:10.1080/09518398.2 014.987852

Vartanian, T. P., Karen, D., Buck, P. W., & Cadge, W. (2007). Early factors leading to college graduation for Asians and non-Asians in the United States. *The Sociological Quarterly, 48*(2), 165–197. doi:10.1111/j.1533-8525.2007.00075.x

Vellymalay, S. K. N. (2012). Parental involvement at home: Analysing the influence of parent's socio-economic status. Studies in Sociology of Science, 3(1), 1–6. doi: 10.3968j.sss.1923018420120301.2048

Wigfield, A., & Eccles, J. S. (2002). The development of competence beliefs, expectancies for success, and achievement values from childhood through adolescence. In A. Wigfield & J. S. Eccles (Eds.), *Development of achievement motivation* (pp. 91–120). San Diego, CA: Academic Press. doi:10.1016/B978-012750053-9/50006-1

Wilder, S. (2014). Effects of parental involvement on academic achievement: A meta-synthesis. *Educational Review, 66*(3), 377–397. doi:10.1080/00131911.201 3.780009

Wingard, L., & Forsberg, L. (2009). Parent involvement in children's homework in American and Swedish dual-earner families. *Journal of Pragmatics, 41*(8), 1576–1595. doi:10.1016/j.pragma.2007.09.010

Xu, J. (2004). Family help and homework management in urban and rural secondary schools. *Teachers College Record*, *106*(9), 1786–1803. doi:10.1111/j.1467-9620.2004.00405.x

Yamamoto, Y., & Holloway, S. D. (2010). Parental expectations and children's academic performance in sociocultural context. *Educational Psychology Review*, *22*(3), 189–214. doi:10.100710648-010-9121-z

Yin, R. K. (2009). *Case study research: Design and methods* (4th ed.). SAGE Publications Inc.

Zhang, Y., Haddad, E., Torres, B., & Chen, C. (2011). The reciprocal relationships among parents' expectations, adolescents' expectations, and adolescents' achievement: A two-wave longitudinal analysis of the NELS data. *Journal of Youth and Adolescence*, *40*(4), 479–489. doi:10.100710964-010-9568-8 PMID:20628796

Zhao, H., & Akiba, M. (2009). School expectations for parental involvement and student mathematics achievement: A comparative study of middle schools in the US and South Korea. *Compare: A Journal of Comparative Education*, *39*(3), 411–428. doi:10.1080/03057920701603347

ADDITIONAL READING

Byrne, B. M. (2010). Structural equation modeling with AMOS: Basic concepts, applications, and programming (2nd ed.). New York, NY: Routledge.

Creswell, J. W. (2009). *Research design: Qualitative, quantitative, and mixed methods approaches* (3rd ed.). SAGE Publications, Inc.

Pallant, J. (2013). *SPSS survival manual* (5th ed.). Australia: Allen & Unwin.

Punch, K. F. (2014). *Introduction to social research: Quantitative and qualitative approaches* (3rd ed.). Great Britain: SAGE Publications Ltd.

KEY TERMS AND DEFINITIONS

CFA: Confirmatory factor analysis.

Parental Perceptions: Attributes such as attitudes, beliefs, aspirations, expectations, academic standards, and values.

Section 6

Anxiety

Chapter 10
The Effect of Examination-Related Anxiety on Career Pathway for High School Graduates

Joyce Mathwasa
University of Fort Hare, South Africa

Lwazi Sibanda
National University of Science and Technology, Zimbabwe

ABSTRACT

It has always been said 'Knowledge is Power' and that knowledge is gained through education, an idea as old as humanity. Learners acquire life skills such as cognitive ability, interpersonal, psychosocial, and social skills that help learners in decision making, problem solving, critical thinking, creative and effective communication. These skills are learnt through the numerous subjects within a curriculum. Dewey's assertion is that education is life itself, but it focuses on the examinations, yet life depends on the examination outcomes. This chapter focuses on how learning institutions use tests and examinations to grade learners which affects their future. The examination process causes anxiety due to lack of relevant information, inadequate preparation, and overloaded curriculum content. The pressure to achieve a certain level of excellence, family pride, academic recognition, and social mobility is stressful. The chapter will also explore the sources of stress, the levels of stress and stress management tactics.

DOI: 10.4018/978-1-7998-0319-5.ch010

INTRODUCTION

Dynamic changes in education, technological advancements and competitive job markets are exerting pressure on learners to gain recognition. The pressure to achieve a certain level of excellence, family pride, academic recognition and social mobility can cause stress to learners worldwide and across cultures. Dewey's (1938) theory was that: 'Education is a social process, Education is growth, and is life itself.' However, assessing how much knowledge has been saturated by the mind to use in life one has to write a test or undergo some form of examination. While education is for life, examination determines the kind of life one lives hence, the tension leads to anxiety before, during and after an examination. The process of examination causes anxiety while the thought of what happens after the examinations is a cause for panic and stress to learners. Moving from one level of learning to the next requires one to sit for an examination at the end of the year through which they choose their career path based on the performance in a specific field of learning.

Anxiety is a normal emotion that one may feel before making an important decision, taking a test or faced with a problem. The literature on test anxiety has rather remained in the periphery of research development and it has so far to be established whether test anxiety, like clinical and high trait anxiety, is also branded by an attentional bias towards corresponding threat stimuli. Test anxiety can be described as a situation-specific form of anxiety, where a person has a more or slighter tendency to assess performance, evaluative situations as threatening and then develop an escalated degree of apprehension (Spielberger & Vagg, 1995). It is widely considered to have distinct cognitive, affective-physiological and behavioural characteristics (Zeidner & Mathews, 2005). The cognitive component, and worrisome thoughts are classically regarded as the defining constituent of test anxiety (Zeidner & Mathews, 2005) because of the negative effect of worry cognitions on performance in examinations, cognitive tasks and other forms of assessment (Chapell et al., 2005; Putwain, 2009). However, if not well managed, anxiety leads to stress which becomes more detrimental to an individual.

Stress is defined in many studies as the inability to cope with a perceived threat which can be real or imagined to one's mental, physical, emotional and spiritual well-being, which results in a series of physiological responses and adaptations (Werner, 2008). The thought of an examination can be the cause of stress especially if the learner's focus is on the outcome of the examination. Stress can even be an outcome of a combination of these factors especially when a person is unable to strike a balance between them. Consequently, stress is a person's response to a stressor, an event that provokes some reaction. Hence, it can be said that stress is the way the body responds to any demand or threat. This reaction is because stress essentially is felt as anxiety and fear. It becomes worse when the person thinks that they have no response that can reduce the threat, as this affects the need for a sense of control in a person (Siegel, 2008). According to Siegel (2008), control is one of the deepest needs people have.

There are various causes of stress, and everyone has different stress triggers. While stress is perceived to be detrimental, it can also be healthy and helpful. Healthy stress, which is also called eustress posits that a certain level of stress is vital for some people to perform well or complete an assigned task. Some people need a tender prod to get them going. Some theories state that without stress, some people would not be able to perform to their optimal level (Dawis, Fruehling & Oldham, 1989). Thus, stress can have both positive and negative consequences. Examination stress is noticeable by highly pitched performance standards, with elevated levels of worry, self-effacement of attention while getting ready for or during the examinations (Altmaier, 1983:52). According to Hudd, Dumlao, Erdmann, Murray, Phan, Soukas, and Yokozuka, (2000), the academic workload requires that students face a series of peak periods such as finals and at the same time there is a relatively constant underlying pressure to complete an upcoming assignment. Woking hours and workload were identified to be the powerful source of academic stress (Tiwari & Balani, 2013).

Students in high school mention that tests, score ranking, homework, academic and achievement expectations are their greatest academic stressors daily in school (Anda, Boskin, Buckwalld & Morgan, 2000; Kempf, 2011; Shankar & Park, 2016). Stress caused by academic activities has been found to lead to several negative outcomes such as ill-health (Mapfumo et al. 2012; Hashim, 2003), depression (Hampel, Meier and Kummel 2008), and therefore poor academic performance (Needham, Crosnoe & Muller 2004; Mclaughlin, 2009). In addition to test related stress, issues such as parental socio-economic state of losing their jobs, inability for parents to provide for essential needs, parental conflict, and illness or death of family member (Kempf 2011; Magwa, 2013). For example, Hussain, Kumar & Husain, (2008) found a substantial positive correlation between the incidence of illness and the quantity of examinations and assignments. Similarly, Lal (2014) found that perceived academic stress was related to anxiety and depression in college students. Nevertheless, while excessive stress can affect student's preparation, concentration, and subsequently performance, but positive stress can be helpful to students by motivating them to peak performance (Deisseroth, 2014).

CHAPTER OUTCOMES

By the end of the chapter one should be able to;

- Define examination-related stress and explain how it affects learners physically, psychologically and emotionally.
- Identify sources of stress and distinguish between healthy and damaging stress
- Explain how the different levels of stress affect learners' academic performance, psychological and social health
- Discuss the coping strategies that educational institutions and learners can adopt to reduce the effect of examination-related stress on learners

DEFINITION OF STRESS AND EXAMINATION STRESS

In the school system it is well-known that examinations as part of academic curricular are a nerve-wracking event among learners. Examinations are indispensable in education as it is conceivably one of the key approaches of measuring students' achievement. Their impact depends on the learner's ability in perceiving and responding to them. Regrettably, some students fear examinations such that their performance is severely impaired. It has been observed that these examinations are always tedious and very stressful for learners at any level of education. Test anxiety is alleged to be the trait that prejudices individuals to react negatively to examinations and tests. Examinations have become the major source of glitches experienced by learners throughout their academic career as they strive for academic achievements for their future life (Abraham, Sridevi & Sembulingam, 2016; Sujatha & Subhalakshmi, 2016; Saqib & Rehman, 2018). The belief is that test anxiety affects performance by increasing vulnerability to distraction from task-unrelated material. Noticeably, is the fact that stressful feelings might change the learner's capacity to think in the course of taking the examinations. Nevertheless, there is scarcity of studies that have directly examined this impairment.

Thus, various scholars agree that stress is a severe emotional reaction to an internal or external change which includes emotional, physiological and personal response to any stimulus. Stress refers to a situation in which an individual is unable to manage challenging issues and over loading tasks and as a result, has to face physical and psychological hyper tension (Malik, 2015). Stress is a condition that goes along with physical, mental or social grievances and emanates from people feeling incapable to bridge a gap with what is required or expected from them. It is imperative to note that stress is a condition and not a disease. People may experience stress due to exposure to a varied range of work pressures and that can contribute to an equally widespread range of consequences, which may affect the individual's health by turning into an injury, illness or changes in their behaviour and way of living (O'Donovan, Doody & Lyons, 2013). Depending on various circumstances, for example, personality, economic conditions and family background, the type and level of stress differs in every individual (Malik, 2015).

Having looked at the definition of stress in general, the question now is: 'What then is examination or academic stress?' Literature has unveiled several definitions of academic stress where Gunnar (as cited in Saqib and Rehman, 2018), explains that academic stress is the anxiety and stress that comes from schooling and education. Academic related stress can be conceptualised as a learner's relations between the environmental stressors, the learner's cognitive assessment of and how they are coping with the academic-stressors, and physiological on psychological retort to the stressors. Academic stress is a persistent problem among learners across nations, cultures, and ethnic groups, and should be viewed in its setting. Every learner desires to follow academic success to gain respect, be the family pride, and have social mobility. In the end, learners, especially adolescents feel extraordinary pressure from extremely high academic demands. As a result of stress, the learners are not able to enjoy their academic life due to the demands placed upon them to perform well in examination turn out to be cumbersome for them (Kumari & Jain, 2014). Due to the stress learners come out of high school with mediocre pass rate that does not warranty them their desired career. Some end up settling for any course available while others never make it to tertiary education.

There is frequently a lot of firmness that comes along with taking up studies. For instance, learners are expected to do homework, tests, laboratory work, reading, quizzes and many other tasks. As a result, learners experience the stress of doing all the school work, balancing the time and finding time for extra-curricular activities. It has been realised that academic stress is highly manifested on learners who are often living away from home for the first time. Studies have shown that teachers expect work to be completed on time whereas learners might miscalculate the amount of time it takes to complete reading and writing tasks (Saqib & Rehman, 2018).

As learners experience stress, they respond to a mild type of demand which can produce good and bad stressors. If anxiety is making the environment positive, learners benefit from the situation as they are motivated to work harder and strive to achieve a stress-free environment; then achieve impressive results in their school work and increase their efforts towards others and towards oneself (Shahzad, Rehman & Saqib, 2018). The stress reaction can only arise if the learner perceives the circumstance or assignments as a stressor. Innumerable demands or stimuli may be referred to as a stressor and may be emotional or psychological in nature. Learners perceive situations differently, and the same occurrence may cause different stress responses from different learners (Saqib & Rehman, 2018).

Anxiety and Stress

There seems to be a thin line separating the terms stress and anxiety hence they are frequently used interchangeably, and there are overlapping issues between stress and anxiety. Stress is usually associated to the same 'fight, flight, or freeze' response like anxiety, and the physical ambiances of anxiety and stress may be very analogous. Similar as they may seem the cause of anxiety and stress are usually different. Stress focuses mainly on external pressures that people finding hard to cope with. People usually know they are stressed about, and the symptoms of stress naturally vanish after the stressful situation is over. On the other hand, it is not always easy to determine anxiety. Anxiety emphases more on worries or fears about things or situations that could be a threat to us, as well as worry about the anxiety itself. Stress and anxiety can both be problems if they left unaddressed for long or have an impact on people's welfare or way of life.

Test and Examination

The terms examination and test are both forms of assessment and are used interchangeably in this chapter. Both the terms have to do with how teachers measure what students have learnt from the teaching and learning activities. Schools use them to measure the progress in learning and achievement and to evaluate the efficacy and efficiency of the educational programmes. Through the examinations and tests learners' careers are streamlined according to their performance and achievements. Learners' achievement from these tests also assist education institutions to evaluate the strength of their curriculum and teaching strategies.

Abraham, Sridevi and Sembulingam, (2016) postulate that basically, there are two categories of learners as far as perception of stress is concerned. That is, one category is a group of learners who take examinations as a challenge and/or fun with less impact of stress and the other category is the group of learners who take examinations as a burden and/or a pressure with more impact of stress. In both the categories, the triggering points are the same, that is, necessity of remembering and recalling large volumes of information for facing the examinations, anticipation and uncertainty of the examination results and anguish and anxiety of parental care. The main difference is the fact that the first category knows how to manage it with proper approach and methodology and the second category does not know or does not attempt to know how to manage the situation (Abraham, Sridevi & Sembulingam, 2016).

Test Anxiety on Student Motivation

Depending on the situation or their outcome tests can enhance or diminish student motivation. Tests are usually a threat or have been found to be unpopular with students because they reveal what they know, what they do not know and how that affects advancement in learning. Hacker, Bol, Horgan, & Rakow (2000) assert that the feedback from examinations can distract the positive feelings students have about themselves and their capabilities, which are often unsuitably positive, especially in the classroom. This feeling of violation can cause students to poorly rate their teachers (Isley & Singh, 2005). In their view Parkes & Stefanou (2010) postulate that every examination has intended positive benefits that are derived and at the same time unanticipated and sometimes detrimental outcomes emerge. The inference from the above scholars is that test can motivate or demotivate students intentionally or inadvertently. However, Shepard (2000) was of the idea that performance from any assessment may encourage higher order thinking and may enhance engagement and motivation.

Causes of Examination Stress

Research studies have revealed that examinations can trigger stress and a lot of anxiety for many learners. There is evidence that academic pressure is one of the factors that cause failure among the learners (Dobson, 2012: Al-Zoubi & Younes 2015). It has been shown that anxiety and examination stress are intellectual and emotional reaction of a learner due to the fear of adverse consequences. Difficult syllabus and improper instructional methods have been found to be the key reasons behind stress among learners as they try to maintain their academic performance. Consequently, when learners think they are unable to perform according to any self-imposed or externally set standard, they experience stress. Similarly, personal and family-oriented issues, gender and demographic factors such as urban and rural background of learners, environmental factors such as economic, political and technical uncertainties including fear of examination failures and low level of self-esteem during leisure activities also result in examination stress (Malik, 2015).

However, Parsons (2008) argues that learners who are inadequately prepared for the examination because of insufficient effort are more likely to suffer from such stress and should therefore not be given too much sympathy. This attitude appears to have been the dominant one among examiners for many years and persists, but it is evident from the literature that even this phenomenon of inadequate preparation can be attributed, at least partly, to examination stress.

Furthermore, it is documented that mind-sets of disturbance, nervousness and downheartedness are amongst the possible effects of an extreme level of anxiety. Stress factors alone do not contribute to frustration and tension but the collaboration amongst stress factors and the learner's individualised environment contribute towards the attainment of a higher level of stress, frustration and downheartedness. (Shahzad, Rehman & Saqib, 2018).

It is indicated in research that most of the teachers give punishment to the learners on their weaknesses and shortcomings. It has also been revealed in literature that most of the teachers do not provide feedback to the learners timely, which may be helpful to overcome their weaknesses and shortcomings. Quite a number of teachers often fail to clarify the objectives of the lesson during instructional delivery which creates a great barrier to understand the objectives and the same later put the learner under stress at the end or in mid-term examinations. Additionally, some teachers lack adequate pedagogical skills, and this contributes to stress among learners. For instance, some teachers highlight wrong answers and give number of exercises and tests to the learners without proper explanation. Lack of subject mastery on the part of the teacher has a negative impact on learners as it creates anxiety in learners during examination preparation. There are indications that some teachers do not avail themselves to the learners during free time for learning purposes, at times learners need clarity on certain concepts as individuals. Hence, unavailability of teachers might lead to learners experiencing stress during examination time since they will not be sure of certain concepts (Shahzad, Rehman & Saqib, 2018).

Nonetheless, Mc Donald (as cited in Malik, 2015) identified the most common reasons of stress as poor study habits, lack of examination preparation and organisation, the failure to adjust time and studying a night before an examination. Getting worried about competition and anticipated results, past performances in examinations, academic probation are also some other reasons of test anxiety in learners. To add on, it has been shown that poor physical and emotional health results in learners losing weight during examinations, their sleeping habits change, and they feel depressed. Furthermore, managing time is a dynamic factor for academic accomplishment among learners. However, in most cases, learners have very busy timetables because they must attend classes, meet deadlines for assignments, examination preparation, along with co-curricular, social and personal activities. Thus, inability of time management and making a balance in all activities is the major source of stress for learners (Malik, 2015).

Zeidner (as cited in Parsons, 2008) alludes that learners who experience examination stress are those:

- with poor study skills (poor organisation and retrieval skills for example) who know they are not prepared;

- who experience blockage and retrieval problems during examinations;
- who have become accustomed to failure because of their personal history (which may of course be because they have low ability);
- whose primary concern is to avoid failure and thus avoid being seen to be failures either in their own eyes or in the eyes of others;
- who deliberately indulge in examination stress as an excuse for failure so that they can blame examination stress rather than their ability or lack of hard work for their failure; and
- who want to do very well, perfectionists, and whose anxiety comes from worrying that they will not do as well as they would like.

Nevertheless, Kumari and Jain (2014) argue that lifestyle issues such as inadequate rest, poor nutrition and insufficient planning of the available time are the major contributors that cause pre-examination stress or anxiety. If a learner fails to budget the available time, he/she will not sufficiently cover the syllabus content on time resulting in stress. Even though reading may be completed, the challenge is when they run out of time to revise the work to ensure they comprehend and remember what was learnt. It is imperative for learners to have essential information such when the examinations are written, the venue, have knowledge of the course content, stationary essential to write the examination in advance. However, lack of this vital information can lead to pre-examination stress. Several learners adopt the studying styles such as attempting to memorise the textbook contents, studying all night before examinations, incompetent and erratic content coverage, and failure to make revision notes which lead to stress

Signs and Symptoms of Examination Anxiety and Stress

The main noticeable indicators of stress in learners before they take an examination entail headache, loss of appetite and temper, change in sleep pattern, tiredness and sick feeling, loss of concentration and sense of restlessness, feeling lonely or sad, feeling aches on whole body, suffering from upset stomach, food cravings and sweaty palms. Conversely, these do not constitute an alarming situation if a person is experiencing such symptoms. Some physiological indications include increased respiration and heartbeats, heightened muscle tension, blood pressure and gastric discomfort. High-risk learners should be recognised early and intervention should be done accordingly (Mohapatra, Panigrahi & Rath, 2012; Kumari & Jain, 2014; Malik, 2015). The symptoms of stress noticeable during examinations as observed by Parsons (2008) involve:

- learners explaining that during the examination, their mind went blank,
- answering papers containing only very short responses to questions,
- quite high-performing learners who seek out the examiner after a result is announced to explain, presumably for the sake of their own self-esteem, that they suffered lack of concentration during the examination,
- some learners who contact the examiner frequently just prior to the examination with long lists of small questions to which they seek `answers' or reassurance that they have it right,
- learners who request a deferred examination just prior to the examination by visiting a doctor complaining of stress or simply of feeling unwell,
- learners who are perfectionist by nature and who under stress in an examination waste time trying to write perfect answers,
- learners who openly state that they suffer from examination stress and find that reproduction of text from memory is the best way to ensure they at least write something `correct' in the examination.

Observations from literature further suggest the indicators of examination stress as:

- not turning up to examinations;
- thinking about other things, staring into space, worrying;
- working fast but inaccurately;
- working slowly and cautiously but accurately;
- procrastination about assignments and study generally; and
- feelings of helplessness and depression often based on previous failures. (Parsons, 2008).

Segal, Smith, Segal and Robinson (2017) categorise the symptoms of examination stress as follows:

Cognitive Symptoms
- Memory problems
- Inability to concentrate
- Poor judgment
- Seeing only the negative
- Anxious or racing thoughts
- Constant worrying

Emotional Symptoms
- Depression or general unhappiness
- Anxiety and agitation

- ◦ Moodiness, irritability, or anger
- ◦ Feeling overwhelmed
- ◦ Loneliness and isolation
- ◦ Other mental or emotional health problems

Physical Symptoms
- ◦ Aches and pains
- ◦ Diarrhoea or constipation
- ◦ Nausea, dizziness
- ◦ Chest pain, rapid heart rate
- ◦ Frequent colds or flu

Behavioural Symptoms
- ◦ Eating more or less
- ◦ Sleeping too much or too little
- ◦ Withdrawing from others
- ◦ Procrastinating or neglecting responsibilities
- ◦ Nervous habits (e.g. nail biting, pacing)

How Examination Stress Affects Learners Physically, Psychologically, and Emotionally

Examination stress can distract learners' learning and their test performance since it might extremely affect mental and emotional health of learners. Stress generates psychological disorders and impairs performance in a wide range of cognitive functions such as `attention, memory, concept formation and problem-solving. The stress can be severe if the past experiences, performances and beliefs of the learner are negative. For instance, a few learners suffer from ludicrous beliefs or demands such as: "If I don't get a good score, I will lose my respect, or I will be worthless". Some learners undergo through disastrous predictions such as: "I will fail no matter how much hard work I do". It is important to realise that higher level of stress may even cause illness. Stressed learners might experience variation in blood pressure

Table 1.

Reflection
1. Define stress 2. What do you understand by examination stress? 3. Discuss the causes of examination stress. 4. How would you identify learners who are experiencing examination stress? 5. Identify the four categories of symptoms of examination stress and examples of symptoms in each category.

and might develop ulcers because of stomach instability. Research studies have indicated that female learners are prone to high level of stress during examinations as compared to their male counterparts (Parsons, 2008; Kumari & Jain, 2014; Malik, 2015; Sujatha & Subhalakshmi, 2016; Saqib & Rehman, 2018).

Stress releases emotional responses ranging from excitement, even when an event is stressful but is manageable, to nervousness, annoyance, discouragement and despair when the situation seems to be helpless. Continuous traumatic situations may start a diversity of emotional retorts reliant on how successful the learner adopts coping mechanism. Anxiety could be characterised as: apprehension, uneasiness, tautness and terror, which may be established by the feeling of emotionlessness, lack of interest in past activities and a sense of estrangement from others. Examination stress can result in a learner engaging in actions that compromise the body's immunity as it attempts to fight off illness, such as recurring chills and headaches (O'Donovan, Doody & Lyons, 2013). Anxiety also has some emotional effects over the learner who experiences it. The emotional effects include feeling of uneasiness, trouble concentration, feeling tense and anticipating the worst, irritability, restlessness, nightmares, obsessions about sensations, and many others (Sujatha & Subhalakshmi, 2016).

Eustress (Healthy) Examination Stress

Stress is a normal human behaviour but if it surpasses to a great extent it could become a problem and could be very hazardous. A high level of stress can be harmful to learners' academic success. Examinations that create a lot of anxiety in learners do not measure the learners' genuine knowledge and abilities. It is recommended that there should be some other less stressful ways to evaluate learners' talents and capabilities (Malik, 2015). Literature suggests two categories of stress which are eustress (positive stress) and distress (negative stress). Eustress is understood as a positive response to the atmosphere that enables growth, which can heighten the learner's capability to work and increase their functional capacity.

Additionally, a mild degree of strain and stress is occasionally beneficial. For instance, if one feels slightly stressed when working on project or an assignment, frequently it drives them to produce a good job, have a better focus and work enthusiastically. Actually, mild stress before an examination is an indication that the learner really cares about their performance and achievement. It compels the students to work hard to achieve a good grade. But then again, if the learners feel intensely stressed pre-examination and during examination process, it has consequences for the mental stability and somatic symptoms. Research studies have established that every year approximately 25,000 students between the ages of 18 to 20 commit suicide during the examination time (Akhtar & Alam 2015).

A certain quantity of examination stress can inspire, empower and stimulate learners, in that way producing positive results. Yet, if this stress is tenacious, intense or constant, and the learner turns out to be unable to cope, it may develop into distress which is an undesirable response to the environment leading to physical and psychological maladaptation. Consequently, a learner may move along a range from emotional state of eustress to modest or severe distress. Nonetheless, it should be noted that stress does not constantly activate psychological distress, which develop only when forced demands are perceived to exceed the ability to cope (O'Donovan, Doody and Lyons, 2013). On the same note, Parsons (2008) further elaborates that some degree of stress is however a normal part of the incentive to perform well and is thus a good thing, but excess stress can be devastating. Thus, mild stress may be beneficial in cognitive tasks and performance.

Damaging Examination Stress

Research indicates that persistently high stress leads to anxiety and depression, which are definable neuropsychiatric disease entities (Singh, Goyal, Tiwari, Ghildiyal, Nattu & Das, 2012). Al-Nahari (2009) corroborates that chronic stressors may induce maladaptive responses leading to psychiatric diseases, such as anxiety and major depression. Owing to elevated stress levels during examination time, learners refrain from socializing and engaged themselves in passive and active relaxation which may further amplify the impact of examination stress. There is also evidence that when anxiety triggered by examination reaches clinical or sub-clinical levels, it interferes with the capacity of the learners to achieve at their potential. The failure to achieve as expected in turn leads to a more severe sense of distress (Kumari & Jain, 2014; Segal, Smith, Segal & Robinson, 2017).

According to Segal et al. (2017) health problems caused or exacerbated by examination stress include:

- Depression and anxiety
- Pain of any kind
- Sleep disorders
- Autoimmune diseases
- Digestive complications
- Skin conditions, such as eczema
- Heart disease
- Weight gain or loss
- Thinking and memory difficulties

Table 2.

Reflection
1. Discuss how examination stress affects learners physically, psychologically and emotionally.
2. How can examination stress be beneficial to the learner?
3. What are the health problems associated with examination stress?
4. How does examination stress affect the career path of a learner?

Stress Coping Mechanism

Coping with stress has been extensively studied in contemporary psychology. Coping strategy denotes to a system of coping accepted as useful in a specific setting. Over time, individuals develop a precise coping panache. This refers to the way an individual respond to any traumatic event. In stress literature the word "coping" has two meanings. Coping signifies the means of dealing with stress or exertion to control situations of challenge, harm or threat when a routine or involuntary response is not readily accessible (Park and Adler, 2003). Explaining coping Lazarus (1997) referred to it as becoming proficient at conditions that levy or exceed adaptive resources. The concept of coping is based on three theoretical components namely: physiological, cognitive and learned. Furthermore, Lazarus (1999) stressed the crucial role of cognitive process in coping activities and the importance of coping in assessing the quality and severity of emotional reactions to stress. Adolescents are having difficulty in coping with various 21st century pressures, hence the appeal to schools to include an element of teaching them how to cope with stress in their educational programmes (Frydenberg et al., 2004). Kumar and Bhukar (2013) also noted that many students faced stress as they attempt to synchronise busy lives, school work having quality time with family and friend. While some students may thrive on stress, it may be dangerous because some stress levels can lead to a terrible effect that completely changes a student's life which may lead to failure.

Thus far, few studies have scrutinised the relationship between students' academic stress and the coping strategies they adopt. Adolescents have been found to be prone to stress due to numerous life events that are unusual and mostly unanticipated such as

- family conflict and parental divorce,
- glitches with peers including bulling, romances and acceptance in the clique
- school-related problems or pressures such as work overload, high standards expected,
- their own opinions, emotional state, or behaviours such as being lonely, depressed or delinquent behaviour that attracts punishments (Nagle & Sharma 2018)

High school learners experience harmful academic stress which leads them to maladaptive behavioural coping retorts such as alcohol and drug abuse, smoking and delinquent conduct (Glozah & Pevalin, 2014). Their common reactions to stressful are anxiety, anger, excitement, fear and sadness, and their behaviour may change. Individuals react differently whereby some isolate themselves, others way scream at others while some actively seek the solace from others. Generally, two foremost ways to cope with stress identified are problem solving and managing emotions. Problem solving involves changing the state of affairs or eliminating the problem. Managing emotions as a way of dealing with stress comprises management the feelings and thoughts that cause the problem. Both methods are effective depending on the source and magnitude of the traumatic situation.

In solving the problem some learners look at the problem positively, adjusting their activities, learning new skills and adopt new strategies. In terms of poor performance at school may mean paying more attention to teachers, learning new study tactics and devoting more time to complete assignments (Kadhiravan and Kumar, 2012). Coping with feeling of isolation may necessitate learning social skills by joining group sporting activities that require team effort to win (Låftman & Östberg, 2006). On the other hand, managing emotions can be beneficial in handling an uncontrollable problem by blowing off steam, avoidance, and distraction which prepares one to directly cope with difficult situations.

Studies show that young adolescents love music and watching movies which helps them to cope with stress (Bland et al., 2010; Pisarczyk, 2018). Music has proved to be a convenient coping strategy due to technology that allows them to play music on their cellphones. It has always been said experience is the best teacher, hence, it helps to resolve stressful situations especially when the young person feels they can derive something good from the problem. Having fun, hanging out with best friends and loved ones, being in resort areas provides respite from stress. It is often called a time to "recharges batteries" so that one is energised for dealing with stress. Nevertheless, there is no "one size fits all" in coping with examination stress and perhaps the prospects of what career one desires to follow may be the best coping strategy which is discussed below.

Career Path

While choosing a career can be daunting, it is also dependent on various factors such as ability, attitude, acumen, parental desires, peer pressure, academic performance and disposition. Pre-examination anxiety may cause a learner to perform below the expected standard or attain lower points which may divert their original planned career. On the same topic Feldman (2003) unveiled quite a few factors, such as low cognitive aptitudes, low levels of self-esteem and self-efficacy, and to be positively interrelated to career indecisiveness that can derail one's career path. There is a possibility of the learner being attracted to one side of the career without considering all its facets. For instance, one may be attracted to nursing because they like the uniform and have done well in the required science subjects, but can they stand blood and death of patience? From an early age some learners already know what they would be when they grow up and work diligently to while some learners reach their dream job (Fizer, 2013). Sadly, though some learners end up settling for a different path due to many factors beyond their control .

SOLUTIONS AND RECOMMENDATIONS

Since individuals are different with some learners being more resilient to stress than others, a "one size fits all" rule cannot be applied to reduce or eliminate stress in high school students. Teachers have to be more sensitive to individual differences in order to help each student to adequately prepare for the examination. While reducing or eliminating stress is a noble idea it may not work for those who need eustress to excel academically. The recommendations made may not be conclusive or considered as prescription but offer guidelines in assisting learners experiencing examination stress in high schools.

1. Every institution should offer guidance and counselling services at all time to assist learners when faced with day-to-day stressful situations and especially during examination time.
2. Teachers should cover the curriculum content so that learners are tested on what they have learnt. They should be available to give extra lessons or reinforcement of what was learnt in form of revision.
3. All teachers should be trained to identify signs and symptoms of stress and anxiety before it escalates to depression. With this vital knowledge they in turn would refer cases of acute stress.
4. Strong teacher-parent collaboration is essential because any behavioural change that parents may miss is picked up by teachers and collectively they help the learner in distress.
5. There is need for education systems to reduce the amount of work which has been brought by new technology, new learning areas (subjects) and curriculum changes introduced in schools
6. There is need for research into how education systems can reduce examination related stress and anxiety

FUTURE RESEARCH DIRECTION

As already indicated that "a one size fits all" strategy may not work in reducing or eliminating stress among high school students, there is need for extensive research that will come up with stratagems that can commonly work equally for students and teachers. While this chapter has focused on students only there is a possibly that teachers are equally stressed by the examination such that the effect is cascaded to their students, hence the need for a longitudinal study that will find out the effect of teacher stress on the students.

CONCLUSION

This chapter looked at the effect of examination-related anxiety on career pathway for high school graduates. Curriculum changes, new innovations and the high demand for excellence in performance are causes of examination stress faced by learners in high school. Besides stress from the desire to achieve high marks, learners have to deal with domestic problems, peer pressure and socio-economic challenges. The chapter highlighted these issues although the list is endless. Key terms were defined and finally the chapter proposed recommendations to reduce stress experienced by high school learners.

REFERENCES

Abraham, S. G. K., Sridevi, G., & Sembulingam, P. (2016). Gender difference in the impact of examination stress on psychological and physiological profiles of dental students. *IOSR Journal of Dental and Medical Sciences*, *15*(9), 101–108.

Akhtar, Z., & Alam, M. (2015). Stress and Suicidal Ideation among School Students. *Journal of the Indian Academy of Applied Psychology*, *41*(2), 236.

Al-Nahari, H. (2009). Effect of academic examination stress on some physiological parameters of medical technology students. *Egyptian Journal of Experimental Biology (Zoology)*, *5*, 481–485.

Al-Zoubi, S. M., & Younes, M. A. B. (2015). Low academic achievement: Causes and results. *Theory and Practice in Language Studies*, *5*(11), 2262–2268. doi:10.17507/tpls.0511.09

Altmaier, E. M. (1983). *Helping students manage stress*. San Francisco: Jossey-Boss Inc.

Anda, D., Baroni, S., Boskin, L., Buckwalld, L., Morgan, J., Ow, J., ... Weiss, R. (2000). Stress, stressors and coping among high school students. *Children and Youth Services Review*, 22(6), 441–463. doi:10.1016/S0190-7409(00)00096-7

Baumeister, R. F. (1984). Choking under pressure: Self-consciousness and paradoxical effects of incentives on skillful performance. *Journal of Personality and Social Psychology*, 46(3), 610–620. doi:10.1037/0022-3514.46.3.610 PMID:6707866

Bland, H. W., Melton, B. F., Welle, P., & Bigham, L. (2012). Stress tolerance: New challenges for millennial college students. *College Student Journal*, 46(2), 362–375.

Chapell, M. S., Blanding, Z. B., Takahashi, M., Silverstein, M. E., Newman, B., Gubi, A., & McCann, N. (2005). Test anxiety and academic performance in undergraduate and graduate students. *Journal of Educational Psychology*, 97(2), 268–274. doi:10.1037/0022-0663.97.2.268

Dawis, R. V., Fruehling, R. T., & Oldham, N. B. (1989). *Psychology: human relations and work adjustment* (7th ed.). New York: Gregg Division, McGraw-Hill.

Deisseroth, K. (2014). Circuit dynamics of adaptive and maladaptive behaviour. *Nature*, 505(7483), 309–317. doi:10.1038/nature12982 PMID:24429629

Dewey, J. (1938). *Experience and education*. New York: MacMillan.

Dobson, C. (2012). *Effects of academic anxiety on the performance of students with and without learning disabilities and how students can cope with anxiety at school*. Northern Michigan University.

Feldman, D. C. (2003). The antecedents and consequences of early career indecision among young adults. *Human Resource Management Review*, 13, 499–531.

Fizer, D. (2013). *Factors affecting career choices of college students enrolled in agriculture* (Unpublished master's thesis). University of Tennessee.

Frydenberg, E., Lewis, R., Bugalski, K., Cotta, A., McCarthy, C., Luscombe-smith, N., & Poole, C. (2004). Prevention is better than cure: Coping skills training for adolescents at school. *Educational Psychology in Practice*, 20(2), 117–134. doi:10.1080/02667360410001691053

Glozah, F. N., & Pevalin, D. J. (2014). Social support, stress, health, and academic success in Ghanaian adolescents: A path analysis. *Journal of Adolescence*, 37(4), 451–460. doi:10.1016/j.adolescence.2014.03.010 PMID:24793393

Hacker, D. J., Bol, L., Horgan, D. D., & Rakow, E. A. (2000). Test prediction and performance in a classroom context. *Journal of Educational Psychology*, *92*(1), 160–170. doi:10.1037/0022-0663.92.1.160

Hampel, P., Meier, M., & Kummel, U. (2008). School-based stress management training for adolescents: Longitudinal results from an experimental study. *Journal of Youth and Adolescence*, *37*(8), 1009–1024. doi:10.100710964-007-9204-4

Hashim, I. H. (2003). Cultural and gender differences in perceptions of stressors and coping skills: A study of Western and African college students in China. *School Psychology International*, *24*(2), 182–203. doi:10.1177/0143034303024002004

Hudd, S. S., Dumlao, J., Erdmann-Sager, D., Murray, D., Phan, E., Soukas, N., & Yokozuka, N. (2000). Stress at college: Effects on health habits, health status and self-esteem. *College Student Journal*, *34*(2).

Hussain, A., Kumar, A., & Husain, A. (2008). Academic stress and adjustment among high school students. *Journal of the Indian Academy of Applied Psychology*, *34*(9), 70–73.

Isley, P., & Singh, H. (2005). Do higher grades lead to favorable student evaluations? *Journal of Economic Education*, *36*(1), 29–42. doi:10.3200/JECE.36.1.29-42

Kadhiravan, S., & Kumar, K. (2012). Enhancing stress coping skills among college students. *Researchers World*, *3*(4), 49.

Kempf, J. (2011). *Recognizing and Managing Stress Coping Strategies for Adolescents* (Doctoral dissertation). University of Wisconsin-Stout.

Kumar, S., & Bhukar, J. (2013). Stress Level and Coping Strategies of College Students. *Journal of Physical Education and Sport Management*, *4*, 5–11.

Kumari, A., & Jain, J. (2014). Examination stress and anxiety: A study of college students. *Global Journal of Multidisciplinary Studies*, *4*(1), 101–108.

Låftman, S. B., & Östberg, V. (2006). The pros and cons of social relations: An analysis of adolescents' health complaints. *Social Science & Medicine*, *63*(3), 611–623. doi:10.1016/j.socscimed.2006.02.005 PMID:16603298

Lal, K. (2014). Academic stress among adolescent in relation to intelligence and demographic factors. *American International Journal of Research in Humanities. Arts and Social Sciences*, *5*(1), 123.

Lazarus, A. A. (1997). *Brief but Comprehensive Psychotherapy: The Multimodal Way*. New York: Springer.

Lazarus, R. S. (1999). *Stress and emotion: A new synthesis*. New York: Springer.

Magwa, S. (2013). Stress and Adolescent Development. *Greener Journal of Educational Research*, *3*(8), 373–380.

Malik, S. (2015). Assessing level and causes of exam stress among university students in Pakistan. *Mediterranean Journal of Social Sciences*, *6*(4), 11–18.

Mapfumo, J. S., Chitsiko, N., & Chireshe, R. (2012). Teaching practice generated stressors and coping mechanisms among student teachers in Zimbabwe. *South African Journal of Education*, *32*(2), 155–166. doi:10.15700aje.v32n2a601

Mclaughlin, C. L. (2009). *Understanding stress: Helping students cope information for educators*. Bethesda, MD: National Association of School Psychologists.

Mohapatra, S., Panigrahi, S. K., & Rath, D. (2012). Examination Stress in Adolescents. *Asian Journal of Paediatric Practice*, *16*(1), 7–9.

Nagle, Y. K., & Sharma, U. (2018). Academic stress and coping mechanism among students: An Indian perspective. *Journal of Child Adolescent Psychology*, *2*(1), 6–8.

Needham, B. L., Crosnoe, R., & Muller, C. (2004). Academic failure in secondary school: The inter-related role of health problems and educational context. *Social Problems*, *51*(4), 569–586. doi:10.1525p.2004.51.4.569 PMID:20354573

O'Donovan, R., Doody, O., & Lyons, R. (2013). The effect of stress on health and its implications for nursing. *British Journal of Nursing (Mark Allen Publishing)*, *22*(16), 969–973. doi:10.12968/bjon.2013.22.16.969 PMID:24037402

Park, C. L., & Adler, N. E. (2003). Coping styles as a predictor of health and well-being across the first year of medical school. *Health Psychology*, *22*(6), 627–631. doi:10.1037/0278-6133.22.6.627 PMID:14640860

Parkes, J., & Stefanou, C. (2010). Does pragmatism trump motivation in college students' preferences for examination formats? *Learning Environments Research*, *13*(3), 225–241. doi:10.100710984-010-9077-4

Parsons, D. (2008). Is there an alternative to exams? Examination stress in engineering courses. *International Journal of Engineering Education*, *24*(6), 1111–1118.

Pisarczyk, K. (2018). *Music and its effect on stress*. Retrieved from http://digitalcommons.augustana.edu/muscstudent/4

Putwain, D. W. (2009). Assessment and examination stress in Key Stage 4. *British Educational Research Journal*, *35*(3), 391–411. doi:10.1080/01411920802044404

Saqib, M., & Rehman, K. U. (2018). Impact of stress on student's academic performance at secondary school level at District Vehari. *International Journal of Learning and Development*, *8*(1), 84–93. doi:10.5296/ijld.v8i1.12063

Segal, J., Smith, M., Segal, R., & Robinson, L. (2017). *Trusted guide to mental, emotional & social health.* Retrieved from: http://www.helpguide.org/articles/healthy-living/how-to-start-exercising-and-stick-to-it.htm

Shahzad, A. H., Rehman, K. U., & Saqib, M. (2018). Does stress impact school students' learning performance? In *6th Asia Pacific Conference on Advanced Research (APCA-2018)*. Melbourne, Australia: Asia Pacific Institute of Advanced Research.

Shankar, N. L., & Park, C. L. (2016). Effects of stress on students' physical and mental health and academic success. *International Journal of School & Educational Psychology*, *4*(1), 5–9. doi:10.1080/21683603.2016.1130532

Shepard, L. A. (2000). The role of assessment in a learning culture. *Educational Researcher*, *29*(7), 4–14. doi:10.3102/0013189X029007004

Siegel, D. (2008). *Mindsight.* Oxford, UK: Oneworld.

Singh, R., Goyal, M., Tiwari, S., Ghildiyal, A., Nattu, S. M., & Das, S. (2012). Effect of examination stress on mood, performance and cortisol levels in medical students. *Indian Journal of Physiology and Pharmacology*, *56*(1), 48–55. PMID:23029964

Spielberger, C. D., & Vagg, P. R. (1995). *Test anxiety. Theory, assessment, and treatment.* Washington, DC: Taylor & Francis.

Sujatha, B., & Subhalakshmi, S. (2016). Effect of stress on exam going first year medical students of Tirunelveli. *International Journal of Medical Research & Health Sciences*, *5*(1), 118–121.

Tiwari, A., & Balani, S. (2013). The Effect of Intervention Program to Reduction Stress. *IOSR Journal of Humanities and Social Science*, *9*, 27–30. doi:10.9790/0837-0942730

Werner, J. (2008). Process-and controller-adaptations determine the physiological effects of cold acclimation. *European Journal of Applied Physiology*, *104*(2), 137–143. doi:10.100700421-007-0608-3 PMID:18026979

Zeidner, M., & Mathews, G. (2005). Evaluation anxiety. In A. J. Elliot & C. S. Dweck (Eds.), *Handbook of Competence and Motivation*. London: Guildford Press.

KEY TERMS AND DEFINITIONS

Anxiety: Can be defined as a normal and frequently healthy feeling of worry, nervousness, or uneasiness about something with an indeterminate consequence. However, when an individual frequently feels inconsistent levels of anxiety, it might develop to a medical disorder. Anxiety disorders form a category of mental health diagnoses that lead to excessive nervousness, fear, apprehension, and worry.

Depression: Is a common but grave mood syndrome which causes severe indications that affect how one feels, thinks, and handles everyday activities, such as eating, sleeping or working. When these symptoms persist for two weeks then that proves that one has depression.

Learning Pattern: Is theorised as a comprehensible whole of learning actions that learners frequently use, what they believe about learning and what motivates them to learn, the entire that is characteristic of them in a certain period. It is a synchronising concept, in which the interrelationships between affective, cognitive and regulative learning activities, beliefs about learning, and learning motivations are unified.

Sleep Disorders: Are variations in the way that one sleeps which affect the overall health, safety, and the quality of life. Sleep disturbances encompass disorders of initiating and maintaining sleep such as DIMS and insomnias, disorders of excessive somnolence the DOES, syndromes of sleep like wake schedule. Sleep disorders affect the learning and attention span of students.

Stress: Is either physical or biological that is an organism's retort to a stressor such as an ecological condition. Stress is the body's technique of responding to a disorder such as a threat, challenge or corporeal and mental barricade.

Teaching Strategies: Are techniques, method or tactics that teachers use to disseminate information which in turn helps students to effectively learn.

Section 7
Bullying

Chapter 11

Homophobic Bullying in South African Schools:
Theory Into Practice Solutions (TIPS)

Johannes Ntshilagane Mampane
University of South Africa, South Africa

ABSTRACT

Homophobic bullying in schools is a global phenomenon. However, on the African continent, the phenomenon is rife because homosexuality is regarded to be un-African and is often linked to Western culture and colonial influence. These misconceptions about homosexuality have resulted in a culture of homophobia being inculcated into major structures of the society including schools. In this regard, this chapter aims to explore and describe the problem of homophobic bullying in South African schools. Particular attention is paid to cases of school-based homophobic bullying as primary sources of data as well as secondary sources of data from extant literature, textbooks, and journals articles. The chapter employs the Epstein Theory of Overlapping Spheres of Influence to proffer practical solutions and recommendations to address the problem of homophobic bullying in South African schools. These are school-, family-, and community-based solutions and recommendations based on the principles of social justice, inclusion, diversity, and equality.

INTRODUCTION

Recently, the South African media has been inundated with media reports on the rising incidents of school-based violence. Bullying is reported as one of these violent incidents in schools. School-based bullying is a widely researched topic in South

DOI: 10.4018/978-1-7998-0319-5.ch011

Africa, however, particular research on homophobic bullying, either in schools or elsewhere, remains dormant. This dearth of research on homophobic bullying on the African continent is mainly attributed to some of the reasons raised by Johnson (2007) which include:

- Denial of the frequency of homosexual behavior in Africa.
- The resistance by African research review panels to approve research on homosexuality.
- A general unwillingness among otherwise rigorous researchers to address issues of same-sex sexuality due to their discomfort with homosexuality.
- The hesitancy of those who are in same-sex relationships to expose themselves to potentially judgmental researchers.
- Homophobic stigmatization faced by researchers themselves when addressing issues of homosexuality.

Homophobia, in simple terms, refers to prejudice, stigmatization, and discrimination of people who are homosexually inclined, particularly gay and lesbian individuals. Peate (2005) describes homophobia as the irrational fear of, hatred against, or disgust towards homosexual people. Nickerson (2016) provides a broader definition of homophobia as:

A pervasive irrational fear of homosexuality. Homophobia includes the fear heterosexuals have of any homosexual feelings within themselves, any overt mannerisms or actions that would suggest homosexuality, and the desire to suppress or stamp out homosexuality. It includes the self-hatred of homosexuals who know what they are but have been taught all of their lives by a heterosexual society that persons like themselves are sick, sinful and criminal. (p. 10)

Bullying on the other hand is defined by the American Psychological Association as a threatening and aggressive behavior directed towards people or individuals who are usually perceived to be smaller or weaker than others (Singh, 2016). Bullying is often characterized by the imbalance of power between perpetrators and victims. For this reason, Rivers (2011) asserts that:

There will always be power relationships in social groups, by virtue of strength or size or ability, force of personality, sheer numbers or recognized hierarchy. Power can be abused; the extent definition of what constitutes abuse will depend upon the social or cultural context, but this is inescapable in examining human behavior. If the abuse is systematic – repeated and deliberate – bullying seems a good name to describe it. (p. 6)

Based on the definitions of homophobia and bullying, homophobic bullying, which is the focus of this chapter, can be defined as conscious, willful, and deliberate hostile behavior that is perpetrated against homosexual people. This kind of behavior is usually influenced by the principles of heterosexism and heteronormativity. Heterosexism refers to an automatic assumption and belief that everyone is and should be heterosexual, and that other sexual orientations are unhealthy, unnatural, and a threat to the society. Heteronormativity on the other hand is an idea, dominant in most societies, that heterosexuality is the only normal sexual orientation, and that only sexual relations between men and women are acceptable (Mampane, 2017).

Based on their sexual orientation and gender non-conformity, homosexual learners are more vulnerable to bullying as compared to their heterosexual counterparts. To corroborate the latter, the United Nations Educational, Scientific and Cultural Organization (UNESCO) (2016) presents following three studies that were conducted in three different countries:

- A study conducted in New Zealand in 2014 discovered that lesbian, gay and bisexual students are three times more likely to be bullied than their heterosexual peers, and that transgender students are five times more likely to be bullied than non-transgender students.
- Data collected in Norway in 2015 found that between 15 per cent and 48 per cent of lesbian, gay and bisexual students reported being bullied, compared to 7 per cent of heterosexual students. The extent to which students experienced bullying depended on their sexual orientation, with 15 per cent of lesbian students, 24 per cent of bisexual male students and 48 per cent of homosexual male students respectively reporting being bullied.
- In a survey in Belgium in 2013, 56 per cent of young homosexual respondents reported at least one experience of homophobic bullying at school, with transgender males and homosexual males experiencing the highest levels of bullying.

Although there is lack of similar studies that have been conducted in South Africa, it is worth noting that the statistics may be higher because homosexuality is highly prohibited on the African continent.

Against this backdrop, this chapter aims to explore and describe the problem of homophobic bullying in South African schools. Particular attention is paid to cases of school-based homophobic bullying as primary sources of data as well as secondary sources of data from extant literature, textbooks and journals articles. The chapter employs the Epstein Theory of Overlapping Spheres of Influence to proffer practical solutions and recommendations to address the problem of homophobic bullying in South African schools. These are school-, family-, and community-based solutions and recommendations based on the principles of social justice, inclusion, diversity, and equality.

Background

Historically, homosexuality on the African continent is surrounded by silence, secrecy, and denial, coupled with prejudice, stigma, and discrimination. Homosexuality is illegal and treated as a criminal offence in 38 out of 54 countries in Africa (LeVasseur, Goldstein, & Welles, 2014). As a result, Altman (1998) argues that African governments have been reluctant to acknowledge that homosexuality exists on the African continent. However, extensive historical and anthropological research has confirmed that homosexuality has long been in existence in Africa (Mampane, 2017). According to Lehne (1995):

Every human society in the world today, from vast industrial nations to the smallest and simplest tribes in remote parts of the world, has some degree of homosexuality... some of these societies accepted homosexuality readily while others severely condemned it, but all human societies have been aware of it because homosexuality has always existed wherever human beings existed. (pp. 327-328)

Hartmann (1998) also contends that "Gays, lesbians and bisexuals are so invisible that at times one may doubt the presence of such individuals at all. But it is generally accepted that between five to ten percent of any given population are homosexually active" (p. 165). Meem, Gibson and Alexander (2010) posit that during much of the twentieth century, psychiatrists throughout the world treated homosexuality as an illness, primarily caused by poor parenting, domineering mothers and/or absent fathers. However, Sigmund Freud (1856-1939), a prominent and renowned Austrian neurologist and psychoanalyst, wrote that:

Homosexuality is assuredly no advantage, but it is nothing to be ashamed of, no vice, no degradation, it cannot be classified as an illness...Many highly respectable individuals of ancient and modern times have been homosexuals, several of the greatest among them (Plato, Michelangelo, Leonardo da Vinci, etc.). It is a great injustice to persecute homosexuality as a crime, and cruelty too. (Meem et al., 2010, p. 52)

In light of the above statement, it is worth noting that in 1973, the American Psychiatric Association declassified homosexuality as a mental disorder from its list of psychiatric disorders. This move was fully supported by the American Psychological Association in 1975 and the American National Association of Social

Workers in 1977 (Mampane, 2017). Consequently, the World Health Organization (WHO) followed suit by also declassifying homosexuality as a mental illness in 1992 (Nel, 2009). The Chinese government did the same in 2001 (Meem et al., 2010). According to Hekma (2006), during the 1960s European countries gradually decriminalized homosexuality. He states that criminal laws that targeted male homosexuals were abolished in many European countries like Britain, Germany, Netherlands, France, and Spain. By the 1990s, same-sex marriages were legalized in countries such as Denmark, Norway, Sweden, and Holland (Richardson & Seidman, 2002). Surprisingly, in 2006, a milestone was reached on the African continent when South Africa became the only country in Africa and the fifth in the world to allow same-sex marriages. It is worth noting that South Africa had already repealed its sodomy laws in the year 1999. Interestingly, South Africa is the first country in the whole world and the only country on the African continent to enshrine the rights of Lesbian, Gay, Bisexual and Transgender (LGBT) people in its Constitution. This is stipulated in Act No. 108 of 1996 Clause 9(3) which states that:

The state may not unfairly discriminate directly or indirectly against anyone on one or more grounds including race, gender, pregnancy, marital status, ethnic or social origin, colour, sexual orientation, age, disability, religion, conscience, belief, culture, language and birth.

Despite these successful milestones for homosexual people in South Africa, it is worth noting that members of the LGBT community in the country still experience high levels of homophobia. According to Hekma (2006), the current liberation and visibility of homosexual people in many societies has triggered an increase in incidents of homophobia being perpetuated against members of the LGBT community. This culture of homophobia has inevitably infiltrated into major structures of the society including schools. In South Africa, incidents of homophobia in schools mainly manifests themselves in the form of homophobic bullying. Homophobic bullying in schools is a global phenomenon. However, on the African continent, the phenomenon is rife because homosexuality is regarded to be un-African and is often linked to western culture and colonial influence. Homophobic bullying in schools is normally perpetrated against learners who are perceived or known to be homosexual. In most cases, victims of homophobic bullying in schools are victimized for not conforming to traditional gender stereotypes and norms of being a heterosexual boy or girl. According to Zinn (1995), "sex roles are rigidly dichotomized with the male conforming to the dominant-aggressive archetype, and the female being the polar opposite – subordinate and passive" (p. 33). In this regard, a boy who resembles a more feminine or effeminate behavior, and a girl who shows more masculine traits, are likely to be perceived to be gay or lesbian and may well become victims of homophobic bullying. The majority of cases of school-based homophobic bullying are usually not reported because victims in many cases fear secondary victimization by school authorities, law enforcement agencies and health care practitioners on grounds of their sexual orientation.

HOMOSEXUAL IDENTITY THEORIES AND MODELS

Human sexuality is a complex phenomenon that is not easily understood. According to Pillard (1996), "the forces shaping human sexual orientation are largely unknown" (p. 115). Over the past century, for example, many sexologists believed that sexual orientation emanated from a biological or genetic basis. For instance, Ellis (as cited in Pillard, 1996, p. 116) argued that "any theory of the etiology of homosexuality which leaves out the hereditary factor cannot be admitted." His opinion was that homosexuality often 'runs in families', meaning that gays and lesbians might have inherited their sexual orientation from either their maternal or paternal relatives. Although some researchers argue that genes probably have an influence on sexual orientation, others contend that the environment is imperative in influencing the sexual orientation of individuals. For example, Fracher and Kimmel (1995) proclaim that sexuality is less a product of biological drives and rather a socialization process which is specific to environmental and cultural experiences and influences. They argue that sexual beings are made and not born, and that people make themselves into sexual beings according to and within their social and cultural being. In addition, they contend that sexuality is socially constructed, and is learned nearly the same way as anything else. This debate on human sexuality has resulted in the initiation of the theory of essentialism *versus* the theory social constructionism coined by scholars of human sexuality. These theories are summarized below.

Theory of Essentialism vs. Theory of Social Constructionism

Essentialism refers to a view that human sexuality can be understood with reference to an inherent essence residing within an individual. According to this perspective, sexual orientation is a fixed phenomenon that is predetermined by genetic, biological or physiological mechanisms and is not subjected to change (Germond & De Gruchy, 1997). This means that a person is either born heterosexual, homosexual or bisexual. Conversely, social constructionism refers to a view that human sexuality can be understood with reference to historical, social, cultural and/or environmental factors. According to this perspective, sexual orientation is influenced by past and/ or present societal norms, experiences and practices where individuals live. In a nutshell, this means that heterosexual, homosexual and bisexual labels are simply 'social constructs' indicating the sexual behavior of people. One of the proponents of the theory of social constructionism, John Gagnon, (as cited in Fracher and Kimmel, 1995, p. 367), contends that:

In any given society, at any given moment, people become sexual in the same way as they become everything else...they pick up directions from their social environment. They acquire and assemble meanings, skills and values from the people around them...People learn when they are quite young a few of the things they are expected to be, and continue slowly to accumulate a belief in who they are and ought to be through the rest of childhood, adolescence, and adulthood.

Table 1. summarizes the differences between the two theories.

In this heterosexually-oriented world, children are raised and socialized to become heterosexual. As a result, those who belong to a non-conforming sexual orientation, particularly that of a homosexual or bisexual nature, struggle to assimilate to the norm. Therefore, researchers have proposed models for describing the process of gay identity formation and development. Although these theories and models are formulated by different researchers and have a different number of stages of identity formation development, Troiden (1988) contends that they exhibit strikingly similar patterns of growth and change within the stages of identity formation development. He points out the following reasons as common elements, characteristics and features that are exhibited by different theories and models:

- Nearly all models view homosexual identity formation as taking place against a backdrop of stigma, and that the stigma surrounding homosexuality affects both the formation and management of homosexual identities.
- Homosexual identities are described as developing over a protracted period and involving a number of 'growth points or changes' that may be ordered into a series of stages.
- Homosexual identity formation involves increasing acceptance of the label 'homosexual' as applied to oneself.

Table 1. Differences between essentialism and social constructionism theories

Essentialism	Social constructionism
Sexual orientation is innate.	Sexual orientation is constructed.
Sexual orientation is fixed or unchangeable.	Sexual orientation is fluid or mutable.
Sexual orientation is not chosen.	Sexual orientation can be chosen.
Sexual orientation is the same universally.	Sexual orientation is different in every culture and society.

- Although 'coming out of the closet' begins when individuals define themselves to themselves as homosexual, individuals typically report an increased desire over time to disclose their homosexual identity to at least some members of an expanding series of audiences. This means that 'coming out of the closet' or homosexual identity disclosure takes place at a number of levels to self, to other homosexual people, to heterosexual friends and family, to colleagues and to the public at large.
- Homosexual people develop 'increasingly personalized and frequent' social contacts with other homosexual people over time.

Although there are other models on homosexual identity theory, the author chooses to discuss the model developed by Cass in 1979 and in 1984 because Troinden (1988) as well as Ritter and Terndrup (2002) argue that it is one of the models that represents current mainstream thinking about homosexual identity formation and development.

The Cass Model of Homosexual Identity Formation and Development

During several years of clinical work with gay and lesbian clients, Australian psychologist Vivienne Cass generated a theoretical model of identity formation that she applied to both men and women of a homosexual orientation. According to Vivienne Cass, "identity is acquired through a developmental process…stability and change in human behavior are dependent within an individual's interpersonal environment" (Terndrup & Ritter, 2002, p. 90). She proposes six stages of development in which homosexuals pass through on the way to fully integrating an identity within an overall self-concept:

Stage 1: Identity Confusion

For people attracted to members of their own sex, the actual process of identity formation begins when they become consciously aware that information regarding homosexuality acquired directly or indirectly somehow applies to them. As they continue to personalize this information, the heterosexual identities they have assumed for themselves and to which they have attempted to conform begin to feel discordant. This incongruency results in emotional tension, often in the form of anxiety, confusion, or both. While experiencing these unpleasant emotions, individuals are privately labelling their thoughts, feelings and fantasies as possibly gay or lesbian. Publicly, however, they are maintaining heterosexual images of themselves which they assume others perceive as well (Ritter & Terndrup, 2002; Troiden, 1988).

Stage 2: Identity Comparison

The second stage of the process occurs when people attracted to members of their own sex can accept the possibility that they might not be heterosexual after all. The ability to admit that they may be gay or lesbian reflects a significant decrease in the confusion they sought to reduce during the first stage of identity formation and marks an initial step toward committing to a gay or lesbian self-image. While feeling less confused about themselves and their experiences, this rising commitment leads them to feel more alienated from others. Accordingly, they develop a sense of not belonging to society at large as well as to specific subgroups such as family and peers. These feelings of alienation may be intensified when individuals are geographically and socially isolated, assume that they are unique in their same-sex attractions, or belong to religious groups which condemn homosexuality. Accepting the possibility of being gay eventually leads many individuals to realize that all the guidelines for behavior, ideals, and expectations for the future that accompany a heterosexual identity are no longer relevant, and most importantly, have not been replaced by others.

The second stage of identity formation can result in several possible outcomes. As with every stage in the process, individuals may foreclose on developing a positive identity. Some people entertain the possibility of bisexuality, whereas others conclude that their same-sex attractions are only temporary or specific to a certain person. Still others complete this phase perceiving themselves as probably gay or lesbian. Of these individuals, some see this probable identity as positive while others see it as negative (Ritter & Terndrup, 2002; Troiden, 1988).

Stage 3: Identity Tolerance

This third stage of the process occurs when people attracted to members of their own sex can admit that they are probably gay or lesbian. Although they only tolerate (rather than fully accept) a gay or lesbian self-image, this greater level of commitment nonetheless alleviates some of the confusion about their identities. The partial relief of their uncertainty enables them to acknowledge their social, emotional and sexual needs. On the other hand, this increased commitment highlights the discrepancy between the way they see themselves and the way they perceive others seeing them. As their feelings of alienation increase, they seek out gay or lesbian individuals and communities in order to reduce their isolation.

More critical for identity formation than establishing contact with other gays and lesbians is the emotional quality of these first encounters. In other words, perceiving these initial experiences as favorable is essential for positive identity development. Many variables, however, may contribute to an individual's negative perceptions of these contacts, for example, poor social skills, shyness, low self-esteem and fear of exposure. When these encounters are perceived as negative, the gay subculture is devalued, contacts with other gays and lesbians are minimized or ceased, and self-esteem is lowered. However, when these experiences are seen as positive, further identification with the gay community is intensified, self-esteem is raised, and ongoing contact with gays is reinforced. According to Cass (1996), "Socialization with homosexuals, at whatever level, allows for the rehearsal of the homosexual role, which then encourages others to identify the individual as a homosexual" (p. 227). Furthermore, socializing with the gay and lesbian community provides people with opportunities to meet potential partners, find positive role models, learn better identity management strategies, practice feeling more comfortable with the subculture, and access ready-made support groups (Ritter & Terndrup, 2002; Troiden, 1988).

Stage 4: Identity Acceptance

The fourth stage of identity formation is characterized by ongoing and additional contacts with other gays and lesbians. These validating and normalizing encounters lead individuals to accept rather than to tolerate a gay or lesbian self-image. As their contacts with others increase in frequency and regularity, individuals discover preferences for same-sex social contexts and start to form friendships within them. The kinds of gay and lesbian community subgroups within which they socialize, however, strongly influence the way they progress through the remaining stages of the process. Whereas some groups espouse attitudes or beliefs that fully legitimize a same-sex orientation, others advocate only a partial legitimization philosophy. Attitudes or beliefs that only partially legitimize homosexuality emphasize fitting in and thus relieve or prevent feelings of incongruency with the heterosexual majority.

A philosophy of full legitimization validates and normalizes the newly formed identities of gay men. Socializing with affirming peers helps them to clarify a more positive self-image and to feel greater security with being gay or lesbian. This affirmation, however, also accentuates the difference between how individuals see themselves (i.e. positively) and how they perceive society as seeing them (i.e. negatively). With newfound friends fully legitimizing their gay identities, prejudiced attitudes toward gays and lesbians become particularly incongruent and offensive. This incongruity of being acceptable in some places and not in others frequently leads them to reject angrily the secrecy and negative status that passing for heterosexual carries with it. The individuals, then, proceed to the fifth stage of identity development in order to resolve these feelings of anger toward a homophobic and heterosexist society (Ritter & Terndrup, 2002; Troiden, 1988).

Stage 5: Identity Pride

Gay and lesbian individuals enter the fifth stage of identity formation with a strong sense of the incongruency between the positive way they have come to accept themselves and society's devaluation of their identities. To manage these discordant feelings, they tend to discriminate between people based on sexual orientation and identification. In other words, they apply strategies that depreciate the significance of heterosexuals and appreciate, if not exaggerate, the importance of other gay men. Thus, they now not only accept but also prefer their new identities to a heterosexual self-image. A strong commitment to the gay community generates feelings of group identity, belonging, and pride. This immersion in the subculture is often characterized by what Cass (1996) refers to as voracious consumption of gay and lesbian media and services. While these dichotomizing strategies relieve internal conflicts for newly identified gays and lesbians, daily encounters with a heterosexist, if not homophobic, outer world generate feelings of anger born out of frustration and alienation. This anger combines with feelings of pride and energizes individuals into becoming activists for the gay and lesbian community. Because this kind of militancy often leads individuals to confront the heterosexual establishment, activists put themselves in positions in which passing strategies are no longer practical. Instead, they adopt disclosure as a coping response.

According to Cass (1996), disclosure has two possible outcomes, depending on its nature and circumstances. First, the more others know about an individual's same-sex orientation, the more that person's gay and lesbian self-image potentially is reflected and reinforced. Second, disclosure allows public and private identities to converge and consolidate into a single self-concept. While disclosure naturally evokes reactions from others, an individual's perception of those responses often determines whether or not identity development proceeds. When derogatory attitudes or behaviors are aroused in others, the person's expectations are confirmed and the 'them versus us' dichotomy is fortified. In these instances, individuals potentially foreclose on their identities, particularly if they are especially fearful of rejection or excessively ashamed. On the other hand, if negative reactions are anticipated and positive responses from others are received, the outcomes are unexpected. This effect often results in gays feeling a sense of discordance or cognitive dissonance. To relieve this inconsistency, some individuals move to the sixth stage of identity formation (Ritter & Terndrup, 2002; Troiden, 1988).

Stage 6: Identity Synthesis

Homosexual people enter this final phase identity with a sense that the formerly adopted 'them versus us' philosophy no longer applies. As this 'heterosexual versus homosexual' dichotomy is relinquished, feelings of anger and pride become less overwhelming. Gays and lesbians now discriminate on the basis of perceived support rather than focusing exclusively on the sexual orientation of another. While greater trust is placed in sensitive and sympathetic heterosexuals, unsupportive heterosexuals are further devalued. Gays and lesbians are now able to acknowledge potential similarities between themselves and heterosexual counterparts, as well as possible differences between themselves and members of their own community. Public and private aspects of self-become synthesized into an integral identity which includes sexual orientation along with many other dimensions. As they feel greater security in their integrated identities, gays and lesbians self-disclose almost automatically. Finally, at peace with themselves, they are free to proceed with the typical developmental tasks of adulthood.

In the process of identity formation, however, Cass (1996) observed individual differences in the rate of progression through the stages, the final stage of development reached, the paths of development taken within each stage, and strategies adopted to cope with the tasks of each stage. Furthermore, she anticipated sex differences resulting from gender role socialization and variances among age groups based on changing social attitudes and assumptions (Ritter & Terndrup, 2002; Troiden, 1988).

The Cass gay identity development and formation model is summarized in Table. 2.

CASE STUDIES OF HOMOPHOBIC BULLYING IN SCHOOLS IN SOUTH AFRICA

The case studies presented in this section were collected during the period when the author was a Researcher based in the Institute for Gender Studies at the University of South Africa.

Types of Homophobic Bullying in Schools in South Africa

Homophobic bullying in South African schools manifests itself mainly as physical, verbal and emotional in nature. Boys are likely to be perpetrators of physical bullying whereas girls are likely to be perpetrators of verbal and emotional bullying (Singh, 2016). However, boys and girls who identify as LGBT fall victim to all these three types of bullying.

Physical Bullying

This type of bullying includes violent activities such as punching, kicking, choking, fighting, stabbing, shoving, poking, hitting and wrestling. According to Singh (2016) girls are more likely to bite, slap, pull hair, scratch, pinch, dig their fingernails into

Table 2. A summary of the Cass gay identity development and formation model

Stages	Description
Stage 1: Identity confusion	Having questions about whether one is gay. If same-sex attraction occurred, explaining it away. Internal conflict about whether one is gay. May have attitudes that being homosexual is incorrect and undesirable, correct but undesirable, or correct and acceptable.
Stage 2: Identity comparison	Accepting possibility that one may be gay. Significant decrease in confusion. Initial commitment to gay self-image. May experience isolation and alienation from others. Developing identity as a gay person rather than straight. Awareness of loss of heterosexual privileges. May still choose to pass as straight.
Stage 3: Identity tolerance	Accepting that one is probably gay. Greater tolerance of being gay. Partial relief because their emotional and relational needs can now be acknowledged. Seeking out gay community and role-models. Getting more support from others. Greater self-esteem.
Stage 4: Identity acceptance	Greater contacts with other gay people. Having more 'normalizing' experiences of homosexuality. Seeing gay community in opposition to straight. Choosing to pass or selectively disclose.
Stage 5: Identity pride	Accepting and preferring being gay. Greater immersion into gay and lesbian subculture. 'Them versus us'. Anger and frustration with homophobic and heterosexist attitudes. Disclosures are more common.
Stage 6: Identity synthesis	Dichotomy of 'them versus us' is let go. Selective contact with allies and supportive heterosexuals. Synthesize public and private aspects of self. Peace with oneself – free to attend to all other aspects of life.

(Source: Smuts, 2009, p. 11)

each other while boys are more likely to punch, choke, kick, throw objects and use dangerous weapons like knives and guns.

Case Study A: Thabo identifies himself as gay. While he was in grade 9 he used to hang-out and play with girls during break times. He avoided hanging-out and playing with other boys because he thought their mannerisms were aggressive in nature. This situation angered a lot of boys in his schools and was assaulted and stabbed with a screwdriver by a group of boys in his school that he ended up in hospital.

Physical bullying in schools in South Africa can also escalate to incidents of sexual violence.

Case Study B: Alex identifies as a lesbian. When she was in high school she was once gang-raped by older boys in school toilets because they wanted to put her in her place as a woman. After that she suffered from post-traumatic stress disorder that she attended counselling sessions on a regular basis. She also had to change schools because she could not face her perpetrators and other school children.

Physical bullying can also be administered by teachers as corporal punishment.

Case Study C: Lerato has an effeminate behavior and identifies himself as gay. His Technology teacher used to hit him with a stick unnecessarily during practical projects because he did not have technical skills like other boys. He tried to explain to his teacher that he is not technically inclined and prefers to be more involved in artistic projects but his plea was not accepted. He ended up failing the subject.

Verbal Bullying

Verbal bullying is one of the common types of homophobic bullying in schools in South Africa. Perpetrators often use derogatory words to belittle, embarrass, humiliate and threaten their victims. The latter includes mocking, name calling, taunting, gossiping, swearing, ridiculing, imitating a lisp or stutter, using sarcasm, spreading rumors and teasing.

Case Study D: Mpho is gay and has a soft voice. Throughout his schools years from primary to high school he has been teased by his classmates for having a voice of a woman. This situation affected him to the point that he ceased to participate in class because he often felt embarrassed by his classmates who laughed at him or imitated him. He was often called a 'trassie' which means a person with both male and female genitals.

Singh (2016) asserts that verbal bullying is also perpetrated by teachers who call learners by undesirable names, use vulgar words or swear, or talk badly about the character of the learner.

Case Study E: Themba identifies as gay. He remembers his schools years as a traumatic ordeal. This is because some of his teachers used to swear at him that he is a devil worshipper and demon possessed because of his sexual orientation. His school mates also used to call him 'sissy boy' because he was part of the gymnastics team at school which was considered a girl's sport.

Emotional Bullying

Emotional bullying is a subtler type of homophobic bullying which is characterized by social ostracism, exclusion, isolation, rejection, shunning and ignoring. It includes non-verbal actions such as continued staring, laughing, rolling of eyes, making faces, using hand signs that imply irreverent and sexual innuendos as well as giving dirty looks and insults or threatening gestures (Singh, 2016). This type of bullying is sometimes referred to as 'invisible' because in many cases the victims suffer privately in silence. According to Singh (2016), girls are more likely than boys to display covert forms of hostility towards others by snubbing or ignoring them or by trying to undermine their relationships or social status.

Case Study F: Tshepo is a lesbian. She is good in soccer and she wanted to participate in the school soccer team but the principal of the school refused by saying that she will be a laughing stock and a disgrace to the school if he allows her as a female to play soccer. Other girls in the school did not want to associate with her because of her masculine mannerisms that makes them uncomfortable. She was always lonely and isolated at school because she could not participate in sport and did not have any friends. She ended up developing an anti-social behavior due to this rejection by peers and teachers.

Case Study G: Vusi identifies as gay. He also had difficult school years. His stationary was always missing due to being stolen by some boys in his class. His belongings were also regularly destroyed by these boys. These boys will often give him dirty looks or laugh at him for no reason. He was diagnosed with depression emanating from this traumatic ordeal and had to change schools to be away from those boys.

The Effects of Homophobic Bullying in schools in South Africa

School learners who are victims of homophobic bullying are susceptible to negative repercussions such as erratic school attendance, truancy, poor academic performance, internalized homophobia, psychological problems, substance abuse and suicide ideation. According to UNESCO (2016):

Homophobic bullying is an unacceptable infringement of basic human rights. In the school setting, homophobia is a direct violation of the right to quality education. It leads to absenteeism, poorer academic performance and achievement, and sometimes to suicide. The right to quality education is not the privilege of a few. It is a universal right. All students – all of them – have the right to quality education in a safe environment. (p. 22)

Homophobic bullying has the following effects on LGBT learners:

The Effect on Educational Progress and Achievement

According to UNESCO (2016), homophobic bullying undermines the educational progress and achievement of LGBT learners. For instance, learners who are victims of homophobic bullying are prone to:

- Disrupted school attendance
- Early drop out from school
- Poor academic performance
- Truancy
- Non-participation in extra-mural educational activities

The Effect on Health and Well-Being

According to UNESCO (2016), homophobic bullying is associated with poor physical and mental health outcomes for LGBT learners. For instance, learners who are victims and survivors of homophobic bullying exhibit the following health problems:

- Loss of appetite for food and loss of weight
- Self-harm
- Increased anxiety
- Stress and depression
- Loss of confidence and low self-esteem
- Suicide ideation

It is worth noting that homophobic bullying does not have negative ramifications only for LGBT learners but also for perpetrators and bystanders. For instance, it is reported that:

We know that exclusion, bullying and violence have immediate, long-term and intergenerational effects. This includes school attendance, performance, and completion…And for those who think that bullying based on sexual orientation and gender identity only affects LGBTI youth. This is wrong. It affects the whole climate of the school and community. (UNESCO, 2016, p. 30)

THE EPSTEIN THEORY OF OVERLAPPING SPHERES OF INFLUENCE

The Epstein theory of overlapping spheres of influence was formulated in the 1990s by Professor Joyce L. Epstein, the Director of the Center on School, Family and Community Partnerships at the Johns Hopkins University, Baltimore, Maryland, United States of America (USA). She identifies the school, family and community as the three spheres of influence that can work together in synergy to bring about change in society. In the education sector, this theory postulates that when these three spheres of influence work in conjunction with each other, there will be a positive outcomes for schools, families and communities (Epstein, 2011). This theory is adopted in this chapter to proffer practical solutions and recommendations to address the problem of homophobic bullying in South African schools. These are school-, family-, and community-based solutions and recommendations based on the principles of social justice, inclusion, diversity, and equality.

SOLUTIONS AND RECOMMENDATIONS

Solutions and recommendations in addressing homophobic bullying in schools are based on the framework of six types of school, family and community partnerships as formulated by Epstein (2011):

- **Offering Parental Support**: Schools as sources of knowledge should assist families and parents of LGBT learners with information on gender and sexual diversity issues in order to create a peaceful and tolerant home environment for learners who identify as LGBT.
- **Open Communication Channels:** There should be open lines of communication between schools and families of LGBT learners regarding learner progress and general wellbeing. Schools should make sure that families of LGBT learners are informed about regular school meetings where teachers and parents of LGBT learners can talk about issues affecting LGBT learners.
- **Encourage Volunteerism:** Involving parents in their children's education has always produced positive outcomes. Parents of LGBT learners should be encouraged to participate in school programs such as extra-mural activities in order to support their children.

- **Foster Learning at Home:** LGBT learners need a positive home environment during out-of-school hours and school holidays in order to their homework and other school projects. In this regard, parents should be able to create a conducive learning environment to their children.
- **Involve Parents in Decision-Making:** Include families as participants in school decisions, governance, and advocacy so that the needs of LGBT learners are not left out to ensure inclusion, diversity and equality.
- **Collaboration with the Community:** Community-based organizations such as LGBT civil society organizations who are at the forefront of LGBT issues should be invited regularly at schools to do outreach and awareness campaigns about gender and sexual diversity issues.

FUTURE RESEARCH DIRECTIONS

The following general directions are made in relation to future research in the field of same-sex sexuality and sexual minorities:

- Researchers should not hesitate to tackle the less explored terrain of homophobia in society due to prejudice and stigma attached to homosexuality.
- African research review panels should not be biased or judgemental in approving research proposals and grants on studies of same-sex sexuality.

CONCLUSION

Homophobic bullying in schools is a worldwide problem. However, many education ministries around the world have turned a blind eye to addressing this problem due to prejudice and stigma attached to homosexuality. This situation has resulted in rising incidents of school-based homophobic bullying in many countries, especially where homosexuality is not accepted. Homophobic bullying in schools has implications for the following milestones:

The Right to Education: Homophobic bullying is a threat to the universal right to education as espoused by Sustainable Development Goals. In South Africa, the National Development Plan Vision 2030 also advocates for the right to education for all people in order for the country to meet its socio-economic development plans. Furthermore, the Constitution of South Africa also states that everyone has the right to education. However, homophobic bullying undermines all three dimensions of a human rights-based approach to education, that is access to education, receiving quality education and respect within the learning environment.

Education for All: Homophobic bullying is a barrier to achieving the Education for All goals related to educational access, retention and achievement. As discussed above, homophobic bullying has a significant impact on school attendance, early school dropout and academic performance and achievement of LGBT learners.

Inclusive Education: Homophobic bullying is a form of discrimination, based on sexual orientation, which is against the global principles of inclusive education. The principles of inclusive education stipulate that all schools should accommodate all learners irrespective of their differences.

REFERENCES

Cass, V. (1996). Sexual orientation identity formation: A western phenomenon. In R. P. Cabaj & T. S. Stein (Eds.), *Textbook of homosexuality and mental health* (pp. 227–251). Arlington, VA: American Psychiatric Association.

Eipstein, J. L. (2011). *School, Family and community partnerships*. Boulder, CO: Westview Press.

Fracher, J., & Kimmel, M. S. (1995). *Hard issues and soft spots: Counseling men about sexuality*. Needham Heights, MA: Allyn & Bacon.

Germond, P., & De Gruchy, S. (Eds.). (1997). *Aliens in the household of God: Homosexuality and Christian faith in South Africa*. Cape Town: David Philip Publishers.

Hartmann, W. (1998). *Homosexuality in Southern Africa*. Windhoek: New Namibia Books.

Hekma, G. (2006). *The gay world: 1980 to present*. New York, NY: Universe Publishing.

Johnson, C. A. (2007). *Off the Map: How HIV/AIDS programming is failing same-sex practising people in Africa*. New York: IGLHRC.

LaVasseur, M., Goldstein, N., & Welles, S. (2014). A public health perspective on HIV/AIDS in Africa: Victories and unmet challenges. *Phatophysiology*, *21*(1), 237–256. PMID:25096828

Lehne, G. K. (1995). *Homophobia among men: supporting and defining the male role*. Needham Heights, MA: Allyn & Bacon.

Mampane, J. N. (2017). *Guidelines for mitigating the risk of HIV-infection among Black men who have sex with men (MSM) in a rural community in South Africa* (Unpublished doctoral dissertation). University of South Africa, Pretoria, South Africa.

Meem, D. T., Gibson, M. A., & Alexander, J. F. (2010). *Finding out: an introduction to LGBT studies*. Thousand Oaks, CA: Sage.

Nel, J. A. (2009). *Same-sex sexuality and health: psychosocial scientific research in South Africa*. Pretoria: HSRC Press.

Nickerson, R. (2016). *Young gay men's experiences of homophobic bullying during adolescence* (Unpublished doctoral dissertation). Alliant International University, San Francisco, CA.

Peate, I. (2005). *Manual of sexually transmitted infections*. London: Whurr Publishers.

Pillard, R. C. (1996). *Homosexuality from a familial and genetic perspective*. Arlington, VA: American Psychiatric Association.

Richardson, D., & Seidman, S. (Eds.). (2002). *Handbook of lesbian and gay studies*. London: Sage.

Rivers, I. (2011). *Homophobic bullying: Research and theoretical perspectives*. Oxford, UK: Oxford University Press. doi:10.1093/acprof:oso/9780195160536.001.0001

Singh, G. D. (2016). *Developing a model to curb bullying in secondary schools in the Uthungulu district of KwaZulu-Natal* (Unpublished doctoral dissertation). University of South Africa, Pretoria, South Africa.

Smuts, L. (2009). *Lesbian identities in South Africa: black and white experiences in Johannesburg* (Unpublished Masters thesis). University of Johannesburg, Auckland Park, South Africa.

Terndrup, A. I., & Ritter, K. (2002). *Handbook of affirmative psychotherapy with lesbians and gay men*. New York, NY: Guildford Press.

Troiden, R. R. (1988). *Gay and lesbian identity: A sociological analysis*. New York, NY: General Hall.

UNESCO. (2016). *Out in the open: Education sector responses to violence based on sexual orientation and gender identity/expression*. Paris: UNESCO.

Zinn, M. B. (1995). *Chicano men and masculinity*. Needham Heights, MA: Allyn & Bacon.

ADDITIONAL READING

Dupper, D. R. (2013). *School bullying: New perspectives on a growing problem.* Oxford: Oxford University Press. doi:10.1093/acprof:oso/9780199859597.001.0001

Harber, C. (2004). *Schooling as violence: How schools harm pupils and societies.* New York, NY: Routledge. doi:10.4324/9780203488423

Rigby, K. (2003). Consequences of bullying in school. *Canadian Journal of Psychiatry*, *48*(9), 583–590. doi:10.1177/070674370304800904 PMID:14631878

Szyndrowski, D. (2005). The impact of domestic violence on adolescent aggression in the schools. *Preventing School Failure*, *44*(1), 9–12. doi:10.1080/10459880009602737

Tabane, R., & Mudau, A. V. (2014). Sexual harassment of female learners in South African schools. *Journal of Sociology and Anthropology*, *5*(1), 37–42. doi:10.108 0/09766634.2014.11885607

KEY TERMS AND DEFINITIONS

Bisexual: A person who is physically and emotionally attracted to both members of the opposite sex as well as members of the same sex.

Gay: Refers to a male homosexual.

Heteronormativity: It is an idea, dominant in most societies, that heterosexuality is the only normal sexual orientation, and that only sexual relations between men and women are normal.

Heterosexism: Refers to an automatic assumption and belief that everyone is and should be heterosexual, and that other sexual orientations are unhealthy, unnatural, and a threat to the society.

Heterosexual: A person who is physically and emotionally attracted to members of the opposite sex.

Homophobia: Refers to prejudice, discrimination and hatred towards homosexual people.

Homosexual: A person who is physically and emotionally attracted to members of the same sex.

Lesbian: Refers to a female homosexual.

LGBT: Is an acronym that stands for Lesbian, Gay, Bisexual and Transgender.

Sexual Orientation: Refers to the concept of whether a person is heterosexually, homosexually or bisexually inclined.

Transgender: A person with a gender identity that differs from their original biological sex, for example, a transgender man (originally a woman at birth) or a transgender woman (originally a man at birth).

Section 8

Support Provision

Chapter 12
Maximizing Students' Learning Success Through Lab-on-Line:
The University of Namibia Experience

Minda M. B. Marshall
LectorSA, South Africa

Simon George Taukeni
University of Namibia, Namibia

Rheinhold Disho Muruti
University of Namibia, Namibia

Gibert Likando
University of Namibia, Namibia

Cynthy Kaliinasho Haihambo
University of Namibia, Namibia

Mathilde Shihako
ⓘ https://orcid.org/0000-0002-9719-0298
University of Namibia, Namibia

Chamelle De Silva
University of Namibia, Namibia

Marshall M.
LectorSA, South Africa

ABSTRACT

This chapter foregrounds the Lab-On-Line project, a technological innovation developed to enhance visual processing skills, improve memory and vocabulary, and increase reading fluency with the explicit aim of improving comprehension. Thirty (30) 3rd year students at one of the University of Namibia campuses participated in the pilot study. A pre-test was conducted for placement purpose. Subsequently, the selected sample commenced with the Lab-On-Line program that consists of 20 lessons that were carried out twice a week over a period of five months. Thereafter a Standardized Reading Evaluation was performed to determine their language proficiency, reading speed per minute and comprehension ability. Results show that the majority of participating students had improved their perceptual development and reading speed (VPF), cognitive development and comprehension skills (CDF), and relative reading efficiency (AIUF).

DOI: 10.4018/978-1-7998-0319-5.ch012

INTRODUCTION

Reading efficacy underscores all academic learning and contributes to the trajectory of a literate identity. A crucial expectation in reading proficiency is that students should learn how to interact critically and creatively with the visual information they have to master in their studies. A successful student is one who gains an extensive knowledge base that affects what they see and how they organize, represent, and interpret the information in their environment. Such knowledge later affects their abilities to remember, to reason, and solve problems. Hence, for experts, knowledge is not merely a list of isolated facts but rather knowledge comes to exist within an extremely organized and contextualized formation. However, researchers revealed that many students enter higher education with limited skills for analytic and critical reading (Boakye & Linden, 2018; Nel, Dreyer & Klopper, 2004; Maree, Fletcher & Sommerville, 2011). As a result, many students grapple to cope with the learning content and its volume. In addition, it is generally observed that students do not participate during class discussions that focus on prescribed reading texts, which can be attributed to lack of understanding.

In order to maximize their academic successes, the students need to be able to 'read-to-learn.' Therefore, reading cannot be separated from language learning and literacy in general (De Silva, 2010). Authors of reading research postulate that reading skills are not hard-wired into the human brain and thus every sub-skill has to be explicitly taught (Noble, Wolmetz, Ochs, Farah & McCandliss, 2006). Students need to be able to read fluently at a gauged speed with good comprehension. Therefore, it is safe to argue that reading fluency is a significant key in learning with good comprehension and should not be underestimated. Dysfluency becomes a barrier as students read less text. The theoretical support for reading fluency as a prerequisite for comprehension is advocated for in the automaticity theory as explained by Samuels, Rasinski and Hiebert (2013). Automaticity has a significant role in reading fluency and is defined as fast, accurate and effortless word identification on a single word level. In referring to automaticity, fluency should also take place within the context of silent reading (Samuels, et al., 2013). In the context of this chapter automaticity theory was adopted to ascertain participants' word reading, speed, and comprehension. The theory helped to measure VPF improvement from level 4 to level 13.

Often, it is assumed that by the time students enter higher education institutions; they have already missed all the windows of opportunity for correct reading and writing skills development. However, the concept of neuroplasticity has changed the way researchers understand reading and comprehension development. Neuroplasticity is defined as the brain's ability to reorganize itself by forming new neural connections throughout life. According to Demarin and Morovic (2014) neuroplasticity depends upon two basic processes, learning, and memory. They further opine that during learning, permanent changes occur in synaptic relationships between neurons. The human brain is constantly making new connections. Connections are reinforced because of focused and continuous use, thus, become stronger. On the other hand, connections that are neglected due to a lack of use become weaker. This then, at a simplistic level, explains why repetition in any form of learning is valuable, irrespective of age. Repetition, as a strategy, can therefore, augment the 'muscle-building' part of the brain; embedded within is a physical basis why repetition strengthens the power of choices and actions. Over time, these actions become automatic (Marshall, 2018).

The question that requires to be answered is how can students be assisted to develop crucial reading, comprehension and writing skills? Academics and leading researchers such as Schmitt, McCallum, Hawkins, Stephenson, and Vicencio, (2018) have explored this much-debated area by employing assistive technology to improve students' reading comprehension. In the similar fashion, researchers such as Masson, Pluchino, and Tornatora, (2016) adopted eye-tracking technology to assess visualization, reading speed, and text interaction. In both these interventions, it was found that participants improved their reading speed and reading comprehension. Therefore, this chapter reports on a project called LAB-on-line, a technological innovation designed to develop and strengthen students' reading comprehension. LAB-on-line is focused on enhancing two factors, namely the visual processing factor (VPF) and the cognitive development factor (CDF). Each of these two factors incorporates measurable sub-elements. The VPF is measured as words per minutes read, while the CDF is measured as a percentage (%) of comprehension against the complexity of content. The combined VPF and CDF lead to an action-interpret-understand (AIU) factor, measured in a grade level of relative efficiency. The CDF is directly dependent on the VPF and it is important to note that students will struggle to be successful in academic reading if there is a deficit in the VPF. Students with a low VPF mostly struggle with automaticity and fluency during silent reading. Visual processing incorporates ocular-motor movements; perception, visual memory, visual accuracy, and interaction between the eye and the brain (Marshall, 2018).

As students work through the 20 lessons embedded in the LAB-on-line course, they develop skills, learn strategies, that helps them to improve their VPF and CDF in order to attain a level of visual processing that enable them to bypass decoding. While reading, novice readers can take up to 80% of their time decoding information. This explains why poor readers spend hours on reading and re-reading, first to decode what they are reading and then trying to extract meaning from text (Marshall, 2018).

If there is no progress or development of skills and actions to automate decoding skills, students struggle to understand what they read. It is posited that working memory can grasp only approximately seven items of distinct bits of information at a time and can hold this information for a mere ten seconds (Delaney & Ericsson,

2016). This is thus the chief reason why readers read slowly and cannot remember most of what they read afterward–they allocate too many resources, also known as 'cognitive load' to the decoding and encoding process. According to the cognitive load theory of Sweller (1988) 'cognitive load' has a bearing on the total amount of mental activity imposed on working memory in any one instant, resulting in a visual processing action, with not enough mental activity to allocate to comprehension.

Within LAB-on-line, the science of neural-wiring is combined with the physics of muscle training to establish muscle memory. This happens through the reading process, namely ocular-motor and whole-brain training, leveraging the plasticity of the brain. Students participating in the LAB-on-line program see more, read faster, and remember better. Since the processing time of orthographical images is shortened it allows the working memory to be focused on understanding what is being read. Now students can start to action higher-order thinking skills, they can focus on convergent and divergent cognitive skills. This chapter is based on the findings of a pilot project aimed to help improve higher education students' reading comprehension.

BACKGROUND

It is expected that every student entering a university should be sufficiently prepared and equipped with the necessary reading skills in order to be successful in all learning activities. To the contrary, the literature reveals that students entering university for further studies have mostly been found to be under-prepared for academic rigor and the demands they may face in further studies (Van Wyk, 2001; Nel, Dreyer, & Klopper, 2004; Maree, Fletcher, & Sommerville, 2011, Marshall, 2016). These can be attributed to poor reading abilities and deficits in critical comprehension skills. How reading is taught has become a much-debated topic in the reading discourse as schools are realizing that many students are not reading at the expected grade levels. One of the most challenging aspects of preparing students for the demands of further studies is the problem of reading (Nel, Dreyer, & Klopper, 2004). This unpreparedness is much more evident within the context of reading, and more specifically academic reading, where students often struggle to complete expected reading assignments, to prepare for classes, prepare for exams and also engage effectively in requisite research projects. Recently, research by Boakye and Linden (2018) found that students' limited reading proficiency negatively affect their academic performance. Additionally, within the African context, and more specifically in Namibia, a further challenge arises–the language of learning is often not the first language of the student as mentioned earlier. This complicates the matter of 'read-to-learn,' and it becomes the first goal to achieve to ensure students are ready for further studies, and eventually becoming lifelong learners.

Reading is seen as an intensive and complex cognitive process involving the decoding of symbols in order to extract meaning from text (Hudson, Pullen, Lane, & Torgesen, 2008). LAB-on-line simulates this complexity to include visual processing, which encapsulates–the eye movement, and perception discerned as the interaction between the eye and the brain. These practices take place in the learning process, within the reading action, inside the eye-brain interaction. In order to understand visual processing, it is necessary to consider the basic skills needed to develop and gain effective reading skills. The human brain is "pre-wired" for spoken language acquisition, but not for written language. Furthermore, most African cultures maintain an oral culture, in which most of the communications happen orally and very little attention is given to the written word. As a result, students come to higher education without a reading culture and have to juggle the complexity of higher education and a new academic sphere in which reading is central. Therefore, the LAB-on-line program accommodates these realities by ensuring that 'accurate wiring' takes place so that the eye-brain interaction is aligned for improved skills and that information is efficiently moved through the brain (Marshall, 2018). LAB-on-line as a technological intervention, have been piloted at various universities in South Africa and it proved to improve students' reading comprehension (Marshal, 2016). Similarly, another technology-based reading intervention was carried out by Fogarty et al. (2017), this study investigated the use of technology at one middle school in the United State of America to determine its impact on students' reading comprehension. Their study found that technological intervention enhanced students' vocabulary, reading comprehension, silent reading efficiency. However, an important question that arises on the promise of technology-based reading interventions such as LAB-on-line is whether it can help students with similar challenges in reading despite their unique backgrounds?

The participants in this pilot study were post-secondary education students at the University of Namibia (UNAM), who come from different environments and backgrounds. Readers have their own cultural and linguistic backgrounds with very specific viewpoints and expectations of learning and education. They live in communities that hold preconceived perceptions, ideas and notions of a particular worldview. Their families subscribe to a particular way of living and have distinct expectations for learning and education. Most of the students come from oral cultures where reading is not a key method of knowledge acquisition. Additionally, the ethos of the institution and the teaching philosophy of lecturers should also be taken into consideration. All these factors engineer a dynamic environment, continually in flux wherein learning takes place. Students have personal past experiences, present skills and a specific developmental level that shape their reading habits. Their lives and thoughts guide their emotions; cultivate their self-esteem, and their motivations and aspirations for being in the classroom and shape the complex persona of the reader in the reading action.

Reading skills within the reading process develop in phases or stages, thus reading skills are never fully perfected. Visual skills and cognition are not an elementary or primary school challenge/ matter, On the contrary, it forms part of lifelong learning skills. It is widely accepted that reading development is not completed at the end of primary school years. Beyond formal school years and further into higher education and corporate levels, there is a need to continually develop visual skills, reading skills, cognitive skills, and strategies in order to unlock the optimum potential of readers. The advancement of critical comprehension skills, the attainment of study skills, an increase in reading speed, and the achievement of flexibility in reading for different purposes is the responsibility of secondary schools. It is at this point, when longer periods of deep reading and independent reading proficiencies are required, that many students begin to fail. Constant re-training and up-skilling to meet the needs of a technological era are the hallmarks of the 21st century and consequently also the fourth Industrial Revolution.

There are two distinct ways of reading, namely; oral and silent reading. Most interventions focus on either the decoding area of reading skills or the language comprehension area. The LAB-on-Line program was developed to sharpen the 'basic' development of reading skills. Oral reading or reading aloud converges every action and interaction. Silent reading fluency is the area of reading that is taught the least, but the efficient ability to read silently is a crucial element for a student's academic performance (Koenig, Du Plessis, & Viljoen, 2015). Within this context, it should be of great value that a reading intervention program addresses students' reading needs in the correct manner. Intervention should concentrate firstly at the tier that is defective or lacking, before focusing on aspects such as comprehension and critical reading, which is layered on top of fluency. Fluency is the ability to read a text quickly and accurately. It remains critical for reading competency, and therefore fundamental in reading success (Rasinski, 2014). In essence, it is the ability to read "automatically" and can be described as a bridge between decoding words (recognizing words for what they are and mean) and understanding what has been read (making the connections between the words to create contextual meaning from a text).

STUDY METHOD

This study used a quantitative descriptive research design as most fitting to meet the objectives of the study. Participants were randomly selected from the list of students doing a Bachelor of Education at the University of Namibia's Rundu Campus. A sample of 30 students whom English was not their tongue took part in the project. All selected respondents were subjected to an English Proficiency Test to determine their levels of proficiency and comprehension. After the test was completed, participants were then officially registered to start the program. LectorSA, the company that runs the Lab-On-Line program then sent the participants login details; usernames and passwords. The Lab-On-Line program consisted of 20 lessons which participants completed over the course of five months from May-August 2018. The program was officially launched on October 15, 2018 at the University of Namibia's Windhoek Main Campus.

THE LAB-ON-LINE PROCESS

The LAB-on-line process considers everything relating to the eyes, the muscles, nerves, and parts of the brain that produce the movements needed for the reading process, as well as the skills needed to be able to become aware and interpret something through the visual senses. LAB-On-Line unlocks students' potential in the following key developmental areas, namely: comprehension, cognitive development, mind activation, memory, perceptual development, and visual processing. It contains 20 lessons that include the following exercises:

1. Eye-Gym
    a. Perceptual Accuracy
    b. Visual Efficiency
    c. Visual Accuracy
    d. Visual Memory
2. Vocabulary development
    a. Improve sight words
    b. Assists a student to develop an understanding of words
    c. Faster decoding skills
3. Silent Reading fluency training area
    a. Develops skills in order to enable the student to read faster and remember more
4. Comprehension skills development
    a. Includes pre-, in-, and post-reading strategy training
5. Downloadable resources
    a. Language development
    b. Comprehension skills and strategy training
    c. Study skills

Perceptual accuracy and visual efficiency is trained through a combination of exercises gauged at the individual's performance on each previous exercise within the Eye-Gym. As students' progress through these exercises, they are being trained to see faster, read better and remember more.

This on-line system initially assists students to work through the process of attention and the working memory in acquiring new information. Information is interpreted with logic and through known information from the long-term memory. The next step is to develop skills and strategies for understanding and comprehension. This is referred to as the cognitive development factor and focuses on improving the cognitive skills through remembering, understanding, applying, analyzing, evaluating, and creating new knowledge. LAB-on-line focuses on the skills and strategies that are required to assist students to arrive at a place of competence in different levels of educational expectations and outcomes. Figure 1 depicts a visual infographic of the process LAB-on-line incorporates in developing visual processing, reading, and cognitive skills.

Figure 1. Visual processing factory

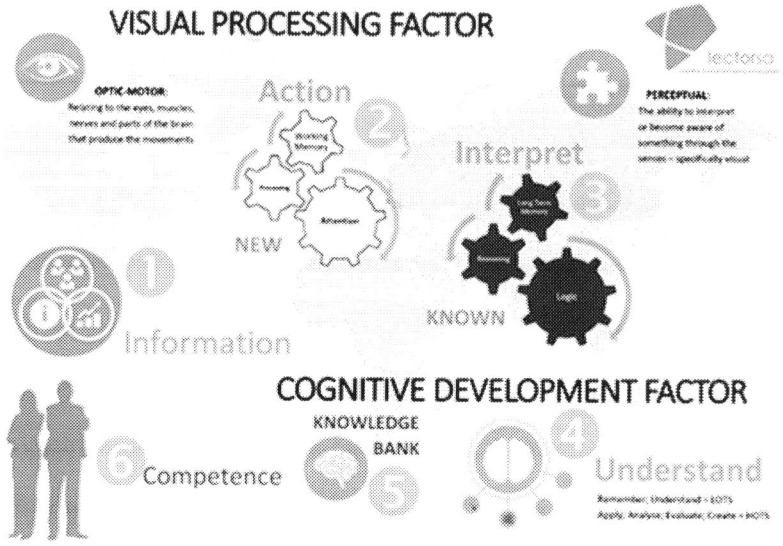

RESULTS AND DISCUSSION

Data generated in this project was sampled from 30 participants. The parameters were set to include data as valid if the participating students have completed at least 15 lessons over the five-month period.

Based upon the criteria, the data in Table 1 reveal that the average improvement was from 117VPF with 60% CDF, which is a relative efficiency or AIUF of Level 1 to 200VPF with 61% CDF, which is a relative efficiency or AIUF of Level 5. This translates to an improvement of 83VPF with 1% CDF, which is a relative improvement of 4 years (AIUF) achieved within the 5-month period that students took part in the project.

In addition, the general research data show that the least improvement achieved in this project was a relative improvement of one year of reading efficiency (from level 1 to level 2 AIUF). While the best improvement achieved was 9 years of relative efficiency (from level 4 to level 13 AIUF).

The results indicate that if a participant's time was extended by a year, the average efficiency would improve exponentially. This is underscored by the fact that the individual scores of some participants have reached 316 VPF and a CDF of 90%, which is a relative improvement of 9 years of reading efficiency (from level 4 to level 13 AIUF). These results collaborate with similar findings in Koenig's et al., (2015) quasi-experimental study that investigated the effect of a reading program on the reading performance of first-year students at a higher institution. Their study involved 120 students who had a low-level reading efficiency upon entry to the institution but improved significantly after being involved in a reading intervention program over a period of time.

Observations in the literature endorse the findings of Maree et al., (2011) who postulate that some students entering further education lack the required level of reading skills. This was evident as observed in the pre-test results of the Lab-on-line study. Therefore, it is important for institutions to provide an enabling environment in which students can improve their visual processing, reading skills, and comprehension

Table 1. Final results lab-on-line project

FINAL RESULTS UNAM STUDENTS: Level 10 – 13 sets				
	VPF	**CDF**	**R.E. Index**	**AIUF**
Lesson 1	117	60%	70	1
Lesson 5	132	50%	66	1
Lesson 10	167	50%	84	2
Lesson 15	200	61%	122	5

outcomes. Creating an equitable enabling environment where each student is given the support and development needed to succeed is an important step towards improving student outcomes and throughput. The lack of such opportunities places some students at risk of dropping out of their studies and not reaching their full potential.

SOLUTIONS AND RECOMMENDATIONS

The findings of this study revealed that, students who participated in this program demonstrated improved reading speed and comprehension with each Lab-online lesson. The more support the participants had in the laboratory, the more they were motivated. It is therefore recommended that, for the Lab-online program to be successful, reliable internet access and hands-on support are key ingredients. Also, incentives for participating students should be built into the program to motivate students. Such incentives will contribute to an increased reading culture and will also help to reduce students' reluctance to participate in web-based learning activities. The incorporation of the LAB-on-line program into the core modules of the university will enhance reading proficiency that leads to improved student results.

FUTURE RESEARCH DIRECTIONS

It will be interesting to, by way of future research, to trace those students who participated in the pilot study to gauge how the program has impacted their studies through improved skills acquired. It will also be important to have the perspective of staff who implemented the program and learn from their experiences prior to the wider implementation of the program at the University of Namibia.

CONCLUSION

How to help a university student who shows a low-level of reading skills?, This chapter addressed the very same question by exploring the results of a LAB-on-line pilot project. LAB-on-line is a technology-enhanced Eye-Brain-Gym aimed at developing students' reading efficiency. This demonstrates clearly that despite it being a concern for a long time, students continue to enter higher education institutions with a low-level reading skill.

The University of Namibia, has multiple entry requirements, one being through 'mature age entry.' Many of these students who gain entry through 'mature age' may have been out of the educational environment for a prolonged period, not using these crucial learning skills. Some students miss the opportunity to develop requisite reading skills at school. Proficiency in reading skills is sustained when such persons are involved in lifelong learning activities (Marshall, 2016). Therefore, it would be prudent, to engage such students in a reading development and intervention program over a period of time. Through this engagement they can improve their reading skills (Koenig et al., 2015) to the desired level. The LAB-on-line pilot project results support this, as most participants' reading level was found to be below that of a university student at the beginning of the project. However, after engaging them in the LAB-on-line program, students were able to improve their visual processing, reading, and cognitive skills from a low to a high level in a short period of time. Therefore, LAB-on-line is one of the systems with proven efficacy to develop students' reading and comprehension skills. Its scaffolder approach to reading development, the built-in student management, and reporting system, make it seamless to monitor students' progress, ensure successful implementation and positive outcomes.

ACKNOWLEDGMENT

This research was approved and supported by the University of Namibia. It was funded by M3line (Research and Development Company, South Africa).

REFERENCES

Boakye, N. A., & Linden, M. M. (2018). Extended strategy-use instruction to improve students' reading proficiency in a content subject. *Reading and Writing*, *9*(1), 1–9. doi:10.4102/rw.v9i1.212

Delaney, P. F., & Ericsson, K. A. (2016). *Long-term working memory and transient storage in reading comprehension: What is the evidence?* Academic Press.

De Silva, C. R. (2010). *The achievement of grade 3 learners' higher order reading skills on a children's literature-based reading programme* (Doctoral dissertation). Cape Peninsula, University of Science and Technology. Retrieved from http://etd.cput.ac.za/handle/20.500.11838/2132

Demarin, V., & Morovic, S. (2014). Neuroplasticity. *Periodicum Biologorum*, *116*(2), 209–211. Retrieved from https://hrcak.srce.hr/126369

Fogarty, M., Clemens, N., Simmons, D., Anderson, L., Davis, J., Smith, A., ... Oslund, E. (2017). Impact of a technology-mediated reading intervention on adolescents' reading comprehension. *Journal of Research on Educational Effectiveness*, *10*(2), 326–353. doi:10.1080/19345747.2016.1227412

Hudson, R. F., Pullen, P. C., Lane, H. B., & Torgesen, J. K. (2008). The Complex Nature of Reading Fluency: A Multidimensional View. *Reading & Writing Quarterly*, *25*(1), 4–32. doi:10.1080/10573560802491208

Koenig, L., Du Plessis, A., & Viljoen, M. (2015). The Effect of a Reading Program on the Reading Performance of First-Year Students at a Higher Education Institution. *International Journal of Educational Sciences*, *10*(2), 297–305. doi:10.1080/0975 1122.2015.11917660

Maree, J., Fletcher, L., & Sommerville, J. (2011). Predicting success among prospective first-year students at the University of Pretoria. *South African Journal of Higher Education*, *25*(6), 1125–1139. Retrieved from https://journals.co.za/content/high/25/6/EJC37734

Marshall, M. (2016). Accurate On-line Intervention Practices for Efficient Improvement of Reading Skills in Africa. *Universal Journal of Educational Research*, *4*(8), 1764–1771. doi:10.13189/ujer.2016.040804

Marshall, M. (2018). *Through the looking glass: Reading skills development from a different perspective.* Retrieved from https://www.linkedin.com/pulse/through-looking-glass-reading-skills-development-from-minda-marshall/

Mason, L., Pluchino, P., & Tornatora, M. C. (2016). Using eye-tracking technology as an indirect instruction tool to improve text and picture processing and learning. *British Journal of Educational Technology*, *47*(6), 1083–1095. doi:10.1111/bjet.12271

Nel, C., Dreyer, C., & Klopper, M. (2004). An analysis of the reading profiles of first-year students at Potchefstroom University : A cross-sectional study and a case study. *South African Journal of Education*, *24*(1), 95–103.

Noble, K. G., Wolmetz, M. E., Ochs, L. G., Farah, M. J., & McCandliss, B. D. (2006). Brain behavior relationships in reading acquisition are modulated by socio-economic factors. *Developmental Science*, *9*(6), 642–654. doi:10.1111/j.1467-7687.2006.00542.x PMID:17059461

Pourhosein Gilakjani, A., & Sabouri, N. B. (2016). How can students improve their reading comprehension skill. *Journal of Studies in Education*, *6*(2), 229–240. doi:10.5296/jse.v6i2.9201

Rasinski, T. (2017). Fluency matters. *International Electronic Journal of Elementary Education, 7*(1), 3–12.

Samuels, S. J., Rasinski, T. V., & Hiebert, E. H. (2011). Eye movements and reading: What teachers need to know. In A. Farstrup & S.J. Samuels (Eds.), What research has to say about reading instruction (4th ed.). Newark, DE: IRA.

Schmitt, A. J., McCallum, E., Hawkins, R. O., Stephenson, E., & Vicencio, K. (2018). The effects of two assistive technologies on reading comprehension accuracy and rate. *Assistive Technology,* 1–11. doi:10.1080/10400435.2018.1431974 PMID:29370581

Sweller, J. (1988). Cognitive load during problem solving: Effects on learning. *Cognitive Science, 12*(2), 257–285. doi:10.120715516709cog1202_4

Taylor, S. E. (2000). Visagraph eye-movement recording system. In Teaching children to read: An evidence-based assessment of the scientific research literature on reading and its implications for reading instructions. Washington, DC: Academic Press.

Van Wyk, A. L. (2001). *The development and implementation of an English language and literature programme for low-proficiency tertiary learners* (Doctoral Thesis). University of the Free State. Retrieved from https://scholar.ufs.ac.za/handle/11660/6337

ADDITIONAL READING

Alvermann, D. E., Unrau, N. J., & Ruddell, R. B. (2013). *Theoretical models and processes of reading* (6th ed.). Newark, DE: International Reading Association. doi:10.1598/0710

Buehl, D. (2011). *Developing readers in the academic disciplines.* Newark, DE: International Reading Association.

Chall, J. S. (1996). *Stages of Reading Development.* Harcourt Brace College Publishers.

Garner Betty, K. (1941). *Getting to "Got it!": helping struggling students learn how to learn.* ASCD.

Meyler, A., Keller, T. A., Cherkasskya, V. L., Gabrielib, J. D. E., & Just, M. A. (2008). *Modifying the brain activation of poor readers during sentence comprehension with extended remedial instruction: A longitudinal study of neuroplasticity.* Elsevier.

Samuels, S. J., & Farstrup, A. E. (2011). *What research has to say about reading instruction* (4th ed.). Newark, DE: International Reading Association. doi:10.1598/0829

Schwartz, S. (1984). *Measuring reading competence: a theoretical-prescriptive approach* (p. 0306417499). New York: Plenum. doi:10.1007/978-1-4899-0387-7

KEY TERMS AND DEFINITIONS

Cognitive Development: Cognitive development is the construction of thought processes. How a person perceives, thinks, and gains an understanding of his or her world through the interaction of genetic and learned factors. Among the areas of cognitive development are information processing, intelligence, reasoning, language development, and memory.

Comprehension: A reader must have a wide range of capacities and abilities to comprehend. This include cognitive capacities (e.g., attention, memory, a critical analytic ability, inferencing, visualization ability), motivation (a purpose for reading, an interest in the content being read, self-efficacy as a reader), and various types of knowledge (vocabulary, domain and topic knowledge, linguistic and discourse knowledge, knowledge of specific comprehension strategies). The process involves simultaneously extracting and constructing meaning through interaction and involvement with text.

Eye Tracking: The eye tracking method is based on the characteristics of eye movements and the "eye-mind" assumption, which suggests that eye movements provide a dynamic trace of where attention is being directed. It is widely agreed that during a complex information processing task such as reading, eye movements and attention are linked. Eye-tracking methods involve information processing, such as reading, seen perception, visual searching, music reading, and typing. Measures of eye movements have revealed the fundamental cognitive processes and mechanisms involved in reading comprehension and visual perception.

Mind Activation: The movement of the eye is important for auditory and visual processing. It is located within the brainstem and between the two other developmental regions of the brain, the forebrain, and the hindbrain. Activation then proceeds from various portions of the brain, but primarily from the reticular formation, the nerve network in the midbrain monitors ingoing and outgoing sensory and motor impulses.

Neural-Wiring: Neural pathways refer to the network of neurons in the brain responsible for visual representation. It activates the visual cortex as the brain views words. Initially, images are stored in the object area of the visual cortex. When the brain encounters a word repeatedly, it builds neural networks for spelling, pronunciation, and the meaning of the word. Neurons function partly on chemistry and partly on electrical impulses. The more often the neurons are activated, the stronger the wiring between neurons.

Perceptual Development: Perception is not a static process but is a dynamic and continually changing based on successive actions and perceptions. For perception to improve, advancing motor skills brings about a more efficient motor activity. The perceptual system recreates the surrounding environment in the brain based on information provided from the senses: vision, hearing, smell, taste, and touch. Therefore, perception provides the experience of the environment and is a means to act according to what is occurring in the environment.

Scaffolded Reading: The role of language in scaffold reading performance is critical because talk is central to learning how to read; it is not an activity that can be learned simply by watching someone else do it. Thus, structuring the task's level of difficulty, jointly participating in problem-solving, focusing the learner's attention to the task, and motivating the learner. The teacher's challenge is transferring responsibility for the task to the learner and therefore hints at the complexity of scaffolding. It is a flexible activity that offers guidance in comprehending, learning, and enjoying literature.

Visual Processing: The visual system is unique as much of visual processing occurs outside the brain within the retina of the eye. The information from the eye is carried by the axons of the retinal ganglion cells to the midbrain. The visual system initiates the processing of external stimuli. It controls eye movements during decision making both by top-down and bottom-up processes; learning significantly influences the speed and accuracy of fixations; decision makers trade-off between fixations and working memory; and fixated information influences decision making more than non-fixated information.

Chapter 13
Guidance and Counselling Through the Teaching of Life Orientation

Nonzukiso Tyilo
University of Fort Hare, South Africa

Jenny Shumba
University of Fort Hare, South Africa

ABSTRACT

The education system in South Africa is exacerbated with challenges that influence the effective teaching and learning in school, for example, discipline, substance abuse, teenage pregnancy, low self-esteem, lack of positive role models, peer pressure, poor study habits, poverty, etc. Guidance and counselling nurture learners to make informed decisions and about life and this deepens learners' self-knowledge, beliefs, interests, etc. Since the dawn of democratic government in South Africa, guidance was phased out in schools and replaced with Life Orientation (LO). LO as a compulsory subject focuses on self in relation to others and society. It addresses skills, knowledge, and values for people to adopt a healthy lifestyle, involved in solving problems and make informed decisions. The teaching LO in schools prepares and empowers learners to become responsible citizens. The chapter aims to help LO teachers to understand the key role of LO in schools, in the midst of the challenges.

DOI: 10.4018/978-1-7998-0319-5.ch013

INTRODUCTION

This chapter aims to explore the role played by Life Orientation (LO) in enhancing guidance and counselling in schools. Learners experience numerous challenges that affect their learning in schools. The challenges include learner discipline, substance abuse, teenage pregnancy, low self-esteem, lack of positive role models, peer pressure, violence, poor study habits, poverty, etc. Despite the prevailing challenges that learners experience in schools, mastery of 21st century skills is of utmost importance. The acquisition of these skills enable learners to become lifelong learners who can cope with demands even beyond school. Through guidance and counselling learners are empowered to live a productive life for them to be able make decisions about life adjustments and careers. However, in South Africa, guidance and counselling services are not available for the majority of learners in schools. Hence, LO as a compulsory subject introduced in South African schools is the only alternative that integrates the elements of guidance and counselling services in schools. The chapter discusses the challenges facing learners in schools, acquisition of 21st century skills, the importance of guidance and counselling services for learners in schools, and teaching of LO in schools. The chapter has some recommendations about guidance and counselling and the teaching of LO in schools.

Chapter Objectives

After you have studied this chapter, you should be able to:

- Identify the challenges affecting the learners in schools.
- Discover how these challenges affect learners in schools.
- Recognize the importance of acquiring 21st century skills.
- Examine the importance of guidance and counselling services for learners in schools.
- Know how the teaching of Life Orientation addresses guidance and counselling.

Background

The South African education system has undergone numerous changes in ensuring that learners in schools receive similar curriculum regardless of their social status. The changes that took place in South Africa started back in 1806 until the country became a democratic country in 1994. From all the education systems, Bantu Education became popular due to the 1976 Soweto uprising where learners protested against Afrikaans as a medium of instruction (Weber, 2008). After 1976, although there were numerous changes made, the inequalities still prevail. When South Africa became a democratic state after 1994, this brought about the introduction of the new curriculum. The aim of this curriculum was to reconcile the divisions in the curriculum as inherited from the previous regime. The new curriculum introduced was Curriculum 2005, and it was stimulated by the country's Constitution (Act 108 of 1996) with the aim to promote democratic values, social justice, and basic human rights; to ensure that the people's quality of life improves. In addition, Curriculum 2005 aims to cater for the majority of South Africans (Department of Basic Education (DoBE), 2011). The Curriculum 2005 encouraged learner-centered classes where new methodologies that promote learner participation and critical thinking are encouraged (Sargeant, 2012).

With the introduction of Curriculum 2005, there were changes made with the subjects. Some subjects were phased out, some integrated while other new subjects were introduced. Guidance is one of the subjects that was phased out due to transformations that took place in South Africa. Guidance was an extra-curricular and non-examinable subject allocated to any person without specialization. This watered down the significance of this subject; some teachers utilized guidance periods for their examinable subjects. This negatively influenced learners in schools as guidance received no attention. In addition, this has deprived learners the opportunities to receive guidance and counselling services to prepare for the outside world. The schools face unsurmountable challenges that could be minimal if such services are available in schools. Even societies inherit the challenges that schools experience, for example, unemployment, job satisfaction, etc.

Although South Africa became a democratic country in 1994, guidance and counselling programmes remain a contentious subject (Maree & Ebersohn, 2002). South Africa, unlike other countries has been without guidance and counselling programmes for the majority of learners particularly in marginalized communities. Only learners from ex-model C schools receive guidance and counselling services. Hence, Veriara (2012) asserts that this difference between the schools in accessing guidance and counselling services is historical, as black schools remain marginalized than their white counterparts due to inequitable resource allocation. This resulted in guidance not gaining its prominence in black schools, resulting in most learners completing high school without having received guidance and counselling services. This affects them when at university, as they do not seek any professional help when experiencing challenges and decide to make irrational decisions. As learners experience challenges, guidance and counselling services empower them to deal with challenges and become responsible citizens. Currently, learners in schools were born during the 21st century, and the acquisition of 21st century skills is necessary for them to cope with the world even beyond school. The essential skills that learners need to acquire include foundational literacies, competencies and character qualities (Bialik & Fadel, 2015). With foundational literacies learners are to apply the essential skills in their everyday life, while with competencies, the focus is on learners' ability to approach multifaceted challenges and with character qualities, the learners should have ways of approaching their changing situations. These skills are essential for learners as they promote lifelong learning and enable learners to cope with the demands of the world of work. This is because learners are allowed to explore ways that make their learning more meaningful in choosing the best ways of learning in fulfilling their goals and needs (Jan, 2017).

When LO was introduced as a compulsory and non-examinable subject in schools its aim was for learners to develop their selves in relation to other people and the society in general (Jacobs, 2011). As stated in World Health Organisation (WHO, 2003), a need for subject like LO was necessary due to the unavailability of life skills programme where learners can be empowered about life and the current changing circumstances. LO aims to address skills, knowledge, and values for people to enable them to adopt healthy lifestyle, as they are involved in solving problems and making decisions about their life. Hence, Magano and Berman (2016) believe that when LO was introduced it aimed at influencing lives of the learners to become balanced and confident to contribute to an unbiased and democratic society for an enriched and equitable life for all. Moreover, LO wishes to raise learners' consciousness of their constitutional rights and responsibilities, tolerate diversity, making informed, ethically sound, and responsible decisions about their physical health, self, career and the society (Magano & Berman, 2016). Through the teaching of LO in schools, there are specific areas that link to guidance and counselling, for example, career and career choices, study skills and development of self.

MAIN FOCUS OF THE CHAPTER

This section examines the core issues of this chapter as mentioned in the introduction. In this section, guidance and counselling services and functions are discussed at length. Furthermore, this section discusses the challenges that learners face in schools and the influence of such challenges to the learners' well-being. The significate of 21st century skills and their acquisition are discussed. Lastly, the chapter examines the teaching of LO in the midst of all what learners go through in schools.

Guidance and Counselling

Guidance and counselling is a process where people receive help in order to develop self-awareness when it comes to the environmental influences (Egenti, 2012). In a way, through guidance and counselling people can develop appropriate ways of behaving and develop acceptable societal norms and values. Through guidance and counselling services, learners are empowered with solving problems and making decisions. The literature suggests that counselling is more involved and it focusses on the person's mental state as it involves emotions, feelings and attitudes of individual learners (Oviogbodu, 2015). Unlike guidance that is more of a preventive drive in preparing learners for what to do, counselling is more personal because of the personal interaction that occurs between the client (learner) and a counsellor. This means that counselling is a one-on-one interaction between two or more people based on the particular problem. Trust in such interactions is key as it serves as a glue that joins the counsellor and counselee for easy sharing of information (Oviogbodu, 2015). Guidance and counselling services are crucial for learners in schools to encourage their understanding of themselves and their interactions with the immediate environment. This is a transformative process because learners can strike the balance between what they have learned in school and outside school. Counselling is a specialized field that requires people to have psychological knowledge because it focusses on the learners' personal problems. Counselling encourages personality inspection where at some point intelligence tests administered aim to identify the learners' problems that affect learning.

Learners experience numerous challenges that affect their learning. The transition from childhood to adolescence is one of the major challenges affecting learners in schools (De Witt, 2016). Learners often have trouble in navigating their paths when faced with such challenges. That is why at times learners often succumb to negative peer pressure that often leads to making irrational decision and commit crime (Ramakrishnan & Jalajakumari, 2013). Families and schools should play a significant role to help learners grow and become self-fulfilled and adjusted individuals when they are adults. In schools, guidance and counselling acceded to this call; hence, it has adopted an important role in shaping the learners for the future and in dealing with the negative peer influences. As learners spend most of the time at school, school has a role to play in nurturing and guiding the learners (Subasinghe, 2016). Hence, Egbo (2013) is of the view that for learners to develop, the environment needs to be conducive for teaching and learning to take place. Schools therefore are centres where the guidance and counselling services are available for the majority of learners to be the recipients of guidance and counselling services.

Guidance and counselling services are important for learners as learners get guidance on solving their problems that are study related. Guidance and counselling enable learners to solve their problems, make decisions and have an increased educational competence. In guidance and counselling services, for guidance learners receive knowledge of what they should do. Guidance targets learners and enable them to identify future personality development processes. While, with counselling, the counsellor needs a specialized knowledge as learners present with problems that need a trained practitioner with a psychological knowledge. Guidance services are precautionary developmental services aimed at supporting learners, while counselling services are more specific as they are more supportive services that provide curative endeavors for those in need (Lai-Yeung, 2014). The counsellor should be the person that the learners are free to talk to, but respected and trusted by the learners. The problems that require counselling services are individualized rather than generic; hence, the client-counsellor relationship needs to be established and maintained for learner's well-being (Martin, 2018). Counselling service is the core element of guidance programme because learners get help in order to achieve self-understanding and adjust in certain contexts.

The Aims of Guidance and Counselling

Guidance and counselling services in schools has aims that it purport to achieve for the betterment of learners. As stated in Heyden (2011), guidance and counselling services in schools aim to:

- Help learners to accomplish their basic physiological needs, self-awareness, and become self- actualized,
- Develop peer relations and maintain balance between school and personal life,
- Encourage learners to become autonomous,
- Provide prominence and strength to educational programs,
- Develop the cognitive ability of learners in order to synchronize their abilities, interests and values,
- Provide learners with relevant information about careers and necessary course requirements, and help them choose feasible careers
- Harness the genuine self-concept with academic competences,
- Minimize the rate of learners' drop out.

The Importance of Guidance and Counselling

The challenges that learners in schools are facing necessitated the importance of guidance and counselling services for learners in schools. In addition, the demands of the world of work are dynamic because of fourth industrial revolution, guidance and counselling services should be addressing such for learners to be prepared when they are out of school. The transition from school to work continues to be difficult for learners, hence, guidance and counselling services ensure that there is smooth transition and learners are well prepared of how to face the world of work (Fuster, 2002). In addition, Fuster (2002) recommends that counselling should expedite changes in behaviour, increasing skills for coping, decision-making and maintaining relationships with other people. Nowadays, learners are overwhelmed with problems and without proper guidance; they continue to struggle with making some adjustments in their life and end-up engaging in anti-social activities. Although they are still young, delicate, flammable with guidance and counselling services there is hope for them.

Guidance and counselling nurture learners to become responsible in making informed decisions and about life even beyond school. This is because through guidance learners get help to make appropriate choices, life adjustments and ability to solve problems. When making choices about careers there numerous factors that they should consider, for example, their strengths and weaknesses, personality, subject combination, hence, guidance is necessary. Through guidance and counselling, learners become aware of themselves, their attitudes, beliefs, interests, etc. Hence, guidance and counselling believes in the promotion of learner's holistic development that focuses on child's psychosocial, cognitive, emotional, and physical development (De Witt, 2016). In addition, guidance and counselling services help learners to acquire 21st century skills to prepare them for the world of work.

21st Century Skills

As stated by Saavedra and Opfer (2012), 21st century skills are the fundamental abilities that the learners receive from schools in order to succeed in today's world. The fundamental competencies include collaboration, digital literacy, problem solving, decision-making, critical thinking, etc. The 21st century skills are the skills that learners have to acquire to devise ways of approaching changing situations. These skills are essential for learners as they promote lifelong learning and enable learners to cope with the demands of the world of work. Some suggestions are made for curriculum developer to integrate the 21st century skills in the curriculum ensure that learners get prepared for life. Kayange and Msiska (2016) suggest that the curriculum should incorporate life and career skills, innovative skills, integration of global awareness and digital skills for learners to cope with competencies of 21st century skills. The skills mentioned above promote learner's self-awareness and independence, as learners have to be themselves. Guidance and counselling services are to ensure that learners acquire such important skills during their school years to be better prepared when they join the working force. Such skills can serve as a foundation for guidance services for learners to be able gain insight of the strengths and weaknesses in terms of the careers to choose. Despite the 21st century skills that learners should possess, learners in schools face numerous challenges.

Challenges Facing Learners in Schools

There are numerous challenges that learners face in schools and as such, the challenges affect teachers, schools and effective teaching and learning in schools. Nowadays, the prevailing challenges include, learner discipline, substance abuse, teenage pregnancy, low self -esteem, lack of positive role models, peer pressure, poor study habits, poverty, violence, etc. (van der Merwe, Dawes & Ward, 2012; van der Merwe, 2015; Makota & Leoschut, 2016). The discipline problem in school is getting worse and the level of bullying is rife in schools. This brings about conflicting views, as others still believe that the situation gets worse in schools because of the abolishment of corporal punishment. In addition, drug abuse is another challenge that makes learners not to focus at school. In some province, learners younger than 20 years are rehabilitated for abusing drugs (Engelbrecht, 2017). This indicates the magnitude of the problem among the school going age children. This situation affects their learning as their physical and mental health decline (DoBE, 2013). Now, there is no definite solution to this, some schools have embarked on drug testing to detect those using drugs. However, this can be seen as stigmatizing and discriminating the learners should they test positive. Guidance and counselling services in school can prepare learners to become responsible and make informed decisions about their learning and life in general. The guidance and counselling services should ensure that learners are protected from using drugs by having empowering programmes for all learners in schools. In addition, the school counsellor can assist the learners who might have started with drugs. South African Schools Act 84 of 1996 concedes that schools should have random search for drugs searching as it can bring about positive results when appropriately done within the guidelines as stipulated in the Act. Hence, with DoBE (2013), drug testing in school should be the last option after having exhausted other avenues.

Risky sexual behaviours are a challenge for adolescents. There has been an increased number of young people engaging in risky sexual behaviors particularly those still at school (Ugoji, 2014). The inter-generational sex is a problem and this increases the vulnerability to HIV transmission, as they cannot communicate safe sex with the partners (Kuo & Oparario, 2011). In South Africa, there is evidence that either their peers or teachers sexually harass some learners in schools (Graham, 2016; Owusu, Colecraft, Aryeetey, Vaccaro, & Huffman, 2016). This subjects learners to failure as they become depressed, not able to focus on their academic work, absent them from school, etc. (Meinck, Cluver, Boyes, Loening-Voysey (2016). The challenges have an influence on the learners themselves and on the teachers in schools. Through guidance and counselling learners can be empowered to deal with the identified challenges and have mechanisms of eliminating the impact that such challenges may have on their academic endeavors. However, majority of South African schools do not have guidance and counselling services. Hence, Life Orientation is the subject offered in South Africa since the dawn of democracy.

Life Orientation Teaching in Schools

Life Orientation (LO) in schools is a compulsory and non-examinable subject introduced to focus on self in relation to others and society (Department of Education, 2002). Life Orientation in schools is the subject offered at Senior and Further Education and Training (FET) phases. From the Foundation and Intermediate phases, Life skills is the subject offered for all the learners in schools. Life Orientation aims to address skills, knowledge, and values for people to enable them to adopt healthy lifestyle as they are involved in solving problems and making decisions about their life. Life Orientation also encourages learners to become balanced and confident and be able to contribute to an unbiased and democratic society for an enriched and equitable life for all (Department of Education, 2003). LO wishes to raise learners' consciousness of their constitutional rights and responsibilities, tolerate diversity, making informed, ethically sound, and responsible decisions about their physical health, self, career and the society. Hence, Manzini (2012) argues that through the teaching of LO learners are empowered on the issues including body image, decisiveness, confidence and knowledge about self. The teaching of LO in schools aims to prepares learners to become responsible citizens through social interaction. In addition, learners are prepared for career choices through LO. In a way, the teaching of LO in schools attempts to address the aspects of guidance and counselling that is not available for all the learners in schools. LO, is better placed and teachers teaching LO should have psychological background. This is because by its nature, LO encompasses that are important for one's development and how to maintain relationships with other people. However, there are noticeable challenges about the teaching of LO.

Although LO was introduced in schools during the dawn of democracy, it has not managed to fully change the learners' behaviours in South African schools (Jonck & Swanepoel, 2015). The challenges that schools, young people and communities had still prevail despite the teaching of LO in schools. Although LO seems to be an important subject in the school curriculum as it focuses more on skills, attitudes and values other than knowledge, researchers believe that the desired outcomes are still not achieved (Diale, Pillay, & Fritz, 2014). The challenges that learners have in schools are rifer than before despite that LO is intended to empower learners in becoming responsible citizens. The literature suggests that the challenges of LO are due to teachers who are not specialized in teaching LO and that teachers are not prepared and supported for the prevailing challenges facing schools nowadays (Diale et al., 2014). In addition, Price-Mitchell (2014) is also of the view that the absence of positive role models for young people can challenge them.

SOLUTIONS AND RECOMMENDATIONS

Challenges in the implementation of LO in schools presented above calls for re-energizing teacher education to capacitate more teachers in the teaching of the subject. More thrust given to both pre-service and in-service teacher education to capacitate all teachers in training with skills in teaching LO. Since LO is not examinable, teachers, parents and learners tend to give it less attention, hence the need for change of attitude for all stakeholders is essential.

FUTURE RESEARCH DIRECTIONS

Life Orientation serves as a tool for offering life skills to learners in Secondary Schools to equip them with the necessary skills to survive the challenges they encounter in life. However, there seem to constraints, as there is perpetuation of unruly behaviour by those who have gone through the system. Society still experiences shocking incidences of violence in schools despite there being LO in schools. With this in mind, it would be prudent for future research to focus on the causes of violence and other social ills and how LO should be tailored to be responsive to the societal needs.

CONCLUSION

The chapter discussed the challenges affecting the learners in schools, the importance of acquiring 21st century skills. In addition, the chapter outlined the importance of guidance and counselling services for learners in schools. The teaching of Life Orientation in addressing guidance and counselling issues in school was the focus of this chapter. The chapter concludes that despite the efforts made to use LO as a tool for guidance and counselling in schools, the challenges are there in its implementation in terms of attitude and lack of knowledge. The subject is not examined hence it attracts little effort from the stakeholders.

REFERENCES

Bialik, M., & Fadel, C. (2015). *Skills for the 21st Century: What Should Students Learn?* Retrieved August 2, 2019, from https://curriculumredesign.org/wp-content/uploads/CCR-Skills_FINAL_June2015.pdf

De Witt, M. W. (2016). *The young child in context: A psychosocial perspective* (2nd ed.). Van Schaik Publishers.

Department of Basic Education. (2011). *Revised National Curriculum Statement.* Pretoria: Government Printer.

Department of Basic Education. (2013). *HIV and AIDS Life Skills Education Programme.* Pretoria: Government Printer.

Department of Education (DoE). (2002). Revised National Curriculum Statement Grades R–9 (schools): Life Orientation. Pretoria, South Africa: DoE.

Department of Education (DoE). (2003). National Curriculum Statement Life Orientation Grades 10-12. DoE.

Diale, B., Pillay, J., & Fritz, E. (2014). Dynamics in the personal and professional development of Life Orientation teachers in South Africa, Gauteng Province. *Journal of Social Sciences, 38*(1), 83–93. doi:10.1080/09718923.2014.11893239

Egbo, A. C. (2013). *Development of Guidance and counselling.* Enugu: Joe Best Publishers.

Egenti, N. T. (2016). The role of Guidance and Counselling in effective teaching and learning in schools. *International Journal of Multidisciplinary Studies, 1*(2), 36–48.

Engelbrecht, R. (2017). *SA drug abuse trends paint a grim picture.* Retrieved August 2, 2019, from https://boksburgadvertiser.co.za/297238/sa-drug-abuse-trends-paint-grim-picture/

Fuster, J. (2002). Frontal Lobe and Cognitive Development. *Journal of Neurocytology, 31*(3/5), 373–385. doi:10.1023/A:1024190429920 PMID:12815254

Graham, S. (2016). Victims of bullying in schools. *Theory into Practice, 55*(2), 136–144. doi:10.1080/00405841.2016.1148988

Heyden, S. M. (2011). *Counselling children and adolescents.* Belmont, CA: Brooks / Cole.

Jacobs, A. (2011). Life Orientation as experience by learners: A qualitative study in North-West Province. *South African Journal of Education, EASA, 31*(1), 212–223. doi:10.15700aje.v31n2a481

Jan, H. (2017). Teacher of 21st Century: Characteristics and Development. *Research on Humanities and Social Sciences, 7*(9), 50–54.

Jonck, P., & Swanepoel, E. (2015). Exploring the perceived role of life orientation teachers with reference to career guidance provided to Grade 10 learners in the Free State, South Africa. *International Journal of Humanities Social Sciences and Education, 2*(5), 229–239.

Kayange, J. J., & Msiska, M. (2016). Teacher education in China: Training teachers for the 21st century. *The Online Journal of New Horizons in Education, 6*(4), 204–210.

Kuo, C., & Oparario, D. (2011). Health of adults caring for orphaned children in an HIV endemic community in South Africa. *AIDS Care, 23*(9), 1128–1135. doi:10.1080/09540121.2011.554527 PMID:21480009

Lai-Yeung, S. W. C. (2014). The need for guidance and counselling training for teachers. *Procedia: Social and Behavioral Sciences, 113*, 36–43. doi:10.1016/j.sbspro.2014.01.008

Magano, M. D., & Berman, A. (2016). Born frees' negotiating the terrain towards selfhood and wellness: A Life Orientation perspective. *Education as Change, 20*(2), 106–122.

Makota, G., & Leoschut, L. (2016). The National School Safety Framework: A framework for preventing violence in South African schools. *African Safety Promotion, 14*(2), 18–23.

Manzini, C. K. S. (2012). *An appreciative enquiry into the Life Orientation program offered in high schools* (Unpublished Master dissertation) University of KwaZulu-Natal.

Maree, J. G., & Eberson, L. (Eds.). (2002). *Life skills and career counselling*. Cape Town: Clysons.

Martin, A. (2018). *The relationship between the counsellor and the client.* Retrieved August 2, 2019, from http://www.thecounsellorsguide.co.uk/relationship-between-counsellor-client.html

Oviogbodu, C. O. (2015). *Perceived impact of guidance and counselling in the development of Niger Delta Region. Paper present at Niger Delta University conference with the theme: education and sustainable development in the Niger Delta region of Nigeria*, Niger Delta University.

Owusu, J. S., Colecraft, E. K., Aryeetey, R. N., Vaccaro, J. A., & Huffman, F. G. (2016). Comparison of two school feeding programmes in Ghana, West Africa. *International Journal of Child Health and Nutrition, 5*(2), 56–62. doi:10.6000/1929-4247.2016.05.02.2

Price-Mitchell, M. (2014). *How role models influence youth strategies for success.* Retrieved August 2, 2019, from https://www.rootsofaction.com/role-models-youth-strategies-success/

Ramakrishnan, V. K., & Jalajakumari, V. T. (2013). Significance of imparting guidance and counselling programmes for adolescent students. *Asia Pacific Journal of Research, 2*(9), 102–112.

Saavedra, A. R., & Opfer, D. P. (2012). Learning 21st -century skills requires 21st century teaching. *Phi Delta Kappan, 94*(2), 8–13. doi:10.1177/003172171209400203

Sargeant, J. (2012). Prioritising learner voice: 'Tween children's perspectives on school success. *International Journal of Primary. Elementary and Early Years Education, 42*(2), 190–200.

South African Schools Act 84 of 1996. (1996) No. 1867.

Subasinghe, W. (2016). An Introduction on Educational Guidance and school Counselling. *International Journal of Scientific Research and Innovative Technology, 3*(10).

Ugoji, F. N. (2014). Determinants of Risky Sexual Behaviours among Secondary School Students in Delta State Nigeria. *International Journal of Adolescence and Youth, 19*(3), 408–418. doi:10.1080/02673843.2012.751040

Van der Merwe, A., Dawes, A., & Ward, C. L. (2012). The development of youth violence: An ecological understanding. In C. L. Ward, A. van der Merwe, & A. Dawes (Eds.), *Youth violence: Sources and solutions in South Africa* (pp. 53–92). Cape Town, South Africa: UCT Press.

Van der Merwe, M. (2015). Knife's edge: How dangerous are South African schools? *Daily Maverick.* Retrieved August 2, 2019, from https://www.dailymaverick.co.za/article/2019-04-06-knifes-edge-how-dangerous-are-south-africas-schools/#.WS0bAut96G4

Veriava, F. (2012). *Rich school, poor school - the great divide persists*. Retrieved August 2, 2019, from https://mg.co.za/article/2012-09-28-00-rich-school-poor-school-the-great-divide-persists

Weber, E. (2008). *Educational Change in South Africa: Reflections of local realities, practices and reforms*. Rotterdam, The Netherlands: Sense Publishers.

World Health Organization. (2003). *Skills for health*. Information series on school health. Document. Geneva: WHO. Retrieved August 2, 2019, from http://www. unicef.org/lifeskills/files/SkillsForHealth230503

ADDITIONAL READING

Dovey, K. (1983). Guidance and Counselling Services in the Republic of South Africa. *The Personnel and Guidance Journal, 61*(8), 2164–4918. doi:10.1111/j.2164-4918.1983.tb00071.x

Jonck, P. (2015). Learner suggestions on improving the subject "life Orientation" with Specific Reference to Career Guidance: A South African case study. *Mediterranean Journal of Social Sciences, 6*(1), 11–19.

Lamb, S., & Snodgrass, L. (2017). A Nonviolent Pedagogical Approach for Life Orientation Teacher Development: The Alternatives to Violence Project. *Educational Research for Social Change, 5*(2), 1–15. doi:10.17159/2221-4070/2017/v6i2a1

Lothar, R. M. (1993). Guidance and counselling in various societies: Structures and developments, problems and solutions. *International Journal for the Advancement of Counseling, 16*(3), 245–264. doi:10.1007/BF01407849

Pillay, J. (2012). Keystone Life Orientation (LO) teachers: Implications for educational, social, and cultural contexts. *South African Journal of Education, 32*(2), 167–177. doi:10.15700aje.v32n2a497

KEY TERMS AND DEFINITIONS

21st Century Skills: Fundamental abilities that empower one to succeed in today's world.

Career Education: The occupational preparation for a particular career that does not only focus on the specialized subjects but more on tools, skills and practical training for one to succeed in a chosen occupation.

Curriculum: A plan used for learning the content in achieving learning outcomes and purpose of an educational programme with planned activities/learning experience in a school.

Decision-Making: An action taken to make essential resolutions.

Democracy: The government elected by the majority of the people.

Guidance and Counselling: A process of helping people to ascertain and improve their well-being, scholastic and occupational competencies to become self-actualized people.

Life-Long Learner: A person with an ongoing self-driven quest of knowledge for both personal and professional gains.

Problem Solving: A premeditated and logical way of identifying and resolving a problem.

Psychological Well-Being: Constructive interactions with others and being autonomous with a purpose and meaning in life.

Responsible Citizen: A change agent who knows the role to play in their communities, their country, and their world.

Self-Awareness: One's ability to know his/her personality including the strengths and weaknesses.

Study Skills: Discrete strategies used when learning that are applicable in most fields of study.

Transformation: A state of complete change that brings about improvement in something or someone.

Chapter 14
Counselling Pupils for Social Justice

Noxolo Mafu
Vaal University of Technology, South Africa

ABSTRACT

Along the dynamic freedoms of democracies of the 21st century, counselling pupils for social justice is a radical democratic process of learning. This is within awareness of metacognitive application of critical thinking that transforms prior obtained frame of reference. It also ignites, without imposing, critical self-reflection as a deliberate cognitive activity on experiences that bring about perspective transformation. Ironically, that school counselling continues to be less regarded as a management role in schools is a misconstrued perspective that not only disadvantages the pupil but also alienates counsellors while also deflating effectiveness of teaching efforts. The teaching and learning process is a collaborative effort that can only succeed when existing school's networks are utilised in the most effective manner especially for a transformative and democratic education. This chapter explores avenues of school counselling along post-constructivist perspectives determining a democratic pupil as sought to be a change catalyst for good citizenship in the society.

INTRODUCTION

This chapter explores the challenges faced by mainly counsellors of the 21st century's pupils and why it has become insurmountable to improve counselling strategies for learner access, retention and success. Many pupils who start school encounter various challenges from diversity, under-resourcefulness or differences at school. Some out before finishing either primary or high school. Research tends to in the

DOI: 10.4018/978-1-7998-0319-5.ch014

teaching and learning. The role of counselling before and after admission of the pupil into school often overlooked. This chapter explores the poor implementation of schools' counselling in the available publications used for school counsellors to impact pupils' lives for achievement at school.

A school is a field to play crucial roles in developing human capital that effects individual's participation and livelihood within societal economic growth and development (Baker & Gerler, 2004; Gysbers, 2004; Herr, 2002; Paisely & Borders, 1995). Thus, a school itself is a system with sub-units with actors connected by an organisational social network for designated goals. The actors, regardless of their own identities have the mandated to carry the agenda on human capital development. The success of the pupils can significantly be attained if only schools have effective access and retention management of the pupils as well as appropriate teaching staff. As for counsellors along teaching and learning, that's the role often overlooked, yet a crucial. Therefore, counselling at school is yet to be reckoned as a crucial tool that engrains social justice across pupils to capacitate them with tools to overpower the pressure to learn, fit in with peers, discipline and morality. This raises an inquisitive mind as to: does school counselling form part of the school's management ascertaining its role in transformative and effective teaching and learning experience for access, retention and success?

As much as the common values in schools, such as access, retention and success are positive and appealing, however, there is a need to review the application of such, along social justice agenda. Increasing diversity across schools implies that transformative teaching capacity, transformative learning, educational assurance and accountability processes, equity have become crucial issues for access, retention and success of, underpriviledged groups. Contextualisation of teaching and learning experience is the basis for effective success, yet a complex endeavour with multi-dimensions requiring collaborative efforts by relevant school's actors.

The discussion of this chapter is guided by inquisitive questions as to: how are the school's existing organisational networks linked to the promotion of social justice counselling for transformative learning and success? The chapter attempts to explain the links between the structure of information and the performance of a school's agents in ensuring effective teaching and learning success. Thus, it also describes how the network theory analysis can be used to clarify the networks in the school that mediate effectiveness for success. The discussion concludes by sharing some research based strategies that can be implemented to improve implementation of social justice counselling.

Along the use of NTA, there's extensive and exponentially an increasing body of literature on networks in studies of organisations (Ahuja, 2000; Bailie, 2006; Borgatti & Foster, 2003; Brass et al, 2004; Merrill, 2006, Merrill et al., 2007, Sleky & Parker, 2005) and while the focus is commended for examining effectively how managing information and improving performance in organisational systems (Kilduff, 2003; Chang & Harrison, 2004; Brass et al, 2000; Zach, 2000; Krebs, 2011b; Cross et al., 2002; Cross & Thomas, 2009; Cross & Parker, 2004; Burton et al, 2010) that provides useful insights to understanding change structures and processes, in education. However, there's lack of literature where the approach is used to study schools' (as agencies') internal institutional structure. Therefore, in this chapter the role of counsellors as actors in teaching and learning is highlighted as active participation and form of collaborative partnerships with teachers for attaining the schools' goals.

POWER AND BEHAVIOUR IN EDUCATION

Within the global contexts of considering education as a vital tool in developing human capital for livelihood and economic growth and development; countries undergo a series of changes to remain relevant in the global economy (CHE, 2016; Thompson, 1990; Ndebele et al, 2005; Powell, 2002). Dynamic increase of pupils' diversity in learning abilities impose educational quality assurance and accountability processes, equity and transformative learning as pressing issues for the access, retention and success of, in particular, under-represented groups (IHEP, 2014; du Toit, 2012; Price, 2005; Zhao & Kuh, 2004; Mcfarlane, 2015; Peeters & Lievens, 2015; Griffiths et al., 2014; Moore, 2005; Jensen 2011; Bundy, 2005). Doggedly, an agreed upon definition and description of transformative learning (TL) or education transformation (ET) and even social justice (SJ) remain enigma, yet to be deconstructed for the interests of the actors pursuing the phenomena. Moreover, education systems across the southern hemisphere remain operating in terms of catching up with international counterparts for societal positioning in the global community. Even the prescripts for international recognition dictate that nations ought to exhibit effective performance on as TL, ET, counselling pupils for social justice as significant freedoms of democracies.

Power relations embedded in transformation processes (Palmer & Biggart; in Baum, 2002), of schools aren't short of controversy. Resistance to transformative quality education and or transformation at large has been such that the power seized through past social, economic, educational and confounding legislative provisions continues to necessitate the status quo.[1] Hegemony necessitates manipulation of the process of education transformation thro advocates of status quo while under the guise of being for and about transformation to benefit underpriviledged groups. The power exerted through schools' networks and the behaviour of actors are crucial as they can be communicative tools for identifying, manipulating and changing power relations between pupils, teachers and staff in school. Education and the discourse practices that it authorises can routinely repress, dominate and disempower diverse groups whose practices differ from the norms that it establishes. Comprehension of, for description of the real lived lives through concepts as, diversity, student success, counselling, social justice, culture, performance which are constructed by discourse in social frameworks if vital for effective school counsellors. When people apply labels to real pupils in situations where important issues are at stake, they always must confirm that people surrounding them (pupils) agree that these expressions can be used to refer to the pupils. Thus, rampant discourse should be constructions born from the very surround; communities, parents, pupils (in consideration of their contexts), teachers along the literature of the counselling discipline. The latter, being the abundant literature may have its own definitions, yet to be customised to fit the identities, values, contexts and local discourse, if the counselling in school, is indeed to be about social justice. Otherwise, persistent popularisation and engraining of discourse contrary to real-life contexts disarm counsellors from making impact in the pupils' lives, not to mention towards the development of a conducive society with responsible citizens.

The Concept of Transformative Learning_

The first major component of transformative learning is meaning perspective as a frame of reference, which includes assumptions and expectations that build through life experiences (Dirkx 2000) and it has two dimensions; "a habit of mind and the resulting points of view" (Cranton & Roy, 2003). According to Mezirow (2000), habits of mind are the broad, general, orienting perspectives that are used to interpret experience, which usually operate below our level of awareness unless considered through critical self-reflection and are accepted as truth. Mezirow lists six perspectives of habits of mind, each overlapping and influencing the other: (1) epistemic habits of mind relate to the way we come to know things and the way we use that knowledge; (2) sociolinguistic perspectives are the way we view social norms, culture, and how we use language; (3) psychological perspectives include our self-concept, personality, emotional responses, and personal images and dreams; (4) moral-ethical habits of mind incorporate our conscience and morality; (5) philosophical habits of mind are based on religious doctrine or world view; and (6) aesthetic habits of mind include our tastes and standards about beauty (as cited in Cranton & Roy, 2003). Each of the six perspectives is expressed as points of view and each point of view comprises of clusters of meaning schemes where meaning schemes are "sets of immediate specific expectations, beliefs, feelings, attitudes and judgements (Mezirow 2000, p. 18).

Dirkx, Mezirow, and Cranton, (2006) view transformative learning as a "rational process of learning within awareness [and] ... a metacognitive application of critical thinking that transforms an acquired frame of reference—a mind-set or worldview of orienting assumptions and expectations involving values, beliefs, and concepts—by assessing its epistemic assumptions" (p.25). Meizirow (2000) stresses that it occurs through a process of critical self-reflection, reflective dialogue and reflective action. Critical self-reflection as a deliberate cognitive activity, forms its heart while reflective actions on experiences bring about perspective transformation.

Critical reflection as a dichotomy between objective (Mezirow, 200) and reflective reframing (Kitchenham, 2008) and notes that transformative learning may be the result of a momentous event or incremental events over time. In 1991, Mezirow distinguished among three types of reflection (content, process and premise) and their roles in transforming meaning schemes and perspectives. He notes that critical reflection on one's premises can result in a much more profound transformation than through content or process reflection (Mezirow, 1991a). Later in 1998, he refined the three types of reflection into two dimensions of critical reflection; the objective and subjective critical reflection on and of assumptions (Mezirow, 1998; Kitchenham, 2008).

While, objective reframing is usually task orientated, it involves reflecting on what happened (previously denoted content reflection) and an examination of the assumptions that were involved in how something happened (previously denoted process reflection) (Kitchenham, 2008). On the other hand, subjective reframing is self-reflecting and involves critiquing a premise on, rather than of, assumptions that a person has defined as a problem (previously denoted premise reflection) (Kitchenham, 2008). Therefore, transformative learning is about making meaning, not just about acquiring knowledge and "meaning is making sense of or giving coherence to our experiences" (Meizirow, 1991a, p. 11). It is about taking ownership of one's learning through critical reflection, rather than mindlessly or unquestioningly acquiring frames of reference through life experiences. Transformative learning, according to Mezirow, can be viewed as "an enhanced level of awareness of the context of one's beliefs and feelings, a critique of one's assumptions, and particularly premises, and an assessment of alternative perspectives" (1991a, p. 161). Recently, Mezirow writes that "transformative learning is learning that transforms problematic frames of reference—sets of fixed assumptions and expectations (habits of mind, meaning perspectives, mindsets)—to make them more inclusive, discriminating, open, reflective, and emotionally able to change" (2003, p. 58).

Cranton (1994) and Daloz (1986) have argued that transformative learning represents a heroic struggle to wrest consciousness and knowledge from the forces of unconsciousness and ignorance. For Cranton (1998) meaning schemes are based on the experiences one has and through these experiences, ne forms habitual expectations about what will happen next. Dirkx (2000) sees it as involving very personal and imaginative ways of knowledge, grounded in a more intuitive and emotional sense of one's experiences. Along this, conceptions of transformative curricular (TC), as well as descriptions of what they entail or do not, are contested. The nature of books, articles, special editions of journals and even campaigning organisations bear varied focal contents that address disparate contexts (Love, 2011). Some highlight how such learning promotes change in pedagogy and teaching practice whilst others are ambiguous (Findlay, 2010)[2]. For example, several African countries and particularly, their education systems have witnessed varied meanings of the concept of transformation throughout history, from colonialism, (in SA, including apartheid) and to date. Accordingly, during colonialism transformation meant situating the colonists across the continent for ownership and differentiating content along racial lines, wealth and power acquisition. In South Africa, during the apartheid era, under the rule of Nationalist Party, transformation meant the displacement of some groups in favour of the elevation of others along racial lines.[3] Since the beginning of the democratic era, the concept has been predominantly refocused to address imbalances inherited from colonial and apartheid influences while also trying to keep abreast with developments in developed economies (Leke et al., 2015). Recently, added to this is that, the latter must occur whilst ensuring relevance and meaningfulness to the local context. This is not unique to South Africa, but an endeavour occurring even across other countries across the continent.

With founded independence across the continent and after the end of apartheid in South Africa, the mandate for the transformation of education has been in accordance with the eradication of previous regimes. These endeavours necessitated series of efforts with reports, laws and programmes introduced, complemented by programmes of execution and timelines of transformation, put into place by various actors and agents to meet the stipulated objectives. Amongst others, the development and implementation of education policies for transformation also gave impetus to the review of education curricular. The process required inter-agency collaboration. However, its magnitude and complexity continue to be contentious as regards what it ought to involve and could be. For over the two decades the contentions challenge the efforts.

Noteworthy, the development and implementation processes, first, required a grasp of the legacy and complexity of the colonialism and or apartheid systems to inform policies and strategies which had to be implemented overtime. Against this, a need for consensus between opposing groups over/for transformation had to involve representability based on race, gender and class. As crucial as such engagements have been, quite limited regard of school counselling as part of either the management of education or crucial part of teaching and learning. TC and or TL have remained core aspects of education transformation (TE) at large.

Along this, some groups engaged in education transformation or TC have focused on health and healing for alternative contexts (Sathe & Geisler, 2015), sustainability (Moore, 2005) and political and economic independence to overcome poverty (Hope & Timmel, 2014). Invariably, to these groups, transformation is about the nature of priviledge and power.[4] Recently a focus on the decolonisation of education has also re-emerged. Amongst other factors, it involves the decolonisation of curriculum. The discourse has to do with removing the negative impact of colonialism. However, according to Lebakeng et al., (2005) education systems across the African countries mirror "western symbols, rituals and behaviours imposed as a result of epistemicide. In this sense … remain stubbornly untransformed even though the new constitution offer space for constructing a discourse that mainstreams local relevance and vocalizes silent voices" (p. 70). Furthermore, Lebakeng (2000; 2001; 2004a) calls for education as crucial "given that [the African countries] are overwhelmingly African in the indigenous sense of the word and its fundamental historical roots, there should be no contradiction between Africanisation and democratisation of the institutions of higher learning" (p. 71.

Doggedly, the discourse on transformative education discourse still tends to be more about the *tolerance* of diversity within institutions and its expansion. While tolerance of one another is necessary, other aspects of human relations are more crucial. However, the context of education transformation been more about mixing colours to have the rainbow schools. Undeniably, other avenues required for the transformation of previously disadvantaged groups still to be reckoned. For instance, acceptance of one another regardless of differences is what should be urged more than *limited* engagement within staff rooms or boardrooms as diverse groups. When boardrooms, staff rooms, faculties, support staff or grounds are regarded as reflecting the 'rainbow nation', institutions are considered as transformative. Despondently, this is short of understanding the actual relevant configurations of teaching and learning that are appealed for in addition to the other factors of education transformation.

There's reticence urge for diverse groups to "engage with/in" diversity, hence the surge for "tolerance" over the decades. Consequently, within persistent contentions, there's tolerance of one another rather than acceptance. For this reason, it is prudent to adhere to the fact that while affirmative action interventions (primarily along racial redress) are necessary in transformation agenda, these, utterances and or transcripts alone are insufficient. If there is to be an understanding of, first what is counselling pupils for social justice within the African context and secondly, whether ET has an impact on a transformative access, retention and success, there needs to be a clear indication of the organisational networks with the actors as champions of the process and their degrees of involvement, as well as factors of networks that hinder or necessitate transformation within schools. These are networks that are developed between persons, groups, schools, organisations, nations, websites or scholarly publications.

Knowers of Knowledge for and Knowledge of

The scholarship of education transformation is constituted by different "intellectual formations" and accordingly, different intellectual and academic identities (Cross, 2011). According to Muller (1997), the formations refer to groups of people that share common epistemic, political and pragmatic interest and common consciousness, that is, they fundamentally share an ideology (a set of beliefs about the social order... or social change) and social-epistemology (a certain conception of knowledge and its relation to society). To clarify the point further, he (Muller) distinguishes between the notions, *knowledge for* and *knowledge of,* to highlight that intellectuals/academics position themselves in the relations of theory vis-à-vis practices, knowledge production vis-à-vis knowledge utilisation or policy development vis-à-vis policy implementation. However, while there's abundance of general research on ET in South Africa (Badat, 2010; CHE, 2016; Reddy, 2006; Soudien, 2010), a gap of studies with a focus on the integration of counselling pupils is evident. Specifically, it remains unclear as to: ***Who are the knowledge actors***? ***What*** is the knowledge for and of (What ***do the actors do?*** ***How*** and ***with What?*** as well as, ***Why***? during the process of ET. For this reason, an examination of intellectual formations involved in promoting or developing relevant ET in and or for schools such as voluntary non-profit agencies, government agencies, and international research partnerships contributing to the discourse within structures and processes of education transformation, in particular; in organisational networks is necessary.

However, to guard against seeming as endorsing Muller's notion of knowledge for and knowledge of in its entirety, at this stage it's vital to dwell on that.

Muller (1995) declares knowledge to be "a chain of interpretations or translations" (p.6), after first indicating that its basis is on "making a distinction where before one was not made," of which, can be systematised and unsystematised (p.1). A demystification of Muller's notion is explicitly presented by Michelson (2004) who departs with highlighting that Muller illustrates Bourdieu's characterisation of Homo Academicus as a "supreme classifier among classifiers" (1988, p.xi). Michelson also stresses that Muller's case exposes him as both a partisan with "accounts to settle" (2000, p.8) and the typically rational man who, considering his so-called "relatively moderate and modest conclusion" (2000, p.162), fails to understand "what all the fuss is about" (p.1). In line with the earlier raised questions as to: ***What is knowledge***? ***Who has situated it within institutional practices***? and ***Why***? Michelson lends value to this inquisitive mind. She indicates that Muller's point is essentially problematic as something important is at stake here, because the future depends on having knowledge that can be trusted. Thus, debates on matters of 'knowledge' need to be pursued with civil dialogue that doesn't overlook apparent representativity for problematic boundaries of which subtly undermine efforts to address concerns in the education policy.

Muller builds his argument with Durkheim's work to highlight that "divisions and distinctions of ideas become knowledge only once they have become systematised or connected to each other" (p.1). Calling this, schemes of classification,[5] of which, he also views, not to be "static but that they constantly move and change" (p.6). However, argues Michelson that Muller undermines opposing perspectives as lacking systematicity necessary for distinctions to become knowledge, as they are non-systematic "knowledge - practical knowledge and local wisdom of all sorts – refers to the effects and uses of knowledge but does not provide basis for reflection upon its bases" (p.1). Moreover, Michelson identifies such views as casting Muller's description of the more efficacious knowledge regards its systemisation: ideas drawn from Durkheim's work, identifying knowledge only when connections have been made between them and they have been formed into "schemes of classification" (2000, p.1).

Through this, she highlights that Muller underestimates his self-coined nonsystematic 'knowledge' as consisted of various kinds of local wisdom, folklore and practical know-how. Bear in mind that, this could refer to knowledge that has not been provided platform to be integrated as part of Western education system.

Michelson also indicates that Muller refers to such knowledge as "crude", "vulgar" and, again tapping into Durkheim's "profane" (2000, pp.13, 77). The problem with profane knowledge, according to Muller, is that it is not "transparent to itself" (2000, p.136); because it does not offer the possibility of interrogation or destabilisation, it is not open to critique or change. He sees this failure as imposing implications that are political as well as epistemological: "systematic idealization is the only way to project benign possible futures. Without it, no concept of social change is possible. . ." (2000, p.90). Muller claims that the 'other' perspectives; "technical and complex" analyses have imposed difficulties for classical disciplines of knowledge resulting into a crisis for knowledge and the disciplines studying (p.1). However, Michelson demystifies Muller's claims by highlighting that he subtly appeals to maintain the status quo by keeping "the boundaries between knowledges well maintained, in the interest of furthering a 'good life' that all South Africans can share".

Muller positions his notion by stressing that knowledge are self-referential distinctions applied upon inconsistencies,[6] thus reflexive (p.2). He substantiates that self-referentiality and reflexivity, the distinctions and their connections are open for destabilisation due to being 'repeatable, transcribable and therefore, revisable by the competent community at large.' Along this, he declares reflexivity to be the "condition for knowledge" as well as, "the means for its motility and destabilization;" a scenario posing "challenges for a responsible and socially aware scientific practice" (p.2). Muller claims that the 20th century's scientific and societal instability along increased "production of new knowledge … [resulting into] a new prominence of science in all facets of our lives" (p.2) occurred. Furthermore, he indicates that the second notion of reflexivity "points at contingency, risk and ambivalence", as well as, "to enhanced individual possibilities and freedom" (p.2). These notions are drawn from the theory of reflexive modernisation which asks: 'what sorts of institutions are possible in an age of chronic contingency, of chronic ambivalence' (Lash, 1999, pp. 13708).

As Muller 1995) compares the perspectives of the modern and the traditional of sociology of knowledge, he reinforces that the former is unable to hold on parallel to both senses of reflexivity while the latter, knowledge and society were viewed as exclusive to one another with society occurring over knowledge from external, bringing interests or values or purposes to bear on it, happening upon knowledge as science might occur upon nature, bending it to a superior position (p.2). Against this, he concludes that one with comprehension of both senses of reflexivity of knowledge would not buy into that notion as intrinsic sociality of knowledge is what needs to be accounted for, for that's where views extremely diverge. For example, he reveals, the rampant differences of perspectives across disciplines studying knowledge, from philosophy and epistemology through sociology, technology, to applied disciplines of innovation and policy reflect that (Muller, 1995).

Primarily, his stance is one of boundary-maintenance. To liven his argument, he exploits the mainstream debate in contemporary theories of knowledge as being based on distinction between "insularity" and "hybridity". Insularity characterised by disciplinary autonomy, purity, fear of transgression and attention to differences between systems of knowledge and criteria of judgment. Hybridity is consisted of permeability of boundaries and the "promiscuity" of meaning domains. Against this, he argues that having no "theory of the boundary", constructivists fall back on what Muller calls "borderless think", a "spurious ideology of boundlessness". Durkheim figures so largely in this analysis because Durkheim is "the exemplary sociologist of the boundary" (2000, pp. 57, 67, 5, 77). Regards educational and curriculum policy, "the border in question here is the one between common-sense knowledge and codified curricular knowledge, between ordinary everyday knowledge and codes, texts and canons, the mastery of which is assessed and certified at school". The hybrid project has to do with creating bridges and bringing students into the exploration of the relationship between school knowledge and the students' own knowledges. Muller poses to be concerned with the "limits to this project" and the "unintended consequences" (2000, p.58). Using school mathematics to explore the limits to hybridity and to defend the boundaries between academic and local knowledges, he argues that constructivists are wrong to insist that "any and all everyday experiences are suitable metaphors for mathematical relations" (2000, p.70); claiming that curriculum symbolises the values and habits of the group that has won the struggle for symbolic mastery. Consequentially, such a notion, requiring the disadvantaged in need of access to that cultural capital, undeniably, foregoing their own cultural capital.

Michelson continues highlighting that Muller subtly appeals to maintain the status quo by keeping "the boundaries between knowledges well maintained, in the interest of furthering a 'good life'" that can be shared by all. She methodically pokes holes with his claims by interrogation of his portrayal of the constructivist perspective and his typical use of a text by feminist mathematics educator Valerie Walkerdine, whom he presents as a counterpoint to constructivism. Michelson highlights the implications of some of Muller's lexicon, which she regards to imply concerns that characterise contemporary academic life. Michelson indicates Muller's articulation that are what in fact crucial questions, as:

- "How can or should the common-sense knowledge of experience and local culture, indeed of the everyday world, relate to the codified knowledge deemed worthy of inclusion and certification in the formal curriculum?"
- "How, and under what conditions, can vertical discourse be assessed outside formal contexts of transmission?"
- What is the proper relationship between world of reason and science and world of "passion and politics, practical activity and everyday life?" (2000, pp.13, 89, 14).

Accordingly, ongoing educational initiatives require that these questions be addressed along reviewing curricular and epistemological assumptions with the recognition of prior informal and integration of disadvantaged groups to have access into formal education (Michelson 2000). Moreover, Michelson declares that it is important to explore the relationships among cultures of knowledge and cognitive domains while "a thoroughgoing answer may well contribute to a rethinking of the role of formal educational institutions given the cognitive demands and requisites of late modernity". She also shares Muller's insight that such answers might "help to explicate how sacred practices lie nested, often unremarked, within the routines of the everyday" (2000, p.89), without beating around the bush on his flaws.

Elaboration on the above debate is beyond the scope of this chapter. Here, a concise presentation is hared to indicate different opinions across existing scholarship on education transformation. However, cognisant of the thesis of this chapter on counselling pupils for social justice, informed by persistent diversity upon inherently inequitable legacy in schools, Muller's stance negating recognition of prior informal and or nonsystemic experience, of primarily disadvantaged groups – is a problematic one. Accordingly, the knowers of knowledge for and of, has for decades been construed to be select, capacitated by hegemony of groups belonging in. Despondently, such stances hinder envisaged goals and subtly maintain status quo as strategically positioned by liberals entrusted with equitable beliefs and practices. Such dynamics also indicate the web and networks of actors of and for, that could be demystified throughout pursuance of deserved equity in education and or schools.

Arguably, social networks can be both enabling and constraining. Research on homophily addresses this quandary. The theory on homophily argues that individuals' social networks are often homogeneous to the extent of being detrimental. Social network groups are often similar as regards socio-demographic, behavioural and interpersonal characteristics (Baile, 2006). Accordingly, homophily in social networks can "limit people's social worlds in a way that has powerful implications for the information they receive, attitudes they form and interactions they experience" (McPherson, Smith-Lovin & Cook, 2001, p. 422). In support of this, Lawrence (2000) claims that people who are structurally similar are powerful and they identify with each other as relevant individuals in their social lives to one another. Thus, therry are more likely to have interpersonal communications (2000) that emphasise the effects of homophily. Since in essence, these are the individuals whose advice and opinions influence others the most, it will be interesting to identify influential individuals within existing networks in the schools. For, their impact to power relations and the ideals of transformation in the school and thus contribute to the literature on the value of organisational network analysis for studying social networks related to social justice practices employed primarily by the schools. Therefore, an exploration of the existing networks in schools and their roles is crucial. The following section offers a comprehensive discussion on the network theory analysis (NTA).

The Nature of Network Theory Analysis

Generally, there's extensive and increasing body of literature on networks in studies of organisations (Ahuja, 2000; Bailie, 2006; Borgatti & Foster, 2003; Brass et al, 2004; Merrill, 2006, Merrill et al., 2007, Sleky & Parker, 2005). The focus is commended for examining effectively how managing information and improving performance in organisational systems (Kilduff, 2003; Chang & Harrison, 2004; Brass et al, 2000; Zach, 2000; Krebs, 2011b; Cross et al., 2002; Cross & Thomas, 2009; Cross & Parker, 2004; Burton et al, 2010) provides useful insights to understanding change structures and processes. However, there's lack of literature where the approach is used to study education agencies' (schools') internal organisational/institutional structure. For this chapter, the schools' counsellors are viewed actors in transformation processes, yet to be reckoned for establishing their active participation, collaborators and partners in attaining the goals that are linked to education success. Thus, network theory analysis (NTA) guides this chapter in exploring the role of networks in schools.

Even though the use of NTA is scarce in the field of education, it is invaluable for making sense of collaborations in strategically important groups such as top leadership networks (Cross et al., 2002) that form part of organisational networks and whose affiliation might influence other networks or vis-a-versa. McGonagall (2005) highlights how it helps when having to critically analyse the designation of actors within a society (as to, *Who are you?*) and in the context of education transformation system (*What is their role?*). Few scholars, for example, Egle and Silinis (2011) used it to analyse the performance of students who have social networks and Evoh (2009) studied networks in collaborative partnerships between schools, entrepreneurs and education officials for ICT resources and the transformation of secondary schools in South African schools. NTA thus, is beneficial for understanding how social networks and organisational networks help clarify processes for ET and their impact on the institution's community. It helps with broad-based understanding of collaborative networks, agreements, actions and the involvement of organisational groups concerned with the envisaged change in schools through existing networks related to the institutional structure and what the effects are at higher and lower levels of the system.[7]

Background on the NTA

The origin of the NTA has been traced to biology (Senge et al., 1999). In contrast to the theory of reductionism, it is grounded on the "whole" of any object as constituted by its parts, highlights the importance of the whole and postulates that its (whole's) meaning cannot be seen entirely by breaking down the parts.[8] Biological theories were first transferred by Jay W. Forrester to other disciplines in his book, Industrial dynamics (Forrester, 1961). The work emerged as a leading source on systems and presented biological patterns to be applied to disciplines outside of biology, including corporate planning, policy design and public management (Baile, 2006). Central to this approach was a focus on developing a theory that urged researchers not to see interrelationships as linear cause-effect chains but to study processes of change rather than snapshots of activity (Senge, Seville, Lovins & Lotspeich, 1999, Jonsson, 1986b, Knoke, 2001, Seybolt, 2000, Moliterno & Mahony 2010). Figure.1 illustrates its origin.

Figure 1 illustrates the evolution of the systemic NTA, since origin, from biological reductionism perspectives throughout the systems theory. This perspective emphasises a conception of a 'system' as constituted by a set of units and their interrelationships. For Bertalanffy (Miller 1965; p. 10) "a system is a set of units with relationships among them". Related to the viewpoint, Miller (1965; p. 12) suggests that "the universe contains a hierarchy of systems, each higher level of system being composed of systems of low levels". In support of this sentiment Simons' (Miller 1965; p. 12) describes

Figure 1. Evolution of systemic network theory
Source: Customised from Baile, 2006

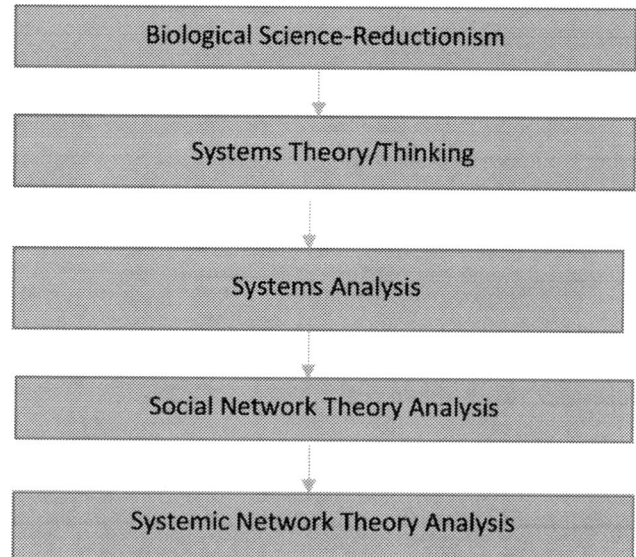

a system through "a hierarchic system, or hierarchy, [as] a system that is composed of interrelated subsystems, each of the latter being, in turn, hierarchic in structure until we reach some lowest level of elementary sub- system". These perspectives led to an increasing interest in the varieties of network analysis. For example, in Seybolt's (2000) view, systemic network theory helps to determine accountability, efficiency and causal relationships. It has four major elements to measure network dependency and effectiveness through feedback; namely, environment, structure, processes and outcomes. This is depicted in Figure 2.

The Figure 2 depicts that a thorough review of these components within the service delivery system offers a platform to theorise how an effective model might be. A school, though not a corporation, operates through contracts between parents and or pupils for service delivery and expectations of agreed upon services. Therefore, the depiction with the above diagram also provides a foundation/start for evaluating service systems. A system's *environment* includes 1) the definition of task requirements (what each agency must do for its stakeholders) and 2) the degree of dependency on other agencies. The degree of dependency an agency has on other agencies and on outside resources has an impact on the structure and process of the network. The degree of dependency is measured by level of complexity, uncertainty, duration and volume of agency's tasks. Dependency itself, including diversity, flux and ambiguity can influence complexity in the organisation (Maznevki et al., 2015).

Figure 2. Elements of a systemic network

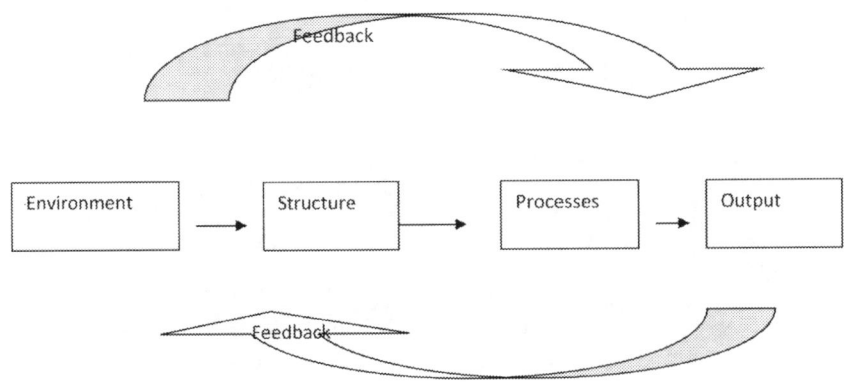

The networks having one single point of access (or source of funding) are far more dependent than those with multiple sources (Seybolt, p. 8). He argues that the degree of independence influences the way services are delivered in the sense that "less regulation allows a system to be more responsive to feedback" (p. 8). Accordingly, external controls influence "to what degree an organisational unit has the freedom to define its own future" (Alter & Hage, 1993: 109).[9]

According to Katz and Kahn (1978) boundaries of an "open-system" become more problematic overtime leading to the next element of organisational networks according to Seybolt's model; structure. The structure is constituted by six components: size, complexity, connectivity, centrality, differentiation, and stability (Atler & Hage, 1993; Burt 1995; Galaskiewicz 1979b; Kenis & Knoke 2002; Nohria & Eccles 1993; Scott 1991; 2000; Seybolt 2000; Wasserman & Faust 1994). Size refers to the number of organisations within the entire network. Then, the complexity of the systemic network is determined by the volume of services and/or products offered by the organisations within the network. On the other hand, connectivity of a network refers to the total number of communication linkages within the system (Atler & Hage 1993: 160).

Centrality is closely related to connectivity, which examines the degree to which information and "total volume of work flows through a single, or a few, core organisations in the network" (Seybolt, 2000, p.9). Seybolt also asserts that the more centralised a system, the fewer connections it has, and therefore; the less adaptive it is. Differentiation of a systemic network measures the amount of functional specialisation each agency maintains. Moreover, it measures the amount of specialisation required to complete functions within any network agency. Then, stability measures the level of turnover in clientele, employees and participating agencies within the network. Stability is highly important in systemic network analysis because if a network is unstable the members are "less likely to trust each, share resources, and develop or maintain a shared vision of the system's goals" (Seybolt, 2000, p.9). Furthermore, if the network is unstable, organizations with similar goals will "compete more aggressively, which will reduce the quality of the output for the system as a whole" (Seybolt, 2000, p.10).

Research reveals that system dynamics has been evolving for over fifty years (Dahl, 1961, Hawley, 1963; Hunter 1953, Parrow 1986). It has enabled practitioners and researchers to better comprehend complex, non-linear, social and environmental systems by applying biological approaches toward the understanding of an organisation as an "organism," consisting of several parts, which craft the whole. For this reason, organisational research tends to identify boundaries[10] between organisations to distinguish them. However, it has become increasingly arguable that the line drawn between organisations and their *environment* is blurred (Galaskiewicz, 1985; Gulati, 1998; Metcaffe, 1981; Perrow, 1986). Jonsson (1986) and others (Nohria & Eccles 1993; Perrow, 1986) indicate how these boundaries became blurred. In the beginning, Jonsson (1986) claimed that, researchers (e.g., Thompson, 1967; Weber, 1947) viewed organisations as closed systems. Accordingly, such analysis encompassed emphasis on self-contained organisational units. Against this, the theory developed into an open system perspective, (Pfeffer & Salancik, 1978; Scott, 1998) which emphasises the influence of the external environment on individual organisations. Furthermore, researchers started reviewing different "organisational sets" using the interaction between different organisations as the unit of analysis tried to identify relevant "sets" (Aldrich & Whetten, 1981; Evan, 1966).

The *process* of interaction is what differentiates a system from a network. Thompson (1967) suggests that if the process of a network is highly adaptive, the quality of the product or service will increase over time. Accordingly, if the system is non-adaptive, the quality of the output will be less linked to the needs of the consumer/client. These principles suggest that, for open systems to provide quality services, they should be adaptive to consumer needs and ensure that the process of interaction with clients and other network members is open to feedback.

Output is indirectly related to the process and the structure of a system. For this reason, *feedback* loops ideally should appear throughout the model, but particularly after an output (service or task) has been produced. Since feedback as a result of outputs can be positive and/or negative, either responses allow the network to adjust by redefining its structure and/or processes in responding to it. After receiving feedback, the process can be altered, thus changing the structure of the system. Specifically, outputs lead to feedback that adjusts the task requirements of the system. Outputs also measure the self -perception of the system. They include the "participating organisations' perceptions of the effectiveness of the systems' structure and process at fulfilling the task requirements" (Seybolt, 2000, p.10). Findings from Thompson

(1967) suggest that if the processes of a network are highly adaptive, the quality of the product or service will increase over time. Alternatively, if the system is non-adaptive, the quality of the output will be less linked to the needs of the consumer/client (Thompson, 1967). Figure 2 illustrates the components of this theory.

Tapping into organisational social networks, as engagement communication tools in schools to identify their usefulness in ET, helps in highlighting the significance of collaborations to effective and transformative educational planning.[11] Specifically, guiding towards revealing *who* does *what* in the process related to the ET, *how*, with *what*, *when* and *why and* whether this happens as stipulated within the transformation discourse is of interest. However, the extent to which education transformation in general has had an impact on TC is thus beyond the scope of the study. The argument is that ET must be responsive and relevant to the conditions in which not only pupils and instructors but also counsellors find themselves as regards local and global demands. Schools' management and programme managers are expected by policy to prioritise creating connections within and between the processes for transformation goals; the pupils, parents and other education stakeholders at large. Therefore, to understand these transformation efforts, Network Theory Analysis (NTA) can offer means to trace the links in the development and implementation of ET.

Interrelated theories such as systems theory and organisational theory, which is extended by information processing theory and network theory oriented by graph and complexity theory are thus invaluable in this regard. The assumption is that the networks of colleagues and experts as well as the institutions' network serve as agencies for service provision. Therefore, NTA for the understanding of internal (social networks) and external (organisational networks) can clarify a school's responsibility to adapt to constitutional imperatives and, how their processes impact on the its community, that is, the individual student who is registered or an employed person. People and institutions (as practice) within the schools are having a responsibility to promote meaningful transformation. However, an examination of their roles using organisational network analysis is yet to be explored for effectively looking at them as a part of organisational social system. By identifying a "systems language" for thinking, communicating and building shared knowledge within the schools, insights can be developed on how the responsibility to adapt to constitutional imperatives and processes used for certain purposes are understood.

Therefore, theoretical stance is useful in making sense of the nature of the current education transformation debates; how the process is addressing the inherited legacy of previous regime and the current demands to make the education relevant to the [new] societal needs. The conscientisation that is hoped for, presupposes that identities of those who have been underpriviledged would be positioned in transformative transcripts and represented/presented accordingly. The degree to which this occurs and whether it does or not across institutions/schools is the subject for investigation.

Research in support of conscientisation regard this aspect as a means to use education to construct critical consciousness to reshape a person and the society (Dirkx, 2000; Cranton & Roy, 2003; Baumgartner, 2001; Freire, 1997; Mezirow, 1997; 2003a; 2003b; Wyandotte & Huh, 2012).

Networks and their Role in School's Effectiveness

Contractor and Eisenberg, (2002) assert that integral to network analysis is that people's beliefs, feelings and behaviours are primarily driven not by the attributes of individuals but by the patterns of relationships among them. The network paradigm is thus regarded as effective for examining socially and organisationally based information flow by focusing attention away from individuals as its independent users to a view of users involved in an interconnected set of interdependent relationships embedded within organisational and social systems (Contrator & Eisenberg 1989). It will be interesting to establish how such patterns of relationships contribute or not to a counselling for social justice within schools.

Galbraith (1973) suggests that information-processing theory builds upon organisational theory by characterising the interactions as an information processing network operating under conditions of uncertainty. Furthermore, Galbraith (1977) argues that such uncertainty reflects the difference between determining the magnitude of information required to perform a task and that already acquired by the Organisation. The quality of output or performance is determined by the nature of this difference and how it is managed. As Carley and Wallace (2001) also explain, this is because information is ubiquitous and distributed widely across multiple agents (people, groups, resources) within institutions (Galbraight, 1974a). By explaining the information flow between the multiple agents within a school and the network model it (the school) has adopted it is possible to identify insights about its performance as an institution involved in the mediation of equitable education through social justice counselling. A conceptual model with five constructions can be observed: The first is the notion of *school education transformation*; the second concept is *transformative or what is recently referred to as a decolonised curriculum*. The third one is *organizational network analysis*, which is about the pursuit for comprehending the complex behaviours in a dynamic educational institution[s] (as organisational system[s]). The fourth concept is *information use,* for the process of transformation, that is, information flows amongst *actors*/agents that are designated and the degrees of connectivity with other agents. The fifth concept focuses on the performance, in this case, that being supposedly counselling pupils for social justice. Is that happening? Who are the actors in the ongoing school's transformation? How does the information flow across actors? If it's not happening what needs to be done?

Accordingly, the nature of organisational theory has a depiction of multilevel systems of relationships (Hitt, Beamish, Jackson, & Mathieu, 2007), hence, a theory that is multilevel in its scope and perspective (Moliterno & Mahony, 2010; Powell et al., 2005). For example, in a hypothetical three-level system, the highest level (Level 3) would represent an inter-organisational network of organisation (e.g., school's system at large) and each actor would have ties representing, for example, joint subjects and activities. Furthermore, each of these institutional actors (i.e., each node in the Level 3 network) would be composed of an intra-organisational network of groups, departments, or divisions. Then, at the Level 2, network ties between the departmental actors may be resource exchange and each group (i.e., each node in the Level 2 network) would represent a network of individuals. Then, at the system's Level 1, advice relationships may form the theoretically relevant network tie (Harary & Batell, 1981; Moliterno & Mahony, 2010).12 It is in this sense that the organisational network analysis can provide both a Visual and a mathematical analysis of complex human systems (Carley & Wallace, 2001) to uncover gaps in information flow and knowledge exchange in an organisation. The revelation can help guide those in counselling leadership find opportunities for improving the flow of information across functional and organisational barriers, connecting isolated teams or individuals and prioritizing areas where improvements will have the most impact as suggested by Merrill et al. (2007). By focusing on links between individuals in an organisational entity (2007) to design and measure relationships between people, groups and organisations' resources, knowledge and work responsibilities, the analysis can provide empirical data to plan for and rationalise the allocation of resources and assist decision-making by highlighting connections between information networks and process performance that is, Service/Performance, which is counselling for social justice and or transformative learning.

Coman, et al., (2016) argue that a network is an interconnected system of things or people. Networks in organisations comprise nodes that represent agents, knowledge, tasks, or resources, and the links that outline relationships between the nodes (Gulati, et al.; in Baum, 2002). While simple in concept, the interdependent "node-link" structure becomes related in multi-faceted ways as networks develop and grow. Therefore, such multi-level networks at one level of the organisational system influence networks at higher and/or lower levels (Kozlowski et al., 2000; Moliterno & Mahony, 2010) and thus link two theoretical perspectives, namely, the notion of systems of nested networks that is used to examine how an observed network structure at one level of the system of organisational networks relates to network structures and notion of the effects of links at higher or lower levels of the system.[13] For this reason, NTA stresses that the environment contributes to or disrupts agency operation. The network structure, environment, process and output all affect its effectiveness. This explains why interagency collaboration is viewed as one way to solve multi-organisational issues. This notion again urges an intriguing question to be asked about schools as: Does the leadership of schools tap into existing interagency for collaborative efforts towards transformation?

Organisational Network Analysis

The organisational network analysis is based on the understanding that organisations are complex systems where various agents interact to shape the environment and the organisation's performance. The agents in this case are the institutional (school's) staff in ET and counselling offices, who operate through observed organisational or social networks, sharing relevant information for operational purposes that have effect on their performance. According to the nature of the scale of analysis, an agent may represent an individual, a project team, a unit, or an entire organisation (Dooley, 2002). These agents might also be linked through social networks. Social networks have been identified to have four broad foci which influence their dynamics: inequality, embedding, contagion, and contingency (Burt, Gabbay, Holt & Moran, 1994). First, inequality addresses the differences in resources available to individuals or groups. Second, embedding describes schools and identities resulting from networks and how they enable transactions Gulati, 1998). Third, contagion exemplifies how social networks can serve as conduits of information. And lastly, contingency approaches suggest how social networks can moderate organisational processes. These four foci were introduced by Burt, et. al (1994) and Gulati (1998) within an organisational, work-related context.

The view that is adopted in this chapter thus suggests that social networks could indeed have an impact on the achievement or enactment of social justice counselling. In the context of school social networks, this means that information about transformation, including access to services and opportunities, as well as counselling would all be affected to some extent by the degree of equity, embedding, contagion and contingency (homophily) within social networks (Ployhart, 2007). The linkages between agents (across units) within a network in an institution inform NTA (Wasserman & Faust, 1994). Theories of organisations, networks and complexity provide models showcasing complex interactional concepts (Dooley, 2002) that make it possible to examine aspects of education provision. Accordingly, these aspects highlight that institutions (schools) are multilevel systems of relationships (Hitt, Beamish, Jackson, & Mathieu, 2007), hence, a network theory of organisation is considered in this chapter to be multilevel in its scope and perspective (Moliterno & Mahony, 2010; Powell et al., 2005).

It is in this sense that the organisational network analysis can provide both a visual and a mathematical analysis of complex human systems that is not possible using probability-based statistical methods (Carley & Wallace, 2001). The technique can uncover gaps in information flow and knowledge exchange in an organisation. This knowledge can help guide those in counselling leadership find opportunities for information improvements, such as smoothing the flow of information across functional and organisational barriers, connecting isolated teams or individuals, and prioritising areas where information improvements will have the most impact. Merrill et al support this by arguing that organisational network analysis is a method of social network analysis, an application focused on links between individuals in an organisational entity (2007).

In their view, it can provide empirical data to plan for and rationalise the allocation of resources and assist decision-making by highlighting connections between information networks and process performance. They thus, regard it as a descriptive, empirical research method for designing and measuring relationships between people, groups and organisations with the resources, knowledge and work responsibilities. According to Harary and Batell (1981) the graph theoretic perspective on systems of nested networks suggests that each node in a network in each level of analysis is itself a network at a lower level of analysis.

This is a missing link between multilevel and social network perspectives on organisations. In consideration of the notion of nested networks, it's advisable to integrate the multilevel and social network theoretical perspectives on organisational analysis to underscore the importance of the perspective of a multilevel theory of the organisation in the attempt to explore how a network structure at one level of the system of organisational networks relates to its network structures and relationships at higher or lower levels (Bliese, 2000; Moliterno & Mahony, 2010). The assumption is that analysing a theoretical perspective through a multilevel notion will strengthen and expand the original theory's insights (Cappelli & Scherer, 1991; Ostroff & Bowen, 2000; Ployhart, 2006). Therefore, to contribute to school counselling leadership scholarship there is a need to provide insights about a path for linking micro and macro levels in organisational network research (Ployhart & Weekely, 2009).

Figure 3 depicts three main concepts upon which this chapter is built around. The first is the notion of organisational *network analysis*, sought for understanding complex behaviours of dynamic and multilevel organisational systems (Baile 2007, Moliterno & Mahony, 2010, Merrill 2003). The second concept is the *information use* in the higher education institution. The third one if *performance*, in this case, that referring to transformational activities for transformative curriculum. The interaction of these concepts (organisational happenings by and use of information) creates a means to study aspects of performance, which depends on how information is used in the complex processes of a public higher education agency.

Network analysis is embedded in general systems theory and is relatively new in terms of theory development and thus, lacks a strong theoretical foundation unique to its ideas. However, the work of Laclau and Mouffe (2001) 'In *Hegemony and*

Figure 3. Conceptual model of schools networks
Conceptual Model of Network Theory Analysis adapted to position education transformation/social justice counselling in schools

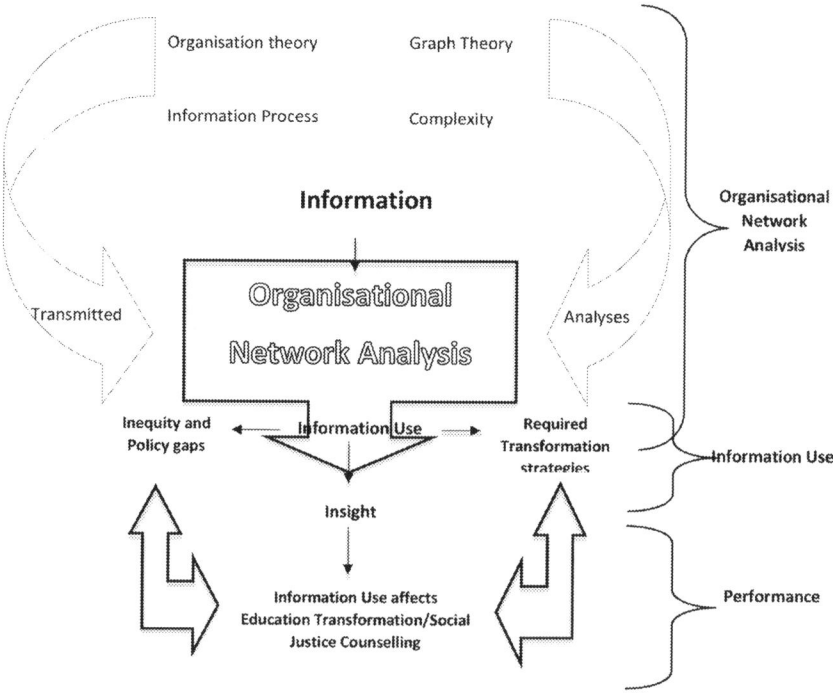

Social Strategy, Laclau and Mouffe (1985)' and later, in Latour's (1985) Actor-Network Theory, that looks at 'articulation' as "any practice establishing a relation among the elements such that their identity is modified as a result of the articulatory practice was sought for understanding of the conceptual implications of network theory analysis.

In Laclau and Mouffe's (2001) view since the nature of the network to be made possible by the content of the transcripts given for actors to articulate; 'articulation' can be understood as, "discursive" practice which does not have a plan of constitution prior to, or outside, the dispersion of the articulated elements" (p. 109). In their view, "every object is constituted as an object of discourse", which means that, although objects certainly do "exist externally to thought", they cannot "constitute themselves as objects outside any discursive condition of emergence" (p. 108). Articulation thus, refers to the ways meaning is fixed within a social arena where everything is discursive. The implication is that actors are never more than "subject-positions: within a discursive structure" (p. 115).

It is in this sense that Laclau and Mouffe (2001) avoid the traditional Marxist approach that links ideology to "a superstructure that is disassociated from actual material institutions, rituals, and practices and that posits a unifying principle like class" (p.56) in the construct of articulation. They link their focus on hegemony to Gramsci, arguing that hegemonic practice has different identities and demands connected along efforts in supporting and challenging, even replacing or modifying the discourse to the satisfaction of those who might have been opposing it, while the identifiers might remain with a generally universal stance (see also Griggs & Howarth 2013). In this case, two contrasting discourses can enter overly conflicting positions, which are then called 'antagonisms' (Ansell & Torfing 2016). Simply what this is highlighting is that regardless of agents' positions in networks, the use (rather, articulations) of discourse within symbolic frameworks (Laclau & Mouffe 2001) and their own practices of it, determines who agents end up being, or what they stand up for, across conflicting stances presented. Apparently, some may just end up being fixed representatives (empty signifiers) holding together the unity of the network without addressing issues at hand. These floating signifiers are ideological elements that are not securely fixed in a discourse and can thus be constructed in diverse ways, whereas empty signifiers are points of symbolic fixation, which provide the representational resources that can hold together multiple and even contradictory demands in a risky unity (Laclau 1990, 1995).

Used in this sense, discourse might be referring to "shared ways of understanding the world" which "enables those who subscribe to it to interpret bits of information and put them together into coherent stories or accounts" (Dryzek 1994, p. 8). As regards this chapter, this implies that, actors in the network do not have prior existence as agents of education transformation nor content for counselling for social justice. It is the stipulations of education and/or counseling (change) social justice through transcripts which determine their communication network. Thus, the discursive practice revolves around ET and/or counselling for social, only when designated as actors of such within schools. Thus, networks for counselling for social justice will reflect social relations defining priviledge/influence within a discourse "discursively constructed" in multiple ways (Laclau & Mouffe 2001).

Organisational Network Analysis

The concept of organisational network analysis refers to an application of social network analysis (a method focused on connections between individuals) of a system (in this case an institution but could be a structure/agency/organisation). It is descriptive and empirical technique for mapping and measuring relationships between people, groups and organisations with the resources, knowledge and tasks that are used to perform work. The technique is built from theories of organisations, networks and complexity to produce models representing the structure of relationships that would be infeasible to describe without relational concepts (Wasserman & Faust, 1994). The results yield insight into organisational behaviour.

That organisational network analysis departs from the perspective of traditional organisation charts and process maps effects its failure in capturing the complex web of information interactions and often missing out true patterns of information exchange that need to be explicit along proper management of organisational processes (Stephenson, 1996). Accordingly, Krebs (2005) identifies that organisational network analysis provides both a graphical and a quantitative analysis of complex human systems to describe the flow of information along existing pathways in organizations. This results into the interpretation of the results of network analysis in relation to formal organisational hierarchies, opportunities for improvement can be discovered.

Information Use

According to Kuhlthau (2001) information use is any activity involving the delivery, accessibility, collection, organisation, or visualisation of information; this might involve initiation of a search for information, selection of information sources, the process of exploration for new or needed information, methods for formulating or focusing information requirements, the process of collecting information, viewing information, or presentation and delivery of information. In support of this notion, the School of Information in the University of Michigan highlights that information use, broadly interpreted, includes how information flows and how information resources and information technologies form, maintain, and serve specific communities of practice (2004). Thus, in the context of the school agency it can include typical business information processing such as text writing, drawing, calculating, filing and communicating information. Primarily, information use is part of specialised tasks such as field investigations, inspections, surveillance, sample collection, or direct provision of education services. Information flow is an aspect of information use in the agency's communication network. This flow of information is essential to public schools' education performance, hence in this chapter associated with education transformation for social justice counselling.

SCHOOL AS A FIELD OF PERFORMANCE

Carley (2002a) indicates that organisational performance is an interaction between organisational knowledge (a function of individual training, knowledge and information processing capabilities) and organisational structure applied to the work of the organisation. If this definition is applied to a public school, then knowledge in any school education agency is a function of staff trained in public school education plus public school's education transformation, data, information and knowledge. Accordingly, schools' education institutional structure is comprised of mission, environment, structural capacity, processes and outcomes (Handler et al., 2001). These elements interact to determine how well public school education institutions can perform their mission: assuring conditions in which pupils can be served efficiently and effectively. In a given public school education agency, performance will be defined by the specific goals that fit that agency's structural capacity and that guide processes for addressing the needs and concerns of the communities served (Turnock & Handler, 2001). Thus, network analysis allows description of organisational complexity within the framework of the information network. The results yield insight into how these interactions may influence performance.

While trends of transformation in education have been witnessed, these, are sluggish in incorporating school counselling agenda, as if achieving schools' goals is exclusive of the role of counsellors. There's an undeniable need for rigorous critical studies of this apparent stagnant progress which remains to be addressed. A sustained body of scholarship with clearly discernible and differentiated theoretical frameworks is currently absent from local public education counselling studies. Even international education studies are often descriptive with a notable paucity in practical, empirically-based research projects capable of building a theoretical knowledge-base for academic research. A compilation and publication of local African focused school counselling studies is needed. Now may just be the right time to incorporate school counselling within ongoing theoretical engagement with the objects of transformation as such have also not yet matured. Despondently, African public education research is so disjointed and needs to be formally organised to offer coherence and to build a strong network of local scholars. From the absence of appreciation, recognition and the power-authority relations across African public education are discouraging for local academics, negatively affects research and leads to a decline in the production of high quality scholarly publications. It can also be argued that studies in African public education is typically atheoretical with a perception that policy texts follow a linear path to implementation in schools. African studies over-dwell on the intended policy, investing it with an importance that is rarely borne out empirically. Scholars tend to expect that policy can and should have its intended impact and are invariably surprised when it fails to materialise.

School as an Agency and its Structure

Understanding the relationship between agent action and institutional structure may yield deeper sociological insight into transformation processes. The importance of the structure/agency relationship as an analytical tool for public education research need recognition. Commonly found studies tend to focus on either the post-apartheid or colonialism curriculum transformation and have a different specific focus. Nevertheless, such also represent recent work on public education studies that suggest that it is worth investigating structure and action as a means for understanding the social relations of power in institutional settings.

Badat suggests that socio-historical research that analyses agency has the potential to illustrate how individuals are implicated in the choices, decisions and strategies that have orientated the trajectory of South African higher education (Badat 2007a, p. 9; Badat 2009). Badat's view on agency stipulated that:

The key actors differ in their interests and roles, in their relation to the state, political parties and other important constituencies, and in strengths and weakness. They employ strategies and tactics of mobilisation and engagement. They differ their involvement in the different domains of change and different phases of the change process -- agenda setting, policy development and formulation, and policy implementation. The actors have histories, different preoccupations, and have differential access to resources, whether knowledge, information, financial or human, or power and influence (Badat 2007b, p. 13)

Referring more directly to the relationship between structure and agent action, Badat argues that "structure and agency" should be part of the ''exciting'' challenge to develop imaginative conceptual frameworks for analysing and theorising ... transformation (Badat 2007b:10). The analysis he offers is thus the most direct appeal for heuristic frameworks that can examine the relationship between agent action and structure in education. Sehoole (2005) provides a detailed empirical account of the relationship between the different dispositions of the "old" and "new" bureaucrats during the reconstitution of the national department of education after 1994. He explains how the newly appointed officials, unaccustomed to the "rules" of bureaucratic policy implementation, struggled to infuse a non-racial post-apartheid ethos into the structures of the new department and notes that officials from the previous era used their institutional memory and experience of the technicalities of government administration as a form of agency to resist transformation. Sehoole's study thus suggests that through an investigation of the manipulation of structures, it is possible to gain deeper insight into agent action in institutional settings (particularly where transformation is the objective). It is apparent that, though the schools have been transforming overtime; a need for attention to the significance of examining institutional history and administrative decision-making processes (structure) for shaping student choices about their academic careers (agency) is necessary.

SYSTEMATIC BIAS IN EDUCATION DISCOURSE

Since the late 1990s there have been significant changes with positive development in the education of previously disadvantaged groups, as well as education about diversity. Research on the trends of international development education has been conducted to date. Teachers' development interventions have been observed. More money ploughed into education systems to improve them. The list of positive developments appears to be endless and beyond the scope of this transcript. The Civil Society Organisations have pursued projects to support education systems nonstop. Against all the giant steps taken to transform education over the years, the results remain comparatively disappointing, hence one is even writing and reading about inequities and or bias of the education discourse.

School counselling is influential means for the possibilities of critical thinking and engaging in the learning process and in one's life to act against institutions (systemic bias) fashioned to promote and sustain inequities. Despondently, schools are bureaucratic platforms with systemic inequities that could be harming pupils. Power, of which an everyday human purpose. The systemic bias embedded in schools is not based on personality traits. They are systems themselves within systems. They are sets of rules, practises, expectations and consequences of which lead to inequitable outcomes affecting specific groups of people of colour, women, homosexuals, underpriviledged and people with disabilities. While the teacher has a public face of a disciplinarian embarking on allocating degrees of competence, the school counsellor has the responsibility to counsel and treat all the same.

The irony of school counselling across, is its focus on pupils, following not only counselling/psychological interventions, but also presented along institutional systemic biases. While school counsellors are for the pupils, teachers with implicit biases upon the children freely roam schools intimidating the children. Who calls on teachers' bias against children for desired success and growth of the pupil? How can schools start addressing this overlooked predicament? The discourse used by counsellors needs not only be, that the entire school community; teachers, parents and the pupils are exposed to and agree with. The systemic bias in education discourse, can be stringent focus and implementation of what has worked in the past, concluded that would work in the present, while disregarding apparent distinctiveness of situations and or individuals/groups. Discourse is consisted of not only the natural language, but also all the practices encountered in life, events and signs of systems. Neither wording nor mutual agreements truly captures reality because each reality depends on the viewpoint of the speaker of which is itself influenced by the discourses that position that speaker (Corson, 2001). In many instances, whenever convenient for some to do so people have rationalised and claimed that to be reasoning (Carson, 2001). Things have been altered and then called to be 'creative' while others have

318

been repressed through language and this called to be 'helpful' (Corson 2001, Edelman 1984). Against this, Foucault presents four cases of children whose families, schools and communities perceive them as misfits. They thought of as 'incorrigible', 'defiant', 'lacking in responsibility' and 'delinquent'. However, Foucault all these expressions could be drastically be reworded for the same children to be regarded differently: 'irrepressible', (instead of incorrigible); 'debunking' (instead of defiant); 'refusing to be sucked in by society (instead of lacking in responsibility)

The power exerted through language is the vehicle for identifying, manipulation and changing power relations between senders of messages and the receivers. The degrees of the emotional and social intelligence within those engaged in the process determines the effectiveness of their engagement. Foucault views power as a network of relations constantly in tension and ever-present in discursive activity. Taking place through production, accumulation, and functioning of various discourses. Along this, Foucault indicates that discourse is the fickle, uncontrollable object of human conflict although no-one is outside it completely or sufficiently independent of discourses to manage them effectively. However, when there's lack of the balance of power, the conflicts that take place over and around discourse can be one-sided (Foucault 1972; 1977; 1980).

Accordingly, people's behaviour tends to be influenced by outward factors aligned with dynamic discourse around them (Corson 2001). Along this, Gramsci identified a non-coercive power though how people have perceptions of themselves and of their roles that make them conform to different influences in their social environments. Moreover, Gramsci highlights that they tend to agree to things under the pressure of invisible cultural power. Contemporary, power is constituted by numerous terms of agreements, hitherto, the non-coercive power penetrates consciousness itself resulting into the dominated being an accomplice in their own domination (1948/1966). Thus, there's always an underlying pressure and measures geared at shaping and informing one's identity to the extent that they are now in. This is, by Gramsci a hegemonic influence reinforced from both sides of power relations. Corson (2001) supports this notion by revealing that: "In their behaviour in any given context, the less powerful tend to adhere to the norms created by powerful others who may be distant from them in time and place. They do this while not always recognizing that they are being 'voluntarily coerced'.

SOCIAL JUSTICE AND COUNSELLING

Although there's generally no fully agreed upon definition of social justice, this humanly viewed endeavour has to do with ideals about legitimacy, fairness, impartiality, political and social consensus, welfare and mutual advantages. Justice itself refers to the way that benefits and burdens are distributed and is usually said to exist when people receive that to which they are entitled to (Barry, 1999). Along this, counselling of course is another humanly oriented endeavour whereby, one creates their own solutions through engagement with a trained counsellor to address rampant issues occurring in their lives. For counselling to be effective, it needs not be linear but more about exchanging ideas and creating one's own meanings and solutions to their problems.

Social Justice Counselling

Local school counselling experiences is such that, one ponders as to: when and where can school counsellors be trained on social justice endeavours? The ongoing engagements of school counselling have been primarily about guidance and counselling on psycho-social issues. For instance, the National Education Policy Investigation report (NEPI, 1992) of South Africa defines guidance and counselling as two different approaches and responsibilities of personnel. Accordingly, guidance involves curriculum activities, while counselling has a separate service provided to pupils besides the curriculum, such as individual counselling, trauma interventions, and parent support and guidance. Along this, a limited research on local school counselling also seem to be more interested in this set-up orientation of school counselling, pinpointing at such issues, overlooking historical background, political framework, inequities as social justice issues as well requiring school counselling.

Internationally, one can observe a wealth of research on school counsellor advocacy addressing issues of social inequity in schools (Bailey, Getch & Chen-Hayes, 2003; Cox & Lee, 2007; Holcomb-McCoy, 2007 House & Martin, 1999). However, their focus has been on the importance of advocacy work on the past school counsellors. Against this, there's limited research addresses the question of how school counsellors can be trained to assume this challenging role (Ratts, DeKruyf & Chen-Hayes, 2007; Trusty &, 2005). In support of this notion, Singh (2010) argues that there's silence of the voices of practising school counsellors in the justice literature in school counselling and calls for qualitative studies to gain significant ways of in-depth understanding of how school counsellors develop and implement advocacy strategies. Singh (2010) also suggests a grounded theory of how school counsellors who identify a social justice agency advocate for systemic change within their school communities.

The international advocacy of school counsellor advocates urged a redress of educational inequities and transformation in academic achievement that may be grounded in issues of race/ethnicity, gender, class, disability status and sexual orientation and that may prevent many students from maximising their academic, social and personal potential (Cox & Lee; Singh 2010). This voice has been supported by ongoing engagements to develop the counselling role from its traditional focus on the intrapsychic concerns of individual students to a broader focus on students' intellectual, social and psychological development (Goodman et al., 2004, Kiselica & Robinson, 2001' Lee, 2007). However, this chapter is not about reviewing that movement's engagement. Only these select school counselling initiatives lend value with groundwork for social justice school counselling:

- In 1996, the Transforming School Counseling Initiative (TSCI), in collaboration with the Education Trust examined the innovative roles for school counsellors. Their conclusion is that, advocacy must be a critical counselling role, especially as it relates to the collection of data to highlight educational disparities (Paisley & Hayes, 2002).
- Then, the American School Counselor Association developed the ASCA National Model to define school counselors' roles as advocates and addresses the question of: "How are students different because of what school counsellors do? The ASCA National Model (2005) which offers a comprehensive framework to guide school counselling programmes is based on the qualities of leadership, advocacy and collaboration, which are intended to lead to systemic change.
- In another engagement, the American Counseling Association (ACA) sanctioned its formal Advocacy Competencies (Lewis, Arnold, House & Toporek, 2003); focusing on competencies that encourage all counsellors to advocate on three levels (student/client, school/community and public arena) to resolve social justice issues rooted in environmental and systemic factors.

The above are interesting models for social justice school counsellors in cognisance of limited research with insights into how school counsellors in the field incorporate social justice agenda into their work. Thus, the challenge of how to infuse social justice orientation into school counsellor training remains.

Counselling

Counselling of course along education, is an endeavour of hope and struggle. When a counsellor engages a child, there is hope for better life while on the other hand, there's a struggle on how to make the child understand and or the counsellors themselves understand the child for relevant engagement and success of that better life. Undeniably, education systems remain arenas with legacy of oppressions, whereby teachers, counsellors, pupils and parents strive to uncover old experiences of dominations, oppression and catastrophe to end up believing that they can be great partakers of a new and relevant history. With that mentality, a realisation of that no counselling is or ever can be innocent is vital, for counselling must be positioned in a cultural context, an historical movement; an economic condition and individuality of a pupil. Counselling must be toward something; it must take a stand; it is either for or against; it must account for the specific within the universal.

Many counsellors also know what it means to counsel against the status quo; oppression, opposition and obstinacy; against the history of evil; against shallow and common-sense assumptions. Counselling of course, functions paradoxically because of its association with and location in schools. While education is about opening doors, opening minds, opening possibilities, the very same arena; school, is often about categorisation/classification and punishing, grading and ranking and certifying. The truth is that, education is unconditional. It's either you take it or leave it. It asks for nothing in return. One either passes or fails. One either has a qualification or doesn't. for one to pass and or have a qualification, they ought to obey school's routinely demands. Undeniably, obedience and conformity are preconditions to attendance. Ironically, education is amazing, disorderly and inquisitive, while the first and fundamental law of school is to follow orders. An educated person has a free mind while a 'schooled' person remains with a bureaucratised brain. Along the educator, a counsellor for social justice releases the suppressive mode of schooling, while a school teacher sometimes starts with an unhealthy obsession with a commitment to classroom management and linear lesson plans.

Contemporary counsellor's duty is so complex as based on its idiosyncratic and improvisational character, with ambiguity as a person's mind or a human heart, as unique and imaginative as a friendship or a love affair, as explosive and unpredictable as a revolution. Does counselling leadership even know what school counselling of nowadays is and or about? The counsellor's duties are about personally experiences, individuality along belongingness, background, environment, setting, surround, position, situation, connection and even some unknowns as well as hidden lot. Importantly, counselling centrally about relationships with this or that person, in this specific world, at a moment. It is dynamic and about one's dynamism.

Looking at how working in schools where the fundamental truths and demands for possibilities of teaching and learning are incomprehensible, reduced and cloudy, along the strong ethical core efforts systematically erased and overlooked; a counsellor for social justice remains with a task to reengage with the large purposes of counselling.

Counselling pupils for social justice is at the core of democratic education. It serves as a reminder not only of the inequities and biases that continue to wear away at the foundation of democratic values, but of the powerful experiences which inspire educators and learners to work toward change and make the world a better place. When issues of social justice are at the heart of teaching and learning, pupils benefit from the rich history of people who didn't settle for the way things are: Nelson Mandela, Samora Machel, Jomo Kenyatta, Patrice Lumumba, Thomas Sankara,

Kwame Nkrumah, Julius Nyerere, Winnie Mandela, Steve Biko, Marcus Mosiah Garvey who are notable freedom fighters and countless union workers, teachers and good neighbours. A focus on counselling for social justice reminds the people that the children need not only a grounding in academics but also practice in how to use those academics to promote a democratic society in which all get to participate fully.

That kind of counselling is consciously for social justice; to counsel for transformation of status quo, for change. Consequentially it has its own complicating elements to the ultimate message, for, its reality isn't in wording, but also about the conveyor of the content and the mannerism of delivery; making it encrusted, solid, challenging to enact. On the other hand, coherent, essential, needed, engaging, influential and ecstatic, for it to be shared. Therefore, counselling for social justice demands dialectical stance: one firmly fixed on the pupils; asking oneself: Who are they? Where are they coming from? What do they have and do not have? Why? What are their aspirations? What are their challenges and stumbling blocks to their success? What excites them? Do they have commitments and if so in what, if not what has hampered chances of having their own commitments? What skills, abilities, talents and capacities does each one bring to the school? The other eye of course, observing unblinkingly at the nature of context within which one operates; its historical trend, cultural environment, economic reality against international demands. Along this, counselling for social justice is counselling that arouses learners, engaging them in an expedition to identify impediments to their full humanity, to their exploration of available freedoms of democracies and act against those hindrances. One way or the other, the fundamental message of a school counsellor for social justice is that: 'You can be change catalyst and change the world.'

CRITICAL REALISM

Contextualisation of Counselling for Education

According to Dahir and Stone (2009), a school counsellor is 'ideally situated in school to serve as social justice advocate to eliminate the achievement gap and focus their efforts on ensuring success for every underserved and underrepresented student' (p:16). This notion is supported by transformation of the roles and responsibilities of a school counsellor (Amatea & Clark, 2005; ASCA, 2003; Baker, Robichaud, Westforth Dietrich, Wells, & Schreck, 2009; Bemak, 2000; Dahir & Stone, 2009; Dollarhide, 2003; Paisley, Ziomek-Daigle, Getch, & Bailey, 2006; Ratts, DeKruyf, & Chen-Hayes, 2007). These authors call for a school counsellor to be leader, advocate and change agent. These roles illustrate a professional for social justice in the school system for holistic effectiveness on pupils' access, retention and success.

323

If school counsellors are to be effective in being social justice advocates, they also need to observe communities' issues as intertwined to the pupils, as well as the discourse and or practices of their colleagues teaching in schools. Accordingly, having the identified roles implies that a school counsellor consistently assesses and is knowledgeable of school and student issues, maintains and involves a collaborative network of stakeholders and mediates at various levels to promote justice, equity and access; in order to close achievement gaps (Ockerman & Mason, 2012). Such a mode of operation depicts a daily theoretical-practical engagement of a school counsellor which is transformed from the counterparts of the past, who traditionally served students only in a one-to-one basis from their offices (Ockerman & Mason, 2012).[14]

Diversity Awareness and Critical Counselling Awareness

The rampant and increasing diversity across communities provides evidence of the need for schools to be aware of dynamics of diversity. Along this, is persistent failure rate across diverse groups in schools (Feldwisch & Whiston, 2015). Awareness of diversity in schools is very helpful, not only for pupils to learn and only about pupils. There are many other things that diverse pupils need to know about diversity, so many in fact that they cannot be listed in this chapter. Actually, awareness of diversity is an endeavour that even counsellor need to constantly upgrade. The nature of critical realism in counselling is such that, a status quo is demystified, using research-based discourse about present and real-life of diverse groups of pupils and the people at large. This is primarily informed about the beneficiaries, as in present and not engraining of what has worked in the past, as ought to work in present.

Feldwich and Whiston (2015) the academic achievement of pupils from diverse backgrounds persistently reflects an unequal education system. This is regardless of various efforts for success and retainment of pupils in schools. Against this, a call for more counsellors exhibiting social justice advocacy have been sought to address the rampant achievement gap (Bemak & Chung, 2005; Dixon, Tucker & Clark, 2010; Lewis, Arnold, House & Toporek, 2003, Hipolito-Delgado & Lee, 2007; Holcomb-McCoy, 2007; Ratts, DeKruyf, & Chen-Hayes, 2007).

Emancipatory Conception of Counselling for Social Justice

Critical realism is an ontology to identify the most basic things that exist, in this context, in a school. According to Bemak and Chung (2008) school counsellors also function to be liked in schools, in fear of raising uncomfortable dialogues across colleagues and pupils. Against such a perception of counsellors, critical realism examines the existing knowledge about anything within the school setting and surround. According to Bhaskar, the most basic evidence we can obtain about the social world is the reasons and accounts that offer people the description of things in their real world that they value and or the things that oppress them. An inquisitive question becomes: Why a school counsellor prioritise being liked in their surround at the expense of pupils in need social justice in schools?

When counsellors are dealing with pupils, they must always be cognisant of existing human agency pupils might be coming from, because such an understanding reflects, also understanding of the fact that, they (human agencies) are influenced by certain social structures that, themselves entail certain actions. Counselling for social justice, is oriented by disparities embedded across individuals and groups, of which might be engrained into entrails of social structures informing their worldviews. Thus, critical realism lends value towards addressing underlying matters through actual and not what the other, in past had done, marrying that to the now-situation.

Along this, Singh et al (2010) argue that practice, training and research are crucial means for social justice counselling. A point to keep in mind with this grounded theory of these researchers is that, it has its own limitations making it not viable for transferability regardless of its (the nature of grounded theory study) nature of having an advantage of not seeking generalisability (Creswell, 2006). Nevertheless, lessons from this study can serve as a means for a relevant research engagement. From their findings, the practice and training lend value to the school counsellors in support of social justice skills in schools. This encompasses tackling difficult discourse along power relations in schools. Continued education of school counsellors also serves a dynamic purpose on relevant social justice content. Moreover, research keep schools abreast about happenings in other areas as well as within their own surround. Counsellors need not wait for other professionals to publish research for them to take as relevant models. The voice of counsellors in research is required as it can offer sound advice and insight born from first-hand experience in dealing with pupils within schools. Moreover, collaborating with colleagues on social justice agenda, especially when it comes to addressing underlying issues in schools, needs to be a planned and intentional practice (Paisley, 2002).

CONCLUSION

While this chapter contributes to the compilation of literature on school counselling, it falls short of offering its own strategies used by school counsellors for social justice. Thus, it raises some interesting questions throughout the sections, towards development of local studies for relevant issues. A call for local research is sought to exonerate the author from being prescribing own perspectives as reality. Perhaps, some of the notions shared can serve as hypothetical statements towards developing studies to lend value to the dire situation of African school counselling.

Mezirow (2000) suggests six perspectives that can be viewed as strategies for transformative learning and for such to even begin situated within schools, the counsellors would need to take a broader role beyond intrapsychic and guidance engagements with pupils. If school counsellors are to be largely taken seriously, their voices need to be heard and research being better means of spreading such voices. Along the limited research in social justice school counselling, there also exists a gap in studies on school counsellors' intentional building of support networks in-out of schools to facilitate the social justice agenda.

REFERENCES

Aldrich, H., & Herker, D. (1977, April). Boundary Spanning Roles and Organization Structure. *Academy of Management Review*, 217–230.

Aldrich, H., & Whetten, D. (1981). Organization-Sets, Action-Sets, and Networks: Making the most of Simplicity. In P. C. Nystrom & W. H. Starbuck (Eds.), *Handbook of Organizational Design* (Vol. 1). New York: Oxford University Press.

Amatea, E. S., & Clark, M. A. (2005). Changing schools, changing counsellors: A qualitative study of school administrators' conceptions of the school counsellor role. *Professional School Counseling, 9*(1), 6–27. doi:10.5330/prsc.9.1.w6357vn62n5328vp

American School Counselor Association. (2005). *The ASCA national model: A framework for school counselling programs* (2nd ed.). Alexandria, VA: Author.

Atler, C., & Hage, J. (1993). *Organizations Working Together*. Newbury Park, CA: Sage Publications.

Baile, C. (2006). *Refugee Social Networks and Organizational Resettlement Networks: Generating an Integrative Model* (PhD Dissertation). The New School.

Bailey, D. F., Getch, Y. Q., & Chen-Hayes, S. (2003). Professional school counsellors as social and academic advocates. In B. T. Erford (Ed.), *Transforming the school counselling profession* (pp. 441–434). Upper Saddle River, NJ: Merrill Prentice Hall.

Bailey, D. F., Getch, Y. Q., & Chen-Hayes, S. (2007). Achievement advocacy for all students through transformative school counselling programs. In B. T. Erford (Ed.), *Transforming the school counselling profession* (pp. 98–120). Upper Saddle River, NJ: Merrill Prentice Hall.

Baker, S. B., & Gerler, E. R. Jr. (2004). *School Counseling for the Twenty-First Century* (4th ed.). North Carolina: Pearson.

Baker, S. B., Robichaud, T. A., Westforth Dietrich, V. C., Wells, S. C., & Schreck, R. E. (2009). School counselor consultation: A pathway to advocacy, collaboration, and leadership. *Professional School Counseling, 12*(3), 200–206. doi:10.5330/ PSC.n.2010-12.200

Bartuner, J. M., & Reynolds, C. (1983). Boundary Spanning and Public Accountant Role Stress. *The Journal of Social Psychology, 121*(1), 65–72. doi:10.1080/00224 545.1983.9924468 PMID:6645425

Baum, J. A. C. (Ed.). (2002). *The Blackwell companion to organizations.* Malden, MA: Blackwell.

Baumgartner, L. M. (2001). An Update on Transformational Learning. *New Directions for Adult and Continuing Education, 2001*(89), 15–24. doi:10.1002/ace.4

Bemak, F. (2000). Transforming the role of the counselor to provide leadership in educational reform through collaboration. Professional School Counseling, 3(5), 323-331 Retrieved from http://www.schoolcounselor.org/content.asp?contentid=235

Bemak, F., & Chung, C. Y. (2005). Advocacy as a critical role for urban school counsellors: Working toward equity and social justice. *Professional School Counseling, 8,* 196.

Bemak, F., & Chung, C. Y. (2006). New professional roles and advocacy strategies for school counsellors: A multicultural perspective to move beyond the nice counsellor syndrome. *Journal of Counseling and Development, 86*(3), 372–381. doi:10.1002/j.1556-6678.2008.tb00522.x

Benson, J. (1975). The Interorganizational Network as A Political Economy. *Administrative Science Quarterly, 20*(2), 229–249. doi:10.2307/2391696

Bertalanffy, L. (1972). The History and Status of General Systems Theory. The Academy of Management Journal, 15(4), 407-426.

Bliese, P. D. (2000). Within-group agreement, non-independence, and reliability: Implications for data aggregation and analysis. In K. J. Klein & S. W. J. Kozlowski (Eds.), *Multilevel theory, research, and methods in organizations, foundations, extensions, and new directions* (pp. 349–381). San Francisco: Jossey-Bass.

Borgatti, S. P., & Foster, P. C. (2003). The network paradigm in organizational research: A review and typology. *Journal of Management, 29*(6), 991–1013. doi:10.1016/S0149-2063(03)00087-4

Brass, D. J., Galaskiewicz, J., Greve, H. R., & Tsai, W. (2004). Taking stock of networks and organizations: A multilevel perspective. *Academy of Management Journal, 47*(8), 795–817.

Bundy, C. (2005). Global patterns, local options? Some implications for South Africa of international changes in higher education. *Perspectives in Education, 23*(2), 85–98.

Burt, R. (1995). *Structural Holes: The Social Structure of Competition.* Cambridge, MA: Harvard University Press.

Burton, P., Wu, Y., & Prybutok, V. R. (2010). Social Network Position and Its Relationship to Performance of IT Professional. Information Science. *The International Journal of an Emerging Transfiscipline., 13,* 121–137.

Cappelli, P., & Scherer, P. (1991). The missing role of context in OB: The need for a meso level approach. In Research in organizational behavior. Greenwich, CT: JAI.

Carley, K. M. (2002). Computational organization science: A new frontier. *National Academy of Science, 99*(Supplement 3), 7257–7262. doi:10.1073/pnas.082080599 PMID:12011404

Carley, K. M., & Wallace, W. A. (2001). Computational organization theory: A new perspective. In S. Gass & C. M. Harris (Eds.), *Encyclopedia of operations research and management science.* Norwich, MA: Kluwer Academic Publishers. doi:10.1007/1-4020-0611-X_143

Chang, M., & Harrison, J. E. (2004). Agent-based models of organizations. Handbook of Computational Economics II: Agent-based. *Computational Economics,* 1273–1377.

Coman, A., Momennejad, I., Geana, A., & Drach, D. R. (2016). Mnemonic convergence in social networks: The emergent properties of cognition at a collective level. *Proceedings of the National Academy of Sciences of the United States of America, 113*(29), 8171–8176. doi:10.1073/pnas.1525569113 PMID:27357678

Constantine, M., Hage, S., Kindaichi, M., & Bryant, R. (2007). Social justice and multicultural issues: Implications for the practice and training of counsellors and counselling psychologists. *Journal of Counseling and Development, 85*(1), 24–29. doi:10.1002/j.1556-6678.2007.tb00440.x

Contractor, N. S., & Eisenberg, E. M. (1990). Communication Networks and New Media in Organizations. In Fulk, J. & Steinfield, C. (eds) Organizations and Communication Technology, pp. 143-171 Sage Publications, Newbury Park. doi:10.4135/9781483325385.n7

Cox, A. A., & Lee, C. C. (2007). Challenging educational inequities: School counsellors as agents of social justice. In C. C. Lee (Ed.), *Counseling for social justice* (2nd ed.; pp. 3–14). Alexandria, VA: American Counseling Association.

Cranton, P. (1994). *Understanding and promoting transformative learning: A guide for educators and adults*. San Francisco: Jossey-Bass.

Cranton, P. A. (1998). Fostering authentic relationships in the transformative classroom. *New Directions for Adult and Continuing Education, 2006*(109), 5–13.

Cranton, P. A. (2002). Teaching for transformation. *New Directions for Adult and Continuing Education, 2002*(93), 63–71. doi:10.1002/ace.50

Cranton, P. A., & Roy, M. (2003). When the bottom falls out of the bucket: A holistic perspective on transformative learning. *Journal of Transformative Education, 1*(2), 86–98. doi:10.1177/1541344603001002002

Creswell, J. W. (2006). *Qualitative inquiry and research design: Choosing among five traditions* (2nd ed.). Thousand Oaks, CA: Sage Publication.

Cross, M. (2011). *An Unfulfilled Promise. Transforming Schools in Mozambique. Organisation for Social Research in Eastern and Southern Africa*. OSSREA.

Cross, R., Borgatti, S. P., & Parker, A. (2002). Making Invisible Work Visible: Using Social Network Analysis to Support Strategic Collaboration. *California Management Review, 44*(2), 25–46. doi:10.2307/41166121

Cross, R., Thomas, R., & Light, D. (n.d.). Creating the Right Decision-Making Networks: Driving Decision Efficiency and Effectiveness through Networks. Academic Press.

Cross, R., & Thomas, R. J. (2009). *Driving Results Through Social Networks: How Top Organizations Leverage Networks for Performance and Growth*. San Francisco: Jossey-Bass.

Cross, R. L., Parker, A., & Cross, R. (2004). *The Hidden Power of Social Networks: Understanding How Work Really Gets Done in Organizations* (1st ed.). Harvard Business Review Press.

Dahir, C. A., & Stone, C. B. (2009). School counsellor accountability: The path to social justice and systemic change. *Journal of Counseling and Development, 87*(1), 12–20. doi:10.1002/j.1556-6678.2009.tb00544.x

Dahl, R. (1961). *Who Governs?* New Haven, CT: Yale University Press.

Daloz, L. (1986). *Effective Teaching and Mentoring: Realizing the Transformational Power of Adult Learning.* Jossey-Bass.

Dirkx, J. M. (1998). Transformative learning theory in the practice of adult education: An overview. *PAACE Journal of Lifelong Learning, 7,* 1–14.

Dirkx, J. M. (2000). Transformative learning and the journey of individuation. *ERIC Digests, 223,* 1–7.

Dirkx, J. M. (2006). Engaging emotions in adult learning: A Jungian perspective on emotion and transformative learning. *New Directions for Adult and Continuing Education, 2006*(109), 15–26. doi:10.1002/ace.204

Dixon, A. L., Tucker, C., & Clark, M. A. (2010). Integrating social justice advocacy with national standards for practice: Implications for school counsellor education. *Counselor Education and Supervision, 50*(2), 103–115. doi:10.1002/j.1556-6978.2010.tb00112.x

Dollarhide, C. T. (2003). School counselors as program leaders: Applying leadership contexts to school counseling. *Professional School Counseling, 6*(5), 304. Retrieved from http://www.schoolcounselor.org/content.asp?contentid=235

Dooley, K. (2002). Organizational complexity, In International encyclopedia of business and management. London: Thomson Learning.

Du Toit, E. (2012). Constructive feedback as a learning tool to enhance students' self-regulation and performance in higher education. *Perspectives in Education, 30*(2), 32–40.

Evan, W. M. (1966). The Organization Set: Toward a Theory of Interorganizational Relationships. In J. D. Thompson (Ed.), *Approaches to Organizational Design* (pp. 175–191). Pittsburgh, PA: University of Pittsburgh Press.

Evoh, C. J. (2009). *Collaborative partnerships and the transformation of secondary schools in South Africa* (Dissertation). The New School of Social Research.

Feldwisch, R. P., & Whiston, S. C. (2015-2016). Examining School Counselors' Commitments to Social Justice Advocacy. *Professional School Counseling, 19*(1), 166–175. doi:10.5330/1096-2409-19.1.166

Field, J. E., & Baker, S. (2004). Defining and examining school counsellor advocacy. *Professional School Counseling, 8,* 56–63.

Findlay, C. M. (2010). Transformative curriculum: changing pedagogy and practice (Master's Thesis). School of Graduate Studies of the University of Lethbridge.

Forrester, J. (1961). *Industrial Dynamics*. Cambridge, MA: Productivity Press Incorporated.

Freire, P. (1997). *The Politics of Education: Culture, Power and Liberation* (1st ed.). Bergin & Garvey Publishers.

Galaskiewicz, J. (1979a). *Exchange Networks and Community Politics* (Vol. 75). Beverly Hills, CA: Sage Publications.

Galaskiewicz, J. (1979b). The Structure of Community Networks. *Social Forces*, *57*(4), 1346–1364. doi:10.1093f/57.4.1346

Galaskiewicz, J. (1985). Interorganizational Relations. *Annual Review of Sociology*, *11*(1), 281–304. doi:10.1146/annurev.so.11.080185.001433

Galbraith, J. R. (1973). *Designing complex organizations*. Reading, MA: Addison-Wesley Publishing Company.

Galbraith, J. R. (1977). *Organization design*. Reading, MA: Addison-Wesley Publishing Company.

Goodman, L. A., Lian, B., Helman, J. E., Latta, R. E., Sparks, E., & Weintraub, S. R. (2004). Training psychologists as social justice agents: Feminists and multicultural principles in action. *The Counseling Psychologist*, *32*, 793–837. doi:10.1177/0011000004268802

Griffiths, N., Aitken, A., & Egea, K. (2014). *A Collaborative Approach to Embedding Academic Literacies in First Year Grant Projects*. Academic Press.

Gulati, R. (1998). Alliances and Networks. *Strategic Management Journal*, *19*(4), 293–317. doi:10.1002/(SICI)1097-0266(199804)19:4<293::AID-SMJ982>3.0.CO;2-M

Gulati, R., Dialdin, D. A., & Wang, L. (2002). Organizational networks. In J. A. C. Baum (Ed.), *The Blackwell companion to organizations* (pp. 281–303). Malden, MA: Blackwell.

Gysbers, N. C. (2004). Comprehensive guidance and counseling programs: The evolution of accountability. *Professional School Counseling*, *8*, 1–14. Retrieved from http://www.schoolcounselor.org/content.asp?contentid=235

Hagedoorn, J. (2006). Understanding the cross-level embeddedness of interfirm partnership formation. *Academy of Management Review*, *31*(3), 670–680. doi:10.5465/amr.2006.21318924

Harary, F., & Batell, M. F. (1981). What is a system? *Social Networks*, *3*(1), 29–40. doi:10.1016/0378-8733(81)90003-4

Hawley, A. (1963). Community Power and Urban Renewal Success. *American Journal of Sociology*, *68*(4), 422–431. doi:10.1086/223399

Hayes, R. L., & Paisley, P. O. (2002). Transforming school counsellor preparation programs. *Theory into Practice*, *41*(3), 169–176. doi:10.120715430421tip4103_5

Herr, E. L. (2002). School reform and perspectives on the role of school counselors: A century of proposals for change. *Professional School Counseling*, *5*(4), 220–234.

Hipolito-Delgado, C. P., & Lee, C. C. (2007). Empowerment theory for the professional school counsellor: A manifesto for what really matters. *Professional School Counseling*, *10*(4), 327–332. doi:10.5330/prsc.10.4.fm1547261m80x744

Hitt, M. A., Beamish, P. W., Jackson, S. E., & Mathieu, J. E. (2007). Building theoretical and empirical bridges across levels: Multilevel research in management. *Academy of Management Journal*, *50*(6), 1385–1399. doi:10.5465/amj.2007.28166219

Holcomb-McCoy, C. (2007). *School counselling to close the achievement gap: A social justice framework to success*. Thousand Oaks, CA: Sage Publications.

Hope, A. E., & Timmel, S. J. (2014). *Training for Transformation in Practice*. Practical Action Publishing.

House, R., & Martin, P. J. (1999). Advocating for better futures for all students: A new vision for school counsellors. *Education*, *119*, 284–291.

Hunter, F. (1953). *Community Power Structure*. Chapel Hill, NC: University of North Carolina Press.

Jensen, U. (2011). *Factors Influencing Student Retention in Higher Education. Summary of Influential Factors in Degree Attainment and Persistence to Career or Further Education for At-Risk/High Educational Need Students*. Honolulu, HI: Kamehema Schools Research & Evaluation Division.

Jonsson, C. (1986). Interoganization Theory and International Organization. *International Studies Quarterly*, *30*(1), 39–57. doi:10.2307/2600436

Katz, D., & Kahn, R. L. (1978). *The social psychology of organizations*. New York: John Wiley.

Kenis, P., & Knoke, D. (2002). How Organizational Field Networks Shape Interorganizational Tie-Formation Rates. *Academy of Management Review*, *27*(2), 275–293. doi:10.5465/amr.2002.6588029

Kilduff, M., & Tsai, W. (2003). *Social networks and organizations*. Thousand Oaks, CA: Sage. doi:10.4135/9781849209915

Knoke, D. (2001). *Changing Organizations: Business Networks in the New Political Economy*. Boulder, CO: Westview Press.

Kozlowski, W. J., & Klein, K. (2000). *Multilevel Theory, research and methods in organizations: Foundations, Extensions, and new directions*. San Francisco: Jossey-Bass.

Krebs, V. E. (2011b). *Network Analysis: Understanding the Connected Economy. Public guest lecture*. Riga, Latvia: Stockholm School of Economics in Riga.

Lawrence, B. S. (2000). *Working Paper- Organizational Reference Groups: How People Constitute the Human Component of their Work Environment*. Los Angeles: Anderson Graduate School of Management, University of California.

Lebakeng, J., Phalane, M. M., & Dalindjebo, N. (2005). *Epistemicide, Institutional Cultures and the Imperative for the Africanasation of Universities in South Africa*. University of South Africa.

Lebakeng, T. J. (2000). Africanasation of the Social Sciences and Humanities in South Africa. In L. A. Kasanga (Ed.), *Challenges and Changes at Historically Disadvantaged Universities*. University of North.

Lebakeng, T. J. (2001). The State, Globalisation and Higher Education. *Southern Africa Political & Economic Monthly, 4*, 7.

Lebakeng, T. J. (2004). *Prospects and Problems of Transforming Universities in South Africa, with Special Refence to the Right to be an African University* (PhD thesis). Department of Sociology, University of the North.

Lee, c. (Ed.). (2007). *Counseling for social justice* (2nd ed.). Alexandria, VA: American Counseling Association.

Leke, A., Fine, D., Dobbs, R., Magwentshu, N., Lund, S., & Jacobson, P. (2015). *South Africa's Big Five: Bold Priorities for Inclusive Growth. McKinsey Report*. McKinsey Global Institute.

Lewis, J., Arnold, M. S., House, R., & Toporek, R. (2003). *Advocacy competencies*. Academic Press.

Love, K. A. (2011). Enacting a Transformative Education. In Critical pedagogy in the Twenty First Century: A new generation of scholars. New York, NY: Age.

Maznevski, M. L., Steger, U., & Amann, W. (2007). *Managing Complexity in Global Organizations*. IMD.

McPherson, M., Smith-Lovin, L., & Cook, J. (2001). Birds of a Feather: Homophily in Social Networks. *Annual Review of Sociology, 27*(1), 415–444. doi:10.1146/annurev.soc.27.1.415

Merril, J., Bakken, S., Rockoff, M., Gebbi, K., & Carley, K. (2007). Description of a method to support public health information management: Organisational network analysis. *Journal of Biochemical Informatics, 40*(40), 422–428.

Metcalfe, L. (1981). Designing Precarious Partnerships. In P. C. Nystrom & W. H. Starbuck (Eds.), *Handbook of Organizational Design* (Vol. 1). New York: Oxford University Press.

Mezirow, J. (1997). Transformative learning: Theory to practice. *New Directions for Adult and Continuing Education, 74*(74), 5–12. doi:10.1002/ace.7401

Mezirow, J. (2003a). Transformative learning as discourse. *Journal of Transformative Education, 1*(1), 58–63. doi:10.1177/1541344603252172

Mezirow. (2003b). Epistemology of transformative learning. In Transformative learning in action: Building bridges across contexts and disciplines (pp. 326-330). Academic Press.

Miller, A., Smith, E., Park, E., & Engle, J. (2014). *Blurring Boundries: Transforming Place, Policies, and Partnerships for Postsecondary Education Attainment in Metropolitan Areas*. Washington, DC: Institute for Higher Education Policy.

Mizruchi, M. S. (1996). What do interlocks do? An analysis, critique, and assessment of research on interlocking directorates. *Annual Review of Sociology, 22*(1), 271–298. doi:10.1146/annurev.soc.22.1.271

Moliterno, P. T., & Mahony, D. M. (2011). Network Theory of Organization: A Multilevel Approach. *Journal of Management, 37*(2), 443–467. doi:10.1177/0149206310371692

Moore, J. (2005). Is Higher Education Ready for Transformative Learning: A question Explored in the Study of Sustainability. *Journal of Transformative Education, 3*(1), 76–91. doi:10.1177/1541344604270862

Muller, J. (1997). Social justice and its renewals: A sociological comment. *International Studies in Sociology of Education, 7*(2), 195–211. doi:10.1080/09620219700200011

Ndebele, N., Sawyer, A., Rowett, J., & Perinbam, L. (2005). The Abertay Conversation. Communique to G 8 Leaders.

Nohria, N., & Eccles, R. G. (Eds.). (1993). *Network and Organizations: Structure, Form and Action*. Boston, MA: Harvard Business School.

Ockerman, M. S., & Mason, E. C. (2012). Developing School Counseling Students' Social Justice Orientation Through Service Learning. DePaul University. Retrieved from: https://files.eric.ed.gov/fulltext/EJ978861.pdf

Ostroff, C., & Bowen, D. E. (2000). Moving HR to a higher level: HR practices and organizational effectiveness. In K. J. Klein & S. W. J. Kozlowski (Eds.), *Multilevel theory, research, and methods in organizations, foundations, extensions, and new directions.* San Francisco: Jossey-Bass.

Paisely, P. O., & Border, L. D. (1995). School Counseling: An Evolving Specialty. Journal of counseling and development. *JCD, 74*(2), 150–153. doi:10.1002/j.1556-6676

Paisley, P. O., & Hayes, R. L. (2002). Transformation in school counsellor preparation and practice. *Counseling and Human Development, 35*(3), 1–10.

Paisley, P. O., Ziomek-Daigle, J., & Getch, Q. Y., & F. Bailey, D. (2006). Using state standards to develop professional school counsellor identity as both counsellors and educators. Guidance & Counseling, 21(3), 143-151. Retrieved from http://www.tandf.co.uk/journals/authors/cbjgauth.asp

Palmer, D. A., & Biggart, W. (2002). Organizational Institutions. In J. A. C. Baum (Ed.), *The Blackwell companion to organizations.* Malden, MA: Blackwell.

Peeters, I., & Lievens, P. (2015). *The ultimate curriculum design for ultimate learning experience in higher education.* At the 6th International Conference of Technology, Education and Development (INTED), Valencia, Spain.

Pennymon, W. (2005). School counselors' perceptions of social advocacy training: Helpful and hindering events: A qualitative study. In N. S. Madu & S. Govender (Eds.), *Mental health and psychotherapy in Africa* (pp. 184–208). Sovenga, South Africa: UL Press of the University of Limpopo-Turfloop Campus.

Perrone, V., Zaheer, A., & McEvily, B. (2003). Free to be Trusted? Organizational Constraints on Trust in Boundary Spanners. *Organization Science, 14*(4), 442–439. doi:10.1287/orsc.14.4.422.17487

Price, D. V. (2005). *Learning Communities and Student Success in Postsecondary Education. MDRC Building Knowledge to Improve Social Policy. DVP-PRAXIS* LTD.

Price, J. H., & Murnan, J. (2004). Research Limitations and the Necessity of Reporting Them. *American Journal of Health Education, 35*(2), 66–67. doi:10.10 80/19325037.2004.10603611

Ratts, M. J., DeKruyf, L., & Chen-Hayes, S. F. (2007). The ACA advocacy competencies: A social justice advocacy framework for professional school counsellors. *Professional School Counseling, 11*(2), 90–97. doi:10.5330/PSC.n.2010-11.90

Salancik, G. R. (1995). WANTED: A good network theory of organization. *Administrative Science Quarterly, 40*, 345–349.

Sathe, L. A., & Geisler, C. C. (2015). The Reverberations of a graduate study abroad course in India. *Journal of Transformative Education*, 55–78.

Scott, J. (1991, 2000). Social Network Analysis: A Handbook (2nd ed.). Thousand Oaks, CA: Sage Publications.

Scott, W. R. (1998). *Organizations: Rational, Natural, and Open Systems* (4th ed.). Englewood Cliffs, NJ: Prentice-Hall.

Senge, P., Seville, D., Lovins, A., & Lotspeich, C. (1999). *Systems Thinking Primer for Natural Capitalism, Chapter 1: The Four Basic Shifts, working paper*. Academic Press.

Seybolt, T. B. (2000). *Systemic Network Analysis of Refugee Relief: A Business-like Approach*. Solna, Sweden: Stockholm International Peace Research Institute.

Simon, H. A. (1973). The organization of complex systems. In H. H. Pattee (Ed.), *Hierarchy theory* (pp. 1–27). New York: Braziller.

Singh, A., Urbano, A., Haston, M., & McMahon, E. (2010). School Counselors' Strategies for Social Justice Change: A Grounded Theory of What Works in the Real World. *Professional School Counseling, 13*(3), 135–145. doi:10.5330/PSC.n.2010-13.135

Steadman, H. J. (1992). Boundary Spanners: A Key Component for the Effective Interactions of the Justice and Mental Health Systems. *Law and Human Behavior, 16*(1), 75–87. doi:10.1007/BF02351050

Wasserman, S., & Faust, K. (1994). *Social Network analysis: methods and applications*. Cambridge, UK: Cambridge University Press. doi:10.1017/CBO9780511815478

Weber, M. (1947). *The Theory of Social and Economic Organization*. New York: Free Press.

Winant, H. (2001). *The World Is A Ghetto Race And Democracy Since World War II*. Basic Books.

Wyandotte, A., & Huh, S. (2012). *Of toads, gardens, and possibilities: A phenomenological approach to transformative education.* Transformational Learning of Three Adult Academicians.

Zack, M. H. (2000). Researching Organizational Systems using Social Network Analysis. *Proceedings of the 33rd Hawai'i International Conference on System Sciences.*

ENDNOTES

[1] Existing power relations, as well as networks can enable or disable imperatives of transformation, hence it's necessary to understand the nature of networks that exist for what purposes and necessitated by whom.

[2] Findlay (2010) conducted a research to investigate how a social studies programme changed curriculum specialists and teachers' perceptions of learning and pedagogy.

[3] See Winant (2001) 'after 1948 elections, the National Party set about instituting apartheid – as a means of legislation and regulated the kind of transformation that was skewed, benefitting non-Blacks.

[4] See Spirit of the Nation: Reflections on South Africa's Educational Ethos by New Africa Education, Human Sciences Research Council and the Department of Education.

[5] See Joas, 1993, p.81, fn.1

[6] See Luhmann, 1998, p.37.

[7] If the intentional design of institutional transformation integrates transformative counseling, schools' transformational goals would have improved.

[8] Note: PARTS vs. WHOLE- Reductionism "finds the ultimate meaning of the 'object' not in its inherent qualities but in the parts which compose it and in the lateral relations of those parts." The whole is equal to the sum of its parts, the significance being that if the whole is the same as the combination of its parts, there is no whole. Only the parts exist. Therefore, one should study the lower level elemental parts as the meaning of the whole instead of regarding the whole as the meaning of its parts. Put simply, "reductionism collapses (or reduces) the higher level of meaning and being into the lower level of elemental parts; when this collapse occurs what is left is not the whole but its parts." Retrieved on 24 October 2016, "The Concept of Reductionism," http://www.princeton.edu/~freshman/art/reduction/reduction.html.

[9] This theory lies in the "resource dependency" literature (Benson, 1975; Pfeffer & Salancik, 1978). In brief, resource dependency asserts the degree

of flexibility, effectiveness, and functionality of network members is a direct result of the external controls of the organizations within it.

[10] For brevity, boundary spanner research has not been directly incorporated into this proposal. For information on people that span the outer edges of organizations (i.e., boundary spanners) (Aldrich & Herker, 1977; Bartuner & Reynolds, 1983; Jonsson, 1986a; Perrone, Zaheer, & McEvily, 2003; Podolny & Baron, 1997; Steadman, 1992; Thompson, 1967; Williams, 2002).

[11] The term *effective* for this research means and that the existing collaboration offers fair platform for participation of designated agents geared at addressing diverse services.

[12] An example of HEI's network that Moliterno & Mahony (2010) offer is a scenario whereby; a Level 3 network of colleges within a university: Each college in turn consists of a Level 2 network of departments within the college, and each department consists of a Level 1 network of individual faculty members. Here, the relevant network ties may be joint faculty appointments (Level 3), serving across departments on doctoral committees (Level 2), and intradepartmental research collaborations (Level 1).

[13] ibid.

[14] Primarily, this requires operating in meaningfully visible and active roles than were historically the norm.

Compilation of References

(1995). Compassion fatigue as secondary traumatic stress disorder: An overview. InFigley, C. R. (Ed.), *Compassion Fatigue: Coping with Secondary Traumatic Stress Disorder in Those Who Treat the Traumatized* (pp. 1–19). New York: Brunner /Mazel.

Abamara, N. (2017). *Factors Precipitating Child Abuse and Neglect Among Nigerians*. Unpublished Thesis.

Abraham, S. G. K., Sridevi, G., & Sembulingam, P. (2016). Gender difference in the impact of examination stress on psychological and physiological profiles of dental students. *IOSR Journal of Dental and Medical Sciences*, *15*(9), 101–108.

Adler, R. B., Rosenfeld, L. B., & Proctor, R. F. (2017). *Interplay: The process of interpersonal communication* (14th ed.). New York, NY: Oxford University Press, Inc.

Ainsworth, M. D. S., Blehar, M., Waters, E., & Wall, S. (1978). *Patterns of attachment*. Hillsdale, NJ: Erlbaum.

Akande, A. (2001). A way of being: A program for aggression control of male children. *Early Child Development and Care*, *167*(1), 127–148. doi:10.1080/0300443011670111

Akhtar, Z., & Alam, M. (2015). Stress and Suicidal Ideation among School Students. *Journal of the Indian Academy of Applied Psychology*, *41*(2), 236.

Akoloh, L., Okenjom, G. P., & Obiahu, C. L. (2016). The effect of child abuse on youths and their academic performance in secondary schools in Bayelsa State, Nigeria. *Greener Journal of Educational Research*, *6*(4), 170–176. doi:10.15580/GJER.2016.4.040916075

Al Dosari, M. N., Ferwana, M., Abdulmajeed, I., Aldossari, K. K., & Al-Zahrani, J. M. (2017). Parents' perceptions about child abuse and their impact on physical and emotional child abuse: A study from primary health care centers in Riyadh, Saudi Arabia. *Journal of Family & Community Medicine*, *24*(2), 79–85. PMID:28566970

Aldrich, H., & Herker, D. (1977, April). Boundary Spanning Roles and Organization Structure. *Academy of Management Review*, 217–230.

Aldrich, H., & Whetten, D. (1981). Organization-Sets, Action-Sets, and Networks: Making the most of Simplicity. In P. C. Nystrom & W. H. Starbuck (Eds.), *Handbook of Organizational Design* (Vol. 1). New York: Oxford University Press.

Ali, N. S., Mahmud, S., Khan, A., & Ali, B. S. (2013). Impact of postpartum anxiety and depression on child's mental development from two peri-urban communities of Karachi, Pakistan: A quasi-experimental study. *BMC Psychiatry*, *13*(1), 274. doi:10.1186/1471-244X-13-274 PMID:24148567

Allen-Meares, P., & Montgomery, K. L. (2014). Global trends and school-based social work. *Children & Schools*, *36*(2), 105–112. doi:10.1093/cs/cdu007

Al-Nahari, H. (2009). Effect of academic examination stress on some physiological parameters of medical technology students. *Egyptian Journal of Experimental Biology (Zoology)*, *5*, 481–485.

Al-shail, E., Hassan, A., Aldowaish, A., Kattan, H., Lazenbatt, A., Cyr, C., & Lutya, T. M. (2012). *Child Abuse and Neglect – – A Multidimensional Approach*. InTech; doi:10.5772/3035

Alsubaie, M. A. (2015). Examples of current issues in the multicultural classroom. *Journal of Education and Practice*, *6*(10).

Altmaier, E. M. (1983). *Helping students manage stress*. San Francisco: Jossey-Boss Inc.

Al-Zoubi, S. M., & Younes, M. A. B. (2015). Low academic achievement: Causes and results. *Theory and Practice in Language Studies*, *5*(11), 2262–2268. doi:10.17507/tpls.0511.09

Amatea, E. S., & Clark, M. A. (2005). Changing schools, changing counsellors: A qualitative study of school administrators' conceptions of the school counsellor role. *Professional School Counseling*, *9*(1), 6–27. doi:10.5330/prsc.9.1.w6357vn62n5328vp

Ambrose, T. K., & Mayne, T. J. (1999). Research review on anger in psychotherapy. *Clinical Psychologist*, *55*(3), 353–363. doi:10.1002/(SICI)1097-4679(199903)55:3<353::AID-JCLP7>3.0.CO;2-B PMID:10321749

American Psychiatric Association. (2000). *Diagnostic and statistical manual of mental disorders* (4th ed.). Washington, DC: Author.

American Psychiatric Association. (2000). *Diagnostic and statistical manual of mental disorders: DSM-IV-TR*. Washington, DC: American Psychiatric Publishing, Inc.

American Psychological Association. (1993). Guidelines for psychological practice with ethnic, linguistic, and culturally diverse populations. *The American Psychologist*, *48*(1), 45–48. doi:10.1037/0003-066X.48.1.45

American School Counselor Association. (2003). *Position statement: Child abuse/neglect prevention: The professional school counselor and child abuse and neglect prevention*. Retrieved from http://www. schoolcounselor.org/content.asp?contentid

American School Counselor Association. (2005). *The ASCA national model: A framework for school counselling programs* (2nd ed.). Alexandria, VA: Author.

Anda, R. F., Croft, J. B., Felitti, V. J., Norenberg, D., Giles, W. H., Williamson, D. R., & Giovino, G. A. (1999). Adverse childhood events and smoking during adolescence and adulthood. *American Medical Association, 282*(17), 1652-1658.

Anda, D., Baroni, S., Boskin, L., Buckwalld, L., Morgan, J., Ow, J., ... Weiss, R. (2000). Stress, stressors and coping among high school students. *Children and Youth Services Review, 22*(6), 441–463. doi:10.1016/S0190-7409(00)00096-7

Anderson, C. M., Hogarty, G. E., & Reiss, D. J. (1980). Family Treatment of Adult Schizophrenic Patients: A Psycho-educational Approach. *Schizophrenia Bulletin, 6*(3), 490–505. doi:10.1093chbul/6.3.490

Anderson, P. M., Butcher, K. F., & Levine, P. B. (2003). Maternal Employment and Overweight Children. *Journal of Health Economics, 22*(3), 477–504. doi:10.1016/S0167-6296(03)00022-5 PMID:12683963

Apebende, E., Umoren, G., & Ukpepi, B. (2010). The Influence of Child Abuse on the Academic Performance of Primary School Pupils in Primary Sci333ence in Cross River State, Nigeria. *An International Multi-Disciplinary Journal, 3*(2), 49–51.

Ardington, C. (2007). *Orphan-hood and schooling in South Africa: Trends in the Vulnerability of Orphans between 1993 & 2005*. Academic Press.

Arredondo, P., Toporek, R., Brown, S. P., Jones, J., Locke, D. C., Sanchez, J., & Stadler, H. (1996). Operationalization of the multicultural counseling competencies. *Journal of Multicultural Counseling and Development, 24*(1), 42–78. doi:10.1002/j.2161-1912.1996.tb00288.x

Arrhur, N. (1988). Counsellor education for diversity: Where do we go from here? *Canadian Journal of Counselling, 32*, 88–103.

Asok, A., Bernard, K., Roth, T. L., Rosen, J. B., & Dozier, M. (2013). Parental responsiveness moderates the association between early-life stress and reduced telomere length. *Development and Psychopathology, 25*(3), 577–585. doi:10.1017/S0954579413000011 PMID:23527512

Assembly, U. G. (1948). *Universal declaration of human rights*. UN General Assembly.

Atkinson, A. B. (1998). *Exclusion, Employment and Opportunity. In Exclusion, Employment and Opportunity. CASE Paper 4*. Centre for Analysis of Social Exclusion, London School of Economics.

Atler, C., & Hage, J. (1993). *Organizations Working Together*. Newbury Park, CA: Sage Publications.

Averill, J. R. (1993). Illusions of anger. In R. B. Felson & J. T. Tedeschi (Eds.), *Aggression and Violence: Social interactionist perspectives* (pp. 171–192). Washington, DC: American Psychological Association. doi:10.1037/10123-007

Ayasse, R. H., & Stone, S. I. (2015). The evolution of school social work services in an urban school district. *Children & Schools, 17*(4), 215–222. doi:10.1093/cs/cdv025

Ayres, J. R. C. M., Paiva, V., & França, I. Junior. (2011). From natural history of disease to vulnerability. In R. Parker & M. Sommer (Eds.), *Routledge handbook in global public health* (pp. 98–107). New York: Routledge.

Baile, C. (2006). *Refugee Social Networks and Organizational Resettlement Networks: Generating an Integrative Model* (PhD Dissertation). The New School.

Bailey, D. F., Getch, Y. Q., & Chen-Hayes, S. (2003). Professional school counsellors as social and academic advocates. In B. T. Erford (Ed.), *Transforming the school counselling profession* (pp. 441–434). Upper Saddle River, NJ: Merrill Prentice Hall.

Bailey, D. F., Getch, Y. Q., & Chen-Hayes, S. (2007). Achievement advocacy for all students through transformative school counselling programs. In B. T. Erford (Ed.), *Transforming the school counselling profession* (pp. 98–120). Upper Saddle River, NJ: Merrill Prentice Hall.

Baker, S. B., & Gerler, E. R. Jr. (2004). *School Counseling for the Twenty-First Century* (4th ed.). North Carolina: Pearson.

Baker, S. B., Robichaud, T. A., Westforth Dietrich, V. C., Wells, S. C., & Schreck, R. E. (2009). School counselor consultation: A pathway to advocacy, collaboration, and leadership. *Professional School Counseling, 12*(3), 200–206. doi:10.5330/PSC.n.2010-12.200

Bala, D., Maji, B., Satapathy, J., & Routray, R. K. (2017). Prevalence of child abuse in eastern India: A tip of iceberg. *International Journal of Contemporary Pediatrics, 2*(4), 353–355.

Bandura, A. (1967). The role of modeling personality development. In C. Lavatelli & F. Stendler (Eds.), *Readings in childhood and development* (pp. 334–343). New York: Harcourt Brace Jovanovich.

Barnett, J. (2018). Setting the stage for bridging disability and trauma studies: Reclaiming narrative in Amy and the Orphans. Word & Text: A Journal of Literary Studies & Linguistics, 8, 129–148.

Barnett, T., & Whiteside. (2002). AIDS in the Twenty First Century: Diseases and Globalization. Palgrave McMillan.

Barrientos, A. (2011). Social protection and poverty. *International Journal of Social Welfare, 20*(3), 240–249. doi:10.1111/j.1468-2397.2011.00783.x

Bartuner, J. M., & Reynolds, C. (1983). Boundary Spanning and Public Accountant Role Stress. *The Journal of Social Psychology, 121*(1), 65–72. doi:10.1080/00224545.1983.9924468 PMID:6645425

Baumeister, R. F. (1984). Choking under pressure: Self-consciousness and paradoxical effects of incentives on skillful performance. *Journal of Personality and Social Psychology, 46*(3), 610–620. doi:10.1037/0022-3514.46.3.610 PMID:6707866

Baumgartner, L. M. (2001). An Update on Transformational Learning. *New Directions for Adult and Continuing Education, 2001*(89), 15–24. doi:10.1002/ace.4

Baum, J. A. C. (Ed.). (2002). *The Blackwell companion to organizations.* Malden, MA: Blackwell.

Beck, C. T. (1996). A meta-analysis of the relationship between postpartum depression and infant temperament. *Nursing Research, 45*(4), 225–230. doi:10.1097/00006199-199607000-00006 PMID:8700656

Beck, R., & Fernandez, E. (1998). Cognitive behavioral therapy in the treatment of anger: A meta-analysis. *Cognitive Therapy and Research, 22*(1), 63–74. doi:10.1023/A:1018763902991

Behere, P. B., & Mulmule, A. N. (2013). Sexual abuse in 8-year-old child: Where do we stand legally? *Indian Journal of Psychological Medicine, 35*(2), 203. doi:10.4103/0253-7176.116256 PMID:24049233

Beitchman, J. H., Zucker, K. J., Hood, J. E., DaCosta, G. A., Akman, D., & Cassavia, E. (1992). A review of the long- term effects of child sexual abuse. *Child Abuse & Neglect, 16*(1), 101–118. doi:10.1016/0145-2134(92)90011-F PMID:1544021

Belsky, J., Schlomer, G. L., & Ellis, B. J. (2012). Beyond cumulative risk: Distinguishing harshness and unpredictability as determinants of parenting and early life history strategy. *Developmental Psychology, 48*(3), 662–673. doi:10.1037/a0024454 PMID:21744948

Bemak, F. (2000). Transforming the role of the counselor to provide leadership in educational reform through collaboration. Professional School Counseling, 3(5), 323-331 Retrieved from http://www.schoolcounselor.org/content.asp?contentid =235

Bemak, F., & Chung, C. Y. (2005). Advocacy as a critical role for urban school counsellors: Working toward equity and social justice. *Professional School Counseling, 8,* 196.

Bemak, F., & Chung, C. Y. (2006). New professional roles and advocacy strategies for school counsellors: A multicultural perspective to move beyond the nice counsellor syndrome. *Journal of Counseling and Development, 86*(3), 372–381. doi:10.1002/j.1556-6678.2008.tb00522.x

Bempechat, J., & Shernoff, D. J. (2012). Parental influences on achievement motivation and student engagement. In S. L. Christenson, A. L. Reschly, & C. Wylie (Eds.), *Handbook of research on student engagement* (pp. 315–342). New York: Springer US. doi:10.1007/978-1-4614-2018-7_15

Ben-Porat, A. (2015). Vicarious post-traumatic growth: Domestic violence therapists versus social service department therapists in Israel. *Journal of Family Violence, 30*(7), 923–933. doi:10.100710896-015-9714-x

Benson, J. (1975). The Interorganizational Network as A Political Economy. *Administrative Science Quarterly, 20*(2), 229–249. doi:10.2307/2391696

Bernstein, M., & Munoz, N. (2012). Position of the Academy of Nutrition and Dietetics: food and nutrition for older adults: promoting health and wellness. *Journal of the Academy of Nutrition and Dietetics, 112*(8), 1255–1277. doi:10.1016/j.jand.2012.06.015 PMID:22818734

Bertalanffy, L. (1972). The History and Status of General Systems Theory. The Academy of Management Journal, 15(4), 407-426.

Bialik, M., & Fadel, C. (2015). *Skills for the 21st Century: What Should Students Learn?* Retrieved August 2, 2019, from https://curriculumredesign.org/wp-content/uploads/CCR-Skills_FINAL_June2015.pdf

Bildik, T. (2002). School period emotional abuse [in Turkish]. *Journal of Children's Forum, 5*, 9–13.

Bilge, F. (2006). Child neglect and abuse, violence in schools and juvenile delinquency. In S. Ercetin (Ed.), *Education and Violence* (pp. 219–260). Ankara: Pegem Publications.

Bird, W., & Spurr, N. (2004). Media representations of baby rape: The case of 'Baby Tshepang'. The rape of young children in Southern Africa, 36-52.

Blackwell, A. (2017, July). *Teaching in the Spirit of Ubuntu.* Paper presented at Public Lecture of the University of Namibia.

Blake, C. S., & Hamrin, V. (2007). Current approaches to the assessment and management of anger and aggression in youth: A review. *Journal of Child and Adolescent Psychiatric Nursing, 20*(4), 209–221. doi:10.1111/j.1744-6171.2007.00102.x PMID:17991051

Bland, H. W., Melton, B. F., Welle, P., & Bigham, L. (2012). Stress tolerance: New challenges for millennial college students. *College Student Journal, 46*(2), 362–375.

Bliese, P. D. (2000). Within-group agreement, non-independence, and reliability: Implications for data aggregation and analysis. In K. J. Klein & S. W. J. Kozlowski (Eds.), *Multilevel theory, research, and methods in organizations, foundations, extensions, and new directions* (pp. 349–381). San Francisco: Jossey-Bass.

Blom Hansen, T. (2009). *Sovereigns beyond the State: On Legality and Authority in Urban India. In Sovereign Bodies: Citizens* (pp. 169–191). Migrants, and States in the Postcolonial World. doi:10.1515/9781400826698.169

Blosnich, J. R., & Anderson, J. P. (2015). Thursday's child: The role of adverse childhood experiences in explaining mental health disparities among lesbian, gay, and bisexual U.S. adults. *Social Psychiatry and Psychiatric Epidemiology, 50*(2), 335–338. doi:10.100700127-014-0955-4 PMID:25367679

Blumenthal, A. (2015). *Child Neglect II : Prevention and Intervention.* Academic Press.

Boakye, N. A., & Linden, M. M. (2018). Extended strategy-use instruction to improve students' reading proficiency in a content subject. *Reading and Writing, 9*(1), 1–9. doi:10.4102/rw.v9i1.212

Bober, T., & Regeher, C. (2006). Strategies for reducing secondary or vicarious trauma: Do they work? *Brief Treatment and Crisis Intervention, 6*(1), 1–9. doi:10.1093/brief-treatment/mhj001

Bolier, L., Haverman, M., Westerhof, G. J., Riper, H., Smit, F., & Bohlmeijer, E. (2013). Positive psychology interventions: A meta-analysis of randomized controlled studies. *BMC Public Health, 13*(1), 119. doi:10.1186/1471-2458-13-119 PMID:23390882

Borgatti, S. P., & Foster, P. C. (2003). The network paradigm in organizational research: A review and typology. *Journal of Management, 29*(6), 991–1013. doi:10.1016/S0149-2063(03)00087-4

Boscarino, J. A., Figley, C. R., & Adams, R. E. (2004). Compassion fatigue following September 11 terrorist attacks: A study of secondary trauma among New York City social workers. *International Journal of Emergency Mental Health, 6*(2), 57–66. PMID:15298076

Bosch, S. (2012). Targeting and prosecuting 'under-aged' child soldiers in international armed conflicts, in light of the international humanitarian law prohibition against civilian direct participation in hostilities. *The Comparative and International Law Journal of Southern Africa, 45*(3), 324–364.

Bowlby, J. (1969). *Attachment and loss* (Vol. 1). New York: Basic Books.

Bowman-Edmondson, C., & Cohen-Conger, J. (1996). A review of treatment efficacy for individuals with anger problems: Conceptual, assessment, and methodological issues. *Clinical Psychology Review, 16*(3), 251–275. doi:10.1016/S0272-7358(96)90003-3

Boyer, B., Bubel, D., Jacobs, S. R., Knolls, M., Harwell, V. D., Goscicka, M., & Keenan, A. (2002). Posttraumatic stress in women with breast cancer and their daughters. *The American Journal of Family Therapy, 30*(4), 323–338. doi:10.1080/01926180290033466

Bradshaw, J. (2015). Healing the Shame That Binds You. *Health Communication.*

Brady, J. L., Guy, J. D., Poelstra, P. L., & Fletcher-Brokaw, B. F. (1999). Vicarious traumatization, spirituality, and treatment of sexual abuse survivors: A national survey of women psychotherapists. *Professional Psychology, Research and Practice, 30*(4), 368–393. doi:10.1037/0735-7028.30.4.386

Branson, D. C., Radu, M. B., & Loving, J. D. (in press). Adverse Childhood Experiences (ACE) scores: When social work students and trauma mix. *The Journal of Baccalaureate Social Work.*

Brass, D. J., Galaskiewicz, J., Greve, H. R., & Tsai, W. (2004). Taking stock of networks and organizations: A multilevel perspective. *Academy of Management Journal, 47*(8), 795–817.

Bride, B. E., Robinson, M. M., Yegidis, B., & Figley, C. R. (2003). Development and validation of the secondary traumatic stress scale. *Research on Social Work Practice, 13*, 1–16.

Briley, D. A., Harden, K. P., & Tucker-Drob, E. M. (2014). Child characteristics and parental educational expectations: Evidence for transmission with transaction. *Developmental Psychology, 50*(12), 2614–2632. doi:10.1037/a0038094 PMID:25285965

British Psychological Society (BPS). (2000). *Code of conduct, ethical principles and guidelines.* Leicester, UK: BPS.

Brito, C. N. D. O., Alves, S. V., Ludermir, A. B., & Araújo, T. V. B. D. (2015). Postpartum depression among women with unintended pregnancy. *Revista de Saude Publica, 49*(0), 33. doi:10.1590/S0034-8910.2015049005257 PMID:26083941

Brown, A., & Haihambo, C. K. (2015). Developmental issues facing the San people of Namibia: Road to de-marginalization in formal education. University of Namibia Press. doi:10.2307/j.ctvgc619h.20

Brown, B. (2006). Shame Resilience Theory: A Grounded Theory Study on Women and Shame. *Families in Society, 87*(1), 43–52. doi:10.1606/1044-3894.3483

Brown, K. (2011). Vulnerability: Handle with care. *Ethics & Social Welfare, 5*(3), 313–321. doi:10.1080/17496535.2011.597165

Bruder-Costello, B., Warner, V., Talati, A., Nomura, Y., Bruder, G., & Weissman, M. (2007). Temperament among offspring at high and low risk for depression. *Psychiatry Research, 153*(2), 145–151. doi:10.1016/j.psychres.2007.02.013 PMID:17651814

Bundy, C. (2005). Global patterns, local options? Some implications for South Africa of international changes in higher education. *Perspectives in Education, 23*(2), 85–98.

Burke-Harris, N. (2018). *The deepest well: Healing the long-term effects of childhood adversity.* London: Bluebird.

Burney, D. M. (2001). *Adolescent Anger Rating Scale: Professional Manual.* Lutz, FL: Psychological Assessment Resources.

Burton, P., Wu, Y., & Prybutok, V. R. (2010). Social Network Position and Its Relationship to Performance of IT Professional. Information Science. *The International Journal of an Emerging Transfiscipline., 13*, 121–137.

Burt, R. (1995). *Structural Holes: The Social Structure of Competition.* Cambridge, MA: Harvard University Press.

Butchart, A., Phinney, A., & Furness, T. (2006). *Preventing child maltreatment: A guide to taking action and generating evidence.* World Health Organization.

Cacioppo, J. T., & Patrick, W. (2008). *Lonliness: Human Nature and the Need for Social Conncetion.* New York: W.W. Norton & Co.

Campano, J. P., & Munakata, T. (2004). *Anger and aggression among Filipino students.* The Free Library Sourced.

Canadian Psychological Association. (1990). *Guidelines for psychological practice with ethnic and culturally diverse populations.* Ottawa, Canada: Author.

Canadian Red Cross. (2019). Retrieved from https://www.redcross.ca/how-we-help/violence-bullying-and-abuse-prevention/educators/child-abuse-and-neglect-prevention/definitions-of-child-abuse-and-neglect

Cappelli, P., & Scherer, P. (1991). The missing role of context in OB: The need for a meso level approach. In Research in organizational behavior. Greenwich, CT: JAI.

CAPTA Reauthorization Act of 2010 (P.L. 111-320), § 5101, Note (§ 3). (n.d.). Retrieved from https://www.childwelfare.gov/pubpdfs/whatiscan.pdf

Carley, K. M. (2002). Computational organization science: A new frontier. *National Academy of Science*, *99*(Supplement 3), 7257–7262. doi:10.1073/pnas.082080599 PMID:12011404

Carley, K. M., & Wallace, W. A. (2001). Computational organization theory: A new perspective. In S. Gass & C. M. Harris (Eds.), *Encyclopedia of operations research and management science*. Norwich, MA: Kluwer Academic Publishers. doi:10.1007/1-4020-0611-X_143

Carter, S. M., & Little, M. (2007). Justifying Knowledge, Justifying Method, Taking Action: Epistemologies, Methodologies, and Methods in Qualitative Research. *Qualitative Health Research*, *17*(10), 1316–1328. doi:10.1177/1049732307306927 PMID:18000071

Case, A., & Ardington, C. (2006). *The impact of Parental Death on School Outcomes: Longitudinal Evidence from South Africa*. Academic Press.

Caserta, T. A. (2017). *The psychosocial wellbeing of orphans and youth in Rwanda: Analysis of predictors, vulnerability factors and buffers* (Academic dissertation). University of Helsinki, Finland: Department of Social Science 36, Social Psychology.

Caska, C. M., & Renshaw, K. D. (2013). Personality traits as moderators of the associations between deployment experiences and PTSD symptoms in OEF/OIF service members. *Anxiety, Stress, and Coping*, *26*(1), 36–51. doi:10.1080/10615806.2011.638053 PMID:22129461

Cass, V. (1996). Sexual orientation identity formation: A western phenomenon. In R. P. Cabaj & T. S. Stein (Eds.), *Textbook of homosexuality and mental health* (pp. 227–251). Arlington, VA: American Psychiatric Association.

Castillo-Eito, L., Rowe, R., & Norman, P. (2018). Interventions to reduce aggressive behaviour in adolescents: A systematic review and meta-analysis. . doi:10.13140/RG.2.2.35740.39041

Catani, C., & Sossalla, I. M. (2015). Child abuse predicts adult PTSD symptoms among individuals diagnosed with intellectual disabilities. *Frontiers in Psychology*, *6*, 1600. doi:10.3389/fpsyg.2015.01600 PMID:26539143

Catherall, D. R. (1992). *Back from the brink: a family guide to overcoming traumatic stress*. New York: Bantam Books.

Cawson, P., Wattam, C., Brooker, S., & Kelly, G. (2000). *Child maltreatment in the United Kingdom: a study of the prevalence of abuse and neglect*. London: NSPCC.

Chan, E., & Ross, V. (2014). Narrative understandings of a school policy: Intersecting student, teacher, parent and administrator perspectives. *Journal of Curriculum Studies*, *46*(5), 656–675. doi:10.1080/00220272.2014.911352

Chang, M., & Harrison, J. E. (2004). Agent-based models of organizations. Handbook of Computational Economics II: Agent-based. *Computational Economics*, 1273–1377.

Chapell, M. S., Blanding, Z. B., Takahashi, M., Silverstein, M. E., Newman, B., Gubi, A., & McCann, N. (2005). Test anxiety and academic performance in undergraduate and graduate students. *Journal of Educational Psychology*, *97*(2), 268–274. doi:10.1037/0022-0663.97.2.268

Cherry, K. (2012). About.com. *Psychology (Irvine, Calif.)*.

Child and Family Services Reviews. (2012). Retrieved from https://training.cfsrportal.acf.hhs.gov/section-2-understanding-child-welfare-system/2984

Child Welfare Information Gateway. (2004). *Child abuse and neglect fatalities: Statistics and interventions*. Available: http://www.childwelfare.gov/ pubs/factsheets/fatality.pdf

Child Welfare Information Gateway. (2017). *Foster care statistics 2015*. Washington, DC: U.S. Department of Health and Human Services, Children's Bureau.

Children's Society. (2008). *The Good Childhood Inquiry: health research evidence*. London: Children's Society.

Chin, L. S., & Ahmad, N. S. B. (2017). Effect of cognitive behavioural therapy (CBT) anger management module for adolescents. *International Journal of Guidance and Counselling*, *3*(2), 68–78.

Chitnis, R. (2018). *Causes of child abuse and neglect*. retrieved from https://parenting.firstcry.com/articles/child-abuse-a-guide-to-parents-caregivers/

Clement, M. E., Berube, A., & Chamberland, C. (2016). Prevalence and risk factors of child neglect in the general population. *Public Health*, *138*, 86–92. doi:10.1016/j.puhe.2016.03.018 PMID:27117500

Coccaro, E. F. (2012). Intermittent Explosive Disorder as a Disorder of Impulsive Aggression for DSM-5. *The American Journal of Psychiatry*, *169*(6), 577–588. doi:10.1176/appi.ajp.2012.11081259 PMID:22535310

Cohen-Katz, J., Wiley, S., Capuano, T., Baker, D. M., Deitrick, L., & Shapiro, S. (2005). The effects of mindfulness-based stress reduction on nurse stress and burnout: A qualitative and quantitative study, part III. *Holistic Nursing Practice*, *19*(2), 78–86. doi:10.1097/00004650-200503000-00009 PMID:15871591

Coman, A., Momennejad, I., Geana, A., & Drach, D. R. (2016). Mnemonic convergence in social networks: The emergent properties of cognition at a collective level. *Proceedings of the National Academy of Sciences of the United States of America*, *113*(29), 8171–8176. doi:10.1073/pnas.1525569113 PMID:27357678

Constantine, M., Hage, S., Kindaichi, M., & Bryant, R. (2007). Social justice and multicultural issues: Implications for the practice and training of counsellors and counselling psychologists. *Journal of Counseling and Development*, *85*(1), 24–29. doi:10.1002/j.1556-6678.2007.tb00440.x

Contractor, N. S., & Eisenberg, E. M. (1990). Communication Networks and New Media in Organizations. In Fulk, J. & Steinfield, C. (eds) Organizations and Communication Technology, pp. 143-171 Sage Publications, Newbury Park. doi:10.4135/9781483325385.n7

Convention on the Rights of the Child (CRC). (2011). Retrieved from https://www.unicef-irc.org/portfolios/general_comments/CRC.C.GC.13_en.doc.html

Cooper, H. M., Lindsay, J. J., & Nye, B. (2000). Homework in the home: How student, family and parenting style differences relate to the homework process. *Contemporary Educational Psychology*, *25*(4), 464–487. doi:10.1006/ceps.1999.1036 PMID:11001787

Cooper, H., Lindsay, J. J., Nye, B., & Greathouse, S. (1998). Relationships among attitudes about homework, amount of homework assigned and completed, and student achievement. *Journal of Educational Psychology*, *90*(1), 70–83. doi:10.1037/0022-0663.90.1.70

Corbin, T. J., Purtle, J., Rich, L. J., Rich, J. A., Adams, E. J., Yee, G., & Bloom, S. L. (2013). The prevalence of trauma and childhood adversity in an urban, hospital-based violence intervention program. *Journal of Health Care for the Poor and Underserved*, *24*(3), 1021–1030. doi:10.1353/hpu.2013.0120 PMID:23974377

Courtney, J. (2010). The Civil War That Was Fought by Children: Understanding the Role of Child Combatants in El Salvador's Civil War 1980-1992. *The Journal of Military History*, *74*(2), 525.

Cox, A. A., & Lee, C. C. (2007). Challenging educational inequities: School counsellors as agents of social justice. In C. C. Lee (Ed.), *Counseling for social justice* (2nd ed.; pp. 3–14). Alexandria, VA: American Counseling Association.

Cranton, P. (1994). *Understanding and promoting transformative learning: A guide for educators and adults*. San Francisco: Jossey-Bass.

Cranton, P. A. (1998). Fostering authentic relationships in the transformative classroom. *New Directions for Adult and Continuing Education*, *2006*(109), 5–13.

Cranton, P. A. (2002). Teaching for transformation. *New Directions for Adult and Continuing Education*, *2002*(93), 63–71. doi:10.1002/ace.50

Cranton, P. A., & Roy, M. (2003). When the bottom falls out of the bucket: A holistic perspective on transformative learning. *Journal of Transformative Education*, *1*(2), 86–98. doi:10.1177/1541344603001002002

Creswell, J. W. (2006). *Qualitative inquiry and research design: Choosing among five traditions* (2nd ed.). Thousand Oaks, CA: Sage Publication.

Cross, R., Thomas, R., & Light, D. (n.d.). Creating the Right Decision-Making Networks: Driving Decision Efficiency and Effectiveness through Networks. Academic Press.

Cross, M. (2011). *An Unfulfilled Promise. Transforming Schools in Mozambique. Organisation for Social Research in Eastern and Southern Africa*. OSSREA.

Cross, R. L., Parker, A., & Cross, R. (2004). *The Hidden Power of Social Networks: Understanding How Work Really Gets Done in Organizations* (1st ed.). Harvard Business Review Press.

Cross, R., Borgatti, S. P., & Parker, A. (2002). Making Invisible Work Visible: Using Social Network Analysis to Support Strategic Collaboration. *California Management Review, 44*(2), 25–46. doi:10.2307/41166121

Cross, R., & Thomas, R. J. (2009). *Driving Results Through Social Networks: How Top Organizations Leverage Networks for Performance and Growth.* San Francisco: Jossey-Bass.

Crowe, S. L., & Blair, R. J. R. (2008). The development of antisocial behavior: What can we learn from functional neuroimaging studies? *Development and Psychopathology, 20*(4), 1145–1159. doi:10.1017/S0954579408000540 PMID:18838035

Crume, T., DiGuiseppi, C., Byers, T. L., Sirotnak, A. P., & Garrett, C. (2002). *Under ascertainment of child maltreatment fatalities by death certificates, 1990–1998.* Available: http://pediatrics. appublications.org/cgi/reprint/110/2/e18.pdf

D'Agostino, A., Covanti, S., Monti, M. R., & Starcevic, V. (2017). Reconsidering Emotion Dysregulation. *The Psychiatric Quarterly, 88*(4), 807–825. doi:10.100711126-017-9499-6 PMID:28194549

D'Andrea, W., Ford, J., Stolbach, B., Spinazzola, J., & van der Kolk, B. A. (2012). Understanding interpersonal trauma in children: Why we need a developmentally appropriate trauma diagnosis. *The American Journal of Orthopsychiatry, 82*(2), 187–200. doi:10.1111/j.1939-0025.2012.01154.x PMID:22506521

Dahir, C. A., & Stone, C. B. (2009). School counsellor accountability: The path to social justice and systemic change. *Journal of Counseling and Development, 87*(1), 12–20. doi:10.1002/j.1556-6678.2009.tb00544.x

Dahl, R. (1961). *Who Governs?* New Haven, CT: Yale University Press.

Daloz, L. (1986). *Effective Teaching and Mentoring: Realizing the Transformational Power of Adult Learning.* Jossey-Bass.

Dandy, J., & Nettelbeck, T. (2002). Research note: A cross-cultural study of parents' academic standards and educational aspirations for their children. *Educational Psychology: An International Journal of Experimental and Educational Psychology, 22*(5), 621–627.

Danese, A., & McEwen, B. S. (2012). Adverse childhood experiences, allostasis, allostatic load, and age-related disease. *Physiology & Behavior, 106*(1), 29–39. doi:10.1016/j.physbeh.2011.08.019 PMID:21888923

Danis, F. S., & Lockheart, L. (2004). *Breaking the silence in social work education. Domestic violence modules for foundation courses.* Alexandria: Council of Social Work Education.

Daral, S., Khokhar, A., & Pradhan, S. (2016). Prevalence and determinants of child maltreatment among school-going adolescent girls in a semi-urban area of Delhi, India. *Journal of Tropical Pediatrics*, *62*(3), 227–240. doi:10.1093/tropej/fmv106 PMID:26769624

Daro, D., & Benedetti, G. (2014). Sustaining progress in preventing child maltreatment: A transformative challenge. In *Handbook of child maltreatment* (pp. 281–300). Dordrecht: Springer. doi:10.1007/978-94-007-7208-3_14

Daruy-Filho, L., Brietzke, E., Lafer, B., & Grassi-Oliveira, R. (2011). Childhood maltreatment and clinical outcomes of bipolar disorder. *Acta Psychiatrica Scandinavica*, *124*(6), 427–434. doi:10.1111/j.1600-0447.2011.01756.x PMID:21848703

Dawis, R. V., Fruehling, R. T., & Oldham, N. B. (1989). *Psychology: human relations and work adjustment* (7th ed.). New York: Gregg Division, McGraw-Hill.

Dawkins, R. (1976). *The Selfish Gene*. Oxford, UK: Oxford University Press.

Day, C. (2008). *A Literature Review into Children Abused and / or Neglected Prior Custody*. Academic Press.

De Bellis, M. D., Keshavan, M. S., Shifflett, H., Iyengar, S., Beers, S. R., Hall, J., & Moritz, G. (2006). Cerebellar volumes in pediatric maltreatment-related posttraumatic stress disorder: A sociodemographically matched study. *Biological Psychiatry*, *52*(11), 1066–1078. doi:10.1016/S0006-3223(02)01459-2 PMID:12460690

De Bellis, M. D., & Van Dillen, T. (2005). Childhood post-traumatic stress disorder: An overview. *Child and Adolescent Psychiatric Clinics of North America*, *14*(4), 745–772. doi:10.1016/j.chc.2005.05.006 PMID:16171701

De Silva, C. R. (2010). *The achievement of grade 3 learners' higher order reading skills on a children's literature-based reading programme* (Doctoral dissertation). Cape Peninsula, University of Science and Technology. Retrieved from http://etd.cput.ac.za/handle/20.500.11838/2132

De Witt, M. W. (2016). *The young child in context: A psychosocial perspective* (2nd ed.). Van Schaik Publishers.

DeBellis, M. D., Broussard, E. R., Herring, D. J., Wexler, S., Moritz, G., & Benitez, J. G. (2001). Psychiatric co-morbidity in caregivers and children involved in maltreatment: A pilot research study with policy implications. *Child Abuse & Neglect*, *25*(7), 923–944. doi:10.1016/S0145-2134(01)00247-2 PMID:11523869

Deb, S., & Walsh, K. (2012). Impact of physical, psychological, and sexual violence on social adjustment of school children in India. *School Psychology International*, *33*(4), 391–415. doi:10.1177/0143034311425225

Deci, E. L., & Ryan, R. M. (1987). The support of autonomy and the control of behavior. *Journal of Personality and Social Psychology*, *53*(6), 1024–1037. doi:10.1037/0022-3514.53.6.1024 PMID:3320334

Deci, E. L., & Ryan, R. M. (1995). Human autonomy: The basis for true self-esteem. In M. Kernis (Ed.), *Efficacy, agency, and self-esteem* (pp. 31–49). New York: Plenum Publishing Co.

Deffenbacher, J. L. (1999). Cognitive-behavioural conceptualisation and treatment of anger. *Journal of Clinical Psychology, 55*(3), 295–309. doi:10.1002/(SICI)1097-4679(199903)55:3<295::AID-JCLP3>3.0.CO;2-A PMID:10321745

Deisseroth, K. (2014). Circuit dynamics of adaptive and maladaptive behaviour. *Nature, 505*(7483), 309–317. doi:10.1038/nature12982 PMID:24429629

Del Vecchio, T., & O'Leary, K. D. (2004). The effectiveness of anger treatments for specific anger problems: A meta-analytic review. *Clinical Psychology Review, 24*(1), 15–34. doi:10.1016/j.cpr.2003.09.006 PMID:14992805

Delaney, P. F., & Ericsson, K. A. (2016). *Long-term working memory and transient storage in reading comprehension: What is the evidence?* Academic Press.

Demarin, V., & Morovic, S. (2014). Neuroplasticity. *Periodicum Biologorum, 116*(2), 209–211. Retrieved from https://hrcak.srce.hr/126369

DePanfilis, D. (2004). *Child neglect: Working to increase safety and well-being.* Presented at the Family Advocacy Training Section, Soldier & Family Support Branch, Department of Preventive Health Services, Army Medical Department Center & School, San Antonio, TX.

DePanfilis, D. (2006). Child neglect: A guide for prevention, assessment, and intervention. US Department of Health and Human Services, Administration for Children and Families, Administration on Children, Youth and Families, Children's Bureau, Office on Child Abuse and Neglect.

DePanfilis, D. (2006). *Child Abuse And Neglect Child Neglect: A Guide for Prevention, Assessment, and (Child Abuse).* Washington, DC: Child Welfare Information Gateway. Retrieved from http://www.childwelfare.gov/pubs/usermanual.cfm

Department of Basic Education. (2011). *Revised National Curriculum Statement.* Pretoria: Government Printer.

Department of Basic Education. (2013). *HIV and AIDS Life Skills Education Programme.* Pretoria: Government Printer.

Department of Education (DoE). (2002). Revised National Curriculum Statement Grades R–9 (schools): Life Orientation. Pretoria, South Africa: DoE.

Department of Education (DoE). (2003). National Curriculum Statement Life Orientation Grades 10-12. DoE.

Detrick, S. (1999). *A Commentary on the United Nations Convention on the Rights of the Child.* Martinus Nijhoff Publishers.

Dewey, J. (1938). *Experience and education.* New York: MacMillan.

Diale, B., Pillay, J., & Fritz, E. (2014). Dynamics in the personal and professional development of Life Orientation teachers in South Africa, Gauteng Province. *Journal of Social Sciences*, *38*(1), 83–93. doi:10.1080/09718923.2014.11893239

DiGiuseppe, R., & Tafrate, R. (2003). Anger treatment for adults: A meta-analysis review. *Clinical Psychology: Science and Practice*, *10*(1), 70–84. doi:10.1093/clipsy.10.1.70

Dirkx, J. M. (1998). Transformative learning theory in the practice of adult education: An overview. *PAACE Journal of Lifelong Learning*, *7*, 1–14.

Dirkx, J. M. (2000). Transformative learning and the journey of individuation. *ERIC Digests*, *223*, 1–7.

Dirkx, J. M. (2006). Engaging emotions in adult learning: A Jungian perspective on emotion and transformative learning. *New Directions for Adult and Continuing Education*, *2006*(109), 15–26. doi:10.1002/ace.204

Dixon, A. L., Tucker, C., & Clark, M. A. (2010). Integrating social justice advocacy with national standards for practice: Implications for school counsellor education. *Counselor Education and Supervision*, *50*(2), 103–115. doi:10.1002/j.1556-6978.2010.tb00112.x

Dlamini, S. L., & Makondo, D. (2017). Effects of Child Abuse on the Academic Performance of Primary School Learners in the Manzini Region, Swaziland. *World Journal of Education*, *7*(5), 58. doi:10.5430/wje.v7n5p58

Dobson, C. (2012). *Effects of academic anxiety on the performance of students with and without learning disabilities and how students can cope with anxiety at school*. Northern Michigan University.

Dollarhide, C. T. (2003). School counselors as program leaders: Applying leadership contexts to school counseling. *Professional School Counseling*, *6*(5), 304. Retrieved from http://www.schoolcounselor.org/content.asp?contentid=235

Donley, J. E. (1911). Psychotherapy and re-education. *The Journal of Abnormal Psychology*, *6*(1), 1–10. doi:10.1037/h0071950

Dooley, K. (2002). Organizational complexity, In International encyclopedia of business and management. London: Thomson Learning.

Du Toit, E. (2012). Constructive feedback as a learning tool to enhance students' self-regulation and performance in higher education. *Perspectives in Education*, *30*(2), 32–40.

Dube, S. R., Anda, R. F., Felitti, V. J., Chapman, D. P., Williamson, D. F., & Giles, W. H. (2001). Childhood abuse, household dysfunction, and the risk of attempted suicide throughout the life span: Findings from the Adverse Childhood Experiences study. American Medical Association, 286(24), 3089-3095.

Dube, S. R., Anda, R. F., Felitti, V. J., Croft, J. B., Edwards, V. J., & Giles, W. H. (2001). Growing up with parental alcohol abuse: Exposure to childhood abuse, neglect, and household dysfunction. *Child Abuse & Neglect, 25*(12), 1627–1640. doi:10.1016/S0145-2134(01)00293-9 PMID:11814159

Dubowitz, H., & Bennett, S. (2007). Physical abuse and neglect of children. *Lancet, 369*(9576), 1891–1899. doi:10.1016/S0140-6736(07)60856-3 PMID:17544770

Dulagil, A., Green, S., & Ahern, M. (2016). Evidence-based coaching to enhance senior students' wellbeing and academic striving. *International Journal of Wellbeing, 6*(3), 131–149. doi:10.5502/ijw.v6i3.426

Dumont, H., Trautwein, U., Lüdtke, O., Neumann, M., Niggli, A., & Schnyder, I. (2012). Does parental homework involvement mediate the relationship between family background and educational outcomes? *Contemporary Educational Psychology, 37*(1), 55–69. doi:10.1016/j.cedpsych.2011.09.004

Duros, P., & Crowley, D. (2014). The body comes to therapy too. *Clinical Social Work Journal, 42*(3), 237–246. doi:10.100710615-014-0486-1

Dweck, C. S. (2008). *Mindset – The new psychology of success.* Ballantine Books.

Dwyer, L. A. (2005). *An investigation of secondary trauma in police wives* (Unpublished doctoral dissertation). Hofstra University, Hempstead, NY.

Egbo, A. C. (2013). *Development of Guidance and counselling.* Enugu: Joe Best Publishers.

Egenti, N. T. (2016). The role of Guidance and Counselling in effective teaching and learning in schools. *International Journal of Multidisciplinary Studies, 1*(2), 36–48.

Eipstein, J. L. (2011). *School, Family and community partnerships.* Boulder, CO: Westview Press.

Eisenberg, N., Cumberland, A., Spinrad, T. L., Fabes, R. A., Shepard, S. A., Reiser, M., ... Guthrie, I. K. (2001). The Relations of Regulation and Emotionality to Children's Externalizing and Internalizing Problem Behavior. *Child Development, 72*(4), 1112–1134. doi:10.1111/1467-8624.00337 PMID:11480937

Eisenberg, N., Ma, Y., Chang, L., Zhou, Q., West, S. G., & Aiken, L. (2007). Relations of Effortful Control, Reactive Under control, and Anger to Chinese *Children's Adjustment. Development and Psychopathology, 19*(02), 385–409. doi:10.1017/S0954579407070198 PMID:17459176

Ekman, P. (1992). An argument for basic emotions. *Cognition and Emotion, 6*(3-4), 169–200. doi:10.1080/02699939208411068

Ellsberg, M., & Heise, L. (2005). *Researching Violence against Women. A Practical Guide for Researchers and Activists.* Washington, DC: World Health Organization, PATH.

Engelbrecht, R. (2017). *SA drug abuse trends paint a grim picture.* Retrieved August 2, 2019, from https://boksburgadvertiser.co.za/297238/sa-drug-abuse-trends-paint-grim-picture/

Enlow, M. B., Blood, E., & Egeland, B. (2013). Sociodemographic risk, developmental competence, and PTSD symptoms in young children exposed to interpersonal trauma in early life. *Journal of Traumatic Stress, 26*(6), 686–694. doi:10.1002/jts.21866 PMID:24490247

Essabar, L., Khalqallah, A., & Dakhama, B. S. B. (2015). Child sexual abuse: Report of 311 cases with review of literature. *The Pan African Medical Journal, 20*(1). PMID:26090005

Evan, W. M. (1966). The Organization Set: Toward a Theory of Interorganizational Relationships. In J. D. Thompson (Ed.), *Approaches to Organizational Design* (pp. 175–191). Pittsburgh, PA: University of Pittsburgh Press.

Evoh, C. J. (2009). *Collaborative partnerships and the transformation of secondary schools in South Africa* (Dissertation). The New School of Social Research.

Ewan, W., & Green, S. (2013). Positive psychology goes to primary school. *Education Today, 13*(4), 22–23. Retrieved from http://www.educationtoday.com.au/article/Positive-psychology-goes-to-primary-school-388

Fan, W., & Williams, C. M. (2010). The effects of parental involvement on students' academic self-efficacy, engagement and intrinsic motivation. *Educational Psychology, 30*(1), 53–74. doi:10.1080/01443410903353302

Fan, W., Williams, C. M., & Wolters, C. A. (2012). Parental involvement in predicting school motivation: Similar and differential effects across ethnic groups. *The Journal of Educational Research, 105*(1), 21–35. doi:10.1080/00220671.2010.515625

Farkas, J. (2015, September). *Recognizing and managing paradoxical reactions from benzodiazepines and propofol.* Retrieved from: https://emcrit.org/pulmcrit/recognizing-and-managing-paradoxical-reactions-from-benzodiazepines-propofol/

Fecser, M. E. (2015). Classroom strategies for traumatized, oppositional students. *Reclaiming Children and Youth, 24*(1), 20–24.

Feindler, E. L., & Engel, E. C. (2011). Assessment and intervention for adolescents with anger and aggression difficulties in school settings. *Psychology in the Schools, 48*(3), 243–253. doi:10.1002/pits.20550

Feldman, D. C. (2003). The antecedents and consequences of early career indecision among young adults. *Human Resource Management Review, 13*, 499–531.

Feldwisch, R. P., & Whiston, S. C. (2015-2016). Examining School Counselors' Commitments to Social Justice Advocacy. *Professional School Counseling, 19*(1), 166–175. doi:10.5330/1096-2409-19.1.166

Felitti, V. J., Anda, R. F., Nordenberg, D., Williamson, D. F., Spitz, A. M., Edwards, V., ... Marks, J. S. (1998). Relationship of childhood abuse and household dysfunction to many of the leading causes of death in adults: The Adverse Childhood Experience (ACE) study. *American Journal of Preventive Medicine, 14*(4), 245–258. doi:10.1016/S0749-3797(98)00017-8 PMID:9635069

Ferrato, D. (2000). *Living with the enemy*. New York: Aperture Foundation.

Field, J. E., & Baker, S. (2004). Defining and examining school counsellor advocacy. *Professional School Counseling, 8*, 56–63.

Findlay, C. M. (2010). Transformative curriculum: changing pedagogy and practice (Master's Thesis). School of Graduate Studies of the University of Lethbridge.

Finkelhor, D., & Korbin, J. (1988). Child abuse as an international issue. *Child Abuse & Neglect, 12*(1), 3–23. doi:10.1016/0145-2134(88)90003-8 PMID:3284612

Finkelhor, D., Ormrod, R. K., Turner, H. A., & Hamby, S. L. (2005). Measuring poly-victimization using the Juvenile Victimization Questionnaire. *Child Abuse & Neglect, 29*(11), 1297–1312. doi:10.1016/j.chiabu.2005.06.005 PMID:16274741

Fizer, D. (2013). *Factors affecting career choices of college students enrolled in agriculture* (Unpublished master's thesis). University of Tennessee.

Foa, E. B., Feske, U., Murdock, R. G., Kozac, M. J., & McCarthy, P. R. (1991). Processing of threat-related material in rape victims. *Journal of Abnormal Psychology, 100*(2), 156–162. doi:10.1037/0021-843X.100.2.156 PMID:2040766

Fogarty, M., Clemens, N., Simmons, D., Anderson, L., Davis, J., Smith, A., ... Oslund, E. (2017). Impact of a technology-mediated reading intervention on adolescents' reading comprehension. *Journal of Research on Educational Effectiveness, 10*(2), 326–353. doi:10.1080/19345747.2016.1227412

Forrester, J. (1961). *Industrial Dynamics*. Cambridge, MA: Productivity Press Incorporated.

Fracher, J., & Kimmel, M. S. (1995). *Hard issues and soft spots: Counseling men about sexuality*. Needham Heights, MA: Allyn & Bacon.

Frattaroli, J. (2006). Experimental disclosure and its moderators: A meta-analysis. *Psychological Bulletin, 132*(6), 823–865. doi:10.1037/0033-2909.132.6.823 PMID:17073523

Fredrickson, B. L. (1998). What good are positive emotions? *Review of General Psychology, 2*(3), 300–319. doi:10.1037/1089-2680.2.3.300 PMID:21850154

Fredrickson, B. L. (2013). Positive emotions broaden and build. *Advances in Experimental Social Psychology, 47*, 1–53. doi:10.1016/B978-0-12-407236-7.00001-2

Freire, P. (1997). *The Politics of Education: Culture, Power and Liberation* (1st ed.). Bergin & Garvey Publishers.

Frydenberg, E., Lewis, R., Bugalski, K., Cotta, A., McCarthy, C., Luscombe-smith, N., & Poole, C. (2004). Prevention is better than cure: Coping skills training for adolescents at school. *Educational Psychology in Practice, 20*(2), 117–134. doi:10.1080/02667360410001691053

Fuster, J. (2002). Frontal Lobe and Cognitive Development. *Journal of Neurocytology, 31*(3/5), 373–385. doi:10.1023/A:1024190429920 PMID:12815254

Galaskiewicz, J. (1979a). *Exchange Networks and Community Politics* (Vol. 75). Beverly Hills, CA: Sage Publications.

Galaskiewicz, J. (1979b). The Structure of Community Networks. *Social Forces, 57*(4), 1346–1364. doi:10.1093f/57.4.1346

Galaskiewicz, J. (1985). Interorganizational Relations. *Annual Review of Sociology, 11*(1), 281–304. doi:10.1146/annurev.so.11.080185.001433

Galbraith, J. R. (1973). *Designing complex organizations.* Reading, MA: Addison-Wesley Publishing Company.

Galbraith, J. R. (1977). *Organization design.* Reading, MA: Addison-Wesley Publishing Company.

Garbarino, J., & Collins, C. C. (1999). Child neglect: The family with a hole in the middle. In H. Dubowitz (Ed.), *Neglected children: Research, practice, and policy* (pp. 1–23). Thousand Oaks, CA: Sage. doi:10.4135/9781452225586.n1

Gaudin, J. (1993). Child neglect: A guide for intervention. Westover Consultants, Inc.

Germond, P., & De Gruchy, S. (Eds.). (1997). *Aliens in the household of God: Homosexuality and Christian faith in South Africa.* Cape Town: David Philip Publishers.

Ghahramanlou, M. A., & Brodbeck, C. (2000). Preditors of secondary trauma in sexual assault counselors. *International Journal of Emergency Mental Health, 1*, 229–240. PMID:11217154

Gherardi, S. A., & Whittlesey-Jerome, W. K. (2018). Role integration through the practice of social work with schools. *Children & Schools, 40*(1), 35–43. doi:10.1093/cs/cdx028

Gilborn, L., Nyonyintoro, R., Kabumbuli, R., & Jwagwe-Wadda, G. (2001). *Making a difference for children affected by AIDS: Baseline findings from operations research in Uganda.* Washington, DC: Population Council.

Glancy, G., & Saini, M. A. (2005). An evidenced-based review of psychological treatments of anger and aggression. *Brief Treatment and Crisis Intervention, 5*(2), 229–248. doi:10.1093/brief-treatment/mhi013

Glozah, F. N., & Pevalin, D. J. (2014). Social support, stress, health, and academic success in Ghanaian adolescents: A path analysis. *Journal of Adolescence, 37*(4), 451–460. doi:10.1016/j.adolescence.2014.03.010 PMID:24793393

Gokler, I. (2002). Child neglect and abuse: The effect of stress on neurobiological development [in Turkish]. *Journal of Child and Youth Mental Health., 9*, 47–57.

Golden, B. R. (2004, January). Healthy anger: How to help your child/teen manage their anger. New Living Magazine.

Gonzalez-DeHass, A. R., Willems, P. P., & Holbein, M. F. D. (2005). Examining the relationship between parental involvement and student motivation. *Educational Psychology Review, 17*(2), 99–123. doi:10.100710648-005-3949-7

Goodman, J. H. (2004). Paternal postpartum depression, its relationship to maternal postpartum depression, and implications for family health. *Journal of Advanced Nursing, 45*(1), 26–35. doi:10.1046/j.1365-2648.2003.02857.x PMID:14675298

Goodman, L. A., Lian, B., Helman, J. E., Latta, R. E., Sparks, E., & Weintraub, S. R. (2004). Training psychologists as social justice agents: Feminists and multicultural principles in action. *The Counseling Psychologist, 32,* 793–837. doi:10.1177/0011000004268802

Graham, S. (2016). Victims of bullying in schools. *Theory into Practice, 55*(2), 136–144. doi:10.1080/00405841.2016.1148988

Green, A. (1996). Child sexual abuse and incest. In M. Lewis (Ed.), *Child and Adolescent Psychiatry* (pp. 41–48). Williams & Wilkins.

Gresham, D., Melvin, G. A., & Gullone, E. (2016). The Role of Anger in the Relationship Between Internalising Symptoms and Aggression in Adolescents. *Journal of Child and Family Studies, 25*(9), 2674–2682. doi:10.100710826-016-0435-4

Griffiths, N., Aitken, A., & Egea, K. (2014). *A Collaborative Approach to Embedding Academic Literacies in First Year Grant Projects.* Academic Press.

Gross, S. (2002). *Causes and Prevention of Child Abuse.* Munich: GRIN Verlag. Retrieved from https://www.grin.com/document/106157

Gross, J. J., & Thompson, R. A. (2007). Emotion regulation: Conceptual foundations. In J. J. Gross (Ed.), *Handbook of emotion regulation* (pp. 3–24). New York: Guilford Press.

Gulati, R. (1998). Alliances and Networks. *Strategic Management Journal, 19*(4), 293–317. doi:10.1002/(SICI)1097-0266(199804)19:4<293::AID-SMJ982>3.0.CO;2-M

Gulati, R., Dialdin, D. A., & Wang, L. (2002). Organizational networks. In J. A. C. Baum (Ed.), *The Blackwell companion to organizations* (pp. 281–303). Malden, MA: Blackwell.

Gysbers, N. C. (2004). Comprehensive guidance and counseling programs: The evolution of accountability. *Professional School Counseling, 8,* 1–14. Retrieved from http://www.schoolcounselor.org/content.asp?contentid=235

Hacker, D. J., Bol, L., Horgan, D. D., & Rakow, E. A. (2000). Test prediction and performance in a classroom context. *Journal of Educational Psychology, 92*(1), 160–170. doi:10.1037/0022-0663.92.1.160

Hagedoorn, J. (2006). Understanding the cross-level embeddedness of interfirm partnership formation. *Academy of Management Review, 31*(3), 670–680. doi:10.5465/amr.2006.21318924

Haihambo, C. K., Brown, A., Ndimwedi, J., & Claassen, P. (2012). *The crisis of education for the San and Ovahimba in Contemporary Namibia.* Conference Paper. Education Conference, University of Namibia, Windhoek, Namibia.

Hall, K. (2012). Validation of experience. *Psychology Central.* Retrieved on August 25 2014 from http://blogs.psychcentral.com/emotionallysensitive/2012/02/levels-of-validation

Hall, K. (2012). What is validation and Why Do I Need to Know? *Psych Central.* Retrieved on October 23, 2014, from http://blogs.psychcentral.com/emotionally-sensitive/2012/02/levels-of-validation

Hall, C. W., Davis, N. B., Bolen, L. M., & Chia, R. (1999). Gender and racial differences in mathematical performance. *The Journal of Social Psychology, 139*(6), 677–689. doi:10.1080/00224549909598248 PMID:10646303

Hall, E. T. (1976). *Beyond trauma.* New York, NY: Anchor Books.

Hampel, P., Meier, M., & Kummel, U. (2008). School-based stress management training for adolescents: Longitudinal results from an experimental study. *Journal of Youth and Adolescence, 37*(8), 1009–1024. doi:10.100710964-007-9204-4

Hanrahan, F., & Banerjee, R. (2017). 'It makes me feel alive': The socio-motivational impact of drama and theatre on marginalised young people. *Emotional & Behavioural Difficulties, 22*(1), 35–49. doi:10.1080/13632752.2017.1287337

Harary, F., & Batell, M. F. (1981). What is a system? *Social Networks, 3*(1), 29–40. doi:10.1016/0378-8733(81)90003-4

Harris, A., & Goodall, J. (2008). Do parents know they matter? Engaging all parents in learning. *Educational Research, 50*(3), 277–289. doi:10.1080/00131880802309424

Harris, N. (2017). Shame in regulatory settings. In P. Drahos (Ed.), *Regulatory Theory: Foundations and applications* (pp. 59–76). Acton, Australia: ANU Press. doi:10.22459/RT.02.2017.04

Hartig, H. (2018, May 18). Republicans turn more negative toward refugees as number admitted to U.S. plummets. *Pew Research Center.* Retrieved from: http://www.pewresearch.org/fact-tank-2018/05/24/republicans-turn-more-negative-towards-refugees-as-number-to-u-s-plummets/

Hartmann, W. (1998). *Homosexuality in Southern Africa.* Windhoek: New Namibia Books.

Hashim, I. H. (2003). Cultural and gender differences in perceptions of stressors and coping skills: A study of Western and African college students in China. *School Psychology International, 24*(2), 182–203. doi:10.1177/0143034303024002004

Hawley, A. (1963). Community Power and Urban Renewal Success. *American Journal of Sociology, 68*(4), 422–431. doi:10.1086/223399

Hayashi, Y., Okamoto, Y., Takagaki, K., Okada, G., Toki, S., Inoue, T., ... Yamawaki, S. (2015). Direct and indirect influences of childhood abuse on depression symptoms in patients with major depressive disorder. *BMC Psychiatry, 15*(1), 244. doi:10.118612888-015-0636-1 PMID:26467656

Hayes, R. L., & Paisley, P. O. (2002). Transforming school counsellor preparation programs. *Theory into Practice, 41*(3), 169–176. doi:10.120715430421tip4103_5

Hays, J. (2012). In OSISA 2012. The Indigenous World 2013. Retrieved from osisa.org/indigenous-peoples/regional/osisa-and-indigenous-world-2013

Heasley, T. (2018). *Experience and impact of a Psychoeducational Anger Management Programme including Positive Psychology Interventions in Adolescent Males: An Interpretative Phenomenological Analysis* (Unpublished master's dissertation). University of East London, London, UK.

Heat. (2002). The EFA 2002 Assessment Country Report, Zimbabwe, Harare.

Hedin, L. W. (2000). Physical and sexual abuse against women and children. *Current Opinion in Obstetrics & Gynecology*, *12*(5), 349–355. doi:10.1097/00001703-200010000-00003 PMID:11111876

Hefferon, K., & Boniwell, I. (2011). *Positive psychology: Theory, research and applications*. Maidenhead, UK: Open University Press.

Hekma, G. (2006). *The gay world: 1980 to present*. New York, NY: Universe Publishing.

Helfer, R. E., & Kempe, C. H. (Eds.). (1987). *The Battered Child* (4th ed.). Chicago: University of Chicago Press.

Helton, J. J., Jackson, D. B., Boutwell, B. B., & Vaughn, M. G. (2018). Household Food Insecurity and Parent-to-Child Aggression. *Child Maltreatment, Volume*, *24*(2), 213–221. doi:10.1177/1077559518819141 PMID:31094579

Henry, C. S., Merten, M. J., Plunkett, S. W., & Sands, T. (2008). Neighborhood, parenting, and adolescent factors and academic achievement in Latino adolescents from immigrant families. *Family Relations*, *57*(5), 579–590. doi:10.1111/j.1741-3729.2008.00524.x

Hepburn, A. (2005). *Early Childhood Mental Health Consultation*. Georgetown University.

Herman-Giddens, M., Brown, G., Verbiest, S., Carlson, P., Hooten, E., Howell, E., & Butts, J. (1999). Under-ascertainment of child abuse mortality in the United States. *Journal of the American Medical Association*, *282*(5), 463–467. doi:10.1001/jama.282.5.463 PMID:10442662

Herman, J. (1997). *Trauma and recovery: The aftermath of violence-from domestic abuse to political terror*. New York, NY: Basic Books.

Herr, E. L. (2002). School reform and perspectives on the role of school counselors: A century of proposals for change. *Professional School Counseling*, *5*(4), 220–234.

Heyden, S. M. (2011). *Counselling children and adolescents*. Belmont, CA: Brooks / Cole.

Hildyard, K. L., & Wolfe, D. A. (2002). Child neglect: Developmental issues and outcomes. *Child Abuse & Neglect*, *26*(6-7), 679–695. doi:10.1016/S0145-2134(02)00341-1 PMID:12201162

Hillis, S., Mercy, J., Amobi, A., & Kress, H. (2016). Global prevalence of past-year violence against children: A systematic review and minimum estimates. *Pediatrics*, *137*(3), 1–13. doi:10.1542/peds.2015-4079 PMID:26810785

Hill, N. E., & Tyson, D. F. (2009). Parental involvement in middle school: A meta-analytic assessment of the strategies that promote achievement. *Developmental Psychology, 45*(3), 740–763. doi:10.1037/a0015362 PMID:19413429

Hipolito-Delgado, C. P., & Lee, C. C. (2007). Empowerment theory for the professional school counsellor: A manifesto for what really matters. *Professional School Counseling, 10*(4), 327–332. doi:10.5330/prsc.10.4.fm1547261m80x744

Hitt, M. A., Beamish, P. W., Jackson, S. E., & Mathieu, J. E. (2007). Building theoretical and empirical bridges across levels: Multilevel research in management. *Academy of Management Journal, 50*(6), 1385–1399. doi:10.5465/amj.2007.28166219

Hodgins, H. S., Weisbust, K. S., Weinstein, N., Shiffman, S., Miller, A., Coombs, G., & Adair, K. C. (2010). The cost of self-protection: Threat response and performance as a function of autonomous and controlled motivations. *Personality and Social Psychology Bulletin, 36*(8), 1101–1114. doi:10.1177/0146167210375618 PMID:20693387

Hoffman-Plotkin, D., & Twentyman, C. (1984). A Multimodal Assessment of Behavioral and Cognitive Deficits in Abused and Neglected Preschoolers. *Child Development, 55*(3), 794–802. doi:10.2307/1130130 PMID:6734318

Holcomb-McCoy, C. (2007). *School counselling to close the achievement gap: A social justice framework to success.* Thousand Oaks, CA: Sage Publications.

Holtin, J. K. (1990). *Black Families and Child Abuse Prevention: An African American Perspective and Approach.* Working Paper No. 852. Chicago: National Committee for Prevention of Child Abuse.

Home Office. (2015). *Definition of domestic abuse.* Retrieved from https://www.gov.uk

Hong, S., & Ho, H. (2005). Direct and indirect longitudinal effects of parental involvement on student achievement: Second-order latent growth modelling across ethnic groups. *Journal of Educational Psychology, 97*(1), 32–42. doi:10.1037/0022-0663.97.1.32

Honkalampi, K., Hintikka, J., Haatainen, K., Koivumaa-Honkanen, H., Tanskanen, A., & Viinamaki, H. (2005). Adverse childhood experiences, stressful life events, or demographic factors: Which are important in women's depression? A 2-year follow-up population study. *The Australian and New Zealand Journal of Psychiatry, 39*(7), 627–632. doi:10.1080/j.1440-1614.2005.01636.x PMID:15996145

Hope, A. E., & Timmel, S. J. (2014). *Training for Transformation in Practice.* Practical Action Publishing.

Hornor, G. (2014). Child neglect: Assessment and intervention. *Journal of Pediatric Health Care, 28*(2), 186–192. doi:10.1016/j.pedhc.2013.10.002 PMID:24559807

House, R., & Martin, P. J. (1999). Advocating for better futures for all students: A new vision for school counsellors. *Education, 119*, 284–291.

Howe, D. (2011). *Attachment across the life course: a brief introduction*. Basingstoke, UK: Palgrave Macmillan. doi:10.1007/978-0-230-34601-7

Howells, K., & Day, A. (2003). Readiness for anger management: Clinical and theoretical issues. *Clinical Psychology Review*, *23*(2), 319–337. doi:10.1016/S0272-7358(02)00228-3 PMID:12573674

Hsieh, Y. P., Shen, A. C. T., Wei, H. S., Feng, J. Y., Huang, S. C. Y., & Hwa, H. L. (2016). Associations between child maltreatment, PTSD, and internet addiction among Taiwanese students. *Computers in Human Behavior*, *56*, 209–214. doi:10.1016/j.chb.2015.11.048

Hudd, S. S., Dumlao, J., Erdmann-Sager, D., Murray, D., Phan, E., Soukas, N., & Yokozuka, N. (2000). Stress at college: Effects on health habits, health status and self-esteem. *College Student Journal*, *34*(2).

Hudson, R. F., Pullen, P. C., Lane, H. B., & Torgesen, J. K. (2008). The Complex Nature of Reading Fluency: A Multidimensional View. *Reading & Writing Quarterly*, *25*(1), 4–32. doi:10.1080/10573560802491208

Hunter, F. (1953). *Community Power Structure*. Chapel Hill, NC: University of North Carolina Press.

Hussain, A., Kumar, A., & Husain, A. (2008). Academic stress and adjustment among high school students. *Journal of the Indian Academy of Applied Psychology*, *34*(9), 70–73.

Hussey, J., Chang, J., & Kotch, J. (2006). Child maltreatment in the United States: Prevalence, risk factors, and adolescent health consequences. *Paediatrics*, *118*(3), 933–942. doi:10.1542/peds.2005-2452 PMID:16950983

Hyde, J. S., Else-Quest, N. M., Alibali, M. W., Knuth, E., & Romberg, T. (2006). Mathematics in the home: Homework practices and mother–child interactions doing mathematics. *The Journal of Mathematical Behavior*, *25*(2), 136–152. doi:10.1016/j.jmathb.2006.02.003

Institute of Medicine and National Research Council. (2014). *New directions in child abuse and neglect research*. Washington, DC: The National Academies Press; doi:10.17226/18331

Ionescu, C. L., & Binţinţan, M. D. B. (2018). Project for the multidisciplinary team and their management in the context of special education. *Palestrica of the Third Millennium Civilization & Sport*, *19*(2), 123–126. doi:10.26659/pm3.2018.19.2.123

Isley, P., & Singh, H. (2005). Do higher grades lead to favorable student evaluations? *Journal of Economic Education*, *36*(1), 29–42. doi:10.3200/JECE.36.1.29-42

Jackson, M. A. (2008). *A study of children and grief: living through bereavement* (Dissertation). University of KwaZulu-Natal.

Jacobs, A. (2011). Life Orientation as experience by learners: A qualitative study in North-West Province. *South African Journal of Education, EASA*, *31*(1), 212–223. doi:10.15700aje.v31n2a481

Jain, A. M. (1999). Emergency department evaluation of child abuse. *Emergency Medicine Clinics of North America*, *17*(3), 575–593. doi:10.1016/S0733-8627(05)70083-3 PMID:10516839

James, M. (1993). Child neglect: A guide for intervention. U.S. Department of Health and Human Services Administration for Children and Families.

Jan, H. (2017). Teacher of 21st Century: Characteristics and Development. *Research on Humanities and Social Sciences*, *7*(9), 50–54.

Jenkins, S., & Baird, S. (2002). Secondary traumatic stress and vicarious trauma: A validation study. *Journal of Traumatic Stress*, *15*(5), 423–432. doi:10.1023/A:1020193526843 PMID:12392231

Jensen, U. (2011). *Factors Influencing Student Retention in Higher Education. Summary of Influential Factors in Degree Attainment and Persistence to Career or Further Education for At-Risk/High Educational Need Students.* Honolulu, HI: Kamehema Schools Research & Evaluation Division.

Jeynes, W. H. (2011). Aspiration and expectations: Providing pathways to tomorrow. In S. Redding, M. Murphy, & P. Sheley (Eds.), *Handbook on family and community engagement* (pp. 57–59). Lincoln, IL: Academic Development Institute.

Jimenez, S. S., Niles, B. L., & Park, C. L. (2010). A mindfulness model of affect regulation and depressive symptoms: Positive emotions, mood regulation expectancies, and self-acceptance as regulatory mechanisms. *Personality and Individual Differences*, *49*(6), 645–650. doi:10.1016/j.paid.2010.05.041

Johnson, C. A. (2007). *Off the Map: How HIV/AIDS programming is failing same-sex practising people in Africa.* New York: IGLHRC.

Jonck, P., & Swanepoel, E. (2015). Exploring the perceived role of life orientation teachers with reference to career guidance provided to Grade 10 learners in the Free State, South Africa. *International Journal of Humanities Social Sciences and Education*, *2*(5), 229–239.

Jonsson, C. (1986). Interoganization Theory and International Organization. *International Studies Quarterly*, *30*(1), 39–57. doi:10.2307/2600436

Kadhiravan, S., & Kumar, K. (2012). Enhancing stress coping skills among college students. *Researchers World*, *3*(4), 49.

Kaplan, S., Pelcovitz, D., & Labruna, V. (1999). Child and adolescent abuse and neglect research: A review of the past 10 years. Part I: Physical and emotional abuse and neglect. *American Academy Child Adolescence Psychiatry*, *38*(10), 1214–1222. doi:10.1097/00004583-199910000-00009 PMID:10517053

Kara, B., Bicer, U., & Gokalp, A. S. (2004). Child abuse [in Turkish]. *Journal of Child Health and Diseases*, *47*, 140–151.

Kashahu, L., Bushati, J., Dibra, G., & Priku, M. (2014). Parental involvement in a teenager's academic achievements in mathematics and native language courses. *European Scientific Journal*, *10*(13), 8–26.

Kashdan, T. B., Goodman, F. R., Mallard, T. T., & Dewall, C. N. (2015). What Triggers Anger in Everyday Life? Links to the Intensity, Control, and Regulation of These Emotions, and Personality Traits. *Journal of Personality*, *84*(6), 737–749. doi:10.1111/jopy.12214 PMID:26248974

Kassai, S. C., & Motta, R. W. (2006). An investigation of the spread of potential Holocaust-related secondary traumatization to the third generation. *International Journal of Emergency Mental Health*, *8*(1), 35–47. PMID:16573251

Kassinove, H., & Sukhodolsky, D. G. (1995). Anger disorders: Basic science and practice issues. In H. Kassinove (Ed.), *Anger disorders: Definition, diagnosis, and treatment* (pp. 1–26). Washington, DC: Taylor & Francis. doi:10.3109/01460869509087270

Kassinove, H., & Tafrate, R. C. (2002). *Anger management: the complete treatment guidebook for practitioners*. Atascadero, CA: Impact.

Katz, D., & Kahn, R. L. (1978). *The social psychology of organizations*. New York: John Wiley.

Katz, I., Kaplan, A., & Buzukashvily, T. (2011). The role of parents' motivation in students' autonomous motivation for doing homework. *Learning and Individual Differences*, *21*(4), 376–386. doi:10.1016/j.lindif.2011.04.001

Kauffman, J. M. (2018). Psychoeducational Technology: Criteria for Evaluation and Control in Special Education. *Focus on Exceptional Children*, *5*(3). doi:10.17161/fec.v5i3.7377

Kaur, B. (2011). Mathematics homework: A study of three grade eight classrooms in Singapore. *International Journal of Science and Mathematics Education*, *9*(9), 187–206. doi:10.100710763-010-9237-0

Kayange, J. J., & Msiska, M. (2016). Teacher education in China: Training teachers for the 21st century. *The Online Journal of New Horizons in Education*, *6*(4), 204–210.

Kellerman, N. (2001). Psychopathology in children of Holocaust survivors: A review of the research literature. *The Israel Journal of Psychiatry and Related Sciences*, *38*(1), 36–46. PMID:11381585

Kelly, M. S., Frey, A., Thompson, A., Klemp, H., Alvarez, M., & Cosner-Berzin, S. (2016). Assessing the National School Social Work Practice Model: Findings from the Second National School Social Work Survey. *Social Work*, *61*(1), 17–28. doi:10.1093wwv044 PMID:26897995

Kempf, J. (2011). *Recognizing and Managing Stress Coping Strategies for Adolescents* (Doctoral dissertation). University of Wisconsin-Stout.

Kendall-Tackett, K. (2002). The health effects of childhood abuse: Four pathways by which abuse can influence health. *Child Abuse & Neglect*, *26*(6-7), 715–729. doi:10.1016/S0145-2134(02)00343-5 PMID:12201164

Kenis, P., & Knoke, D. (2002). How Organizational Field Networks Shape Interorganizational Tie-Formation Rates. *Academy of Management Review*, *27*(2), 275–293. doi:10.5465/amr.2002.6588029

Kent, A., & Waller, G. (1998). The impact of childhood emotional abuse: An extension of the child abuse and trauma scale. *Child Abuse & Neglect*, *22*(5), 393–399. doi:10.1016/S0145-2134(98)00007-6 PMID:9631251

Kernis, M. H., Grannemann, B. D., & Barclay, L. C. (1989). Stability and level of self-esteem as predictors of anger arousal and hostility. *Journal of Personality and Social Psychology*, *56*(6), 1013–1022. doi:10.1037/0022-3514.56.6.1013 PMID:2746456

Kerr, M. A., & Schneider, B. H. (2008). Anger expression in children and adolescents: A review of the empirical literature. *Clinical Psychology Review*, *28*(4), 559–577. doi:10.1016/j.cpr.2007.08.001 PMID:17884263

Keskin, G., & Cam, O. (2005). Psychodynamic nurse approach towards child sexual abuse (in Turkish). *New Symposium*, *43*(3), 118-125.

Kilduff, M., & Tsai, W. (2003). *Social networks and organizations*. Thousand Oaks, CA: Sage. doi:10.4135/9781849209915

King, E., De Silva, M., Stein, A., & Patel, V. (2009). Interventions for improving the psychosocial well-being of children affected by HIV and AIDS. Cochrane Database of Systematic Reviews, 2. doi:10.1002/14651858.CD006733.pub2

King, L. A. (2001). The health benefits of writing about life goals. *Personality and Social Psychology Bulletin*, *27*(7), 798–807. doi:10.1177/0146167201277003

Kirk, C. M., Lewis-Moss, R. K., Nilsen, C., & Colvin, D. Q. (2011). The role of parent expectations on adolescent educational aspirations. *Educational Studies*, *37*(1), 89–99. doi:10.1080/03055691003728965

Kisely, S., Abajobir, A. A., Mills, R., Strathearn, L., Clavarino, A., & Najman, J. M. (2018). Child maltreatment and mental health problems in adulthood: Birth cohort study. *The British Journal of Psychiatry*, *213*(6), 698–703. doi:10.1192/bjp.2018.207 PMID:30475193

Kithakye, M., Morris, A. S., Terranova, A. M., & Myers, S. S. (2010). The Kenyan political conflict and children's adjustment. *Child Development*, *81*(4), 1114–1128. doi:10.1111/j.1467-8624.2010.01457.x PMID:20636685

Knoke, D. (2001). *Changing Organizations: Business Networks in the New Political Economy*. Boulder, CO: Westview Press.

Koenig, L., Du Plessis, A., & Viljoen, M. (2015). The Effect of a Reading Program on the Reading Performance of First-Year Students at a Higher Education Institution. *International Journal of Educational Sciences*, *10*(2), 297–305. doi:10.1080/09751122.2015.11917660

Koski, A., Clark, S., & Nandi, A. (2017). Has child marriage declined in sub-Saharan Africa? An analysis of trends in 31 countries. *Population and Development Review*, *43*(1), 7–29. doi:10.1111/padr.12035

Kottler, J. A. (1993). *On being a therapist* (2nd ed.). San Francisco: Jossey-Bass.

Kozlowski, W. J., & Klein, K. (2000). *Multilevel Theory, research and methods in organizations: Foundations, Extensions, and new directions*. San Francisco: Jossey-Bass.

Krebs, V. E. (2011b). *Network Analysis: Understanding the Connected Economy. Public guest lecture*. Riga, Latvia: Stockholm School of Economics in Riga.

Kruczek, A. (2017). Relationship of self-image and self-acceptance with the expression of anger in girls diagnosed with conduct disorder. *Psychiatria I Psychologia Kliniczna*, *17*(4), 314–324. doi:10.15557/PiPK.2017.0035

Kumari, A., & Jain, J. (2014). Examination stress and anxiety: A study of college students. *Global Journal of Multidisciplinary Studies*, *4*(1), 101–108.

Kumar, S., & Bhukar, J. (2013). Stress Level and Coping Strategies of College Students. *Journal of Physical Education and Sport Management*, *4*, 5–11.

Kuo, C., & Oparario, D. (2011). Health of adults caring for orphaned children in an HIV endemic community in South Africa. *AIDS Care*, *23*(9), 1128–1135. doi:10.1080/09540121.2011.554527 PMID:21480009

Kuo, J. R., Goldin, P. R., Werner, K., Heimberg, R. G., & Gross, J. J. (2011). Childhood trauma and current psychological functioning in adults with social anxiety disorder. *Journal of Anxiety Disorders*, *25*(4), 467–473. doi:10.1016/j.janxdis.2010.11.011 PMID:21183310

Kutlu, L., Batmaz, M., Bozkurt, G., Gencturk, N., & Gul, A. (2007). Punishment methods towards mothers in their childhood and their own punishment methods towards their children [in Turkish]. *Anatolian Journal of Psychiatry*, *8*, 22–29.

Låftman, S. B., & Östberg, V. (2006). The pros and cons of social relations: An analysis of adolescents' health complaints. *Social Science & Medicine*, *63*(3), 611–623. doi:10.1016/j.socscimed.2006.02.005 PMID:16603298

Lai-Yeung, S. W. C. (2014). The need for guidance and counselling training for teachers. *Procedia: Social and Behavioral Sciences*, *113*, 36–43. doi:10.1016/j.sbspro.2014.01.008

Lal, K. (2014). Academic stress among adolescent in relation to intelligence and demographic factors. *American International Journal of Research in Humanities. Arts and Social Sciences*, *5*(1), 123.

Lam, K. Y.-I. (2015). Disclosure and psychological well-being of sexually abused adolescents in Hong Kong. *Journal of Child Sexual Abuse*, *24*(7), 731–752. doi:10.1080/10538712.2015.1077364 PMID:26479960

Langdridge, D., & Hagger-Johnson, G. (2013). *Introduction to research methods and data analysis in psychology*. Harlow: Pearson Prentice Hall.

LaVasseur, M., Goldstein, N., & Welles, S. (2014). A public health perspective on HIV/AIDS in Africa: Victories and unmet challenges. *Phatophysiology*, *21*(1), 237–256. PMID:25096828

Lawrence, B. S. (2000). *Working Paper- Organizational Reference Groups: How People Constitute the Human Component of their Work Environment*. Los Angeles: Anderson Graduate School of Management, University of California.

Laye-Gindhu, A., & Schonert-Reichl, K. A. (2005). Nonsuicidal self-harm among community adolescents: Understanding the "whats" and "whys" of self-harm. *Journal of Youth and Adolescence*, *34*(5), 447–457. doi:10.1007 10964-005-7262-z

Lazarus, A. A. (1997). *Brief but Comprehensive Psychotherapy: The Multimodal Way*. New York: Springer.

Lazarus, R. S. (1999). *Stress and emotion: A new synthesis*. New York: Springer.

Leary, M. R., & MacDonald, G. (2003). Individual differences in self-esteem: A review and theoretical integration. In M. R. Leary & J. P. Tangney (Eds.), *Handbook of self and identity* (pp. 401–418). New York, NY: Guilford Press.

Lebakeng, T. J. (2004). *Prospects and Problems of Transforming Universities in South Africa, with Special Refence to the Right to be an African University* (PhD thesis). Department of Sociology, University of the North.

Lebakeng, J., Phalane, M. M., & Dalindjebo, N. (2005). *Epistemicide, Institutional Cultures and the Imperative for the Africanasation of Universities in South Africa*. University of South Africa.

Lebakeng, T. J. (2000). Africanasation of the Social Sciences and Humanities in South Africa. In L. A. Kasanga (Ed.), *Challenges and Changes at Historically Disadvantaged Universities*. University of North.

Lebakeng, T. J. (2001). The State, Globalisation and Higher Education. *Southern Africa Political & Economic Monthly*, *4*, 7.

Lee, c. (Ed.). (2007). *Counseling for social justice* (2nd ed.). Alexandria, VA: American Counseling Association.

Lehne, G. K. (1995). *Homophobia among men: supporting and defining the male role*. Needham Heights, MA: Allyn & Bacon.

Leke, A., Fine, D., Dobbs, R., Magwentshu, N., Lund, S., & Jacobson, P. (2015). *South Africa's Big Five: Bold Priorities for Inclusive Growth. McKinsey Report*. McKinsey Global Institute.

Lench, H. C. (2004). Anger Management: Diagnostic Differences and Treatment Implications. *Journal of Social and Clinical Psychology*, *23*(4), 512–531. doi:10.1521/jscp.23.4.512.40304

Leung, F. K. S. (2012). What can and should we learn from international studies of mathematics achievement? In J. Dindyal, L. P. Cheng & S. F. Ng (Eds.), *Mathematics education: Expanding horizons. 35th Annual Conference of the Mathematics Education Research Group of Australasia Inc.* (pp. 34–60). Singapore: MERGA.

Lewis, D. O. (1992). From abuse to violence: Psychophysiological consequences of maltreatment. *J American Child Adolescence Psychiatry, 31,* 383–391.

Lewis, H. B. (1971). *Shame and guilt in neurosis.* New York: International Universities Press.

Lewis, J., Arnold, M. S., House, R., & Toporek, R. (2003). *Advocacy competencies.* Academic Press.

Libov, B. G., Nevid, J. S., Pelcovitz, D., & Carmony, T. M. (2002). Posttraumatic stress symptomology in mothers of pediatric cancer survivors. *Psychology & Health, 19*(4), 501–511. doi:10.1080/0887044022000004975

Livingston, R. (1987). Sexually and physically abused children. *Journal of the American Academy of Child and Adolescent Psychiatry, 26*(3), 413–415. doi:10.1097/00004583-198705000-00023 PMID:3597298

Loewus, L. (2017, August 15). The nation's teaching force is still mostly white and female. *Education Week.* Retrieved from: http://www.edweek.org/articles/2017/08/15/the-nations-teaching-force-is-still-mostly.html

Lok-Dessallien, R. (2000). *Review of Poverty Concepts and Indicators.* New York: United Nations Development Programme.

Lombardo, M. (2005). *Secondary trauma in individuals exposed to a person with a serious medical illness* (Unpublished doctoral dissertation). Hofstra University, Hempstead, NY.

Lombardo, K., & Motta, R. W. (2008). Secondary trauma in children of parents with mental illness. *Traumatology, 14*(3), 57–67. doi:10.1177/1534765608320331

Lotfali, S., Moradi, A., & Ekhtiari, H. (2016). On the Effectiveness of Emotion Regulation Training in Anger Management and Emotional Regulation. *Difficulties in Adolescents. Modern Applied Science, 11*(1), 114. doi:10.5539/mas.v11n1p114

Love, K. A. (2011). Enacting a Transformative Education. In Critical pedagogy in the Twenty First Century: A new generation of scholars. New York, NY: Age.

Loveday, P. M., Lovell, G. P., & Jones, C. M. (2016). The Best Possible Selves Intervention: A Review of the Literature to Evaluate Efficacy and Guide Future Research. *Journal of Happiness Studies, 19*(2), 607–628. doi:10.100710902-016-9824-z

Luther, S. (2004). *Resilience and Vulnerability (Adaptation in the context of childhood Adversities).* Cambridge University Press. Retrieved from assets.cambridge.org/97805218/07012sample/97 80521807012wspdf.PDF

Luyckx, K., Vansteenkiste, M., Goossens, L., & Duriez, B. (2009). Basic need satisfaction and identity formation: Bridging self-determination theory and process-oriented identity research. *Journal of Counseling Psychology, 56*(2), 276–288. doi:10.1037/a0015349

Lyons, J. A. (1987). Posttraumatic stress disorder in children and adolescents: A review of the literature. *Developmental and Behavioral Pediatrics, 8*(6), 349–356. doi:10.1097/00004703-198712000-00007 PMID:3323244

Lyubomirsky, S. (2008). *The How of Happiness: A practical guide to getting the life you want.* London: Sphere.

Maccoby, E. E., & Martin, J. A. (1983). Socialization in the context of the family: Parent–child interaction. In P. H. Mussen & E. M. Hetherington (Eds.), Handbook of child psychology (Vol. 4, pp. 1–101). New York: John Wiley and Sons.

Magano, M. D., & Berman, A. (2016). Born frees' negotiating the terrain towards selfhood and wellness: A Life Orientation perspective. *Education as Change, 20*(2), 106–122.

Magura, S., & Moses, B. S. (1986). Outcome measures for child welfare services. Washington, DC: Child Welfare League of America.

Magwa, S. (2013). Stress and Adolescent Development. *Greener Journal of Educational Research, 3*(8), 373–380.

Makota, G., & Leoschut, L. (2016). The National School Safety Framework: A framework for preventing violence in South African schools. *African Safety Promotion, 14*(2), 18–23.

Malik, S. (2015). Assessing level and causes of exam stress among university students in Pakistan. *Mediterranean Journal of Social Sciences, 6*(4), 11–18.

Mampane, J. N. (2017). *Guidelines for mitigating the risk of HIV-infection among Black men who have sex with men (MSM) in a rural community in South Africa* (Unpublished doctoral dissertation). University of South Africa, Pretoria, South Africa.

Maniglio, R. (2013). Child sexual abuse in the etiology of anxiety disorders: A systematic review of reviews. *Trauma, Violence & Abuse, 14*(2), 96–112. doi:10.1177/1524838012470032 PMID:23262751

Manzini, C. K. S. (2012). *An appreciative enquiry into the Life Orientation program offered in high schools* (Unpublished Master dissertation) University of KwaZulu-Natal.

Mapfumo, J. S., Chitsiko, N., & Chireshe, R. (2012). Teaching practice generated stressors and coping mechanisms among student teachers in Zimbabwe. *South African Journal of Education, 32*(2), 155–166. doi:10.15700aje.v32n2a601

Maree, J. G., & Eberson, L. (Eds.). (2002). *Life skills and career counselling.* Cape Town: Clysons.

Maree, J., Fletcher, L., & Sommerville, J. (2011). Predicting success among prospective first-year students at the University of Pretoria. *South African Journal of Higher Education, 25*(6), 1125–1139. Retrieved from https://journals.co.za/content/high/25/6/EJC37734

Marschall, D., Sanftner, J., & Tangney, J. P. (1994). *The state shame and guilt scale.* Fairfax, VA: George Mason University.

Marshall, M. (2018). *Through the looking glass: Reading skills development from a different perspective.* Retrieved from https://www.linkedin.com/pulse/through-looking-glass-reading-skills-development-from-minda-marshall/

Marshall, M. (2016). Accurate On-line Intervention Practices for Efficient Improvement of Reading Skills in Africa. *Universal Journal of Educational Research, 4*(8), 1764–1771. doi:10.13189/ujer.2016.040804

Marshall, R. D., & Galea, S. (2004). Update on posttraumatic stress disorder. *Journal of Clinical Psychology, 65*(Suppl1), 37–43.

Martin, A. (2018). *The relationship between the counsellor and the client.* Retrieved August 2, 2019, from http://www.thecounsellorsguide.co.uk/relationship-between-counsellor-client.html

Martinez-Cobo. (1984). Study of the Problem of Discrimination against Indigenous Populations. Final report submitted by the Special Rapporteur. United Nations, Department of Economic and Social Affairs.

Mason, L., Pluchino, P., & Tornatora, M. C. (2016). Using eye-tracking technology as an indirect instruction tool to improve text and picture processing and learning. *British Journal of Educational Technology, 47*(6), 1083–1095. doi:10.1111/bjet.12271

Masten, A. S., & Wright, M. O. (1998). Cumulative risk and protection models of child maltreatment. *Journal of Aggression, Maltreatment & Trauma, 2*(1), 7–30. doi:10.1300/J146v02n01_02

Matengu, K. K., Likando, G., & Haihambo, C. K. (in press). Inclusive education in marginalised contexts: The San and Ovahimba learners in Namibia. *British Council.*

May-Chahal, C., & Cawson, P. (2005). Measuring child maltreatment in the United Kingdom: A study of the prevalence of child abuse and neglect. *Child Abuse & Neglect, 29*(9), 969–984. doi:10.1016/j.chiabu.2004.05.009 PMID:16165212

Maznevski, M. L., Steger, U., & Amann, W. (2007). *Managing Complexity in Global Organizations.* IMD.

McCann, I. L., & Pearlman, L. A. (1990). Vicarious traumatization: A framework for understanding the psychological effects of working with victims. *Journal of Traumatic Stress, 3*(1), 131–150. doi:10.1007/BF00975140

McClintock, S. M., Husain, M. M., Greer, T. L., & Cullum, C. M. (2010). Association between depression severity and neurocognitive function in major depressive disorder: A review and synthesis. *Neuropsychology, 24*(1), 9–34. doi:10.1037/a0017336 PMID:20063944

McCrann, D. (2017). *An Exploratory Study of Child Sexual Abuse in Tanzania.* Doctoral thesis.

Mclaughlin, C. L. (2009). *Understanding stress: Helping students cope information for educators.* Bethesda, MD: National Association of School Psychologists.

Mcmahon, J. (2013). Child Neglect. *Impact and Interventions Impact of Neglect on Brain Development and Attachment, 18*(1), 1–9.

McNally, R. J., Kaspi, S. P., Riemann, B. C., & Zeitlin, S. B. (1990). Selective processing of threat cues n posttraumatic stress disorder. *Journal of Abnormal Psychology, 99*(4), 398–402. doi:10.1037/0021-843X.99.4.398 PMID:2266215

McNeal, R. B. Jr. (2012). Checking in or checking out? Investigating the parent involvement reactive hypothesis. *The Journal of Educational Research, 105*(2), 79–89. doi:10.1080/00220 671.2010.519410

McPherson, M., Smith-Lovin, L., & Cook, J. (2001). Birds of a Feather: Homophily in Social Networks. *Annual Review of Sociology, 27*(1), 415–444. doi:10.1146/annurev.soc.27.1.415

McSherry, D. (2007). Commentary: Understanding and addressing the "neglect of neglect": Why are we making a mole-hill out of a mountain? *Child Abuse & Neglect, 31*(6), 607–614. doi:10.1016/j.chiabu.2006.08.011 PMID:17602743

Meem, D. T., Gibson, M. A., & Alexander, J. F. (2010). *Finding out: an introduction to LGBT studies.* Thousand Oaks, CA: Sage.

Mehrabian, A. (1981). *Silent messages: Implicit communication of emotions and attitudes* (2nd ed.). Belmont, CA: Wadsworth.

Mennen, F. E., Kim, K., Sang, J., & Trickett, P. K. (2010). Child neglect: Definition and identification of youth's experiences in official reports of maltreatment. *Child Abuse & Neglect, 34*(9), 647–658. doi:10.1016/j.chiabu.2010.02.007 PMID:20643482

Merril, J., Bakken, S., Rockoff, M., Gebbi, K., & Carley, K. (2007). Description of a method to support public health information management: Organisational network analysis. *Journal of Biochemical Informatics, 40*(40), 422–428.

Mesa-Gresa, P., & Moya-Albiol, L. (2011). Neurobiología del maltrato infantil: El ciclo de la violencia [Neurobiology of child abuse: The 'cycle of violence']. *Revista de Neurología, 52*(8), 489–503. doi:10.33588/rn.5208.2009256 PMID:21425102

Metcalfe, L. (1981). Designing Precarious Partnerships. In P. C. Nystrom & W. H. Starbuck (Eds.), *Handbook of Organizational Design* (Vol. 1). New York: Oxford University Press.

Mezirow. (2003b). Epistemology of transformative learning. In Transformative learning in action: Building bridges across contexts and disciplines (pp. 326-330). Academic Press.

Mezirow, J. (1997). Transformative learning: Theory to practice. *New Directions for Adult and Continuing Education, 74*(74), 5–12. doi:10.1002/ace.7401

Mezirow, J. (2003a). Transformative learning as discourse. *Journal of Transformative Education*, *1*(1), 58–63. doi:10.1177/1541344603252172

Miller, S. (2016). Child Soldiers in the Salvadoran Civil War. *Xavier Journal of Undergraduate Research, 4*(2). Available at: https://www.exhibit.xavier.edu/xjur/vol4/iss1/2

Miller, A., Smith, E., Park, E., & Engle, J. (2014). *Blurring Boundries: Transforming Place, Policies, and Partnerships for Postsecondary Education Attainment in Metropolitan Areas.* Washington, DC: Institute for Higher Education Policy.

Miller-Cribbs, J. E., Wen, F., Coon, K. A., Jelley, M. J., Foulks-Rodriguez, K., & Stearns, J. (2016). Adverse childhood experiences and inequalities in adult health care access. *International Public Health Journal, 8*(2), 257–270.

Mineka, S., & Zinbarg, R. (2006). A contemporary learning theory perspective on the Etiology of anxiety disorders. *The American Psychologist, 61*(1), 10–26. doi:10.1037/0003-066X.61.1.10 PMID:16435973

Mizruchi, M. S. (1996). What do interlocks do? An analysis, critique, and assessment of research on interlocking directorates. *Annual Review of Sociology, 22*(1), 271–298. doi:10.1146/annurev. soc.22.1.271

Mohapatra, S., Panigrahi, S. K., & Rath, D. (2012). Examination Stress in Adolescents. *Asian Journal of Paediatric Practice, 16*(1), 7–9.

Moliterno, P. T., & Mahony, D. M. (2011). Network Theory of Organization: A Multilevel Approach. *Journal of Management, 37*(2), 443–467. doi:10.1177/0149206310371692

Moore, J. (2005). Is Higher Education Ready for Transformative Learning: A question Explored in the Study of Sustainability. *Journal of Transformative Education, 3*(1), 76–91. doi:10.1177/1541344604270862

Moradi, I., Ghahari, S., Gheytarani, B., & Safari, R. (2016). The relationship between identity style, fear of negative evaluation with social acceptance. *Social Sciences, 11*(14), 3549–3553. doi:10.3923science.2016.3549.3553

Moroni, S., Dumont, H., Trautwein, U., Niggli, A., & Baeriswyl, F. (2015). The need to distinguish between quantity and quality in research on parental involvement: The example of parental help with homework. *The Journal of Educational Research, 2015*, 1–15. doi:10.1080/00220671.20 14.901283

Motta, R. W., Hafeez, S., Sciancalepore, R., & Diaz, A. B. (2001). Discriminant validation of the Secondary Trauma Scale. *Journal of Psychotherapy in Independent Practice, 24*, 17–24.

Motta, R. W., Joseph, J. M., Rose, R. D., Suozzi, J. M., & Leiderman, L. (1997). Assesment of secondary trauma with a modified Stroop procedure. *Journal of Clinical Psychology, 53*, 895–903. doi:10.1002/(SICI)1097-4679(199712)53:8<895::AID-JCLP14>3.0.CO;2-F PMID:9403392

Motta, R. W., Newman, C. L., Lombardo, K. K., & Silverman, M. A. (2004). Objective assessment of secondary trauma. *International Journal of Emergency Mental Health, 6*(2), 67–74. PMID:15298077

Mullen, P. E., Martin, J. L., Anderson, J. C., Romans, S. E., & Her-bison, G. P. (1996). The long-term impact of the physical, emotional, and sexual abuse of children: A community study. *Child Abuse & Neglect, 20*(1), 7–21. doi:10.1016/0145-2134(95)00112-3 PMID:8640429

Muller, J. (1997). Social justice and its renewals: A sociological comment. *International Studies in Sociology of Education, 7*(2), 195–211. doi:10.1080/09620219700200011

Muller, R. T., Hunter, J. E., & Stollak, G. (1995). The intergenerational transmission of corporal punishment: A comparison of social learning and temperament models. *Child Abuse & Neglect, 19*(11), 1323–1335. doi:10.1016/0145-2134(95)00103-F PMID:8591089

Munroe, J. F., Shay, J., Fisher, L. M., Makary, L. M., Rapperport, K., & Zimering, R. T. (2003). Preventing compassion fatigue: A team treatment model. In C. R. Figley (Ed.), *Compassion Fatigue: Coping with Secondary Traumatic Stress Disorder in Those who treat the traumatized* (pp. 209–231). Brunner /Mazel.

Murayama, K., Pekrun, R., Suzuki, M., Marsh, H. W., & Lichtenfeld, S. (2016). Don't aim too high for your kids: Parental overaspiration undermines students' learning in mathematics. *Journal of Personality and Social Psychology, 111*(5), 766–779. doi:10.1037/pspp0000079 PMID:26595715

Murphy, A., Roberts, K., & Hoffman, D. (2002). Article. *Journal of Child and Family Studies, 11*(2), 191–202. doi:10.1023/A:1015177609382

Mwoma, T., & Pillay, J. (2015). Psychosocial support for orphans and vulnerable children in public primary schools: Challenges and interventions strategies. *South African Journal of Education, 35*(3), 1–9. doi:10.15700aje.v35n3a1092

Nagle, Y. K., & Sharma, U. (2018). Academic stress and coping mechanism among students: An Indian perspective. *Journal of Child Adolescent Psychology, 2*(1), 6–8.

Nasir, R., & Ghani, N. A. (2014). Behavioral and Emotional Effects of Anger Expression and Anger Management among Adolescents. *Procedia: Social and Behavioral Sciences, 140,* 565–569. doi:10.1016/j.sbspro.2014.04.471

National Association of Social Workers. (2010). *Social workers in schools: Kindergarten through 12 grade occupational profile. NASW Center for Workforce Studies and Social Work Practices.* Washington, DC: Author.

National CASA Volunteer Manual. (2015). Retrieved from https://pgcasa.org/wp-content/uploads/2015/07/ch4.pdf

National Clearinghouse on Child Abuse and Neglect Information. (2001). *What is child maltreatment?* Washington, DC: National Clearinghouse on Child Abuse and Neglect.

National Research Council. (1993). *Understanding Child Abuse and Neglect*. Washington, DC: The National Academies Press; doi:10.17226/2117

Ndebele, N., Sawyer, A., Rowett, J., & Perinbam, L. (2005). The Abertay Conversation. Communique to G 8 Leaders.

Ndimwedi, J. (2014). *Educational Barriers and Employment Advancement among the Marginalized People in Namibia: The case of the OvaHimba and OvaZemba in the Kunene Region* (Master's dissertation). University of the Western Cape.

Nebes, R. D., Butters, R. D., Mulsant, B. H., Pollock, B. G., Zmuda, M. D., Houck, P. R., & Reynolds, C. F. (2000). Decreased working memory and processing speed mediate cognitive impairment in geriatric depression. *Psychological Medicine*, *30*(3), 679–691. doi:10.1017/S0033291799001968 PMID:10883722

Needham, B. L., Crosnoe, R., & Muller, C. (2004). Academic failure in secondary school: The inter-related role of health problems and educational context. *Social Problems*, *51*(4), 569–586. doi:10.1525p.2004.51.4.569 PMID:20354573

Neighbors, C., Vietor, A. N., & Knee, C. R. (2002). A Motivational Model of Driving Anger and Aggression. *Personality and Social Psychology Bulletin*, *28*(3), 324–335. doi:10.1177/0146167202286004

Nel, C., Dreyer, C., & Klopper, M. (2004). An analysis of the reading profiles of first-year students at Potchefstroom University : A cross-sectional study and a case study. *South African Journal of Education*, *24*(1), 95–103.

Nel, J. A. (2009). *Same-sex sexuality and health: psychosocial scientific research in South Africa*. Pretoria: HSRC Press.

Nelson, B. S., & Wampler, K. S. (2000). Systemic effects of trauma in clinic couples: An exploratory study of secondary trauma resulting from childhood abuse. *Journal of Marital and Family Therapy*, *26*(2), 171–184. doi:10.1111/j.1752-0606.2000.tb00287.x PMID:10776604

Ngisa, F. S., Muriungi, P., & Mwenda, E. (2017). Impact of Child Abuse on Academic Performance of Pupils in Public Primary Schools in Kieni West Sub-County. *Nyeri County.*, *6*(9), 62–72.

Nicholl, P (2001). An exploration of the social work response to police referred cases of domestic violence within the four community Health and Social Services Trusts in the Eastern Health and Social Services Board area. (unpublished)

Nickerson, R. (2016). *Young gay men's experiences of homophobic bullying during adolescence* (Unpublished doctoral dissertation). Alliant International University, San Francisco, CA.

Noble, K. G., Wolmetz, M. E., Ochs, L. G., Farah, M. J., & McCandliss, B. D. (2006). Brain behavior relationships in reading acquisition are modulated by socio-economic factors. *Developmental Science*, *9*(6), 642–654. doi:10.1111/j.1467-7687.2006.00542.x PMID:17059461

Nohria, N., & Eccles, R. G. (Eds.). (1993). *Network and Organizations: Structure, Form and Action*. Boston, MA: Harvard Business School.

Norcross, J. C., & Kobayashi, M. (1999). Treating anger in psychotherapy: Introduction and cases. *Journal of Clinical Psychology*, *55*(3), 275–282. doi:10.1002/(SICI)1097-4679(199903)55:3<275::AID-JCLP1>3.0.CO;2-M PMID:10321743

Norman, R. E., Byambaa, M., De, R., Butchart, A., Scott, J., & Vos, T. (2012). The long-term health consequences of child physical abuse, emotional abuse, and neglect: A systematic review and meta-analysis. *PLoS Medicine*, *9*(11), e1001349. doi:10.1371/journal.pmed.1001349 PMID:23209385

Nour, N. M. (2006). Health consequences of child marriage in Africa. *Emerging Infectious Diseases*, *12*(11), 1644–1649. doi:10.3201/eid1211.060510 PMID:17283612

Ntshuntshe, Z. (2012). *An assessment of the implementation of intervention programmes which ensure the right to education for orphans in King William's Town District* (Unpublished Master of Education dissertation). University of Fort Hare.

Nurius, P. S., Green, S., Logan-Greene, P., Longhi, D., & Song, C. (2016). Stress pathways to health inequalities: Embedding ACEs within social and behavioral contexts. *International Public Health Journal*, *8*(2), 241–256. PMID:27274786

Nyarko, K., Amissah, C. M., Addai, P., & Dedzo, B. Q. (2014). The effect of child abuse on children's psychological health. *Psychology and Behavioral Sciences*, *3*(4), 105–112. doi:10.11648/j.pbs.20140304.11

Nyawasha, T. (2006). Psychosocial Support to Orphans and Vulnerable children. Rapports. AIDS in Africa: UNAIDS country by country.

O'Brien, L. M., Heycock, E. G., Hanna, M., Jones, P. W., & Cox, J. L. (2004). Postnatal depression and faltering growth: A community study. *Pediatrics*, *113*(5), 1242–1247. doi:10.1542/peds.113.5.1242 PMID:15121936

O'Donnell, M., Nassar, N., Leonard, H., Mathews, R., Patterson, Y., & Stanley, F. (2010). Monitoring child abuse and neglect at a population level: Patterns of hospital admissions for maltreatment and assault. *Child Abuse & Neglect*, *34*(11), 823–832. doi:10.1016/j.chiabu.2010.04.003 PMID:20888637

O'Donovan, R., Doody, O., & Lyons, R. (2013). The effect of stress on health and its implications for nursing. *British Journal of Nursing (Mark Allen Publishing)*, *22*(16), 969–973. doi:10.12968/bjon.2013.22.16.969 PMID:24037402

Ockerman, M. S., & Mason, E. C. (2012). Developing School Counseling Students' Social Justice Orientation Through Service Learning. DePaul University. Retrieved from: https://files.eric.ed.gov/fulltext/EJ978861.pdf

Office of the United Nations High Commissioner for Human Rights. Convention on the Rights of the Child: Adopted and opened for signature, ratification and accession by General Assembly resolution 44/25 of 20 November 1989. Geneva: UN; c1997–2003 [cited 2008 Oct 24]. (n.d.). Available from: http://www. unhchr.ch/html/menu3/b/k2crc.htm

Olegbeleye, A. O. (2013). *Predictors of the Mental Health of Orphans and Vulnerable Children in Nigeria.* Ife Psychologia. Retrieved from http://www.readperiodicals.com/201309/3093274031.html

Olukoshi, A. (2017). *The conceptual and legal basis for inclusive democracy and integration/mainstreaming of marginalized groups in society. Paper presented on 16 February 2019.* Windhoek: International IDEA.

Onolemhenmhen,, P. E., & Osunde, Y. (2018). Child Neglect as Predictor of Academic Performance among Senior Secondary School Students in Edo State, Nigeria. *International Journal of Humanities and Social Science, 7*(4), 75–84.

Ostroff, C., & Bowen, D. E. (2000). Moving HR to a higher level: HR practices and organizational effectiveness. In K. J. Klein & S. W. J. Kozlowski (Eds.), *Multilevel theory, research, and methods in organizations, foundations, extensions, and new directions.* San Francisco: Jossey-Bass.

Oviogbodu, C. O. (2015). *Perceived impact of guidance and counselling in the development of Niger Delta Region. Paper present at Niger Delta University conference with the theme: education and sustainable development in the Niger Delta region of Nigeria,* Niger Delta University.

Owusu, J. S., Colecraft, E. K., Aryeetey, R. N., Vaccaro, J. A., & Huffman, F. G. (2016). Comparison of two school feeding programmes in Ghana, West Africa. *International Journal of Child Health and Nutrition, 5*(2), 56–62. doi:10.6000/1929-4247.2016.05.02.2

Ozturk, S. (2007). *Psychological Abuse Towards Children* (in Turkish) (MA Thesis). Elazig: Firt University.

Paisely, P. O., & Border, L. D. (1995). School Counseling: An Evolving Specialty. Journal of counseling and development. *JCD, 74*(2), 150–153. doi:10.1002/j.1556-6676

Paisley, P. O., Ziomek-Daigle, J., & Getch, Q. Y., & F. Bailey, D. (2006). Using state standards to develop professional school counsellor identity as both counsellors and educators. Guidance & Counseling, 21(3), 143-151. Retreived from http://www.tandf.co.uk/journals/authors/cbjgauth.asp

Paisley, P. O., & Hayes, R. L. (2002). Transformation in school counsellor preparation and practice. *Counseling and Human Development, 35*(3), 1–10.

Palidofsky, M., & Stolbach, B. C. (2012). Dramatic healing: The evolution of a trauma-informed musical theatre program for incarcerated girls. *Journal of Child & Adolescent Trauma, 5*(3), 239–256. doi:10.1080/19361521.2012.697102

Palmer, D. A., & Biggart, W. (2002). Organizational Institutions. In J. A. C. Baum (Ed.), *The Blackwell companion to organizations.* Malden, MA: Blackwell.

Park, C. L., & Adler, N. E. (2003). Coping styles as a predictor of health and well-being across the first year of medical school. *Health Psychology*, *22*(6), 627–631. doi:10.1037/0278-6133.22.6.627 PMID:14640860

Parkes, J., & Stefanou, C. (2010). Does pragmatism trump motivation in college students' preferences for examination formats? *Learning Environments Research*, *13*(3), 225–241. doi:10.100710984-010-9077-4

Park-Taylor, J., Walsh, M. E., & Ventura, A. B. (2007). Creating healthy acculturation pathways: Integrating theory and research to inform counselors' work with immigrant children. *Professional School Counseling*, *11*(1), 25–34. doi:10.5330/PSC.n.2010-11.25

Parsons, D. (2008). Is there an alternative to exams? Examination stress in engineering courses. *International Journal of Engineering Education*, *24*(6), 1111–1118.

Parsons, J., Kehle, T. J., & Owen, S. V. (1990). Incidence of behavior problems among children of Vietnam war veterans. *School Psychology International*, *11*(4), 253–259. doi:10.1177/0143034390114002

Patall, E. A., Cooper, H., & Robinson, J. C. (2008). Parent involvement in homework: A research synthesis. *Review of Educational Research*, *78*(4), 1039–1101. doi:10.3102/0034654308325185

Patterson, M. (2013). *Vulnerability: A short review* (ICR Working Paper No. 3). Retrieved from Vancouver Island University website: www2.viu.ca/icr/files/2012/06/VulnerabilityLiterature-review-SSHRC-partnership-grant.pdf

Pearlman, L. A., & MacIan, P. S. (1995). Vicarious traumatization: An empirical study of the effects of trauma work on trauma therapists. *Professional Psychology, Research and Practice*, *26*(6), 558–565. doi:10.1037/0735-7028.26.6.558

Pearlman, L. A., & Saakvitne, K. W. (1995). Treating therapists with secondary traumatic stress disorders. In C. R. Figley (Ed.), *Compassion fatigue: Coping with secondary traumatic stress disorder in those who treat the traumatized* (pp. 150–177). New York: Brunner/Mazel.

Peate, I. (2005). *Manual of sexually transmitted infections*. London: Whurr Publishers.

Peeters, I., & Lievens, P. (2015). *The ultimate curriculum design for ultimate learning experience in higher education*. At the 6th International Conference of Technology, Education and Development (INTED), Valencia, Spain.

Pennebaker, J. W. (1997). Writing about emotional experiences as a therapeutic process. *Psychological Science*, *8*(3), 162–166. doi:10.1111/j.1467-9280.1997.tb00403.x

Pennymon, W. (2005). School counselors' perceptions of social advocacy training: Helpful and hindering events: A qualitative study. In N. S. Madu & S. Govender (Eds.), *Mental health and psychotherapy in Africa* (pp. 184–208). Sovenga, South Africa: UL Press of the University of Limpopo-Turfloop Campus.

Perlstein, P. (2010). *An evaluation of potential transgenerational transmission of Holocaust trauma in the third generation* (Doctoral dissertation). Hofstra University, Hempstead, NY.

Perrone, V., Zaheer, A., & McEvily, B. (2003). Free to be Trusted? Organizational Constraints on Trust in Boundary Spanners. *Organization Science*, *14*(4), 442–439. doi:10.1287/orsc.14.4.422.17487

Petalas, M., Hastings, R. P., Nash, S., Dowey, A., & Reilly, D. (2009). "I like that he always shows who he is": The perceptions and experiences of siblings with a brother with Autism Spectrum Disorder. *International Journal of Disability Development and Education*, *56*(4), 381–399. doi:10.1080/10349120903306715

Pezdek, K., Berry, T., & Renno, P. A. (2002). Children's mathematics achievement: The role of parents' perceptions and their involvement in homework. *Journal of Educational Psychology*, *94*(4), 771–777. doi:10.1037/0022-0663.94.4.771

Phillips, D. A., & Shonkoff, J. P. (Eds.). (2000). *From neurons to neighborhoods: The science of early childhood development*. National Academies Press.

Phillips-Hershey, E., & Kanagy, B. (1996). Teaching students to manage personal anger constructively. *Elementary School Guidance & Counseling*, *30*(3), 229–234.

Phillipson, S. (2010). Parental role in relation to students' cognitive ability towards academic achievement in Hong Kong. *The Asia-Pacific Education Researcher*, *19*(2), 229–250. doi:10.3860/taper.v19i2.1594

Phillipson, S. (2013). Parental expectations: The influence of the significant other on school achievement. In S. Phillipson, K. Y. L. Ku, & S. N. Phillipson (Eds.), *Constructing educational achievement: A sociocultural perspective* (pp. 87–104). Routledge.

Phillipson, S., & Phillipson, S. N. (2007). Academic expectations, belief of ability, and involvement by parents as predictors of child achievement: A cross-cultural comparison. *International Journal of Experimental and Educational Psychology*, *27*(3), 329–348. doi:10.1080/01443410601104130

Phillipson, S., & Phillipson, S. N. (2012). Children's cognitive ability and their academic achievement: The mediation effects of parental expectations. *Asia Pacific Education Review*, *13*(3), 495–508. doi:10.100712564-011-9198-1

Phipps, A. B., & Mitchell, K. (2003). Brief interventions for secondary trauma: Review and recommendations. *Stress and Health*, *19*(3), 139–147. doi:10.1002mi.970

Pierce, L., & Bozalek, V. (2008). Child Abuse in South Africa: An examination of how child abuse and neglect are defined. *Child Abuse & Neglect*, *28*(8), 817–832. doi:10.1016/j.chiabu.2003.09.022 PMID:15350767

Pillard, R. C. (1996). *Homosexuality from a familial and genetic perspective*. Arlington, VA: American Psychiatric Association.

Pillay, J. (2014). Challenges educational psychologists face working with vulnerable. In T. Corcoran (Ed.), *Psychology in Education: Critical Theory-Practice*. Rotterdam: Sense Publishers. doi:10.1007/978-94-6209-566-3_7

Pisarczyk, K. (2018). *Music and its effect on stress*. Retrieved from http://digitalcommons. augustana.edu/muscstudent/4

Polansky, N. L. (1979). The Absent Father in Child Neglect. *The Social Service Review, 63*–74.

Polat, O. (2002). *Children and Violence*. Istanbul: Der Publications. (in Turkish)

Pollak, S. (2004). The impact of child maltreatment on the psychosocial development of young children. In Encyclopedia on Early Childhood Development, (pp. 1-6). Academic Press.

Pomerantz, E. M., Moorman, E. A., & Litwack, S. D. (2007). The how, whom and why of parents' involvement in children's academic lives: More is not always better. *Review of Educational Research, 77*(3), 373–410. doi:10.3102/003465430305567

Porter, R. J., Bourke, C., & Gallagher, P. (2007). Neuropsychological impairment in major depression: Its nature, origin and clinical significance. *The Australian and New Zealand Journal of Psychiatry, 41*(2), 115–128. doi:10.1080/00048670601109881 PMID:17464689

Pourhosein Gilakjani, A., & Sabouri, N. B. (2016). How can students improve their reading comprehension skill. *Journal of Studies in Education, 6*(2), 229–240. doi:10.5296/jse.v6i2.9201

Power, R. A., Lecky-Thompson, L., Fisher, H. L., Cohen-Woods, S., Hosang, G. M., Uher, R., ... McGuffin, P. (2013). The interaction between child maltreatment, adult stressful life events and the 5-HTTLPR in major depression. *Journal of Psychiatric Research, 47*(8), 1032–1035. doi:10.1016/j.jpsychires.2013.03.017 PMID:23618376

Prevent Child Abuse America. (2001). *Child maltreatment*. Available from: http://www.who. int/topics/childabuse/en/2007

Price, D. V. (2005). *Learning Communities and Student Success in Postsecondary Education. MDRC Building Knowledge to Improve Social Policy. DVP-PRAXIS* LTD.

Price, J. H., & Murnan, J. (2004). Research Limitations and the Necessity of Reporting Them. *American Journal of Health Education, 35*(2), 66–67. doi:10.1080/19325037.2004.10603611

Price-Mitchell, M. (2014). *How role models influence youth strategies for success*. Retrieved August 2, 2019, from https://www.rootsofaction.com/role-models-youth-strategies-success/

Propper, R. W., Stickgold, R., Keeley, R., & Christman, S. D. (2007). Is television traumatic? Dreams, stress, and media exposure in the aftermath of September 11, 2001. *Psychological Science, 18*(4), 334–340. doi:10.1111/j.1467-9280.2007.01900.x PMID:17470259

PROTECT. (2016). *Indicators of child abuse and neglect*. Retrieved from https://www. education.vic.gov.au/Documents/about/programs/health/protect/ChildSafeStandard5_ WarningSignsSchoolStaff.pdf

Putwain, D. W. (2009). Assessment and examination stress in Key Stage 4. *British Educational Research Journal*, *35*(3), 391–411. doi:10.1080/01411920802044404

Qiao, D. P., & Chan, Y. C. (2005). Child abuse in China: A yet-to-be-acknowledged 'social problem' in the Chinese Mainland. *Child & Family Social Work*, *10*(1), 21–27. doi:10.1111/j.1365-2206.2005.00347.x

Qiao, D. P., & Xie, Q. W. (2017). Public perceptions of child physical abuse in Beijing. *Child & Family Social Work*, *22*(1), 213–225. doi:10.1111/cfs.12221

Raby, K. L., Roisman, G. I., Labella, M. H., Martin, J., Fraley, R. C., & Simpson, J. A. (2018). The legacy of early abuse and neglect for social and academic competence from childhood to adulthood. *Child Development*. doi:10.1111/cdev.13033 PMID:29336018

Radcliff, E., Racine, E., Brunner Huber, L., & Whitaker, B. E. (2012). Association between family composition and the well-being of vulnerable children in Nairobi, Kenya. *Maternal and Child Health Journal*, *16*(6), 1232–1240. doi:10.100710995-011-0849-y PMID:21750894

Radford, L., Corral, S., Bradley, C., & Fisher, H. L. (2013). The prevalence and impact of child maltreatment and other types of victimization in the UK: Findings from a population survey of caregivers, children and young people and young adults. *Child Abuse & Neglect*, *37*(10), 801–813. doi:10.1016/j.chiabu.2013.02.004 PMID:23522961

Rahman, K. (2013). Belonging and learning to belong in school: The implications of the hidden curriculum for indigenous students. *Discourse (Abingdon)*, *34*(5), 660–672. doi:10.1080/0159 6306.2013.728362

Ramakrishnan, V. K., & Jalajakumari, V. T. (2013). Significance of imparting guidance and counselling programmes for adolescent students. *Asia Pacific Journal of Research*, *2*(9), 102–112.

Ramphele, M. (2012). *Conversations with my sons and daughters*. Johannesburg: Penguin Books.

Rasinski, T. (2017). Fluency matters. *International Electronic Journal of Elementary Education*, *7*(1), 3–12.

Ratts, M. J., DeKruyf, L., & Chen-Hayes, S. F. (2007). The ACA advocacy competencies: A social justice advocacy framework for professional school counsellors. *Professional School Counseling*, *11*(2), 90–97. doi:10.5330/PSC.n.2010-11.90

Redford, J. (Producer). (2015, September 21). *ACES primer* [Video file]. Retrieved from https://vimeo.com/139998006

Regehr, C. (2018). *Stress, trauma, and decision-making for social workers*. New York, NY: Columbia University Press. doi:10.7312/rege18012

Regehr, C., & Glancy, G. (2014). *Mental health social work practice in Canada* (2nd ed.). Toronto, Canada: Oxford University Press.

Rehan, W., Antfolk, J., Johansson, A., Jern, P., & Santtila, P. (2017). Experiences of severe childhood maltreatment, depression, anxiety and alcohol abuse among adults in Finland. *PLoS One*, *12*(5), e0177252. doi:10.1371/journal.pone.0177252 PMID:28481912

Reid, J. A., Baglivio, M. T., Piquero, A. R., Greenwald, M. A., & Epps, N. (2017). Human trafficking of minors and childhood adversity in Florida. *American Journal of Public Health*, *107*(2), 306–311. doi:10.2105/AJPH.2016.303564 PMID:27997232

REPSSI. (2013). *REPSSI launches Teacher's Diploma Course in Psychosocial Care, Support and Protection in Zambia*. Retrieved from http://www.repssi-launces-teachers-diploma-course-in-psychosocial-care-support-in-Zambia

REPSSI. (2013). *REPSSI launches Teacher's Diploma in Psychosocial Care, Support & Protection*. Retrieved from http://www.riatt-esa.org/updates/repss-launces-teachers-diploma-psychosocial-care-support-and-protection

Reyes, C. (2010, October 22). *What is psycho-education? Psycho-educational teacher for students with behavioral issues*. Retrieved from http://thepsychoeducationalteacher.blogspot.co.uk/2010/10/what-is-psycho-education.html

Rhodes, S., & Parra, M. A. (2017). Executive Functioning. doi:10.1007/978-981-287-082-7_275

Riber, K. (2017). Trauma complexity and child abuse: A qualitative study of attachment narratives in adult refugees with PTSD. *Transcultural Psychiatry*, *54*(5-6), 840–869. doi:10.1177/1363461517737198 PMID:29130379

Richard, L. A., & Sosa, L. V. (2014). School social work in Louisiana: A model of practice. *Children & Schools*, *16*(4), 211–220. doi:10.1093/cs/cdu022

Richardson, C., & Halliwell, E. (2008). Boiling point: problem anger and what we can do about it. London: Mental Health Foundation.

Richardson, D., & Seidman, S. (Eds.). (2002). *Handbook of lesbian and gay studies*. London: Sage.

Richter, L. M. (2003). Baby rape in South Africa. *Child Abuse Review*, *12*(6), 392–400. doi:10.1002/car.824

Richter, L., Foster, G., & Sherr, L. (2006). *Where the heart is: Meeting psychological needs of young children in the context of HIV/AIDS*. The Hague, The Netherlands: Bernard van Leer Foundation.

Righetti, F., & Visserman, M. (2017). I Gave Too Much: Low Self-Esteem and the Regret of Sacrifices. *Social Psychological & Personality Science*, *9*(4), 453–460. doi:10.1177/1948550617707019

Risk and protective factors. (n.d.). Retrieved from http://www.prokids.org/wp-content/uploads/2017/01/Chap-9-Dec-2016.pdf

Rivers, I. (2011). *Homophobic bullying: Research and theoretical perspectives*. Oxford, UK: Oxford University Press. doi:10.1093/acprof:oso/9780195160536.001.0001

Romero-Martínez, A., Figueiredo, B., & Moya-Albiol, L. (2014). Childhood history of abuse and child abuse potential: The role of parent's gender and timing of childhood abuse. *Child Abuse & Neglect, 38*(3), 510–516. doi:10.1016/j.chiabu.2013.09.010 PMID:24269330

Rosenheck, R., & Nathan, P. (1985). Secondary traumatization in the children of Vietnam veterans with posttraumatic stress disorder. *Hospital & Community Psychiatry, 36,* 538–539. PMID:4007811

Rostami, M., Abdi, M., & Heidari, H. (2014). Study of Various Types of Abuse during Childhood and Mental Health. *Procedia: Social and Behavioral Sciences, 159,* 671–676. doi:10.1016/j.sbspro.2014.12.463

Rothbart, M. K., Ahadi, S. A., & Hershey, K. L. (1994). Temperament and social behavior in childhood. *Merrill-Palmer Quarterly, 40,* 21–39.

Ryan, R. (1992). Agency and organization: Intrinsic motivation, autonomy, and the self in psychological development. Nebraska Symposium on Motivation. *Nebraska Symposium on Motivation, 40,* 1–56. PMID:1340519

Ryan, R. L., & Deci, E. L. (2000). Self-determination theory and the facilitation of intrinsic motivation, social development, and well-being. *The American Psychologist, 55*(1), 68–78. doi:10.1037/0003-066X.55.1.68 PMID:11392867

Ryan, R. M., & Brown, K. W. (2003). Why we don't need self-esteem: On fundamental needs, contingent love, and mindfulness. *Psychological Inquiry, 14,* 71–76.

Ryan, R. M., Stiller, J., & Lynch, J. H. (1994). Representations of relationships to teachers, parents, and friends as predictors of academic motivation and self-esteem. *The Journal of Early Adolescence, 14*(2), 226–249. doi:10.1177/027243169401400207

Saavedra, A. R., & Opfer, D. P. (2012). Learning 21st-century skills requires 21st century teaching. *Phi Delta Kappan, 94*(2), 8–13. doi:10.1177/003172171209400203

Safta, C. G. (2017). Between flexibility and conventionalism. Elements of hidden curriculum with implications in managing conflicts in education. *Jus et Civitas, 68*(1), 95–101.

Saigh, P. A. (1987). In vitro flooding of childhood posttraumatic stress disorder. *School Psychology Review, 16,* 203–211.

Saini, M. (2009). A meta-analysis of the psychological treatment of anger: Developing guidelines for evidence-based practice. *The Journal of the American Academy of Psychiatry and the Law, 37,* 473–488. PMID:20018996

Salancik, G. R. (1995). WANTED: A good network theory of organization. *Administrative Science Quarterly, 40,* 345–349.

Saluja, G., Kotch, J., & Lee, L. C. (2003). Effects of child abuse and neglect: Does social capital really matter? *Archives of Pediatrics & Adolescent Medicine, 157*(7), 681–686. doi:10.1001/archpedi.157.7.681 PMID:12860791

Samuels, S. J., Rasinski, T. V., & Hiebert, E. H. (2011). Eye movements and reading: What teachers need to know. In A. Farstrup & S.J. Samuels (Eds.), What research has to say about reading instruction (4th ed.). Newark, DE: IRA.

Sanchez, C. (2017, February 23). English language learners: How your state is doing. *NPR*. Retrieved from: http://www.npr.org/sections/ed2017/02/23/512451228-5-million-english-language-learners-a-vast-pool-of-at -risk

Sanchez, S. E., Pineda, O., Chaves, D. Z., Zhong, Q. Y., Gelaye, B., Simon, G. E., ... Williams, M. A. (2017). Childhood physical and sexual abuse experiences associated with post-traumatic stress disorder among pregnant women. *Annals of Epidemiology, 27*(11), 716–723. doi:10.1016/j.annepidem.2017.09.012 PMID:29079333

Saqib, M., & Rehman, K. U. (2018). Impact of stress on student's academic performance at secondary school level at District Vehari. *International Journal of Learning and Development, 8*(1), 84–93. doi:10.5296/ijld.v8i1.12063

Sargeant, J. (2012). Prioritising learner voice: 'Tween children's perspectives on school success. *International Journal of Primary. Elementary and Early Years Education, 42*(2), 190–200.

Sathe, L. A., & Geisler, C. C. (2015). The Reverberations of a graduate study abroad course in India. *Journal of Transformative Education*, 55–78.

Savi, F. (1999). *Psychological Abuse Towards Adoles- cents and its Relationship Between Sense of Self and Anxiety Level* (in Turkish) (MA Thesis). Bursa: Uludag University.

Schaefer, R. T. (2016). *Sociology: A brief introduction* (12th ed.). New York, NY: McGraw-Hill Companies, Inc.

Schauben, L. J., & Frazier, P. S. (1995). Vicarious trauma: The effects on female counselors of working with sexual violence survivors. *Psychology of Women Quarterly, 19*(1), 49–54. doi:10.1111/j.1471-6402.1995.tb00278.x

Schetky, D. H., & Green, A. H. (1988). *Child Sexual Abuse: A Handbook for Health Care and Legal Professional*. New York: Brunner/Mazel.

Schmitt, A. J., McCallum, E., Hawkins, R. O., Stephenson, E., & Vicencio, K. (2018). The effects of two assistive technologies on reading comprehension accuracy and rate. *Assistive Technology*, 1–11. doi:10.1080/10400435.2018.1431974 PMID:29370581

Schudlich, T. D. R., Youngstrom, E. A., & Martinez, M. (2015). Physical and sexual abuse and early-onset bipolar disorder in youths receiving outpatient services: Frequent, but not specific. *Journal of Abnormal Child Psychology, 43*(3), 453–463. doi:10.100710802-014-9924-3 PMID:25118660

Scott, J. (1991, 2000). Social Network Analysis: A Handbook (2nd ed.). Thousand Oaks, CA: Sage Publications.

Scott, W. R. (1998). *Organizations: Rational, Natural, and Open Systems* (4th ed.). Englewood Cliffs, NJ: Prentice-Hall.

Segal, J., Smith, M., Segal, R., & Robinson, L. (2017). *Trusted guide to mental, emotional & social health*. Retrieved from: http://www.helpguide.org/articles/healthy-living/how-to-start-exercising-and-stick-to-it.htm

Segal, E. A., Gerdes, K. E., & Steiner, S. (2019). *An introduction to the profession of social work* (6th ed.). Boston, MA: Cengage Learning.

Seligman, M. E. P. (2002). *Authentic happiness: Using the new positive psychology to realize your potential for lasting fulfilment*. New York: Simon & Schuster Australia.

Seligman, M. E. P., Steen, T. A., Park, N., & Peterson, C. (2005). Positive psychology progress: Empirical validation of interventions. *The American Psychologist, 60*(5), 410–421. doi:10.1037/0003-066X.60.5.410 PMID:16045394

Seligman, M. E., & Csikszentmihalyi, M. (2000). Positive psychology: An introduction. *The American Psychologist, 55*(1), 5–14. doi:10.1037/0003-066X.55.1.5 PMID:11392865

Senge, P., Seville, D., Lovins, A., & Lotspeich, C. (1999). *Systems Thinking Primer for Natural Capitalism, Chapter 1: The Four Basic Shifts, working paper*. Academic Press.

Seybolt, T. B. (2000). *Systemic Network Analysis of Refugee Relief: A Business-like Approach*. Solna, Sweden: Stockholm International Peace Research Institute.

Shahzad, A. H., Rehman, K. U., & Saqib, M. (2018). Does stress impact school students' learning performance? In *6th Asia Pacific Conference on Advanced Research (APCA-2018)*. Melbourne, Australia: Asia Pacific Institute of Advanced Research.

Shamshikova, O. A., Ermolova, E. O., & Belashina, T. V. (2018). *Expression of Individual Psychological Personality Traits Depending on the Level of Anger Repression (A Case Study of a Sample Group of Law Enforcement Officers). DEStech Transactions on Social Science, Education and Human Science*. doi:10.12783/dtssehs/ichss2017/19577

Shankar, N. L., & Park, C. L. (2016). Effects of stress on students' physical and mental health and academic success. *International Journal of School & Educational Psychology, 4*(1), 5–9. doi:10.1080/21683603.2016.1130532

Shepard, L. A. (2000). The role of assessment in a learning culture. *Educational Researcher, 29*(7), 4–14. doi:10.3102/0013189X029007004

Shilubana, M., & Kok, J. C. (2004). Learners without adult care at home who succeed in school. *Education as Change, 9*(1), 101–107. doi:10.1080/16823200509487105

Shinebourne, P. (2011). Interpretative Phenomenological Analysis. In N. Frost (Ed.), *Qualitative Research Methods in Psychology: Combining core approaches* (p. 4465). Open University.

Siegel, D. (2008). *Mindsight*. Oxford, UK: Oneworld.

Silove, D., Mohsin, M., Tay, A. K., Steel, Z., Tam, N., Savio, E., ... Rees, S. (2017). Six-year longitudinal study of pathways leading to explosive anger involving the traumas of recurrent conflict and the cumulative sense of injustice in Timor-Leste. *Social Psychiatry and Psychiatric Epidemiology, 52*(10), 1281–1294. doi:10.100700127-017-1428-3 PMID:28825139

Simon, H. A. (1973). The organization of complex systems. In H. H. Pattee (Ed.), *Hierarchy theory* (pp. 1–27). New York: Braziller.

Simon, N. M., Herlands, N. N., Marks, E. H., Mancini, C., Letamendi, A., Li, Z., ... Stein, M. B. (2009). Childhood maltreatment linked to greater symptom severity and poorer quality of life and function in social anxiety disorder. *Depression and Anxiety, 26*(11), 1027–1032. doi:10.1002/da.20604 PMID:19750554

Singer, M. L., Flannery, D. J., Guo, S., Miller, D., & Leibbrandi, S. (2004). Exposure to violence, parental monitoring and television as contributors to children's psychological trauma. *Journal of Community Psychology, 32*(5), 489–504. doi:10.1002/jcop.20015

Singh, G. D. (2016). *Developing a model to curb bullying in secondary schools in the Uthungulu district of KwaZulu-Natal* (Unpublished doctoral dissertation). University of South Africa, Pretoria, South Africa.

Singh, A., Urbano, A., Haston, M., & McMahon, E. (2010). School Counselors' Strategies for Social Justice Change: A Grounded Theory of What Works in the Real World. *Professional School Counseling, 13*(3), 135–145. doi:10.5330/PSC.n.2010-13.135

Singh, R., Goyal, M., Tiwari, S., Ghildiyal, A., Nattu, S. M., & Das, S. (2012). Effect of examination stress on mood, performance and cortisol levels in medical students. *Indian Journal of Physiology and Pharmacology, 56*(1), 48–55. PMID:23029964

Sin, N. L., & Lyubomirsky, S. (2009). Enhancing well-being and alleviating depressive symptoms with positive psychology interventions: A practice-friendly meta-analysis. *Journal of Clinical Psychology, 65*(5), 467–487. doi:10.1002/jclp.20593 PMID:19301241

Sirvani, H. (2007). The effect of teacher communication with parents on students' mathematics achievement. *American Secondary Education, 36*(1), 31–46.

Skinner, D., & Davids, A. (Eds.). (2006). *A situational Analysis of Orphans and Vulnerable Children in Districts of South Africa.* HSRC Press.

Smith, J. A., & Osborn, M. (2009). Interpretative Phenomenological Analysis. In J.A. smith (Ed.), Qualitative psychology: A practical guide to research methods. London, UK: Sage.

Smith, J. A., Flowers, P., & Larkin, M. (2013). *Interpretative phenomenological analysis: theory, method and research.* London: Sage.

Smuts, L. (2009). *Lesbian identities in South Africa: black and white experiences in Johannesburg* (Unpublished Masters thesis). University of Johannesburg, Auckland Park, South Africa.

South African Schools Act 84 of 1996. (1996) No. 1867.

Spera, C. (2005). A review of the relationship among parenting practices, parenting styles, and adolescent school achievement. *Educational Psychology Review*, *17*(2), 125–146. doi:10.100710648-005-3950-1

Sperry, D. M., & Widom, C. S. (2013). Child abuse and neglect, social support, and psychopathology in adulthood: A prospective investigation. *Child Abuse & Neglect*, *37*(6), 415–425. doi:10.1016/j.chiabu.2013.02.006 PMID:23562083

Spielberger, C. D. (1999). *State-Trait Anger Expression Inventory-2 (STAXI-2)*. Odessa, FL: Psychological Assessment Resource Inc.

Spielberger, C. D., Johnson, E. H., Russell, S. F., Crane, R. J., Jacobs, G. A., & Worden, T. J. (1985). The experience and expression of anger: Construction and validation of an anger expression scale. In M. A. Chesney & R. H. Rosenman (Eds.), *Anger and hostility in cardiovascular and behavioral disorders* (pp. 5–30). New York, NY: Hemisphere.

Spielberger, C. D., Krasner, S. S., & Solomon, E. P. (1988). The experience, expression and control of anger. In M. P. Janisse (Ed.), *Health psychology: Individual differences and stress* (pp. 89–108). New York, NY: Springer-Verlag. doi:10.1007/978-1-4612-3824-9_5

Spielberger, C. D., & Vagg, P. R. (1995). *Test anxiety. Theory, assessment, and treatment*. Washington, DC: Taylor & Francis.

Sroufe, L. A., & Fleeson, J. (1986). Attachment and the Construction of Relationships. In W. W. Hartup & Z. Rubin (Eds.), *Relationships and Development*. New York: Cambridge University Press.

Steadman, H. J. (1992). Boundary Spanners: A Key Component for the Effective Interactions of the Justice and Mental Health Systems. *Law and Human Behavior*, *16*(1), 75–87. doi:10.1007/BF02351050

Sternberg, K. (1993). Child maltreatment: Implications for policy from cross-cultural research. In D. Cichette & S. Roth (Eds.), *Child abuse, child development and social policy* (pp. 192–212). Norwood, NJ: Ablex Publishers.

Stoltenborgh, M., Bakermans-Kranenburg, M. J., & van Ijzendoorn, M. H. (2013). The neglect of child neglect: A meta-analytic review of the prevalence of neglect. *Social Psychiatry and Psychiatric Epidemiology*, *48*(3), 345–355. doi:10.100700127-012-0549-y PMID:22797133

Stowman, S. A., & Donohue, B. (2005). Assessing child neglect; *A review of standardized measures. Aggression and Violent Behavior*, *10*(4), 491–512. doi:10.1016/j.avb.2004.08.001

Stroop, J. R. (1935). Studies of interference in serial verbal reactions. *Journal of Experimental Psychology*, *18*(6), 643–661. doi:10.1037/h0054651

Subasinghe, W. (2016). An Introduction on Educational Guidance and school Counselling. *International Journal of Scientific Research and Innovative Technology*, *3*(10).

Substance Abuse and Mental Health Services Administration. (2014). *Trauma-Informed Care in Behavioral Health Services. Treatment Improvement Protocol (TIP) Series 57. HHS Publication No. (SMA) 13-4801.* Rockville, MD: Author.

Sue, D. W., Rasheed, M. N., & Rasheed, J. M. (2016). *Multicultural social work practice: A competency-based approach to diversity and social justice* (2nd ed.). Hoboken, NJ: John Wiley & Sons.

Sue, S., & Okazaki, S. (1990). Asian-American educational experience. *The American Psychologist, 45*(8), 913–920. doi:10.1037/0003-066X.45.8.913 PMID:2221563

Sujatha, B., & Subhalakshmi, S. (2016). Effect of stress on exam going first year medical students of Tirunelveli. *International Journal of Medical Research & Health Sciences, 5*(1), 118–121.

Sullivan, P. (2011). *Teaching Mathematics: Using research-informed strategies. Australian Education Review,* 59.

Sullivan, S. (2000). *Child neglect: Current definitions and models—A review of child neglect research, 1993-1998.* Ottawa, Canada: National Clearinghouse on Family Violence.

Suozzi, J., & Motta, R. W. (2004). The relationship between combat exposure and the transfer of trauma-like symptoms to offspring of veterans. *Traumatology, 10*(1), 17–37. doi:10.1177/153476560401000103

Swaminath, G. (2009). Psychoeducation. *Indian Journal of Psychiatry, 51*(3), 171–172. doi:10.4103/0019-5545.55082 PMID:19881043

Sweller, J. (1988). Cognitive load during problem solving: Effects on learning. *Cognitive Science, 12*(2), 257–285. doi:10.120715516709cog1202_4

Tafrate, R. (1995). Evaluation of treatment strategies for adult anger disorders. In H.

Taillieu, T. L., Brownridge, D. A., Sareen, J., & Afifi, T. O. (2016). Childhood emotional maltreatment and mental disorders: Results from a nationally representative adult sample from the United States. *Child Abuse & Neglect, 59*, 1–12. doi:10.1016/j.chiabu.2016.07.005 PMID:27490515

Tangney, J. P., Stuewig, J., & Mashek, D. J. (2007). Moral Emotions and Moral Behavior. *Annual Review of Psychology, 58*(1), 345–372. doi:10.1146/annurev.psych.56.091103.070145 PMID:16953797

Tangney, J. P., Wagner, P., Fletcher, C., & Gramzow, R. (1992). Shamed into anger? The relation of shame and guilt to anger and self-reported aggression. *Journal of Personality and Social Psychology, 62*(4), 669–675. doi:10.1037/0022-3514.62.4.669 PMID:1583590

Tassie, A. K. (2015). Vicarious resilience from attachment trauma: Reflections of long-term therapy with marginalized young people. *Journal of Social Work Practice, 29*(2), 191–204. doi:10.1080/02650533.2014.933406

Taukeni, S. (2011). *A phenomenological study of orphaned learners' experiences with regard to psychosocial support provisioning in Endola Circuit, Namibia* (PhD thesis). University of Fort Hare.

Taylor, S. E. (2000). Visagraph eye-movement recording system. In Teaching children to read: An evidence-based assessment of the scientific research literature on reading and its implications for reading instructions. Washington, DC: Academic Press.

Teicher, M. H., Samson, J. A., Polcari, A., & McGreenery, C. E. (2006). Sticks, stones, and hurtful words: Relative effects of various forms of childhood maltreatment. *The American Journal of Psychiatry, 163*(6), 993–1000. doi:10.1176/ajp.2006.163.6.993 PMID:16741199

Telfer, E. (1980). *Happiness*. New York: St. Martin's Press. doi:10.1007/978-1-349-16325-0_2

Terndrup, A. I., & Ritter, K. (2002). *Handbook of affirmative psychotherapy with lesbians and gay men*. New York, NY: Guildford Press.

Thabet, A. A. M., Karim, K., & Vostanis, P. (2006). Trauma exposure in pre-school children in a war zone. *The British Journal of Psychiatry, 188*(2), 154–158. doi:10.1192/bjp.188.2.154 PMID:16449703

The Regional Psychosocial Support Initiative (REPSSI). (2012). *Mainstreaming Psychosocial Support within the Education Sector*. Author.

Theron, L. C. (2012). Resilience research with South African Youth: Caveats and ethical complexities. *South African Journal of Psychology. Suid-Afrikaanse Tydskrif vir Sielkunde, 42*(3), 33–345. doi:10.1177/008124631204200305

Thomas, S. P. (2001). Teaching Healthy Anger Management. *Perspectives in Psychiatric Care, 37*(2), 41–48. doi:10.1111/j.1744-6163.2001.tb00617.x PMID:15521301

Thompson, R. (1991). Emotional Regulation and Emotional Development. *Educational Psychology Review, 3*(4), 269–307. doi:10.1007/BF01319934

Tiwari, A., & Balani, S. (2013). The Effect of Intervention Program to Reduction Stress. *IOSR Journal of Humanities and Social Science, 9*, 27–30. doi:10.9790/0837-0942730

Tomlinson, B. E. (1941). *The Psycho-educational Clinic by Brian E*. New York, NY: MacMillan Co.

Tomlinson, B. E. (1941). *The psychoeducational clinic*. New York, NY: MacMillan. doi:10.1037/11457-017

Tomoda, A., Suzuki, H., Rabi, K., Sheu, Y. S., Polcari, A., & Teicher, M. H. (2009). Reduced prefrontal cortical gray matter volume in young adults exposed to harsh corporal punishment. *NeuroImage, 47*, T66–T71. doi:10.1016/j.neuroimage.2009.03.005 PMID:19285558

Topor, D. R., Keane, S. P., Shelton, T. L., & Calkins, S. D. (2010). Parent involvement and student academic performance: A multiple mediational analysis. *Journal of Prevention & Intervention in the Community, 38*(3), 183–197. doi:10.1080/10852352.2010.486297 PMID:20603757

Tracy, J. L., Robins, R. W., & Tangney, J. P. (2008). *The self-conscious emotions: theory and research*. New York: Guilford.

Trautwein, U. (2007). The homework–achievement relation reconsidered: Differentiating homework time, homework frequency, and homework effort. *Learning and Instruction*, *17*(3), 372–388. doi:10.1016/j.learninstruc.2007.02.009

Trautwein, U., Lüdtke, O., Kastens, C., & Köller, O. (2006). Effort on homework in grades 5 through 9: Development, motivational antecedents, and the association with effort on classwork. *Child Development*, *77*(4), 1094–1111. doi:10.1111/j.1467-8624.2006.00921.x PMID:16942508

Troiden, R. R. (1988). *Gay and lesbian identity: A sociological analysis*. New York, NY: General Hall.

Tsheko, G. N. (Ed.). (2007). *Our Children Our Future. From Vision to Innovative Impact. Community Responses to Vulnerable Children. Qualitative Research Report on Orphans and Vulnerable Children in Palapye*. Botswana: HSRC Press.

Tuffour, I. (2017). A Critical Overview of Interpretative Phenomenological Analysis: A Contemporary Qualitative Research Approach. *Journal of Health Communication*, *2*, 52. doi:10.4172/2472-1654.100093

Types of child abuse. (n.d.). Retrieved from http://www.childrenservices.org/cms/files/File/WearBlue2016definitions.pdf

U.S. Department of Health and Human Services (NCCAN). (1996). Child maltreatment, 1994: Reportfrom the states to the National Center on Child Abuse and Neglect. Washington, DC: Government Printing Office.

U.S. Department of Health and Human Services. Administration for Children and Families, Administration on Children, Youth and Families, & Children's Bureau. (2011). *Child Maltreatment 2010*. Washington, DC: Author. Retrieved from http://archive.acf.hhs.gov/programs/cb/pubs/cm10/cm10.pdf

Ugoji, F. N. (2014). Determinants of Risky Sexual Behaviours among Secondary School Students in Delta State Nigeria. *International Journal of Adolescence and Youth*, *19*(3), 408–418. doi:10.1080/02673843.2012.751040

UK types. (n.d.). Retrieved from https://www.ncl.ac.uk/studentambassadors/assets/documents/NSPCCDefinitionsandsignsofchildabuse.pdf

Ule, M., Zivoder, A., & du Bios-Reymond, M. (2015). 'Simply the best for my children': Patterns of parental involvement in education. *International Journal of Qualitative Studies in Education: QSE*, *28*(3), 329–348. doi:10.1080/09518398.2014.987852

Ulugtekin, S. (1991). *Hükümlü Çocuk ve Yeniden Toplum- sallasma*. Ankara: Bizim Büro.

UNAIDS. (2006). *Report on the global AIDS Epidemic 2006*. Retrieved from http://www.unaids.org./en/HIVdata/2006GlobalReport/default.asp

UNAIDS. (2013). *Global report: UNAIDS report on the global AIDS epidemic*. Geneva: UNAIDS.

UNAIDS/UNICEF. (2007). *Global Study on Child Poverty and Disparities 2007-2008*. Author.

UNESCO. (2000). The Dakar framework for action. In Education for all: meeting our collective commitments. Paris: UNESCO.

UNESCO. (2016). *Out in the open: Education sector responses to violence based on sexual orientation and gender identity/expression*. Paris: UNESCO.

UNICEF, UNAIDS, & PEPFAR. (2006). Africa and Vulnerable Generation: Children Affected by AIDS. Authors.

UNICEF. (1989). *Convention on the Rights of the Child*. UNICEF.

UNICEF. (2006). *Africa's orphaned and Vulnerable Generations: Children affected by AIDA*. New York: United Nations Children's Fund.

UNICEF. (2007). *State of the World's Children*. Author.

UNICEF. (2019). UNICEF Humanitarian. *Action for Children*.

United Nations Children's Fund. (2014). *Ending Child Marriage: Progress and Prospects*. New York: UNICEF.

United Nations High Commissioner for Refugees. (2018). *Turn the tide: Refugee education in crisis*. Geneva, Switzerland: UNHCR UN Refugee Agency.

United Nations Office of the High Commissioner on Human Rights. (2014). *Preventing and eliminating child, early and forced marriage*. Available at http://www.ohchr.org/EN/HRBodies/ HRC/RegularSessions/Session26/Documents/A-HRC-26-22_en.doc

Urquiza, A. J., & Winn, C. (1994). *Treatment for Abused and Neglected Children: Infancy to Age 18*. U.S. Department of Health and Human Services; doi:10.1042/BJ20021886\nBJ20021886

van der Kolk, B. (2014). *The body keeps the score: Brain, mind, and body in the healing of trauma*. New York, NY: Penguin Books.

van der Kooij, I. W., Nieuwendam, J., Bipat, S., Boer, F., Lindauer, R. J., & Graafsma, T. L. (2015). A national study on the prevalence of child abuse and neglect in Suriname. *Child Abuse & Neglect*, *47*, 153–161. doi:10.1016/j.chiabu.2015.03.019 PMID:25937450

Van der Merwe, M. (2015). Knife's edge: How dangerous are South African schools? *Daily Maverick*. Retrieved August 2, 2019, from https://www.dailymaverick.co.za/article/2019-04-06-knifes-edge-how-dangerous-are-south-africas-schools/#.WS0bAut96G4

Van der Merwe, A., Dawes, A., & Ward, C. L. (2012). The development of youth violence: An ecological understanding. In C. L. Ward, A. van der Merwe, & A. Dawes (Eds.), *Youth violence: Sources and solutions in South Africa* (pp. 53–92). Cape Town, South Africa: UCT Press.

Van Wyk, A. L. (2001). *The development and implementation of an English language and literature programme for low-proficiency tertiary learners* (Doctoral Thesis). University of the Free State. Retrieved from https://scholar.ufs.ac.za/handle/11660/6337

Vanalstine, J., Cox, S. R., & Roden, D. M. (2015). Cultural diversity in the United States and its impact on human development. *Journal of the Indiana Academy of the Social Sciences, 18,* 125–143.

Vartanian, T. P., Karen, D., Buck, P. W., & Cadge, W. (2007). Early factors leading to college graduation for Asians and non-Asians in the United States. *The Sociological Quarterly, 48*(2), 165–197. doi:10.1111/j.1533-8525.2007.00075.x

Vellymalay, S. K. N. (2012). Parental involvement at home: Analysing the influence of parent's socio-economic status. Studies in Sociology of Science, 3(1), 1–6. doi: 10.3968j. sss.1923018420120301.2048

Veriava, F. (2012). *Rich school, poor school - the great divide persists.* Retrieved August 2, 2019, from https://mg.co.za/article/2012-09-28-00-rich-school-poor-school-the-great-divide-persists

Vertovec, S. (2019). Talking around super-diversity. *Ethnic and Racial Studies, 42*(1), 125–139. doi:10.1080/01419870.2017.1406128

Vinnerljung, B., Hjern, A., & Lindblad, F. (2006). Suicide attempts and severe psychiatric morbidity among former child welfare clients–a national cohort study. *Journal of Child Psychology and Psychiatry, and Allied Disciplines, 47*(7), 723–733. doi:10.1111/j.1469-7610.2005.01530.x PMID:16790007

Vogelstein, R. B. (2013). *Ending Child Marriage: How Elevating the Status of Girls Advances U.S. Foreign Policy Objectives.* New York: Council of Foreign Relations.

W.H.O. (2003). *Caring for children and adolescents with mental disorders.* Setting WHO directions. Geneva: World Health Organization. Available at: http://www.who.int/mental_health/media/en/785.pdf

Walker, J. A. (2012). Early marriage in Africa: Trends, harmful effects and interventions. *African Journal of Reproductive Health, 16*(2), 231–240.

Wasserman, S., & Faust, K. (1994). *Social Network analysis: methods and applications.* Cambridge, UK: Cambridge University Press. doi:10.1017/CBO9780511815478

Waterman, A. S. (1993). Two conceptions of happiness: Contrasts of personal expressiveness (eudaiomina) and hedonic enjoyment. *Journal of Personality and Social Psychology, 64*(4), 678–691. doi:10.1037/0022-3514.64.4.678

Waters, L. (2011). A review of school-based positive psychology interventions. *The Educational and Developmental Psychologist, 28*(2), 75–90. doi:10.1375/aedp.28.2.75

Waterston, T., & Mok, J. (2008). Violence Against Children. The UN Report. *Archives of Disease in Childhood, 93*–85. PMID:17804588

Watson, J. (2005). Child neglect Literature review. Centre for Parenting & Research NSW Department of Community Services.

Watson, S., Gallagher, P., Dougall, D., Porter, R., Moncrieff, J., Ferrier, I. N., & Young, A. H. (2014). Childhood trauma in bipolar disorder. *The Australian and New Zealand Journal of Psychiatry*, *48*(6), 564–570. doi:10.1177/0004867413516681 PMID:24343193

Waysman, M., Mikulinger, M., Solomon, Z., & Weisenberg, M. (1993). Secondary traumatization among wives of posttraumatic combat veterans: A family topology. *Journal of Family Psychology*, *7*(1), 104–118. doi:10.1037/0893-3200.7.1.104

Weber, E. (2008). *Educational Change in South Africa: Reflections of local realities, practices and reforms*. Rotterdam, The Netherlands: Sense Publishers.

Weber, M. (1947). *The Theory of Social and Economic Organization*. New York: Free Press.

Wehmeyer, M. L., & Abery, B. (2013). Self-determination and choice. *Intellectual and Developmental Disabilities*, *51*(5), 399–411. doi:10.1352/1934-9556-51.5.399 PMID:24303826

Weinstein, D., Staffelbach, D., & Biaggio, M. (2000). Attention deficit hyperactivity disorder and posttraumatic stress disorder: Differential diagnosis in childhood sexual abuse. *Clinical Psychology Review*, *20*(3), 359–378. doi:10.1016/S0272-7358(98)00107-X PMID:10779899

Werner, J. (2008). Process-and controller-adaptations determine the physiological effects of cold acclimation. *European Journal of Applied Physiology*, *104*(2), 137–143. doi:10.100700421-007-0608-3 PMID:18026979

WHO. (1999). *Definition of child abuse and neglect*. Retrieved from http://www.yesican.org/definitions/who.html

Wigfield, A., & Eccles, J. S. (2002). The development of competence beliefs, expectancies for success, and achievement values from childhood through adolescence. In A. Wigfield & J. S. Eccles (Eds.), *Development of achievement motivation* (pp. 91–120). San Diego, CA: Academic Press. doi:10.1016/B978-012750053-9/50006-1

Wihbey, J. (2011). Global prevalence of child sexual abuse. Journalist Resource. Available from: Journalistsresource. org/studies/./global-prevalence-child-sexual-abuse

Wilder, S. (2014). Effects of parental involvement on academic achievement: A meta-synthesis. *Educational Review*, *66*(3), 377–397. doi:10.1080/00131911.2013.780009

Willingham, A. J. (2018). US schools now have more security guards than social workers. *CNN*. Retrieved from: http://www.cnn.com/ampstories/us/us-schools-now-have-more-security-guards-than-social workers

Winant, H. (2001). *The World Is A Ghetto Race And Democracy Since World War II*. Basic Books.

Wingard, L., & Forsberg, L. (2009). Parent involvement in children's homework in American and Swedish dual-earner families. *Journal of Pragmatics, 41*(8), 1576–1595. doi:10.1016/j.pragma.2007.09.010

Women's Leadership Center. (2017). *CEDAW through San Young Women's Eyes: Claiming out Rights! Demanding dignity!* Olof Palme International Center.

World Health Organization (WHO). (2014). *Child maltreatment.* Geneva: WHO. Available at: http://www.who.int/mediacentre/factsheets/fs 150/en/

World Health Organization. (2003). *Skills for health.* Information series on school health. Document. Geneva: WHO. Retrieved August 2, 2019, from http://www.unicef.org/lifeskills/files/SkillsForHealth230503

Wyandotte, A., & Huh, S. (2012). *Of toads, gardens, and possibilities: A phenomenological approach to transformative education.* Transformational Learning of Three Adult Academicians.

Xu, J. (2004). Family help and homework management in urban and rural secondary schools. *Teachers College Record, 106*(9), 1786–1803. doi:10.1111/j.1467-9620.2004.00405.x

Yagci, E. (2006). Positive Learning Environments and the Child. In S. Ercetin (Ed.), *Education and Violence* (pp. 139–175). Ankara: Pegem Publications.

Yamamoto, Y., & Holloway, S. D. (2010). Parental expectations and children's academic performance in sociocultural context. *Educational Psychology Review, 22*(3), 189–214. doi:10.100710648-010-9121-z

Yin, R. K. (2009). *Case study research: Design and methods* (4th ed.). SAGE Publications Inc.

Young, J. (1990, July 15). Child Soldiers. Sunday Herald Sun, p. 1.

Yucel, M. (1993). *Prevention of Child Neglect and Abuse.* Academic Press. (in Turkish)

Zack, M. H. (2000). Researching Organizational Systems using Social Network Analysis. *Proceedings of the 33rd Hawai'i International Conference on System Sciences.*

Zastrow, C., & Kirst-Ashman, K. K. (2015). *Empowerment series: Understanding human behavior and the social environment* (10th ed.). Boston, MA: Cengage Learning.

Zeidner, M., & Mathews, G. (2005). Evaluation anxiety. In A. J. Elliot & C. S. Dweck (Eds.), *Handbook of Competence and Motivation.* London: Guildford Press.

Zerrudo, M. R. (2016). Theater of disaster, folk stories as vehicles for healing and survival. *Teaching Artist Journal, 14*(3), 161–170. doi:10.1080/15411796.2016.1209073

Zhang, Y., Haddad, E., Torres, B., & Chen, C. (2011). The reciprocal relationships among parents' expectations, adolescents' expectations, and adolescents' achievement: A two-wave longitudinal analysis of the NELS data. *Journal of Youth and Adolescence, 40*(4), 479–489. doi:10.100710964-010-9568-8 PMID:20628796

Zhao, H., & Akiba, M. (2009). School expectations for parental involvement and student mathematics achievement: A comparative study of middle schools in the US and South Korea. *Compare: A Journal of Comparative Education, 39*(3), 411–428. doi:10.1080/03057920701603347

Zinn, M. B. (1995). *Chicano men and masculinity*. Needham Heights, MA: Allyn & Bacon.

Zuravin, S. J. (1991). Suggestions for Operationally Defining Child Physical Abuse and Physical Neglect. In R. H. Starr & D. A. Wolfe (Eds.), *The Effects of Child Abuse & Neglect New York*. Guilford Press.

About the Contributors

Simon Taukeni is an academic, book editor, and researcher. His research interest mainly is in field of psychology and public health.

* * *

Dana Branson is an assistant professor for the Social Work Program, housed in the Department of Criminal Justice, Social Work, and Sociology. Dr. Branson earned her Ph.D. in Psychology from Northcentral University in 2011, received her Master of Social Work (child and family emphasis) from the University of Kansas in 1995, and completed her undergraduate work at Southwest Baptist University, obtaining a Bachelor of Science in Psychology and Sociology, with a minor in Counseling in 1993. Dr. Branson has been a licensed practitioner (LCSW) and a member of NASW since 1997. Dr. Branson joined Southeast Missouri State after 21 years of clinical experience with substance use disorders, mental health, co-occurring disorders, and trauma-informed care. Dr. Branson's practice is focused primarily with women and adolescents and incorporates the many diverse dynamics of rural social work. Dr. Branson regularly serves as a conference presenter, providing workshops, breakout sessions, and guided discussions on trauma (primary, secondary, and vicarious), adolescent substance abuse trends, and military social work. Dr. Branson has participated in international social work opportunities in Ireland and Belarus.

Stephen Oluwaseun Emmanuel is a young, male professional school counselor. He has a bachelor degree in guidance and counseling from Obafemi Awolowo University, Ile-Ife, Nigeria. He completed the professional training course for counselors, organized by Indiana University School of Social Work, USA. He has a number of professional publications in counseling and educational journals, made a significant number of peer-reviewed presentations while some of his articles are undergoing peer review in referred academic journals. He serves as a Section Editor for Psychocentrum Review: An International Journal. Universitas Indraprasta PGRI, Jarkata, Indonesia. Emmanuel Stephen is concerned with helping students and teachers increase their self-efficacy as well as responding effectively to ac-culturation pressure, cultural adjustment, discrimination, major life transitions, career choice and other stresses that are so typical and so often neglected among adolescents and young adults. He is investigating cultural, social, and psychological indicators of adolescent risk behaviour, teacher education, and bicultural involve-ment. He currently serves as a guidance counselor at St. Patrick Catholic College, Ogun State, Nigeria. As part of his community service, he serves as an advocate for gender vanguard in his community. His roles include; advocating for girl child education, discouraging Female Genital Mutilation, Sensitizing the community on gender issues. This has exposed him to several cultures, thereby providing him with the needed skills and techniques at tailoring counseling interventions to align with clients' cultural background. Although, a Christian, he has recorded successful counselling sessions with clients from religions other than his, such as Muslims, African traditional Religion among others. He has successfully used therapy to as-sist clients who face educational, psychological and social challenges ranging from truancy, anxiety, etc. He is currently undergoing cross-cultural collaborative research projects with scholars from Iran, India and Nepal respectively.

Cynthy Kaliinasho Haihambo is currently a Senior Lecturer and researcher in the Faculty of Education, University of Namibia. She is an academic who in-vests her energy into ensuring that diverse populations of learners receive quality, equitable and inclusive education. She strives to remove barriers and inequalities facing learners in early childhood, primary, secondary and tertiary phases through both scholarly and non-scholarly work. She tries to plant seeds of inclusion in her teaching, publications and community work.

Tanya Heasley originally from Essex, England is an award-winning coach and entrepreneur with over 18 years experience in a successful and progressive career within mental health and personal development. A trained Counsellor, Positive Psychology Coach, Coaching Psychologist and a specialist in Anger Management, Tanya has worked closely with young people, teachers and support staff within education, as well as vulnerable adults in the private sector. In her private practice, Tanya works as a Positive Anger Coach supporting and improving the development of relationships through actively promoting the art of anger as a communicative emotion.

Noxolo Mafu is a generalist academic with background and expertise in edu-cation, communication and psychology. Currently teaching social and emotional intelligence with an upcoming book in the same topic.

Johannes Mampane, PhD, is an Academic and a Researcher at the University of South Africa. His research interests lie in the fields of Gender, Health and Sexuality. He advocates for social justice, inclusivity, equality and diversity issues concerning marginalized, disenfranchised and minority populations in society.

Minda Marshall is an educationalist and researcher focusing on visual processing and cognitive development through the processes of reading. She has developed and implemented such solutions for schools, universities and various other organisations for more than 20 years with tremendous success. Me Marshall, wife and mother of three children, is a Director in various educational and development companies. She serves Compass Academy of Learning, a registered Private FET College, oversee a registered private school and is the co-owner and a director of Lectorsa a South African company. She is also the co-founder of M3Line and has developed the LAB-on-line solution through 30 years of research in her specific field. Lectorsa is partnering with various Tertiary Institutions i.e. Stellenbosch University, University Pretoria, University of the Free Sate, University of Namibia and also various public and private schools to assist students in developing their visual processing, reading and cognitive skills. The on-line solution is the results of 100's of case studies and hours of research compiled into a simplistic user friendly, accurately gauged on-line development system. Her qualifications include a BA degree, various international leadership training programs, and Occupational Directed Education and Training Practitioning Skills. She has authored and co-authored articles, academic articles and books. Minda is passionate about educating and empowering teachers, educators, parents and learners to discover their own internal strengths to maximize their abilities. She trains teachers and leaders around the world.

Joyce Mathwasa began her career in education after obtaining a teaching certificate specialising in Infant classes. She taught in the Early Childhood for twenty years raising through the ranks to headship of primary schools for fifteen years. She furthered her education attaining a Bachelor of Educational Administration, Planning and Policy studies (University of Zimbabwe); Master's in Educational Administration, Planning and Policy studies (Zimbabwe Open University) and PhD (University of Fort Hare). Currently she is a Postdoctoral Fellow in the Early Childhood Development Niche area with the University of Fort Hare. Dr Mathwasa is also an Adjunct lecturer with Lupane State University in Zimbabwe and supervisor in the Unisa Teaching Practice Unit for SDAC students (Zimbabwe). She has a teaching experience extending from early childhood to tertiary education. She has several journal articles in accredited journals and two book chapters that are in-press.

Robert Motta is a Professor of Psychology and Director of the Doctoral Program in School-Community Psychology at Hofstra University in New York. He is also Director of the Child and Family Trauma Institute at Hofstra. He has over 100 publications primarily in peer review journals and is a practicing psychologist.

R. Disho Muruti is a researcher and an academic working for the University of Namibia at Rundu Campus. He teach educational technology courses to students specializing in education.

Zoleka Ntshuntshe is an educator by profession. She holds a Primary Teacher's Diploma from Dr W.B Rubusana College of Education; a Bachelor of Arts; a Bachelor of Education; a Post Graduate Diploma in HIV/AIDS Management from Stellenbosch University; a Master of Education and a Doctor of Philosophy in Education from Fort Hare University and an Advanced Certificate in Early Childhood Development from Wheelock College, Boston. She has spent over twenty-three years teaching English in High School and is currently working as a lecturer at the University of Fort Hare in East London Campus. Her interest is in Inclusive Education and in particular psycho-social support. She has contributed book chapters for publication in ECD related book projects both nationally and internationally.

Jenny Shumba holds a PhD in Education, MEd in Curriculum Studies, BEd in Shona and Curriculum Theory, Certificate in Education (infant education), Post-Graduate Certificate in ECD. Has published extensively in education and more specifically in Contemporary Curriculum Issues.

Lwazi Sibanda began her career in education after obtaining a diploma in education to teach in primary schools. She taught in primary schools for eighteen years and moved to Secondary Teacher Education College as a Professional Studies lecturer for three years. She advanced her education attaining a Bachelor of Education degree in Educational Administration, Planning and Policy Studies (University of Zimbabwe); Master of Education degree in Educational Management (Midlands State University) and PhD in Education (University of Fort Hare). Currently she is a lecturer at the National University of Science and Technology, Faculty of Science and Technology Education and Acting Chairperson in the Department of Science, Mathematics and Technology Education. Dr Sibanda has vast teaching experience extending from primary to higher education. She has published quite a number of journal articles in accredited journals.

Nonzukiso Tyilo is a Senior Lecturer in the Faculty of Education, from the University of Fort Hare. Obtained B.Ped; BED (Hons); Social Sciences Hons

(Psychology) from University of Fort Hare and Post Graduate Diploma (HIV and AIDS Management) and M.Phil from Stellenbosch University. Has published with students and colleagues. Involved in numerous projects within the faculty (ECD, Mathematics and Science Project, and Commonwealth of Learning). Research interests include digital learning, educational psychology, inclusive education, curriculum, ECD and HIV and AIDS.

Daya Weerasinghe is a lecturer (Mathematics) and teacher educator working in the School of Education at the Berwick Campus of Federation University Australia. He joined the University in 2018 after completing his PhD studies at Monash University. He has experience as a Mathematics/ICT teacher in a number of metropolitan and regional secondary schools in Victoria. Daya has a life-long interest in teaching and learning Mathematics and is committed to the development of future mathematicians and mathematics teachers. His research interests include parental involvement in children's education, pre-service teacher education, and pathway programs in tertiary studies. He has published and presented his research at national and international conferences.

400

Index